HISTORIC PHOTOS OF
MONTANA

TEXT AND CAPTIONS BY GARY GLYNN

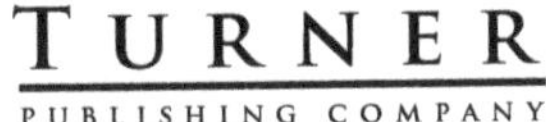

TURNER
PUBLISHING COMPANY

The 1863 discovery of "color" in Alder Gulch set off a gold rush from Bannack to what would soon be Virginia City. Within two years Virginia City had become the territorial capital and boasted a population in the thousands. Seen here near the end of the nineteenth century, Virginia City today is a popular Old West tourist destination.

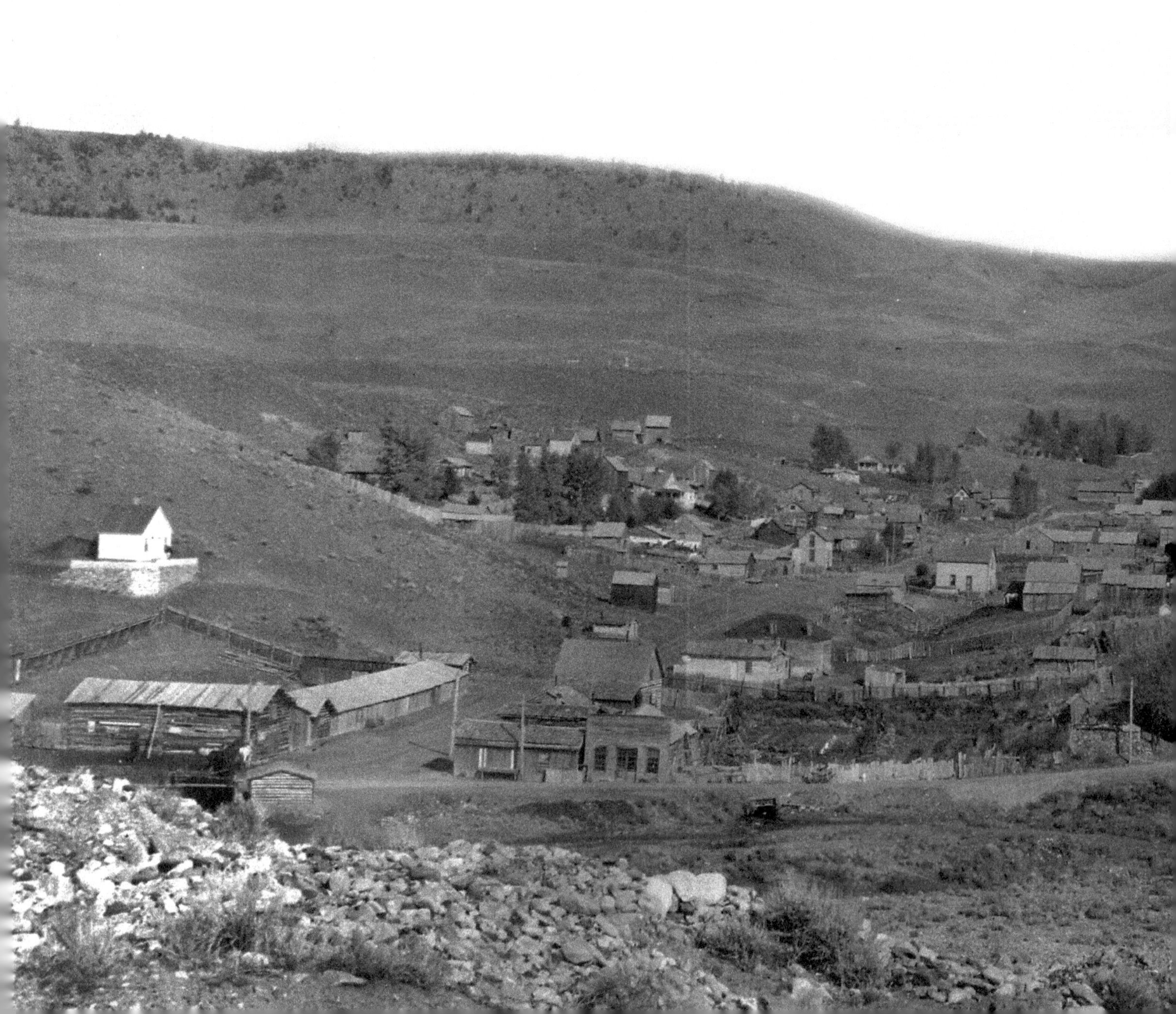

HISTORIC PHOTOS OF
MONTANA

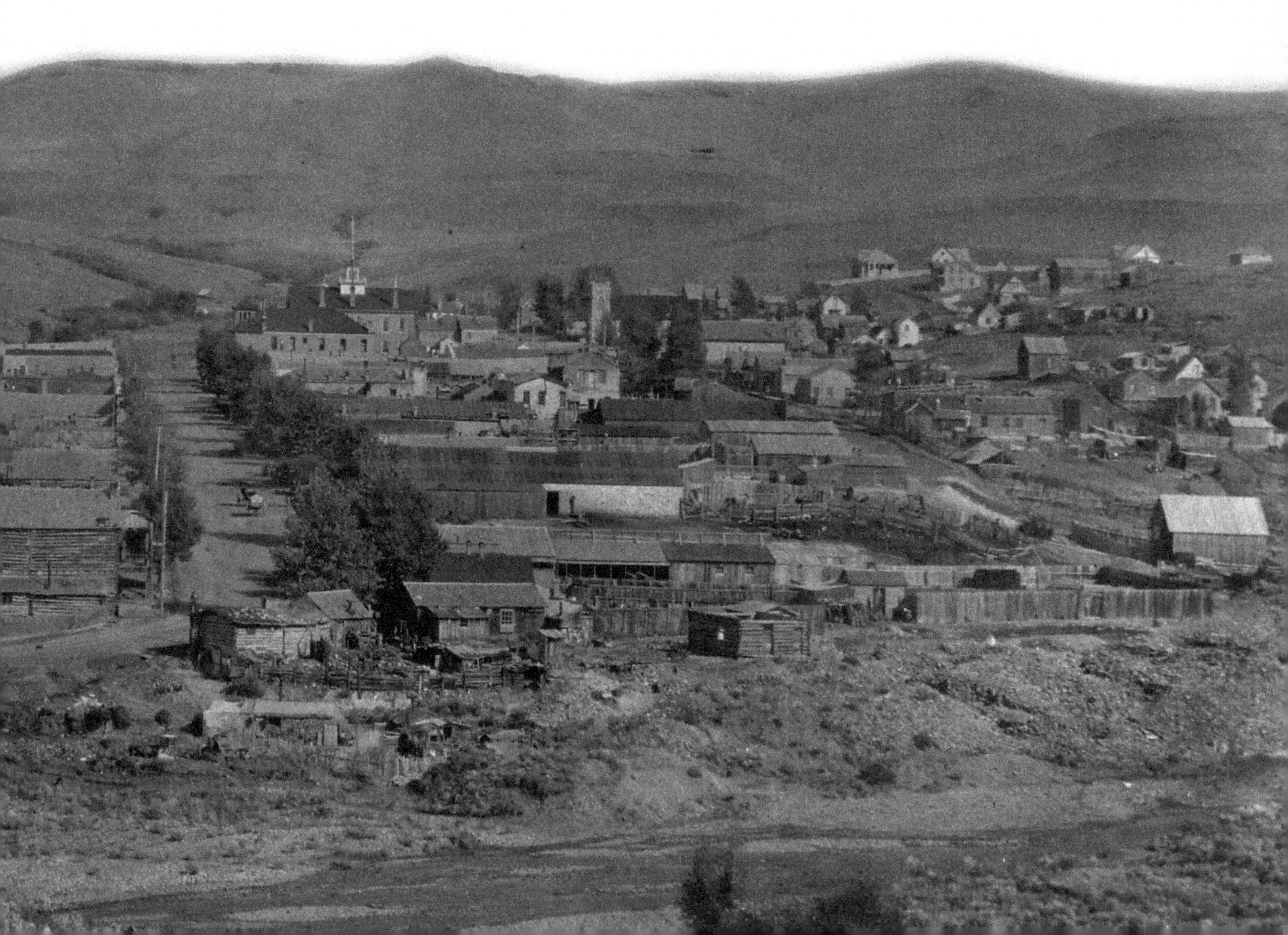

Turner Publishing Company
www.turnerpublishing.com

Historic Photos of Montana

Copyright © 2009 Turner Publishing Company

Library of Congress Control Number: 2008901853

ISBN-13: 978-1-59652-460-6

Printed in the United States of America

ISBN 978-1-68442-038-4 (hc)

CONTENTS

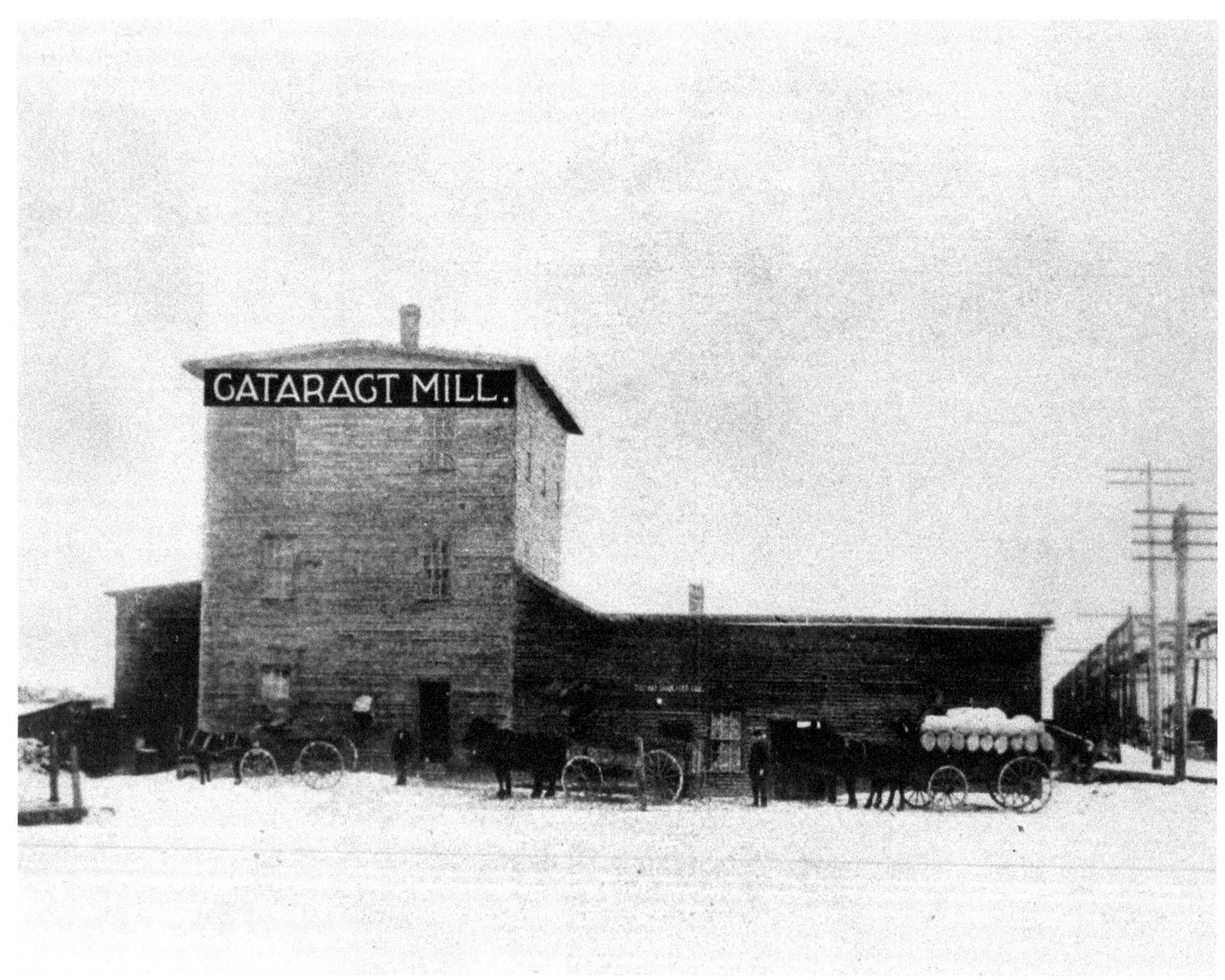

Wagons wait outside the Cataract Mill in Great Falls. Paris Gibson, the founding father of Great Falls, had been a partner in the first flour mill in Minneapolis, and in 1884 he brought H. O. Chowen from Minnesota to organize a branch of the Cataract Mill Company in the young Montana town.

Acknowledgments

This volume, *Historic Photos of Montana,* is the result of the cooperation and efforts of many individuals, organizations, and corporations. It is with great thanks that we acknowledge the valuable contribution of the following for their generous support:

Mansfield Library, Archives and Special Collections, The University of Montana-Missoula
The Historical Museum at Fort Missoula
Library of Congress
Amy Casamassa, Mansfield Library
Mark Fritch, Mansfield Library

The writer would like to thank Daniel Cooper of Turner Publishing for his cogent editing; Dale Johnson, former archivist at the Mansfield Library, for Hallways to History; and all the photographers, professional and amateur, known and unknown, who preserved the history of the Treasure State on film. Of special note are R. H. McKay, who faithfully chronicled the landscapes of western Montana, Edward Curtis, who obsessively recorded the culture of the American Indian, and photojournalist Stan Healy, who roamed the gritty streets of downtown Missoula with camera in hand.

The contributions of Mary Lyndes, Kelsey Glynn, and Connor Glynn made this book possible.

PREFACE

Montana has thousands of historic photographs that reside in archives, both locally and nationally. This book began with the observation that, while those photographs are of great interest to many, they are not easily accessible. During a time when Montana is looking ahead and evaluating its future course, many people are asking, How do we treat the past? These decisions affect every aspect of the state—architecture, public spaces, commerce, infrastructure—and these, in turn, affect the way that people live their lives. This book seeks to provide easy access to a valuable, objective look into the history of Montana.

The power of photographs is that they are less subjective than words in their treatment of history. Although the photographer can make decisions regarding subject matter and how to capture and present it, photographs do not provide the breadth of interpretation that text does. For this reason, they offer an original, untainted perspective that allows the viewer to interpret and observe.

This project represents countless hours of review and research. The researchers and writer have reviewed thousands of photographs in numerous archives. We greatly appreciate the generous assistance of the individuals and organizations listed in the acknowledgments of this work, without whom this project could not have been completed.

The goal in publishing this work is to provide broader access to this set of extraordinary photographs that seek to inspire, provide perspective, and evoke insight that might assist people who are responsible for determining Montana's future. In addition, the book seeks to preserve the past with adequate respect and reverence.

With the exception of touching up imperfections caused by the damage of time and cropping where necessary, no other changes have been made to the photographs in this volume. The focus and clarity of many images is limited to the technology and the ability of the photographer at the time they were taken.

The work is divided into eras. Beginning with some of the earliest known photographs of Montana, the first section records photographs through the end of the nineteenth century. The second section spans the beginning of the twentieth century through World War I. Section Three moves from the 1920s to the end of the Great Depression. The last section covers the World War II years and the first decades of the postwar era.

In each of these sections we have made an effort to capture various aspects of life through our selection of photographs. People, commerce, transportation, infrastructure, religious institutions, and educational institutions have been included to provide a broad perspective.

We encourage readers to reflect as they go walking in Montana, strolling through its parks, its countryside, and the neighborhoods of its cities. It is the publisher's hope that in utilizing this work, longtime residents will learn something new and that new residents will gain a perspective on where Montana has been, so that each can contribute to its future.

—Todd Bottorff, Publisher

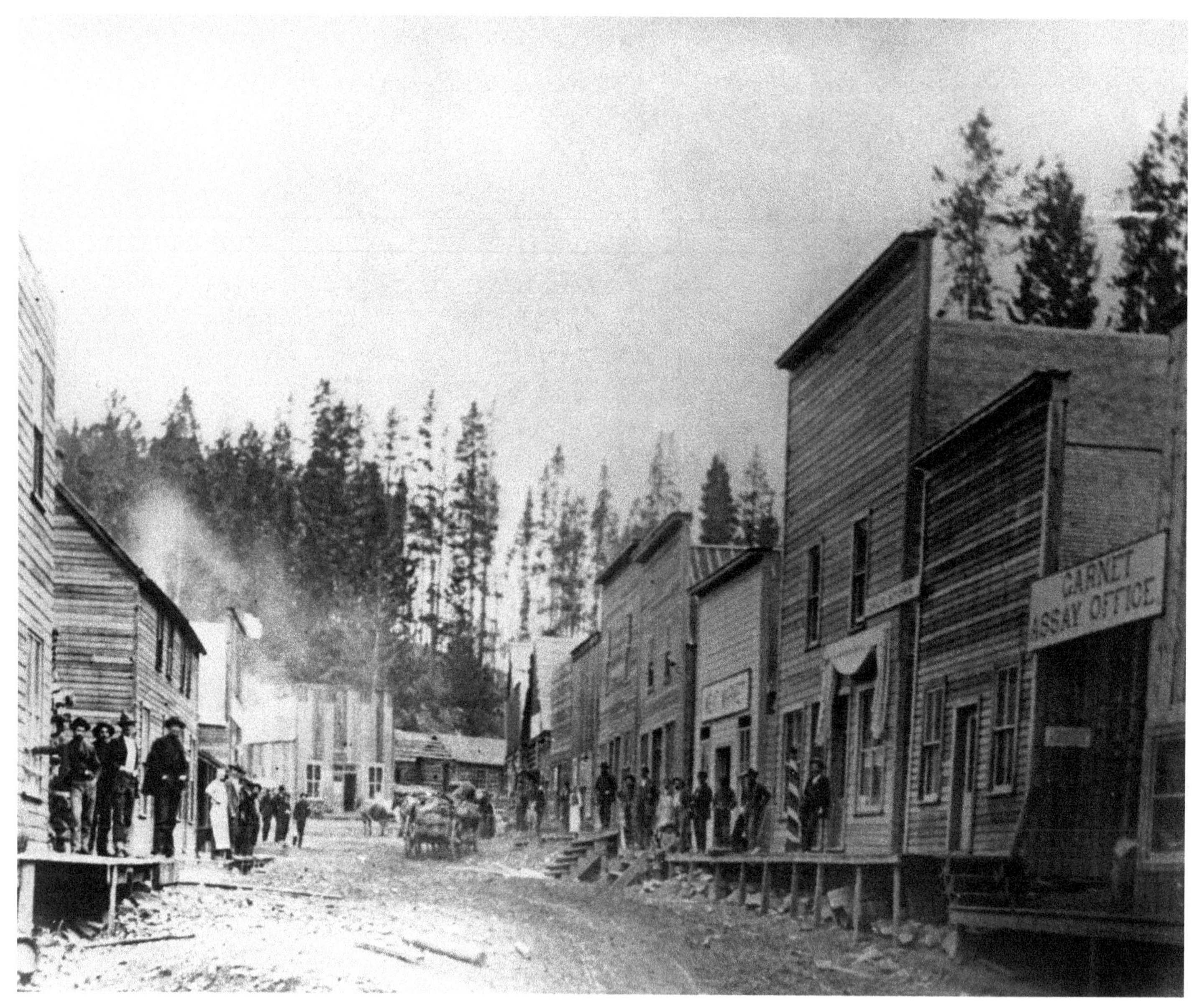

Seen here in its heyday around 1895, Garnet today is one of Montana's best-preserved ghost towns. The district's 50 mines produced almost $10 million in precious metals between 1862 and 1916. The Garnet Preservation Association has been instrumental in protecting much of the town.

State Origins in a Century of Change

(1860–1899)

Named after the Spanish word for mountain, Montana was first introduced to the American people by members of the Lewis and Clark expedition. Adventurous souls were intrigued by the explorers' descriptions of towering mountains and vast plains, a land populated by seemingly limitless herds of elk and bison. Soon after Lewis and Clark returned east, fur trappers followed in their footsteps to Montana, eager to harvest the wealth of what would become known as the Treasure State. There was only one problem—Montana was already occupied.

The Gros Ventre, Assiniboine, and Sioux roamed the eastern plains, while the powerful Blackfeet and Crow tribes controlled large swaths of central Montana. Salish, Kootenai, and Pend d'Oreille occupied the western valleys, and roaming bands of Nez Perce, Northern Cheyenne, Chippewa, and Cree often visited the state. The native tribes soon realized their traditional way of life was threatened by the influx of newcomers.

Among the earliest trappers to reach Montana were a group of Iroquois Indians, who intrigued the Salish with their tales of the "Black Robes," or Catholic priests. The Salish sent word to St. Louis asking that Black Robes be sent to them, and as a result, St. Mary's Mission was built in 1841. It was the first white settlement in Montana. Established in 1847, the Missouri River trading post of Fort Benton (originally Fort Clay) became an important transportation hub, especially after the discovery of gold at Alder Gulch and Nevada Gulch in the 1860s. Montana became a territory in 1864.

Sioux and Cheyenne leaders forcefully resisted government efforts to place them on reservations and handily defeated the 7th Cavalry at the Battle of the Little Big Horn. This defeat shocked the American public, and by 1877, when Chief Joseph of the Nez Perce led his people through Montana on an epic journey for freedom, the U.S. Army was already hard at work constructing a number of new military posts, including Fort Keogh, Fort Custer, and Fort Missoula.

The 1880s brought railroads and increased industrialization, especially in Butte, the state's largest city. The copper from Butte's mines was a critical component in the emerging technologies of electrical lighting and the telephone. Statehood in 1889 brought an epic battle between Marcus Daly and William A. Clark, the powerful copper kings of Butte, over the location of the new state capital. Daly advocated Anaconda, while Clark favored Helena, which was eventually chosen.

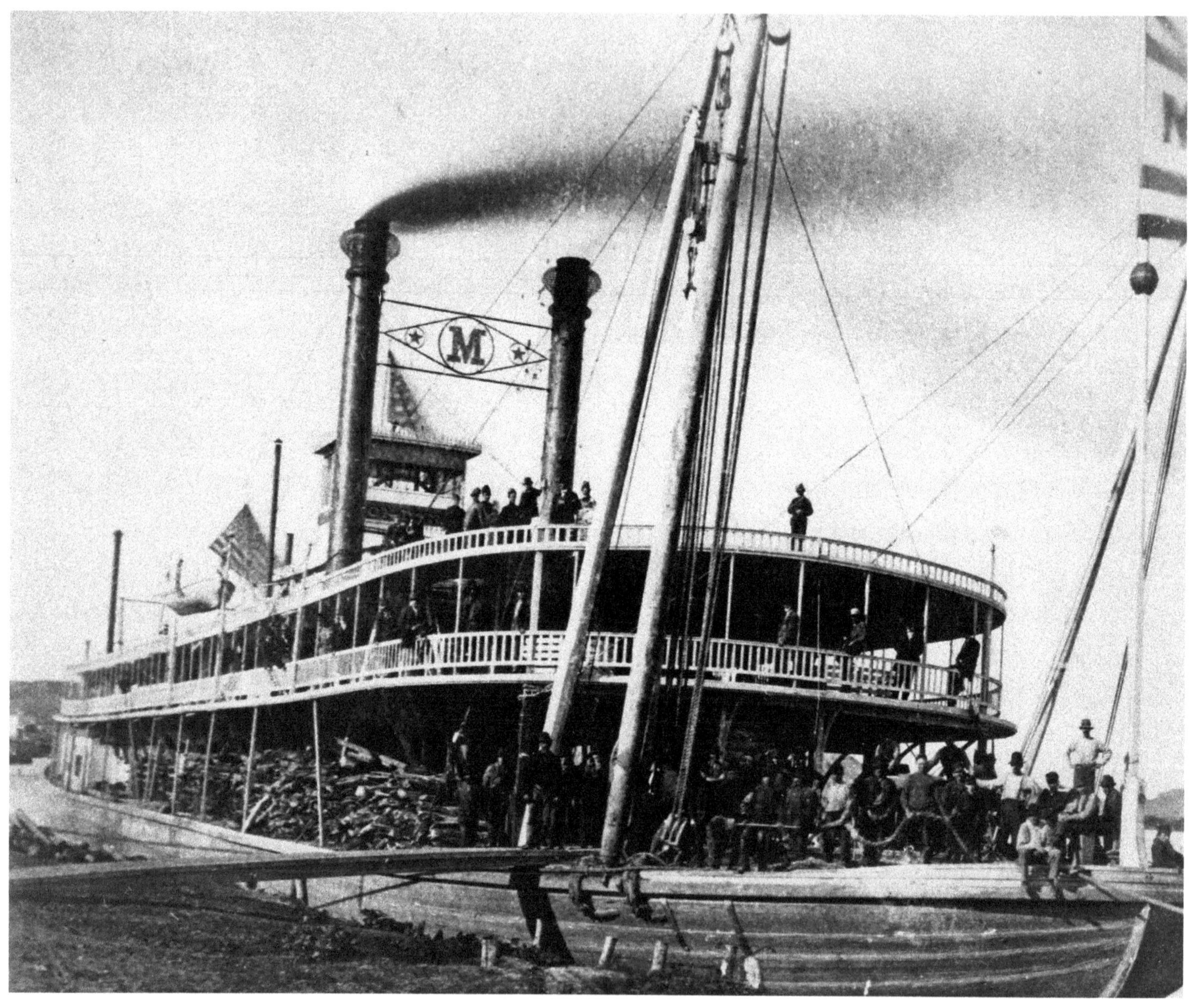

Fort Benton served as a major steamboat port for travelers to Montana for nearly 30 years. This photo shows the three-story paddle wheeler *Montana* in 1879. The largest ship to reach Fort Benton, it ran aground in 1884 on the banks of the lower Missouri.

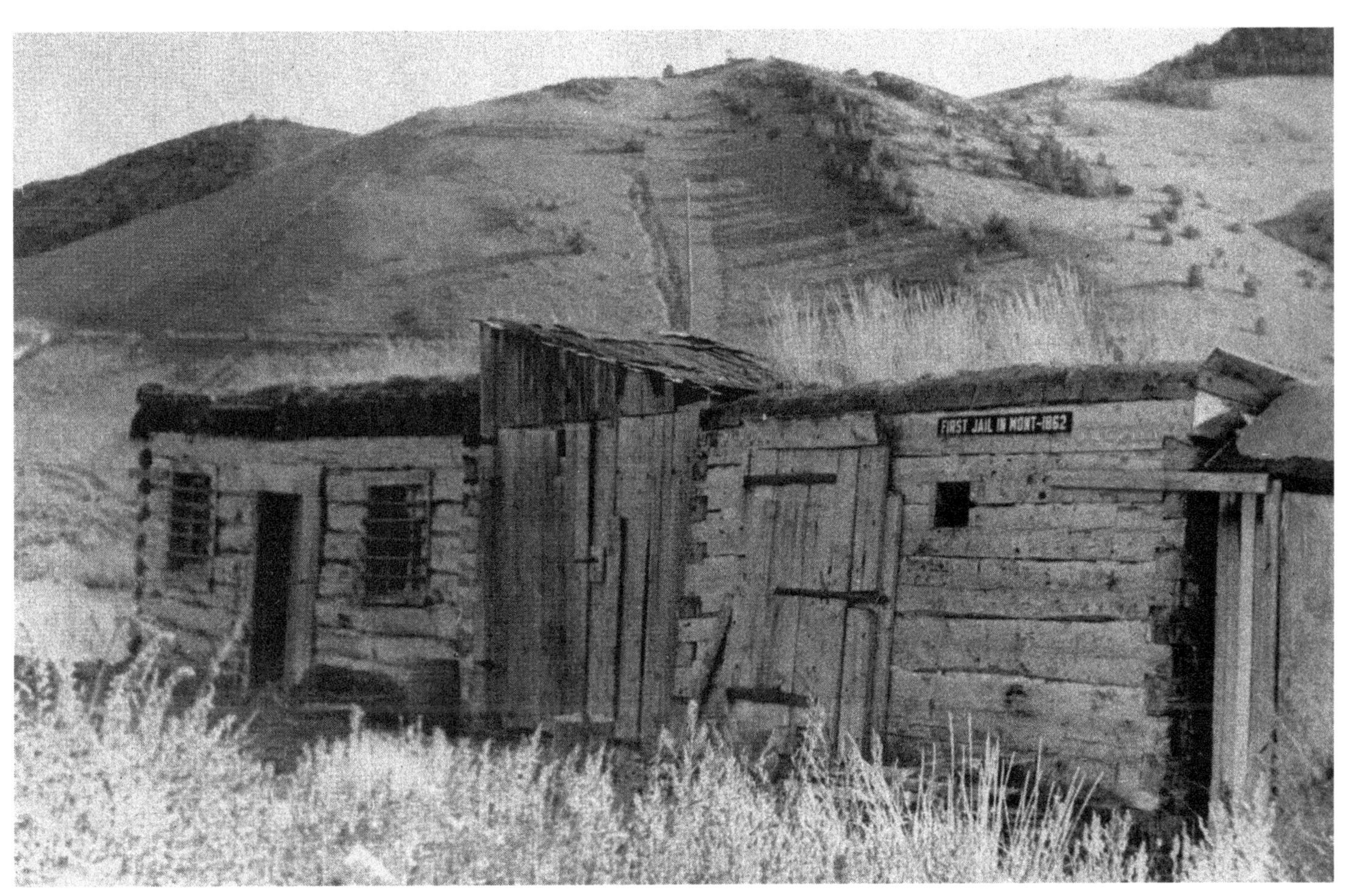

Sheriff Henry Plummer built the first jail in Montana by soliciting donations from the residents of Bannack, a gold rush camp with 3,000 residents, in 1863 (not 1862, as indicated on the sign in this photo). Suspecting that Plummer was actually the leader of a vicious gang of road agents, vigilantes hanged him in 1864.

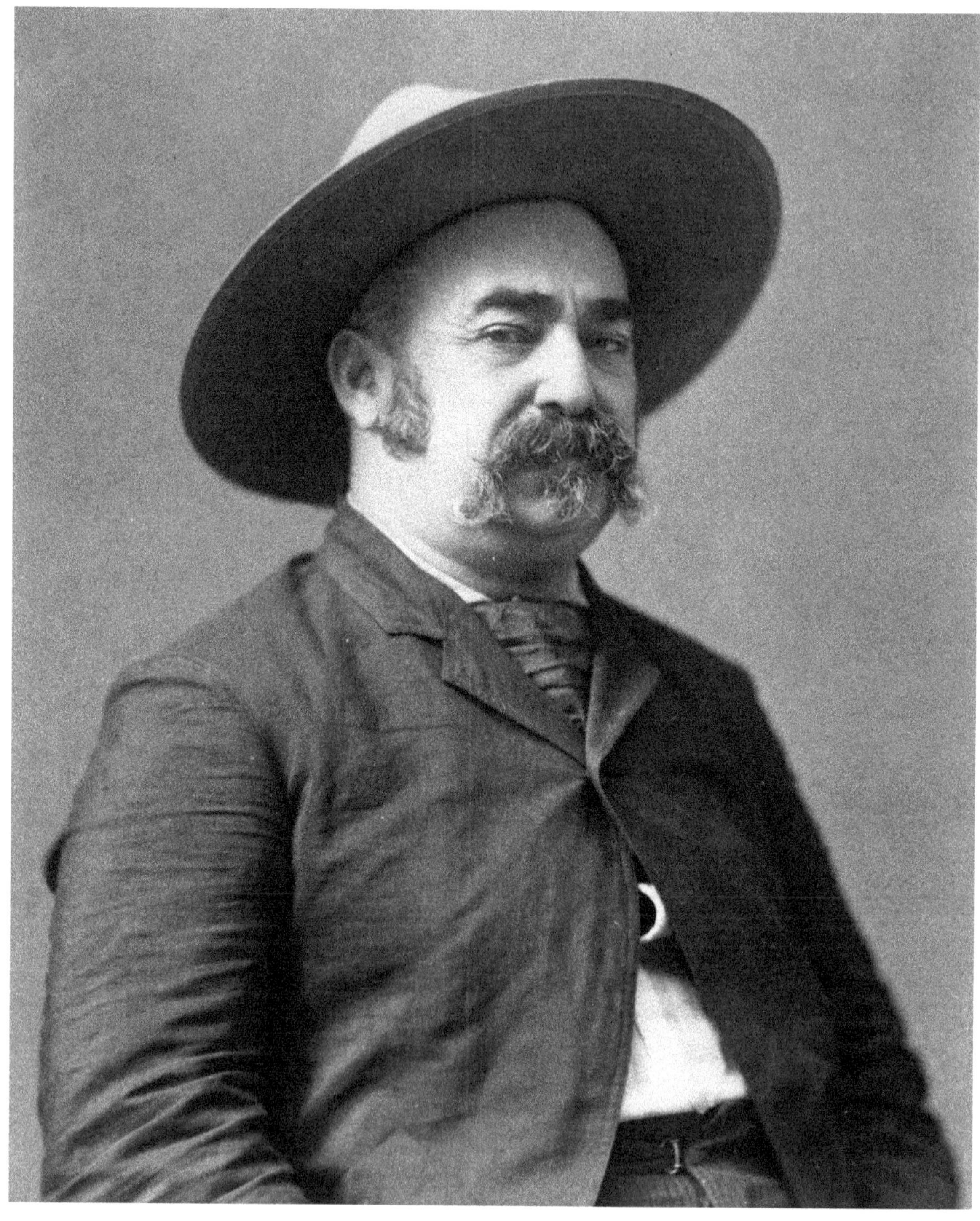

John X. Biedler was an active member of the Vigilance Committee and was responsible for hanging at least five outlaws in Bannack and Virginia City in 1864. Known simply as X, he later became a stagecoach guard and deputy U.S. marshal.

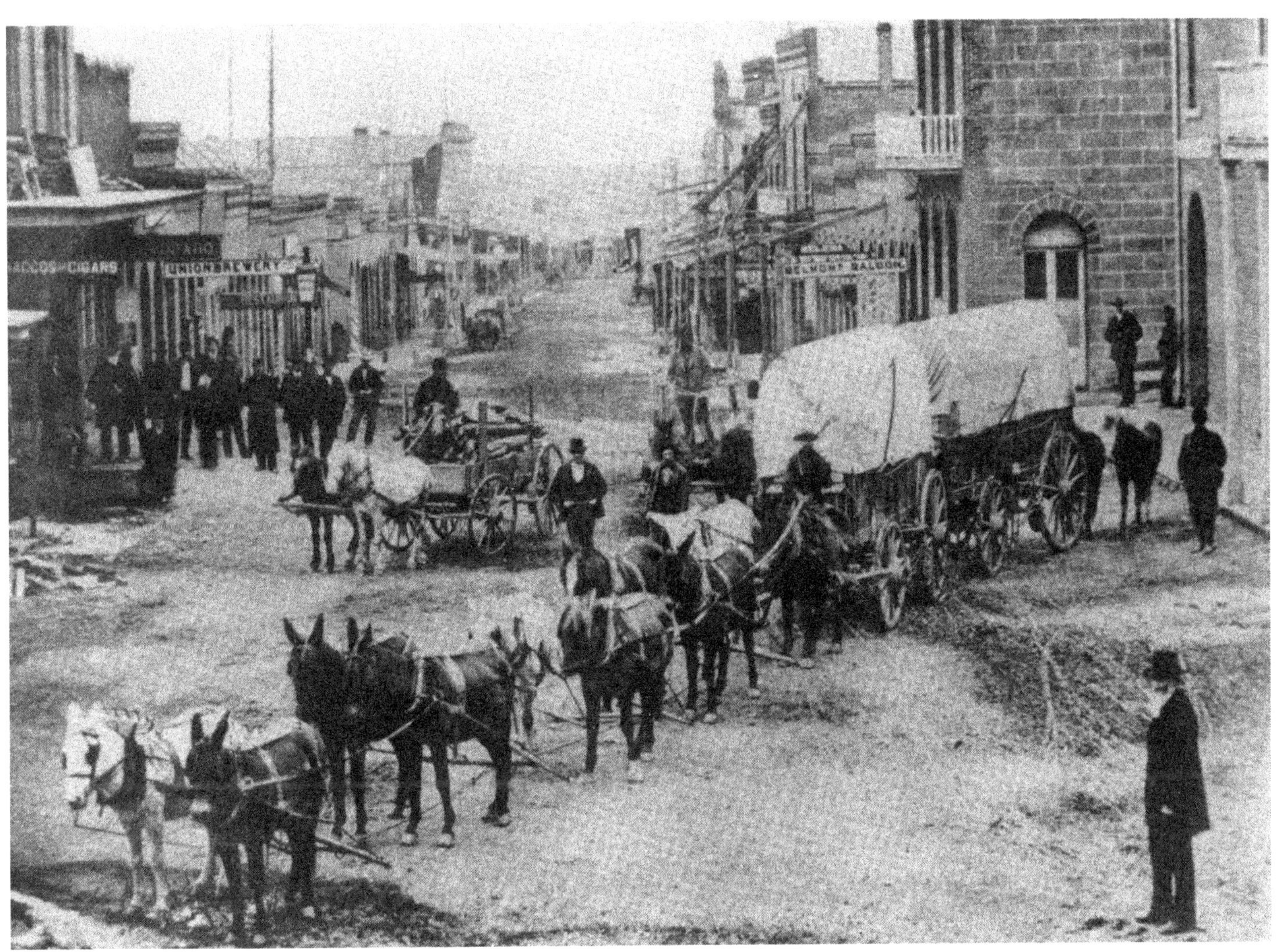

A muddy creek dubbed Last Chance Gulch by four discouraged prospectors became the main street of Montana's capital city. This photo shows the thriving city, Helena, in 1880. Today the area is home to a pedestrian mall.

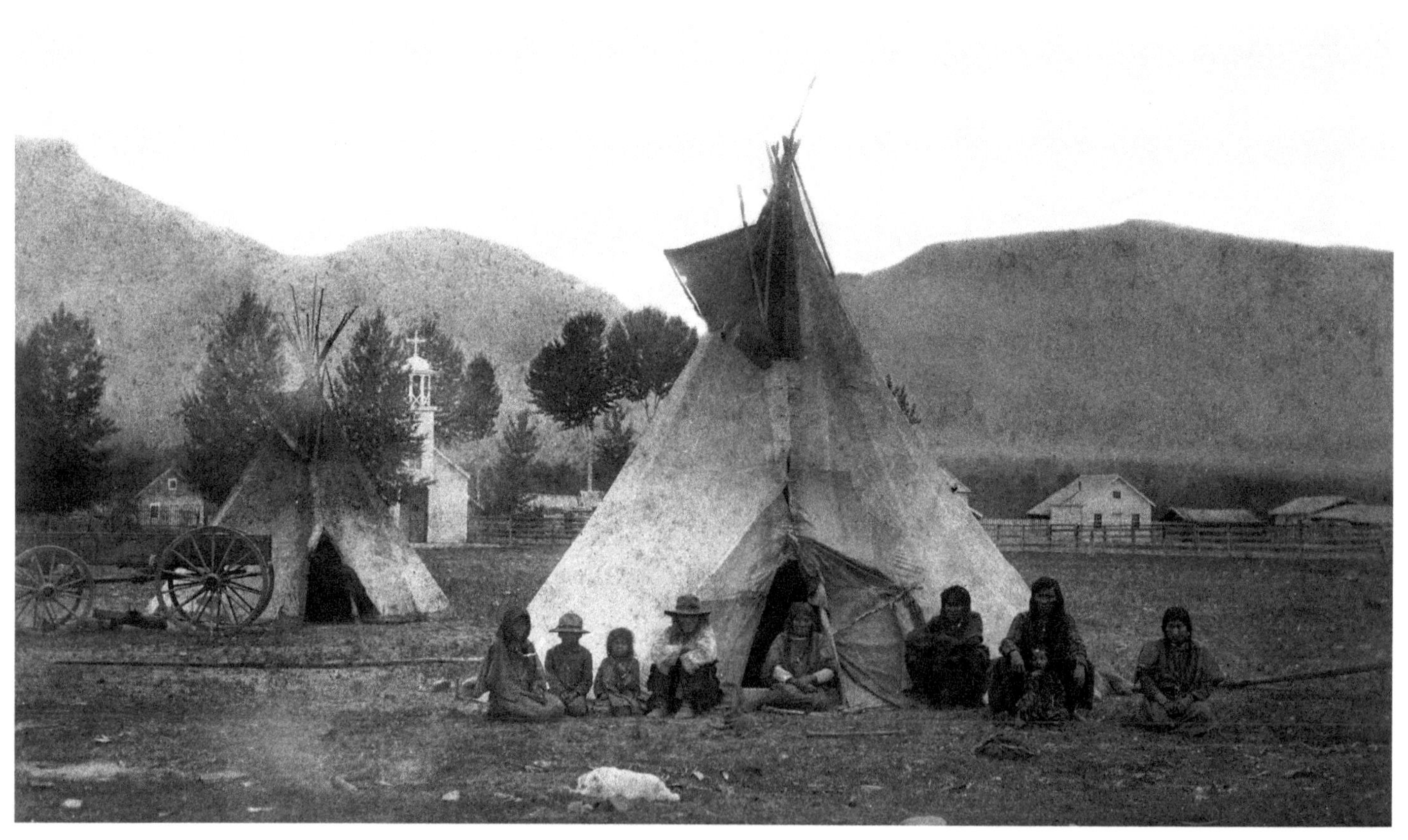

In 1831 four Salish Indians traveled to St. Louis to ask the Catholic Church to send priests to Montana. In 1841 several "Black Robes" arrived in the Bitterroot Valley and built St. Mary's Mission. The mission church can be seen behind the tepees in this 1880s photo.

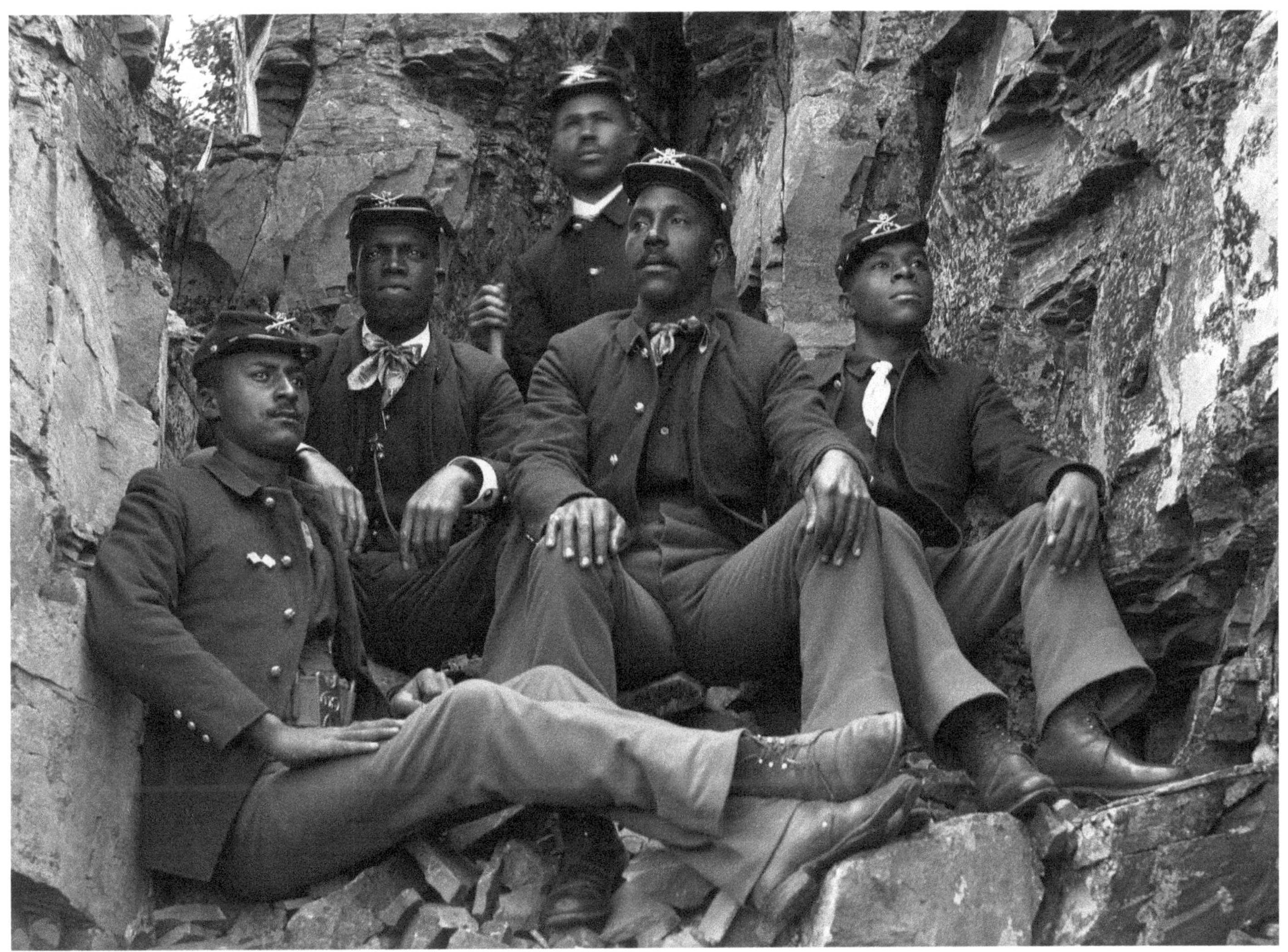

The 25th Infantry Regiment, an African American unit, arrived in Montana in 1888. Given the name Buffalo Soldiers by the American Indians, the troops were stationed at Fort Custer, Fort Shaw, and at Fort Missoula, where these soldiers were photographed. The regiment left Montana in 1898 upon the outbreak of the Spanish-American War.

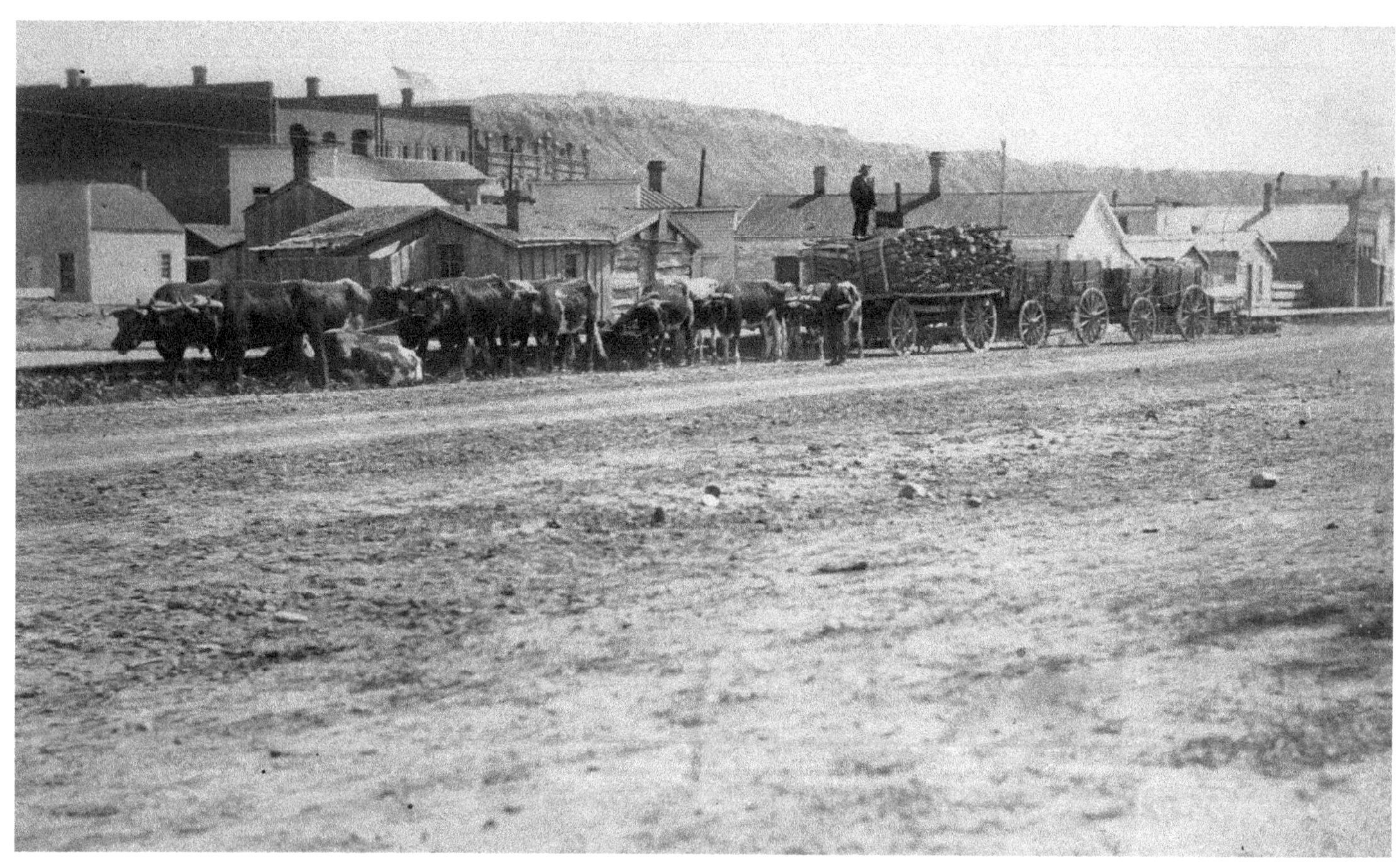

The American Fur Company established a trading post on the upper Missouri in 1847, and Fort Benton soon became an important steamboat port. The freight was off-loaded from the steamboats to wagons like this Fort Benton bull outfit driven by John Giesey.

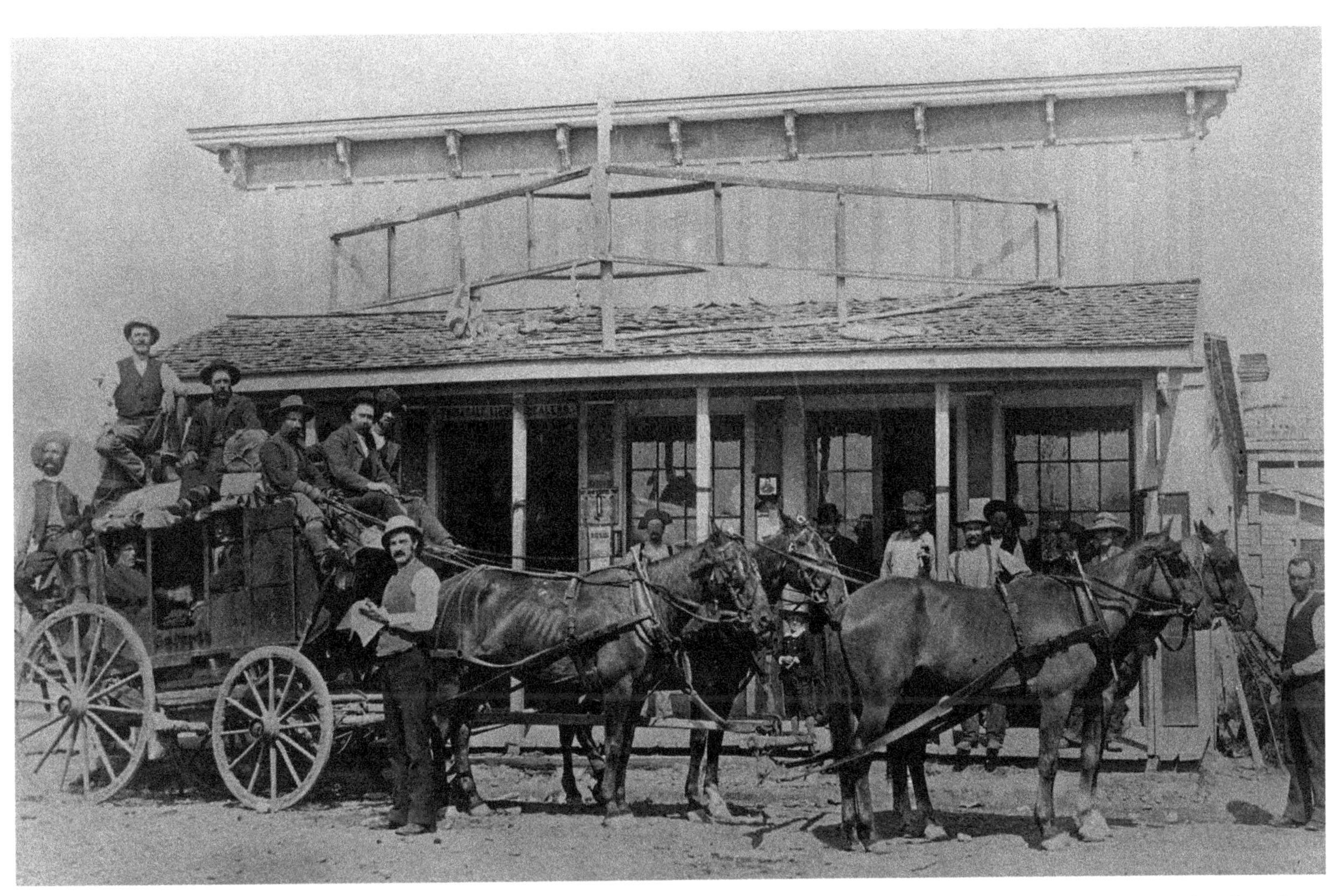

Passengers aboard a Concord Coach prepare to depart from George Steele's store in Sun River Cross in 1885. The Benton and Helena Stage operated for a number of years until the coming of the railroad finally doomed the era's steamboats and stagecoaches.

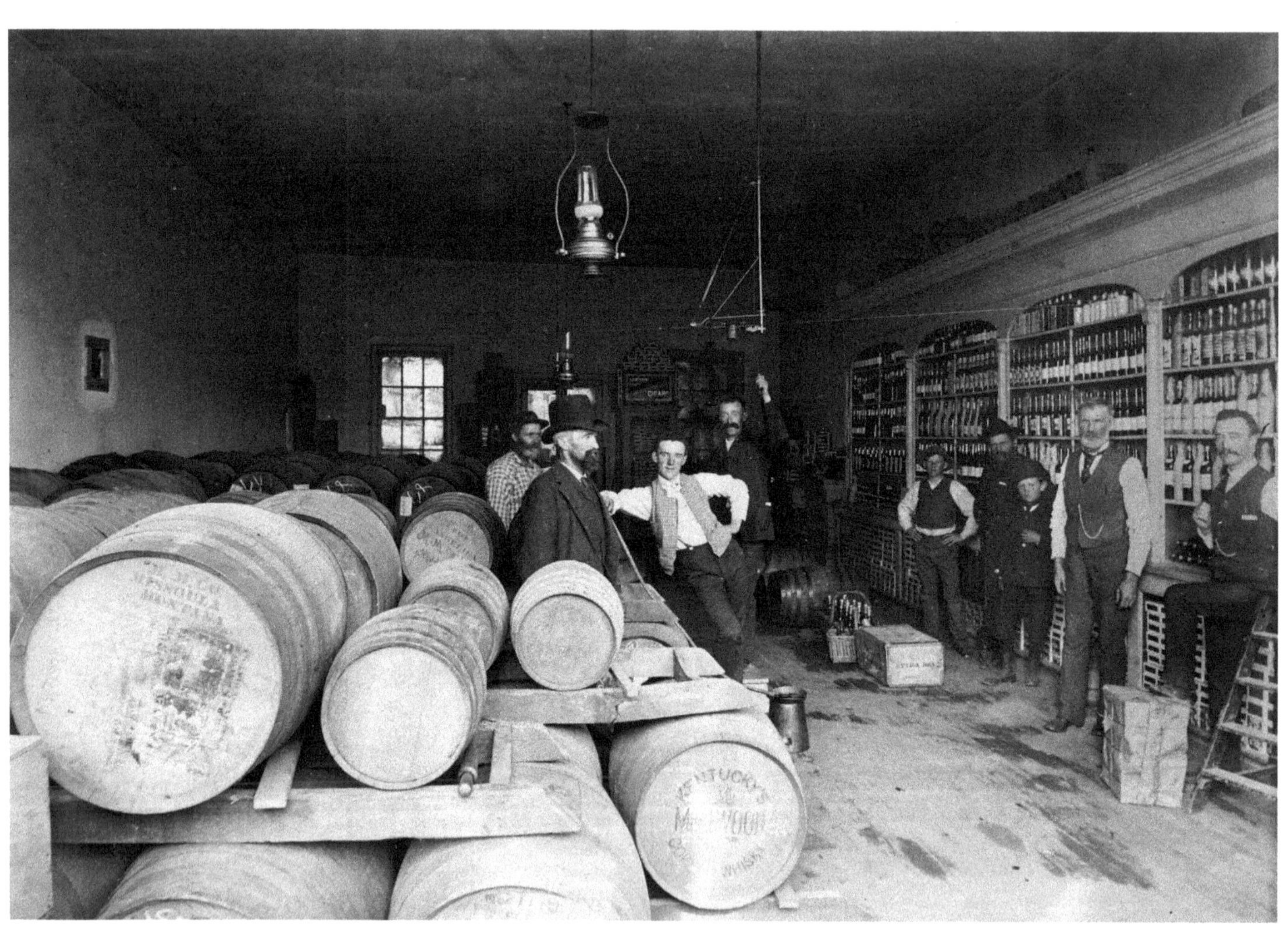

The interior of the Missoula Mercantile is seen here as it looked in 1890. The Nez Perce War broke out during the building's construction in 1877, and Missoula citizens sought shelter behind its brick walls. The extensively remodeled building is now home to a Macy's department store.

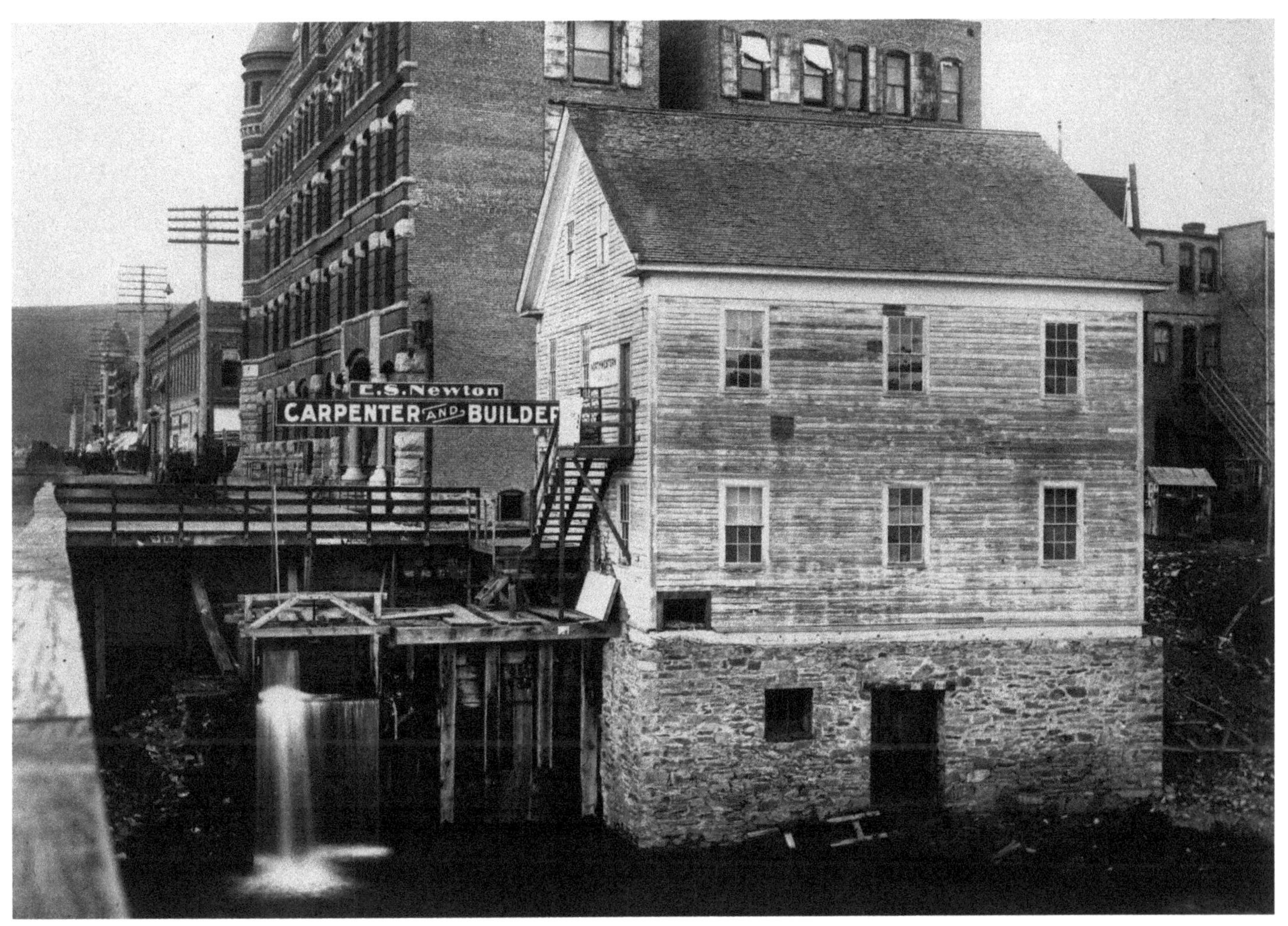

Worden and Company constructed the Missoula Mills gristmill in 1866, but by the 1890s, when seen here, it was used as a carpentry shop by local contractor C. S. Newton, who liked to decorate his building with American flags on patriotic holidays. The mill was torn down in 1912.

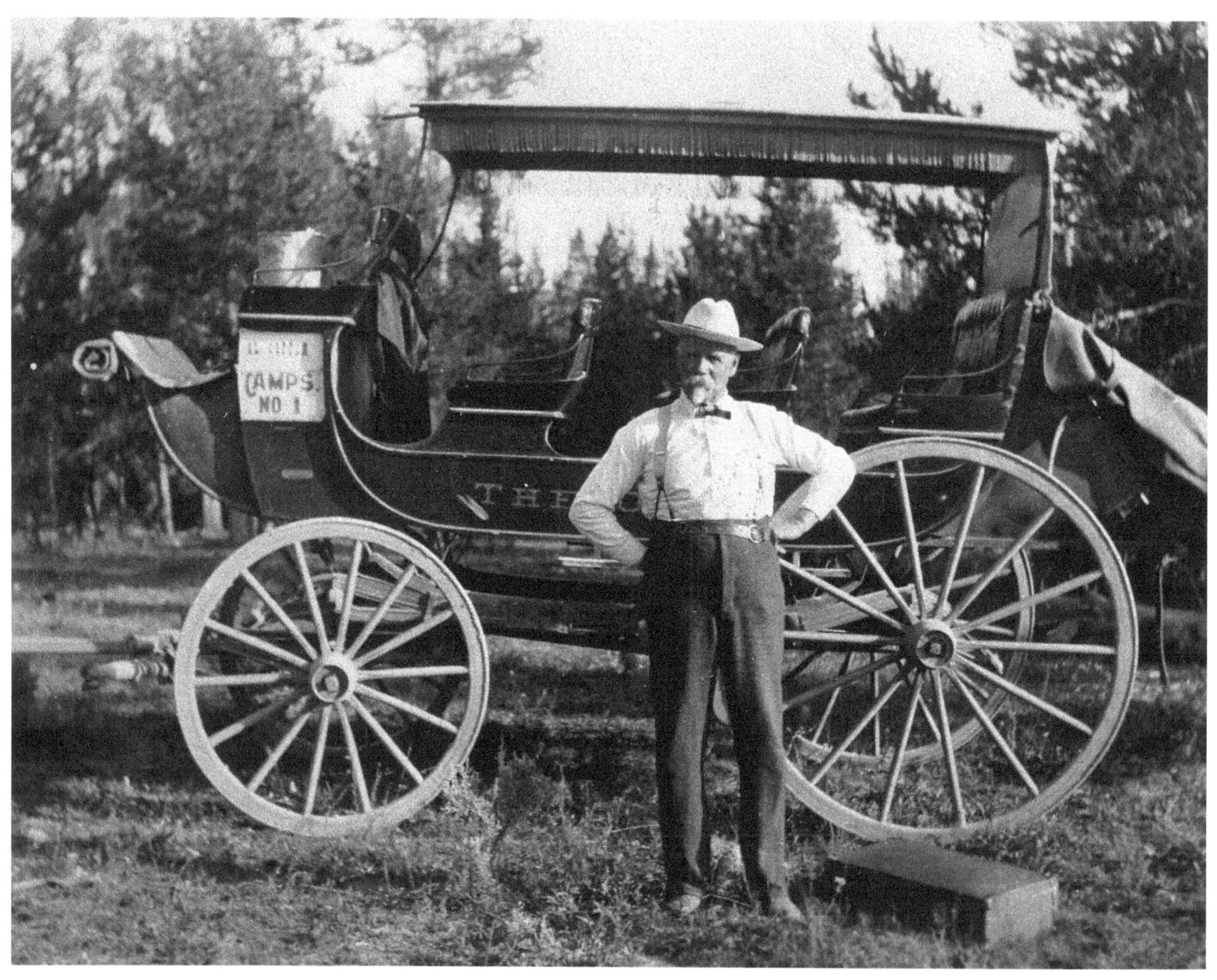

Bozeman resident George W. Wakefield began operating the first stage line into Yellowstone National Park in the 1880s. The former gold prospector charged $40 for a 10-day, all-expenses-paid camping tour of the park aboard one of his 10-passenger Concord Coaches.

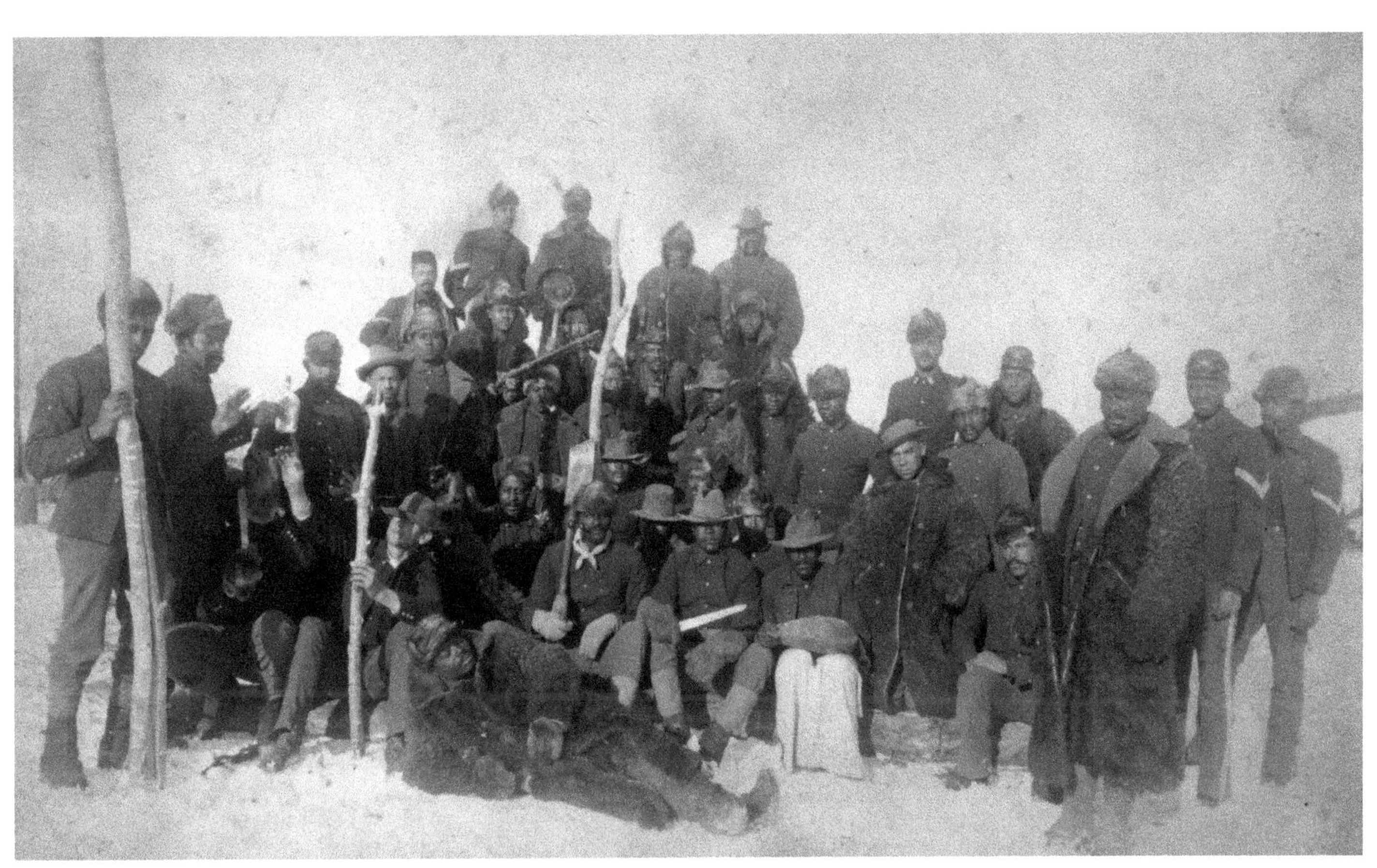

Four companies of the 25th Infantry spent several cold months stationed at Fort Keogh during the Sioux uprising of 1890 but never saw action. Named for one of Custer's officers, Fort Keogh is today a United States Department of Agriculture livestock and range research lab.

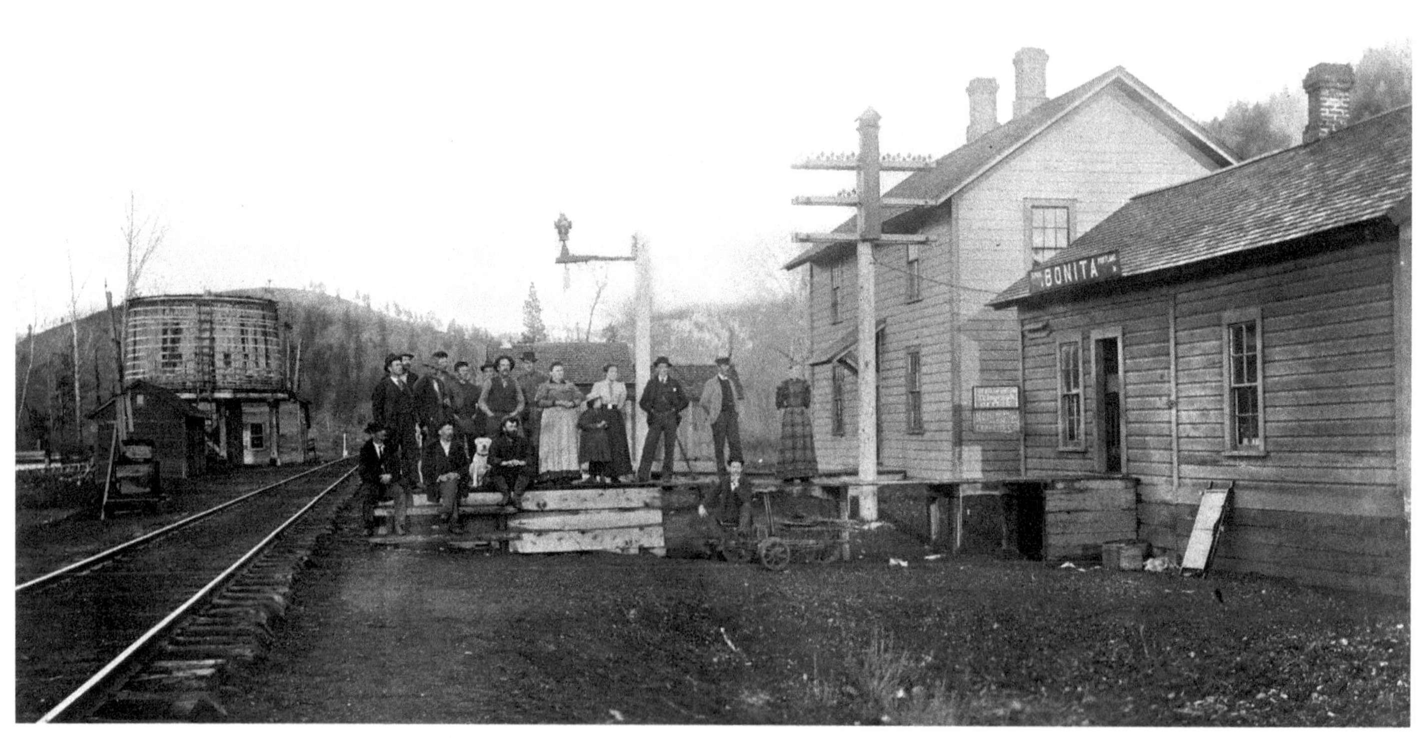

This photo of the railroad siding at Bonita, located near Beavertail Hill, was taken in the years prior to the tracks washing away during the 1908 flood of the Clark Fork River. The Bonita post office closed in 1942, and little trace of the town can be seen today.

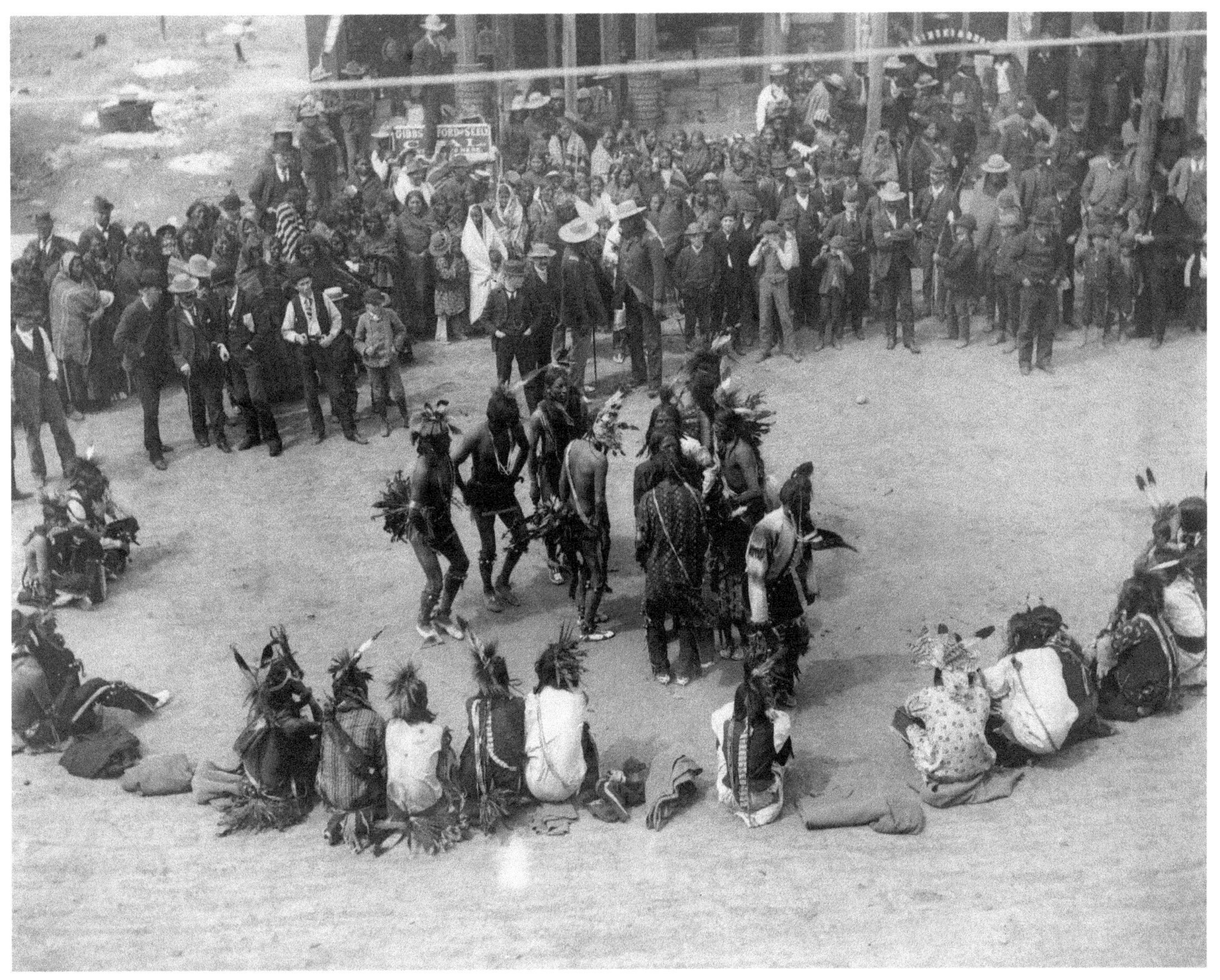

Northern Cheyenne perform the grass dance, also known as the Omaha dance, around 1891. Several different versions of this ceremonial dance still exist and are performed by a number of tribes. Each summer, Cheyenne and other native tribes follow the traditional powwow circuit.

The sun dance was the most important communal and religious celebration of the Plains Indians. Each tribe had its own customs, and the celebration could often last as long as a week. A sun dance pole is visible here at center, with a large tepee behind.

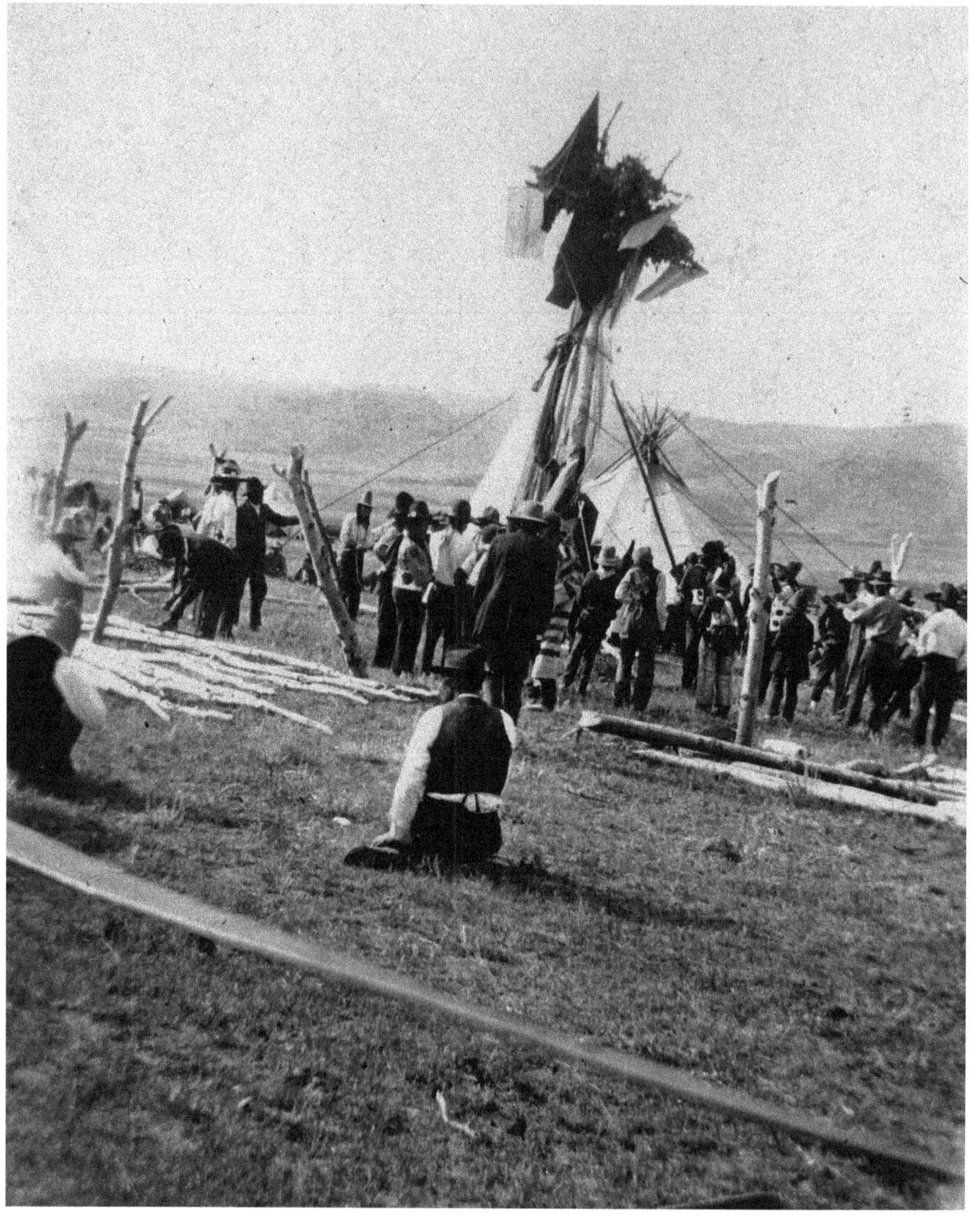

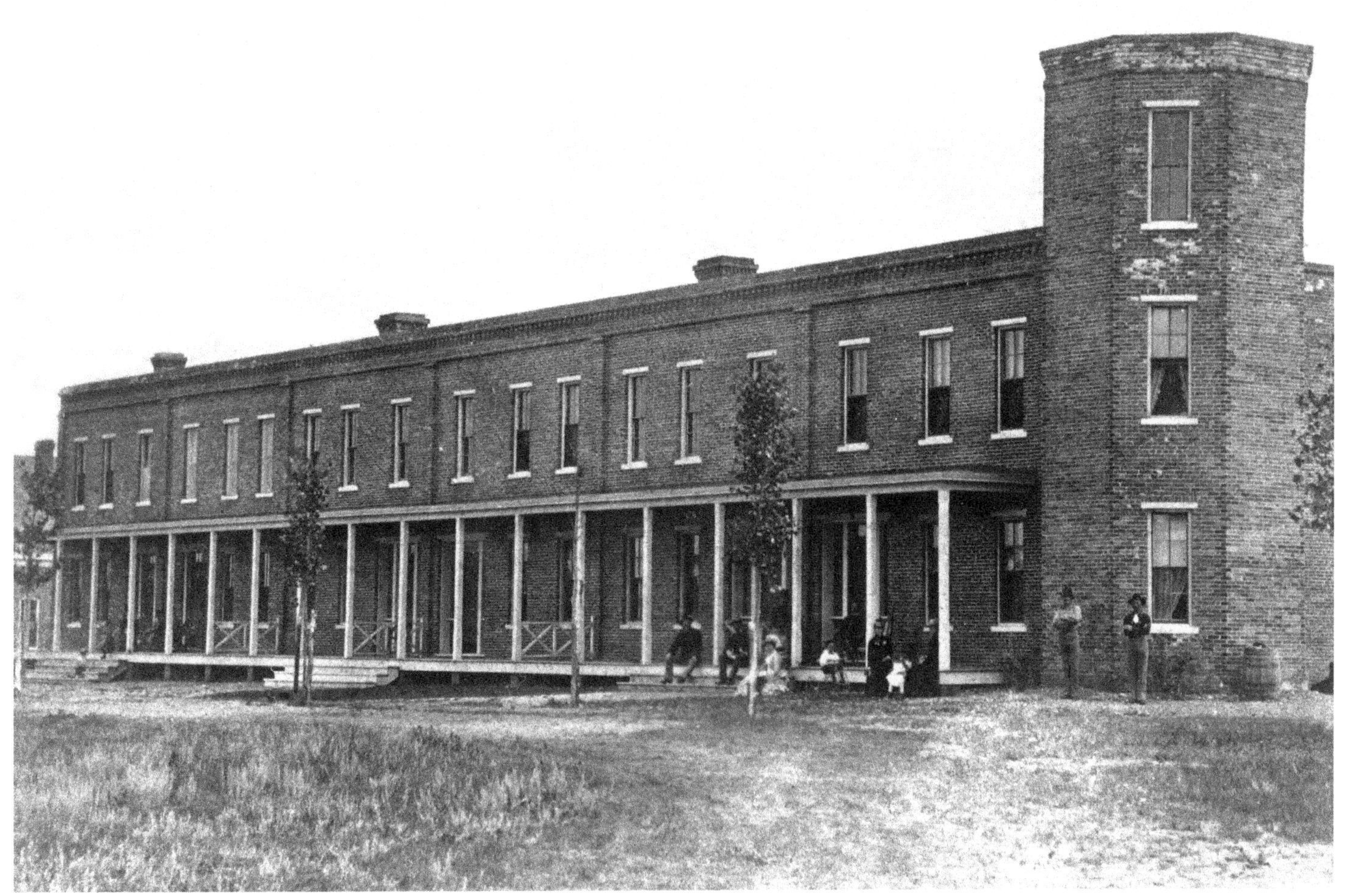

Fort Assiniboine was built in 1879 near present-day Havre. Housing more than 500 men, it was the largest military post in the state. Seen here around 1890, it was abandoned in 1911 and is now an agricultural research station. Some original fort buildings remain, including this officers' quarters.

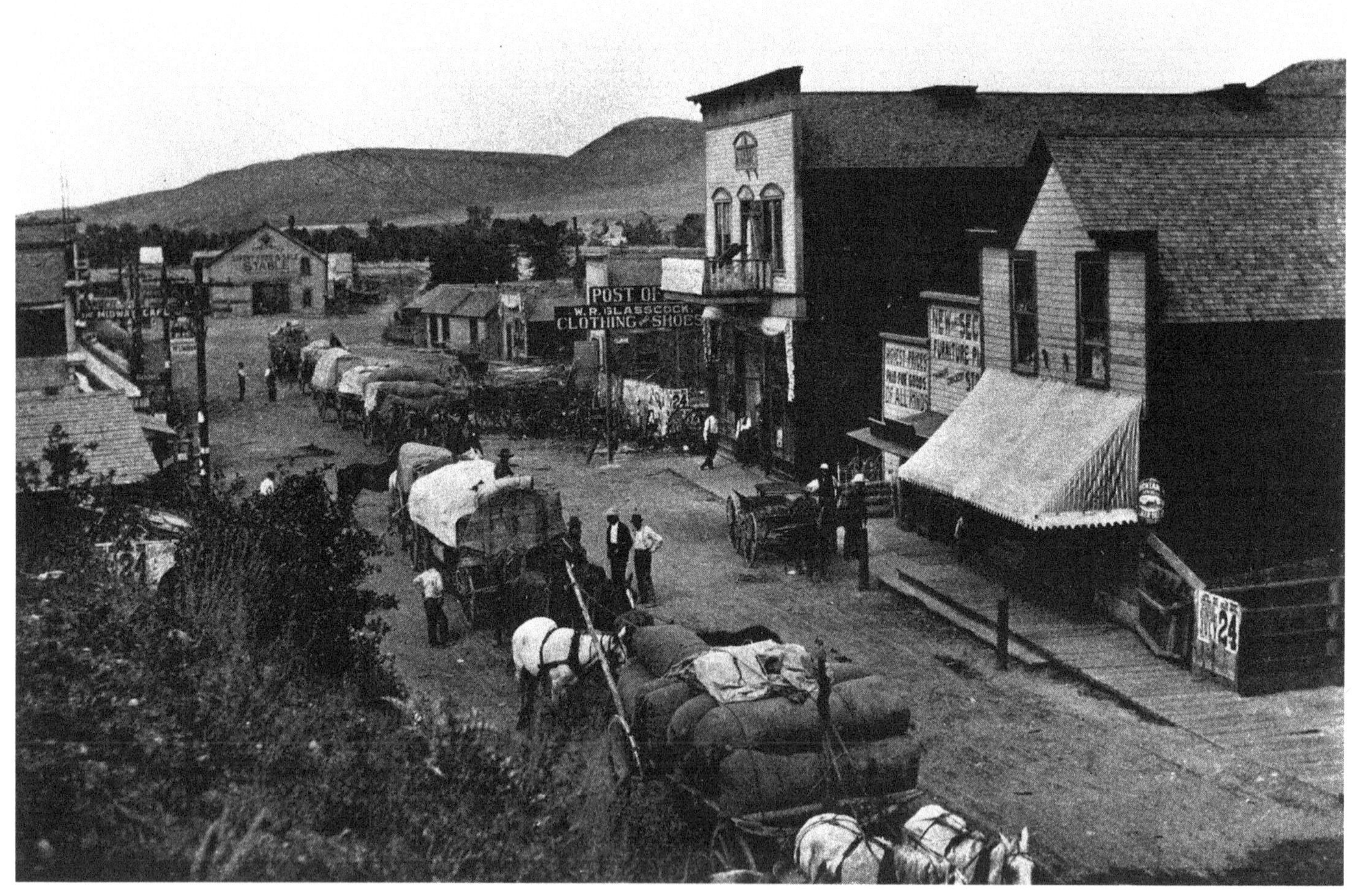

Wagons carrying wool pass through Belt on their way to Great Falls. Belt was a thriving mining town that supplied coal to the Anaconda Mining Company and to the steamboats at Fort Benton. By the 1880s, hundreds of thousands of sheep were being driven into central Montana.

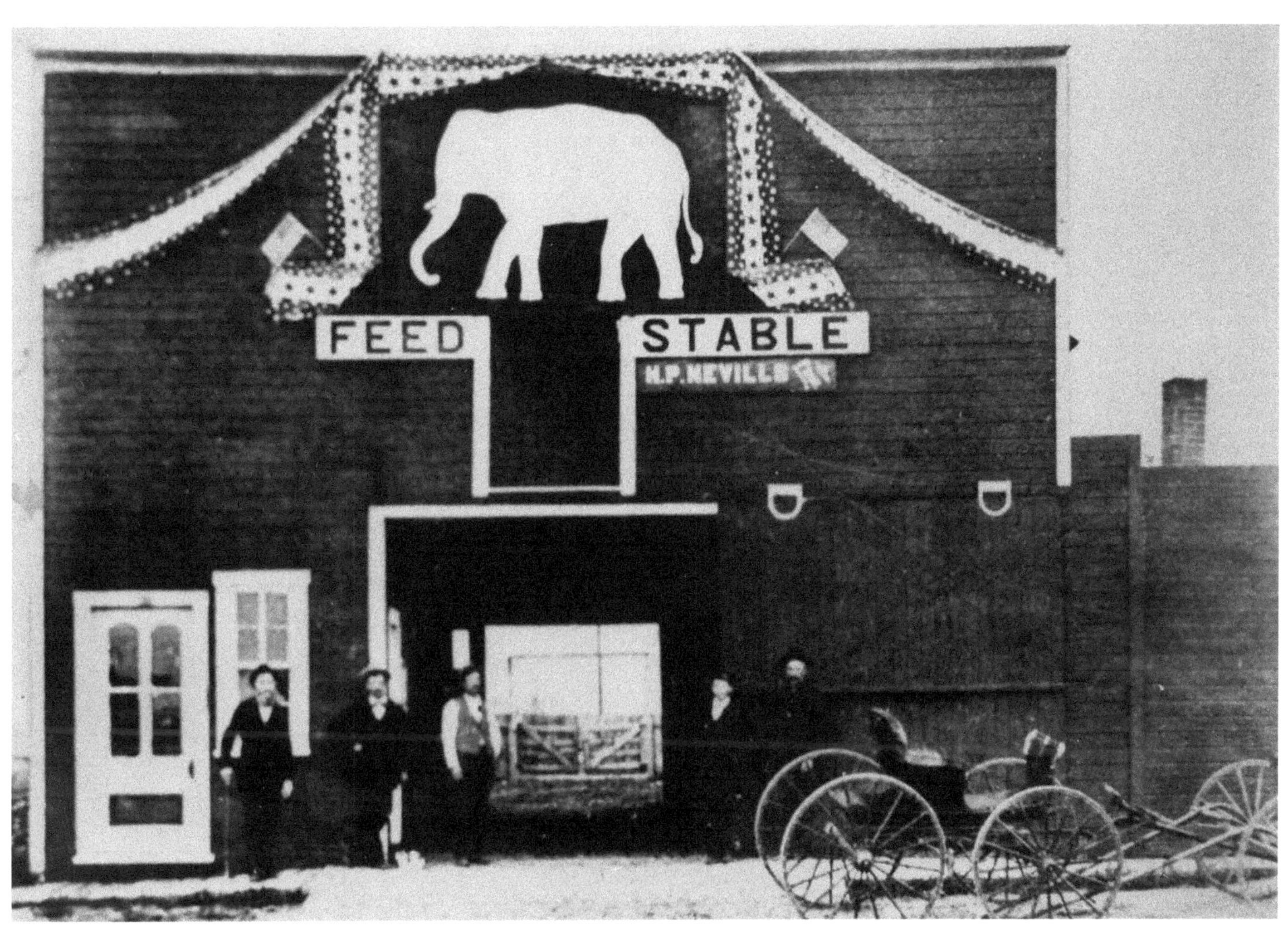

Apparently the H. P. Nevills feed stable in Great Falls was a staunchly Republican enterprise—or else the business was advertising its willingness to serve customers larger than horses.

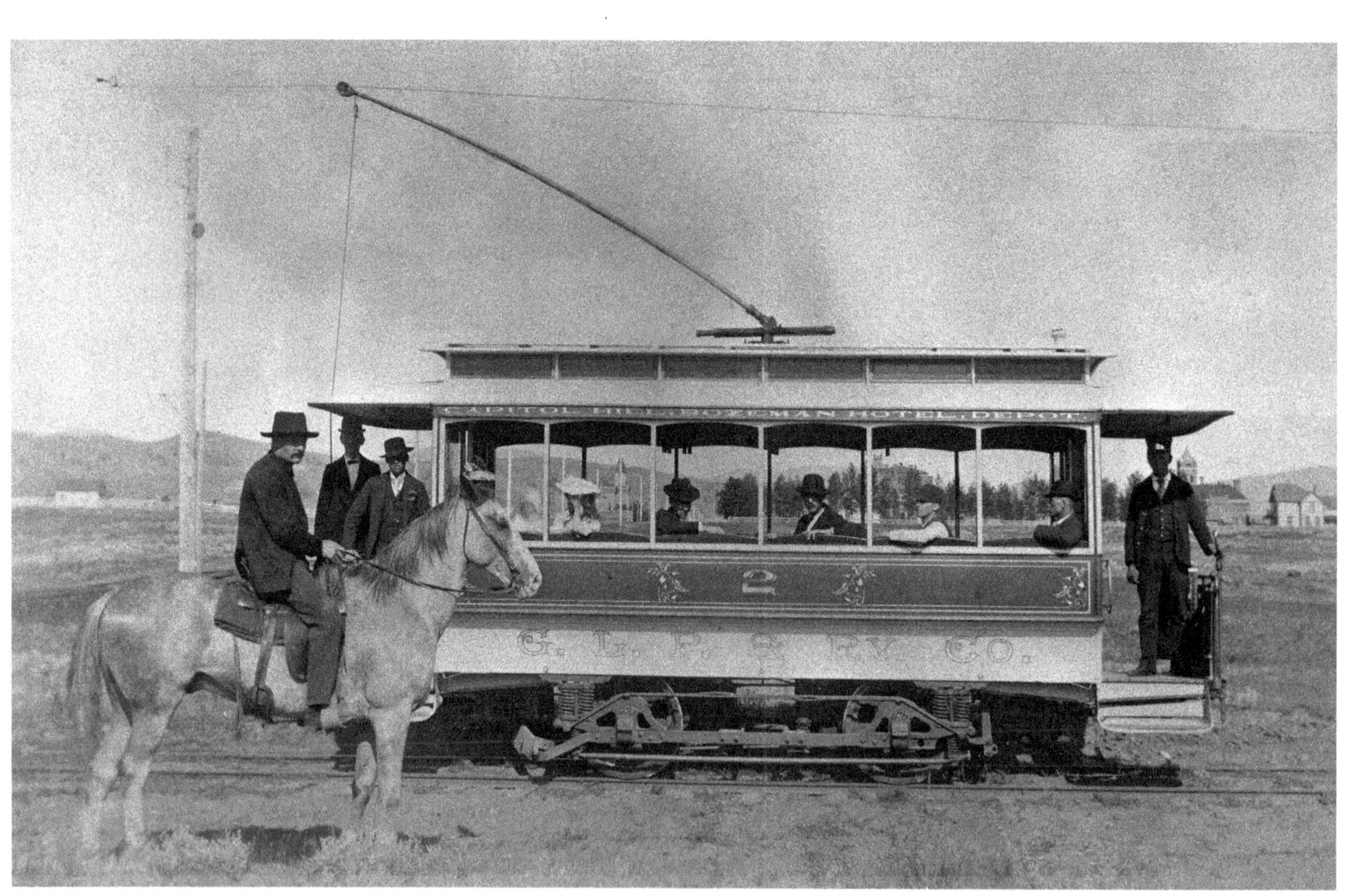

An electric streetcar belonging to the Gallatin Light, Power and Railway Company sits on its track in Bozeman. The line was installed in 1892, not long before this photo was taken, and ran until 1921. Most of Montana's larger cities operated electric streetcars during the 1890s.

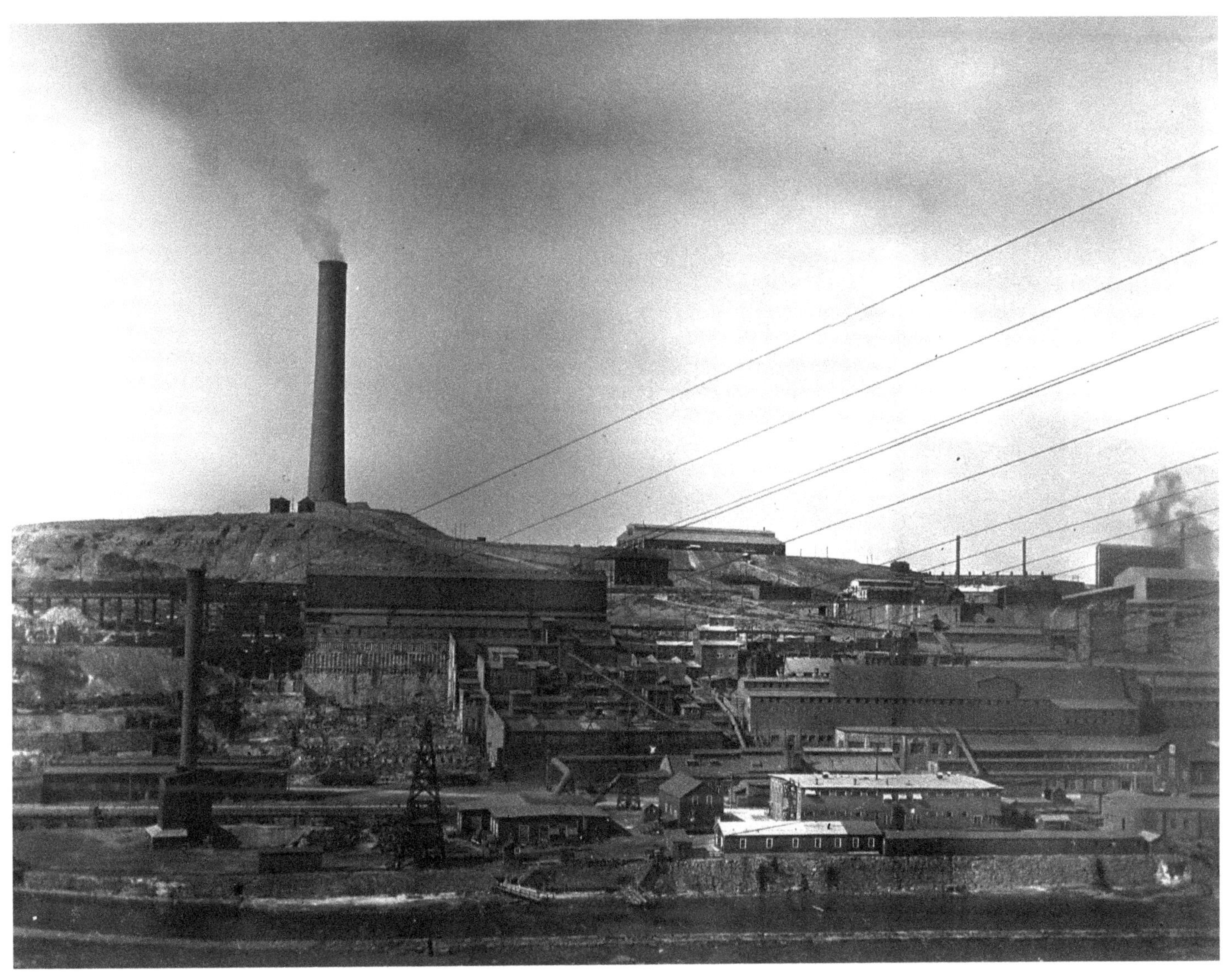

The Boston and Montana Company copper smelter at Black Eagle opened in 1893. Bought by the Anaconda Mining Company in 1910, the plant employed 2,000 men but proved to be an environmental disaster. An audience of 40,000 watched when the big stack was dynamited in 1982.

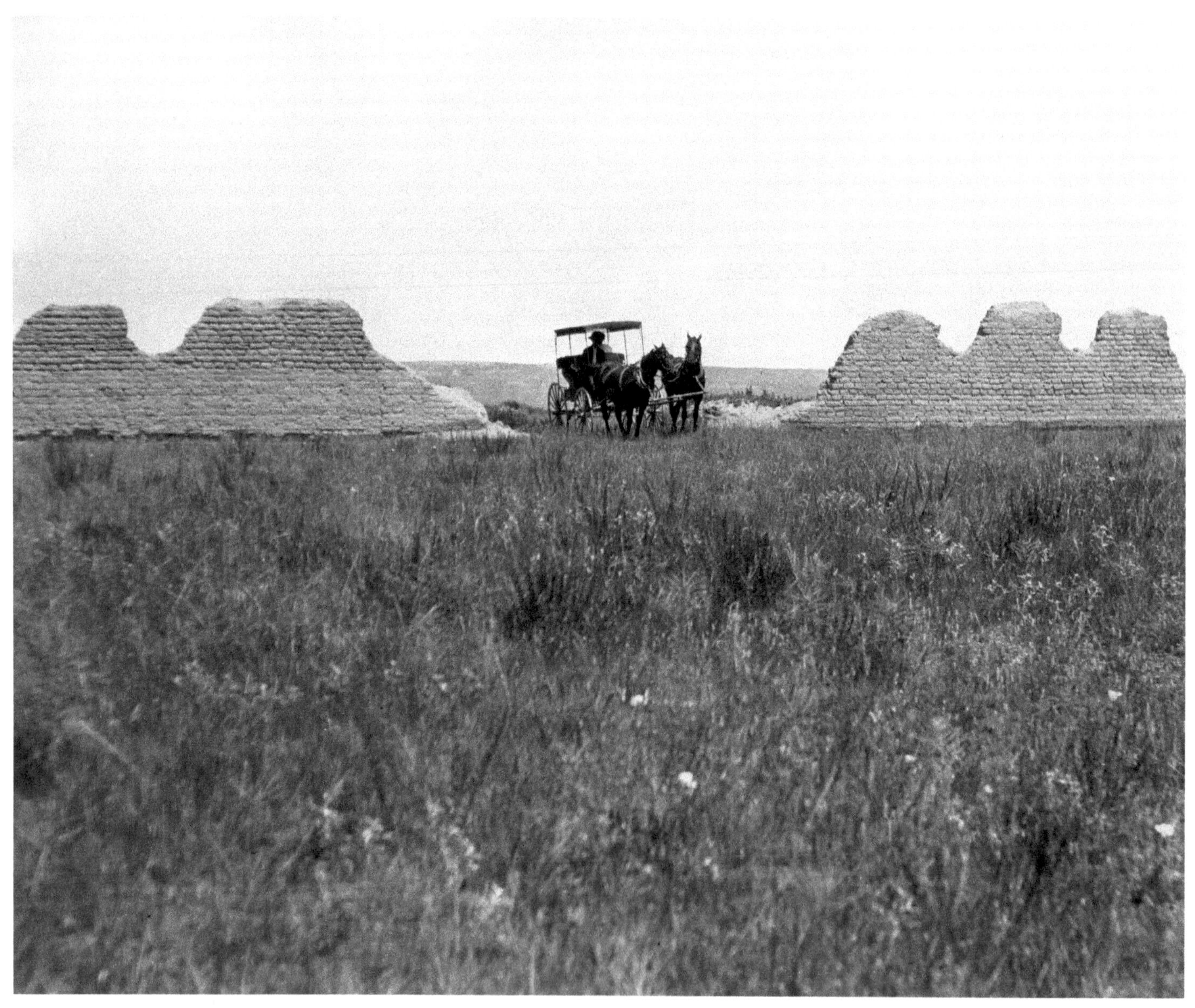

A wagon picks its way through the remains of Fort C. F. Smith. Located on the Big Horn River, the fort was built in 1866 to protect travelers along the Bozeman Trail from hostile Indians who claimed the area. Cut off for months at a time, the garrison abandoned the post in 1868.

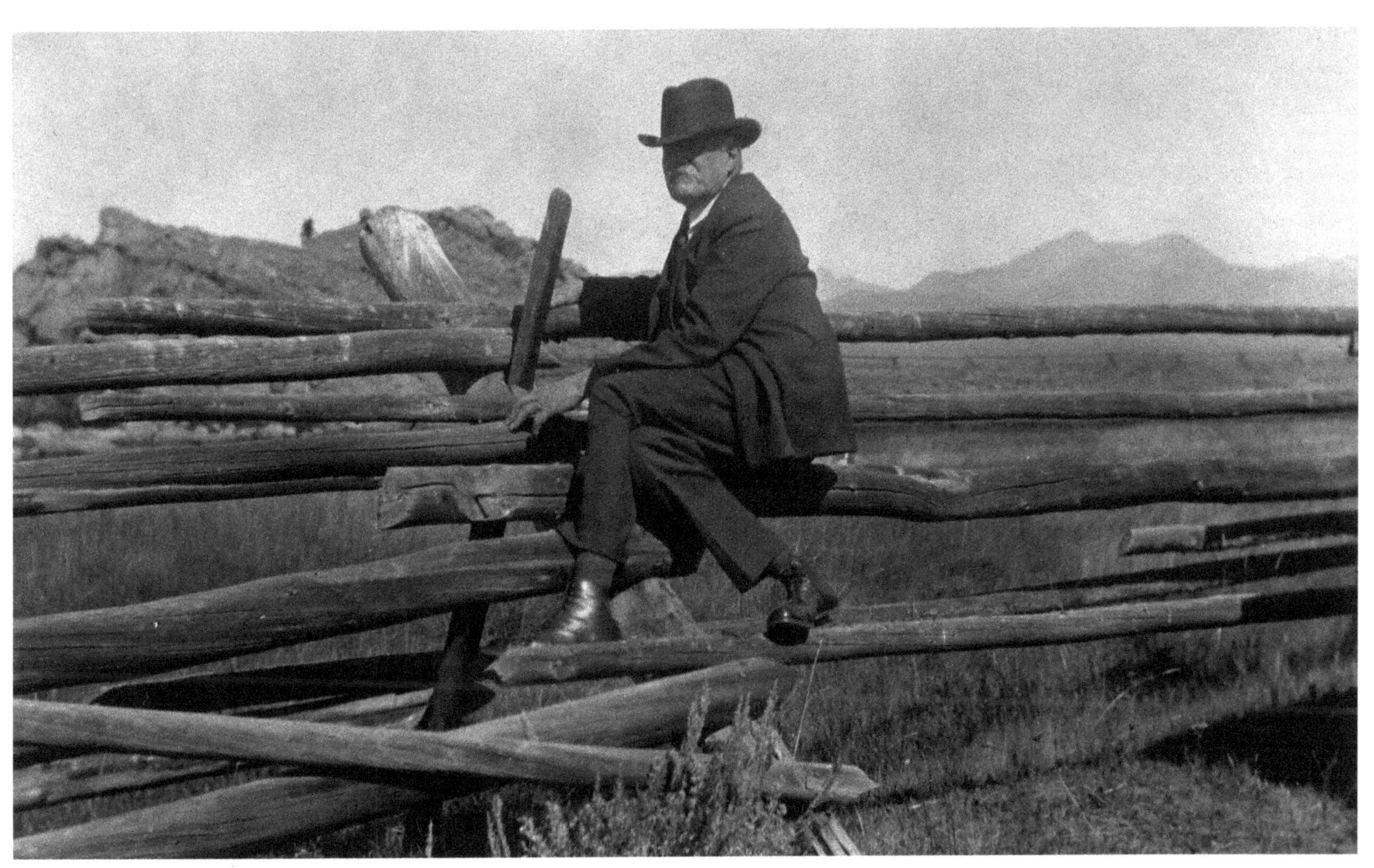

Copper king Marcus Daly of the Anaconda Mining Company poses on a buck-rail fence at his Bitterroot Stock Farm. He bought the property for a summer home in 1886 and turned the 22,000-acre spread into one of the world's premier centers for breeding and training racehorses before his death in 1900.

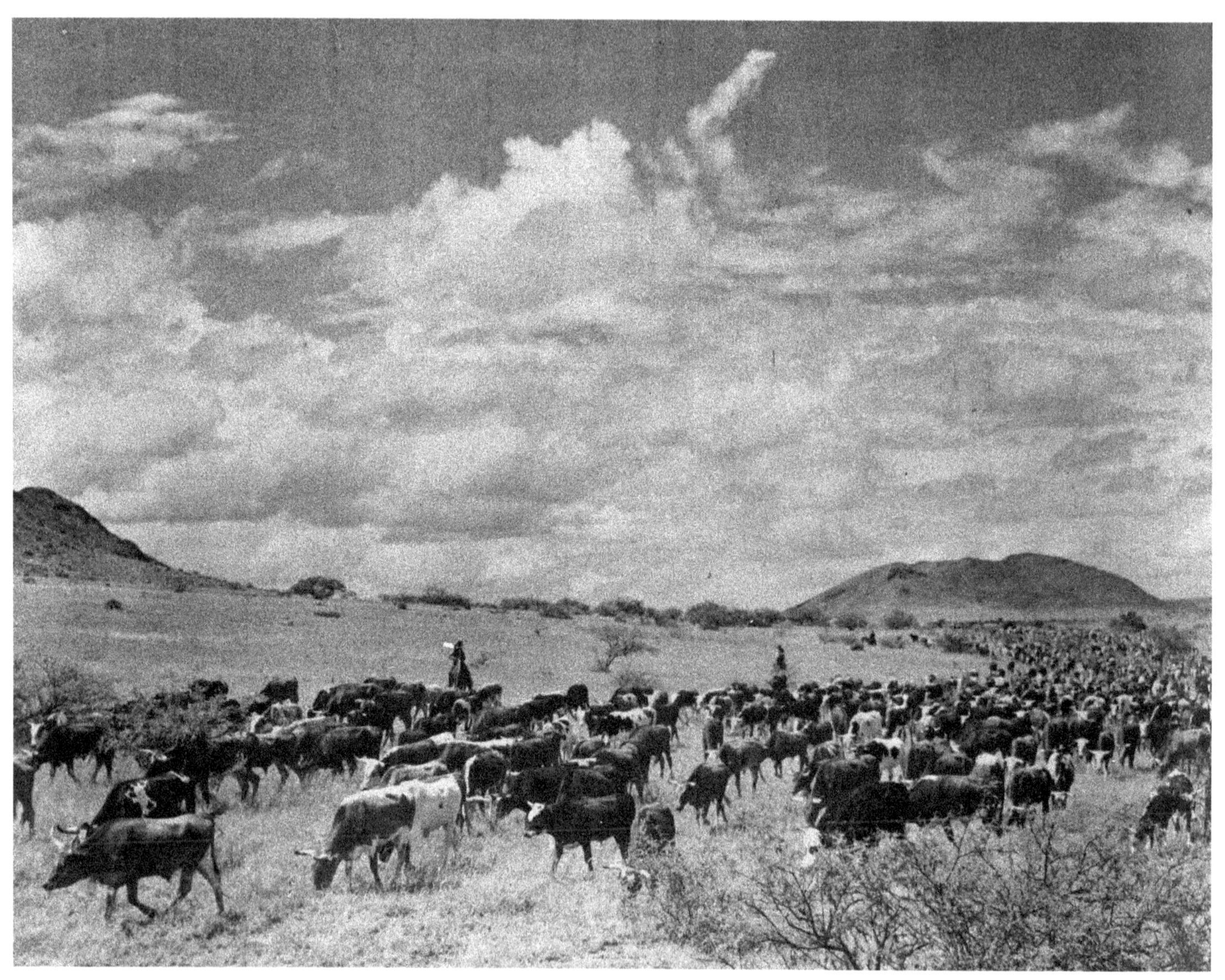

Cowboys drive a herd of shorthorn cattle under the big sky in this iconic photo. Pioneer cattleman Conrad Kohrs introduced shorthorns to Montana in 1871. The death of hundreds of thousands of cattle during the hard winter of 1886 brought an end to the open range.

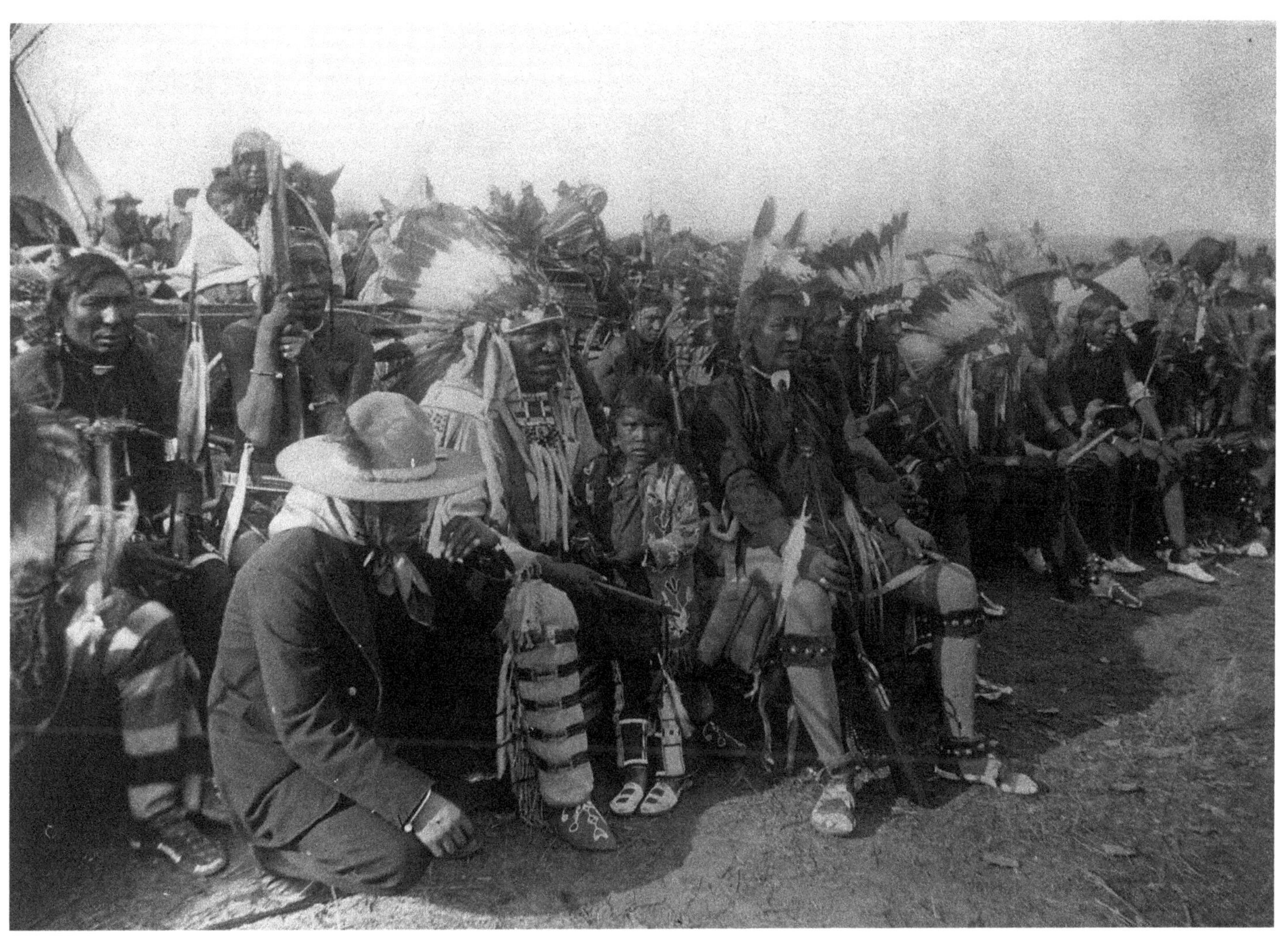

Two Leggings, Chief Plenty Coups, and other Crow elders pose in powwow dress. The Crow prefer to be known as Apsáalooke, which means "big-beaked bird." The Crow Fair remains one of the oldest and largest powwows in the country.

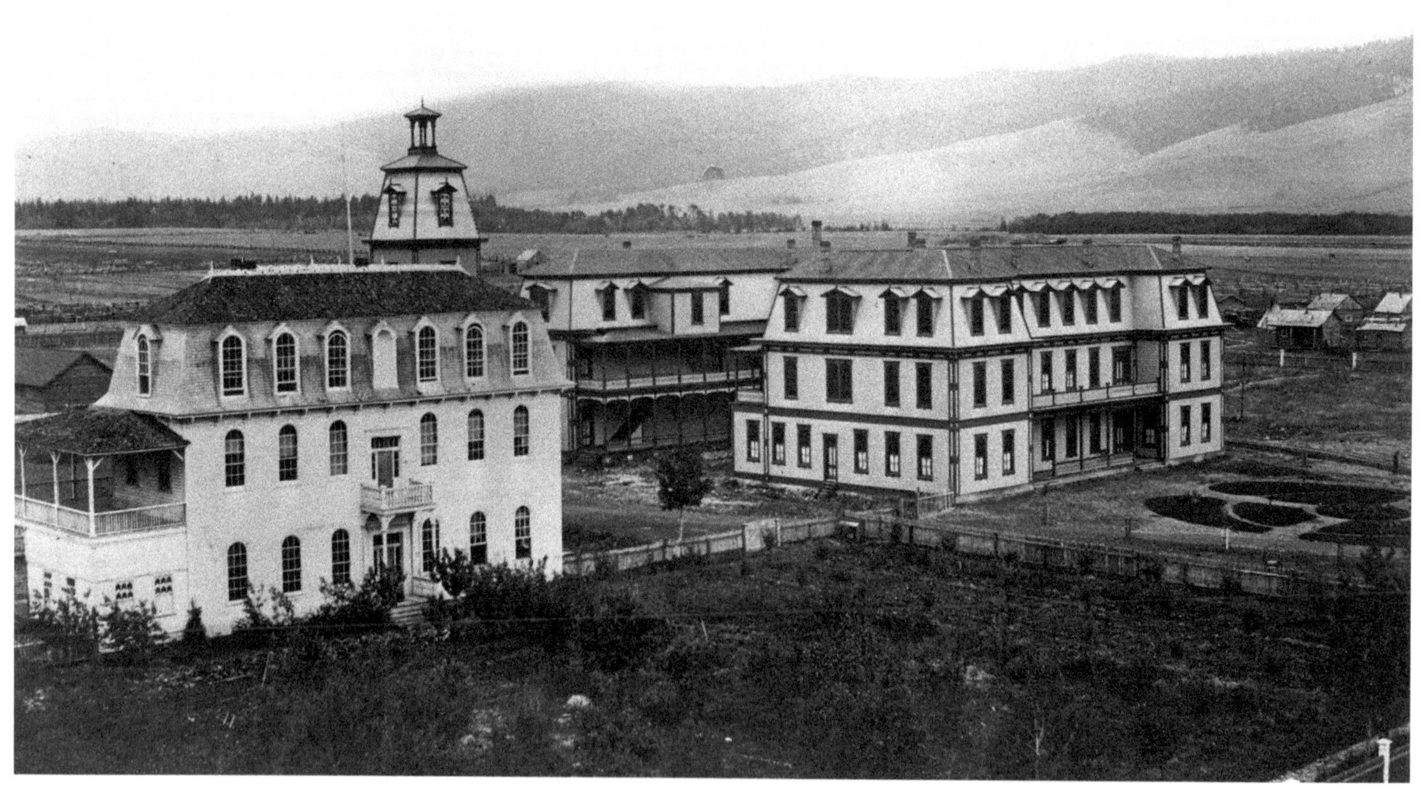

The St. Ignatius Mission was built in 1854. Within a year nearly 1,000 Indians lived nearby. This photo, taken around 1890, shows the boys' barracks at the boarding school. A new mission church built in the early 1890s included murals painted by Brother Carignano and remains a popular tourist destination today.

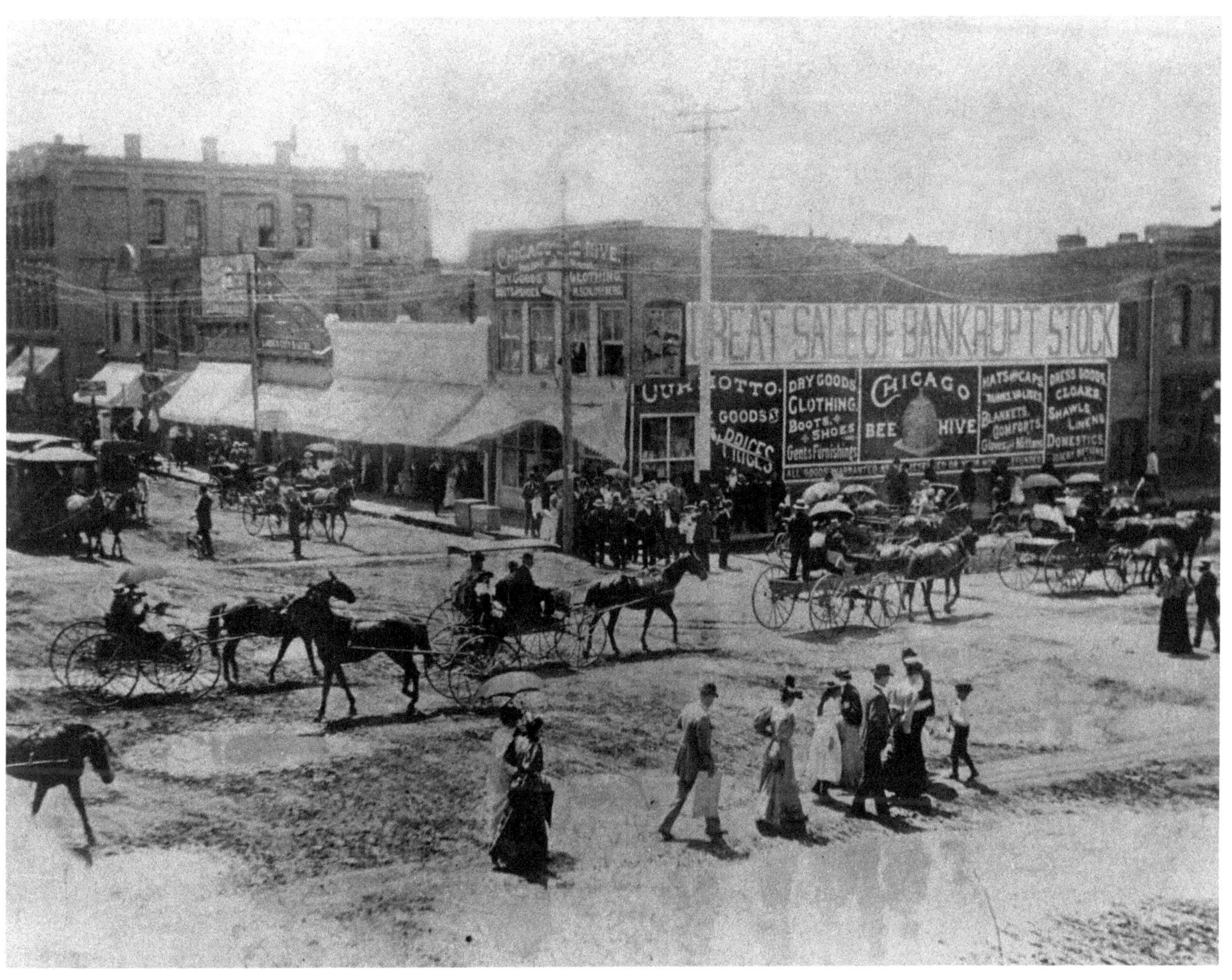

This 1894 street scene depicts the corner of Higgins and Main in Missoula. Pedestrians cautiously pick their way across the muddy street while horse-drawn buggies wend their way through traffic. Bicycles were also increasing in popularity during the 1890s.

In 1881 the 2nd Cavalry constructed this granite memorial to honor the 7th Cavalry troopers who died with General George A. Custer at the Little Big Horn. The remains of many of the soldiers lie under this monument, which was photographed about 1894. A nearby monument honors the Indian casualties.

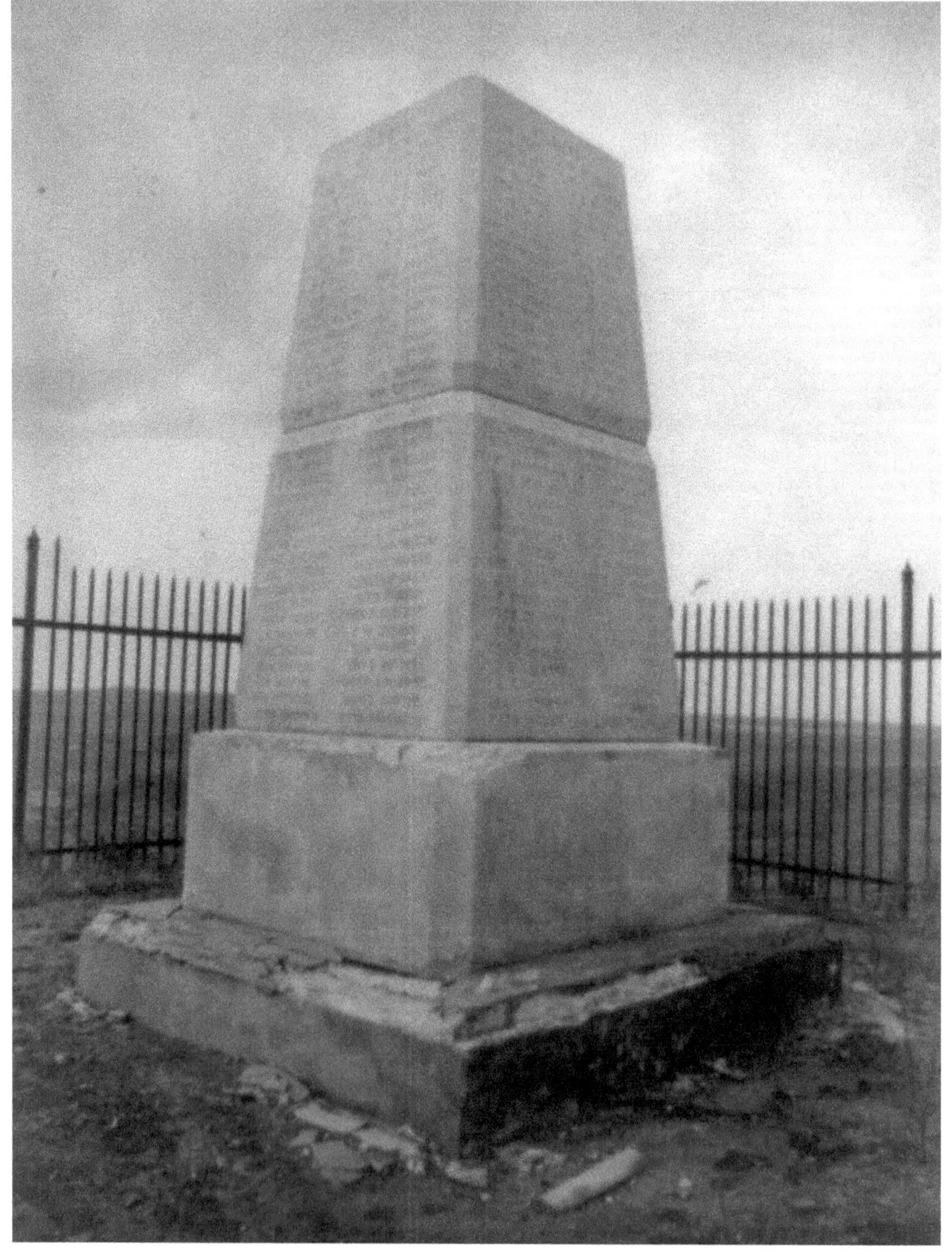

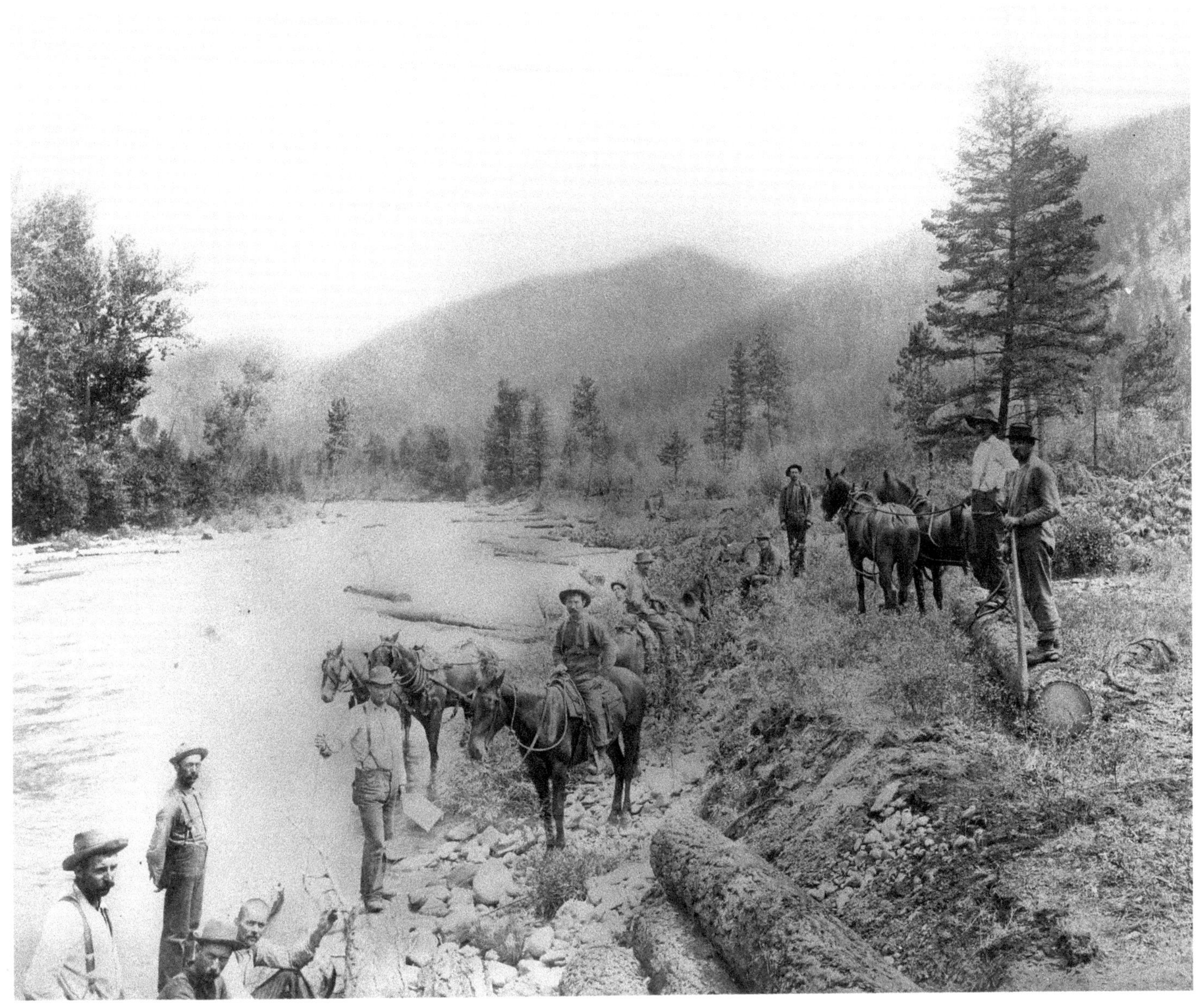

A lumber crew floats logs down lower Rock Creek near Quigley, in Granite County, in 1896. The logs were bound for a road construction project. The area is now a world-famous destination for fly fishermen.

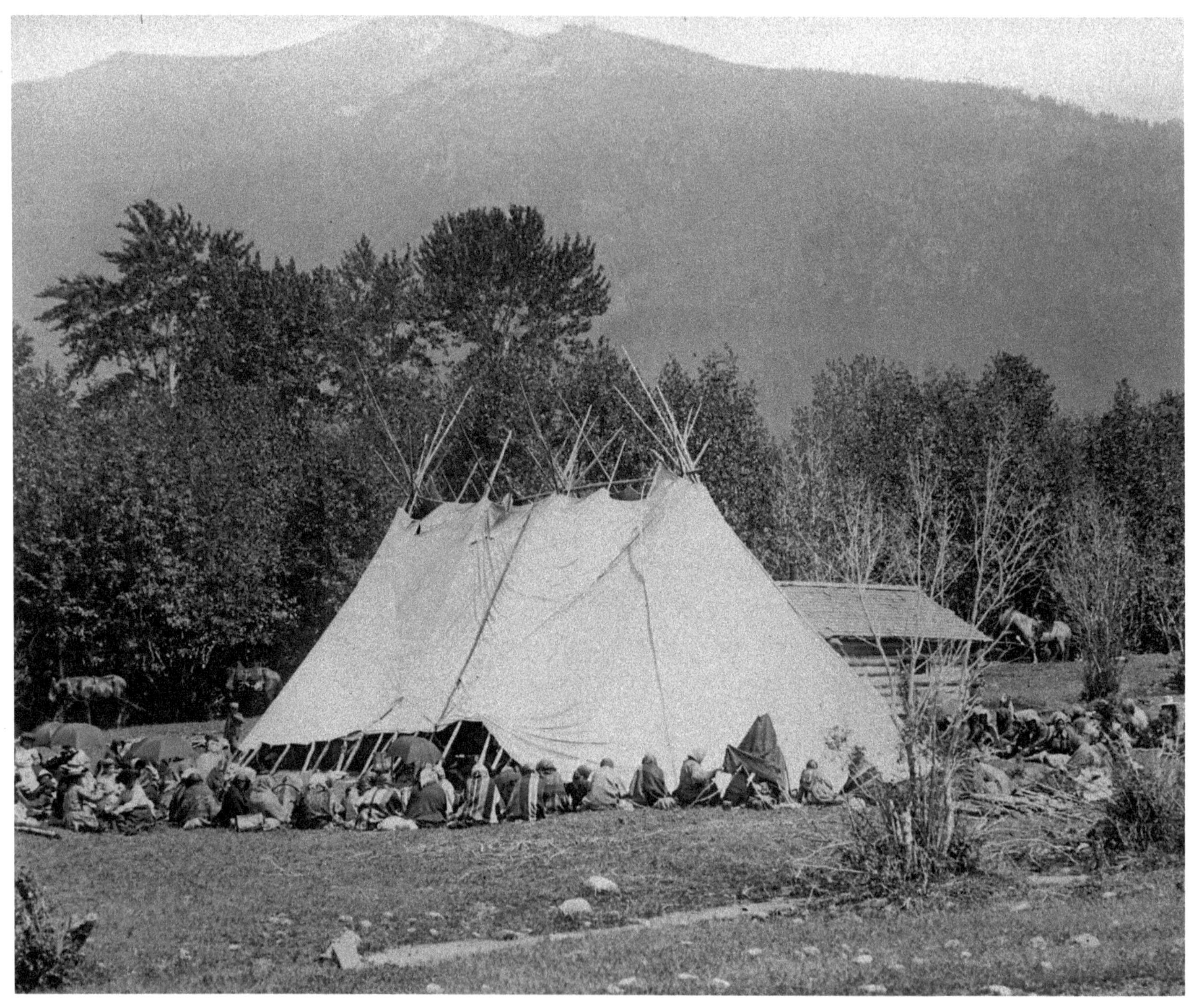

An overflow crowd sits outside a large tepee on the Flathead Reservation as tribal members mourn the recently deceased son of a chief. Home to the Confederated Salish, Kootenai, and Pend d'Oreille, the reservation was established by the Hellgate Treaty of 1855.

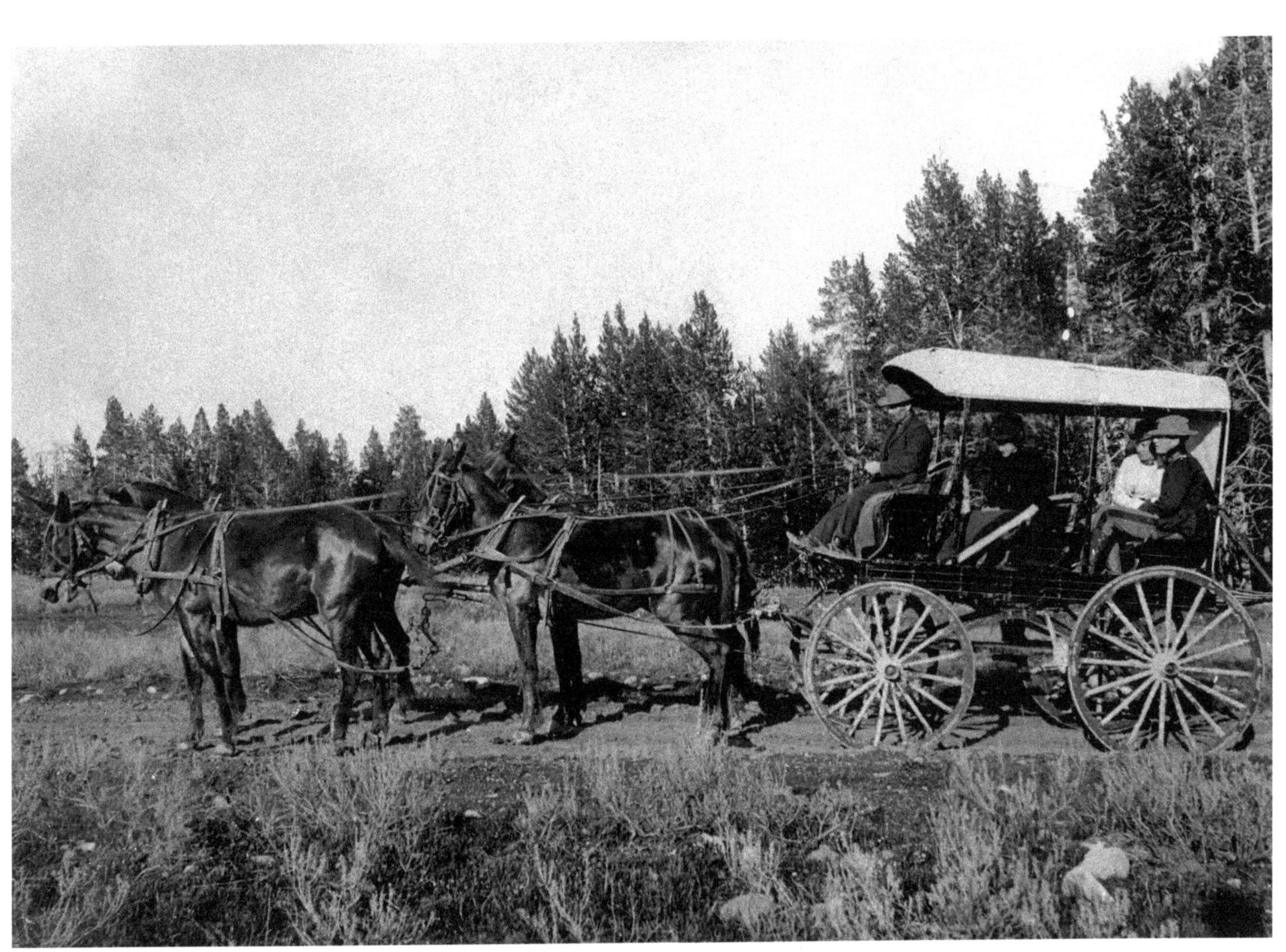

Almost 5,000 people, including this fishing party aboard a mountain wagon, visited Yellowstone National Park in 1897, by which time America's first national park was a quarter-century old. While the railroad reached Gardiner in 1902, the first automobile did not venture into the park until 1915.

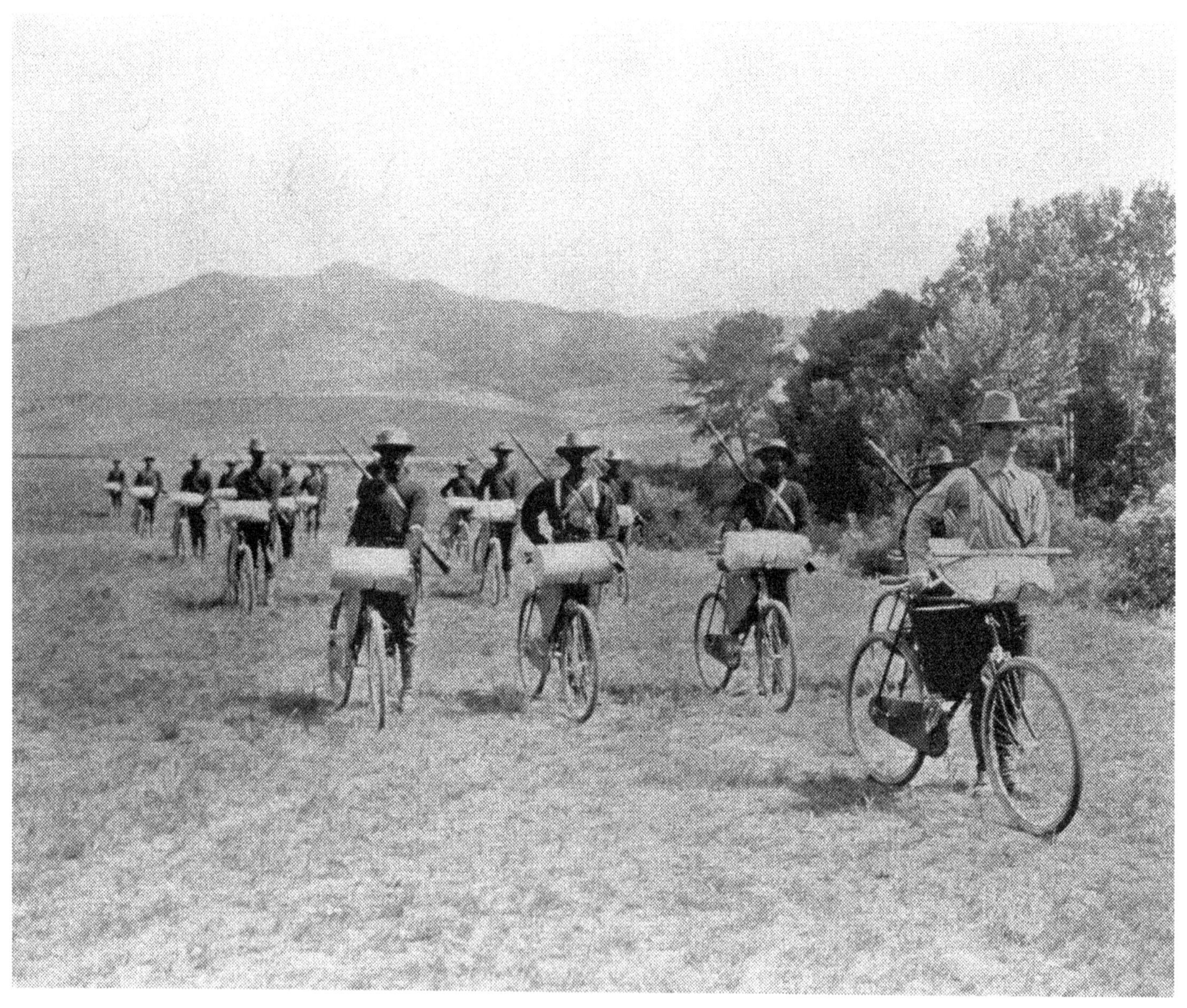

Lieutenant James Moss of the 25th Infantry formed the Fort Missoula Bicycle Corps in 1895. Moss and his men pedaled 1,900 miles to St. Louis in 1897 to evaluate the military potential of the two-wheeled machines. The outbreak of the Spanish-American War ended the experiment.

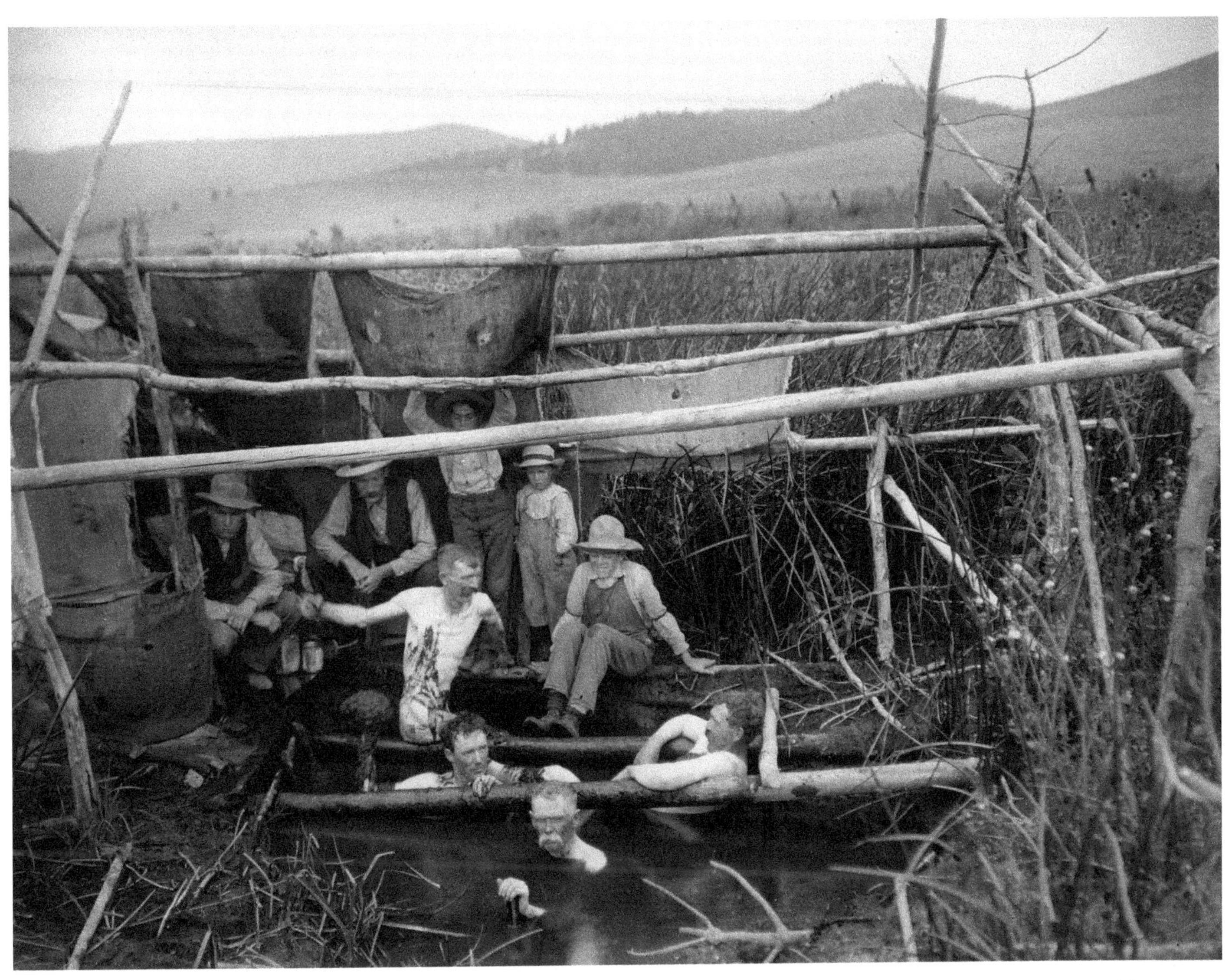

A group of men enjoy a mud bath near Hot Springs. Settlers and Indians alike shared a belief in the rejuvenating powers of the springs.

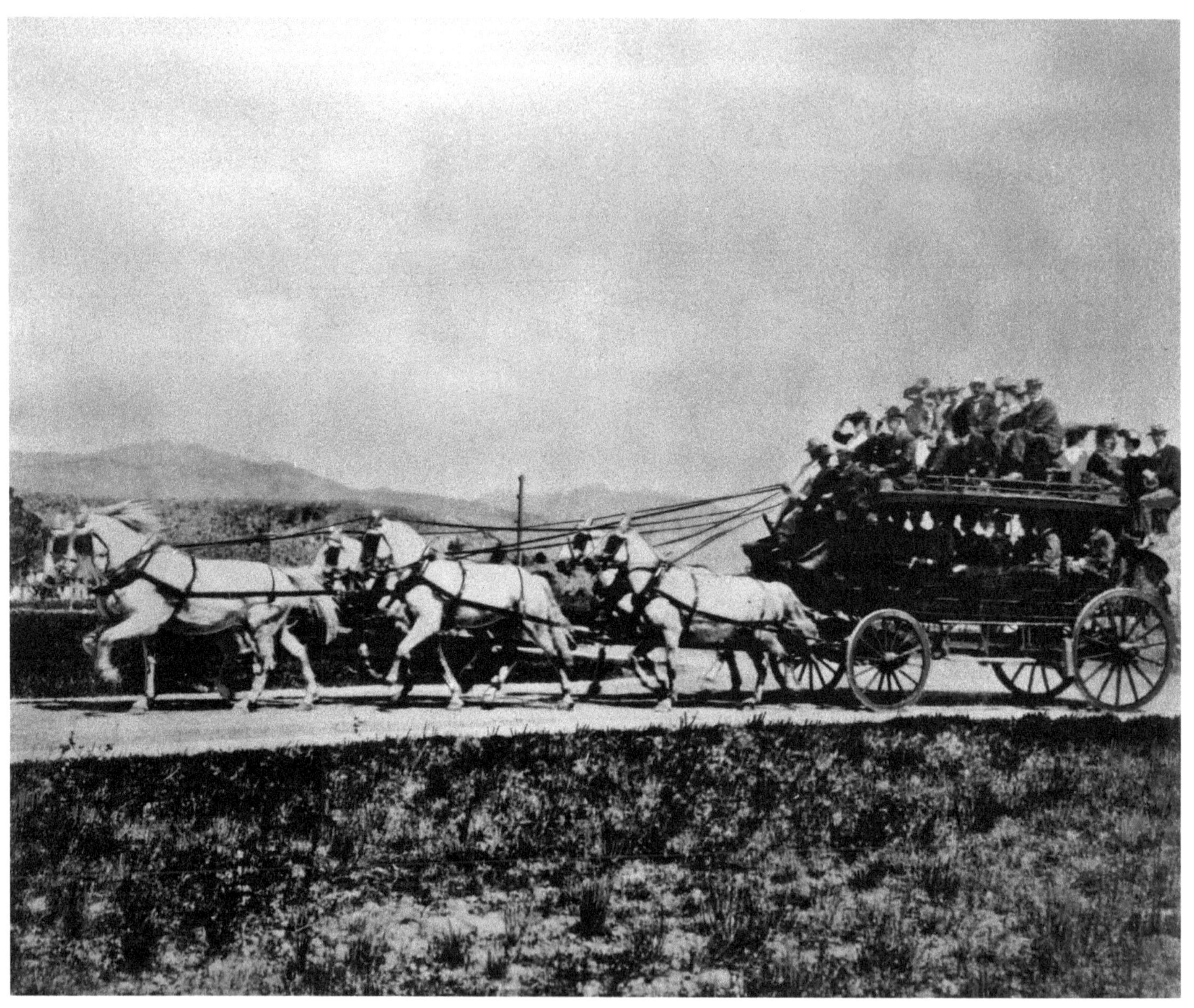

Early on, tourists visited Yellowstone National Park aboard six-horse Concord Coaches. This coach carried passengers from Gardiner to Mammoth Hot Springs. Built to handle rough roads, the coaches had seats on the roof and suspensions made of twisted bull-hide.

Montana's Copper Collar

(1900–1919)

The war of the copper kings continued after Marcus Daly's death in 1900, as William A. Clark and Fritz Heinze battled each other and the Amalgamated Copper Company for control of Butte's fabulous wealth. The ultimate victor was the Anaconda Copper Mining Company, which was formed from the Amalgamated holdings in 1915. For the next half century Anaconda, referred to simply as the "Company," wielded extraordinary and often unscrupulous influence over Montana, buying newspaper editors, legislators, and judges as needed.

Acquiring enough mine timbers to construct the tunnels of Butte required the Company to invest in large-scale logging operations, and railroad spurs were soon snaking into many of the timbered drainages of western Montana. The crucial timber supplies were threatened in 1910 when cataclysmic forest fires burned across the Northwest. At the same time, George B. Grinnell and others' efforts to protect an area he called the "Crown of the Continent" from logging and mining were rewarded when Glacier National Park was created. Grinnell and photographer Edward Curtis both endeavored in the early years of the twentieth century to record the culture and history of the Plains Indian before it disappeared.

The Chicago, Milwaukee, and St. Paul Railroad entered Montana in 1906 and built the first long-distance electric rail line in the country. The Enlarged Homestead Act of 1909 increased the acreage available to prospective farmers at cut-rate prices, and railroads like the Milwaukee vigorously promoted Montana to homesteaders. Tens of thousands of hopeful farmers flocked to Montana and ultimately laid claim to 32 million acres of the state.

Montana women received the right to vote in 1914, and two years later they helped elect Jeannette Rankin as the first woman to serve in the U.S. House of Representatives. She voted against U.S. entry into World War I (and eventually World War II), to no avail. The Montana National Guard was called to service, and 40,000 Montanans enlisted or were drafted. Anti-German sentiment ran high in Montana during the war, and many German immigrants were harassed, or worse.

The labor tension that had been simmering across the state in the prewar years came to a head in 1917, when a series of violent strikes threatened to cripple the lumber and mining industries. Using whatever means it deemed necessary, the Anaconda Company attempted to divide and weaken Montana's powerful labor unions.

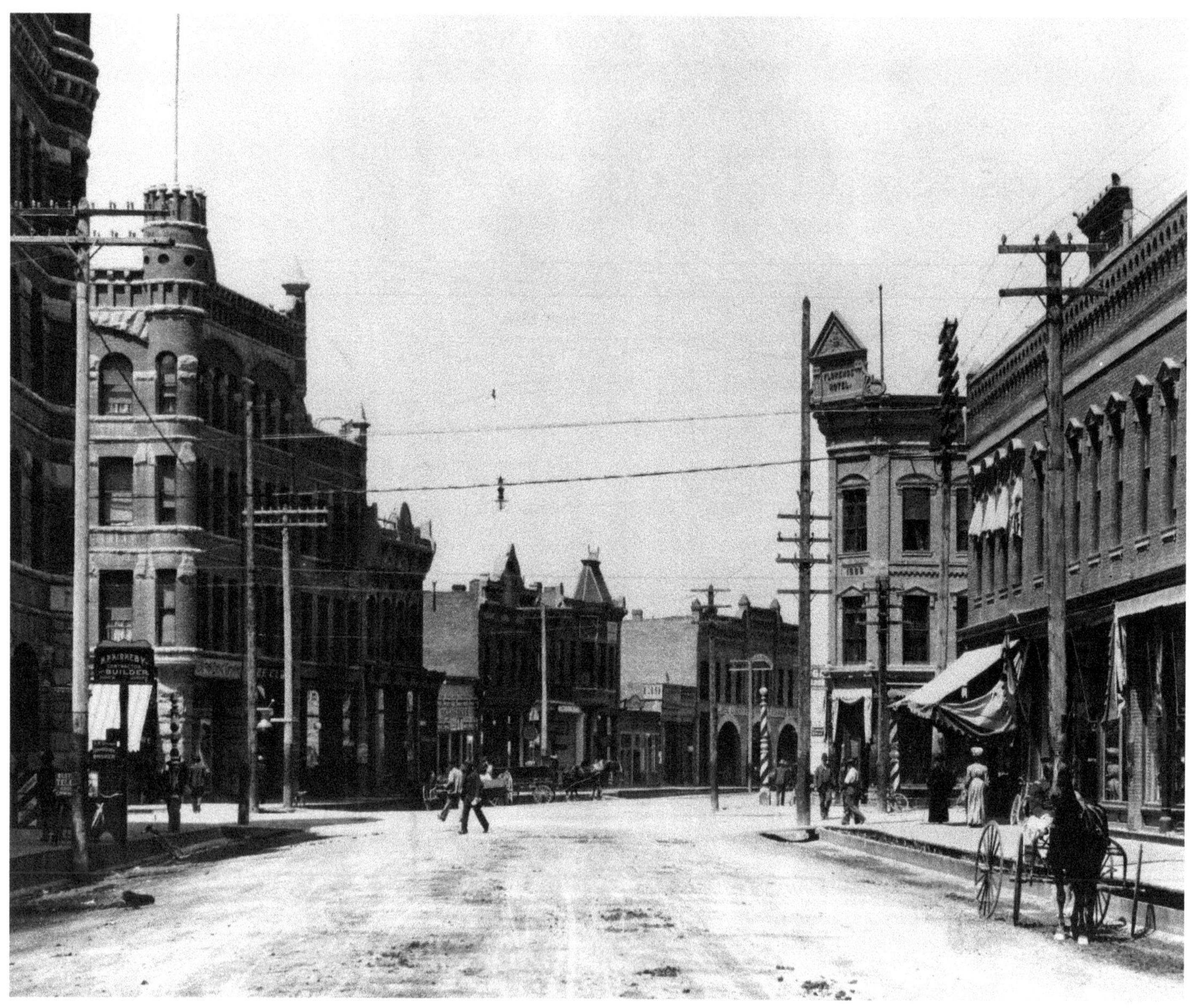

This view of Front Street in Missoula was taken around 1900. Front Street followed the course of the Mullan Road, established between Fort Benton and Walla Walla, Washington, in 1860, and was the heart of Missoula's red-light district at the time.

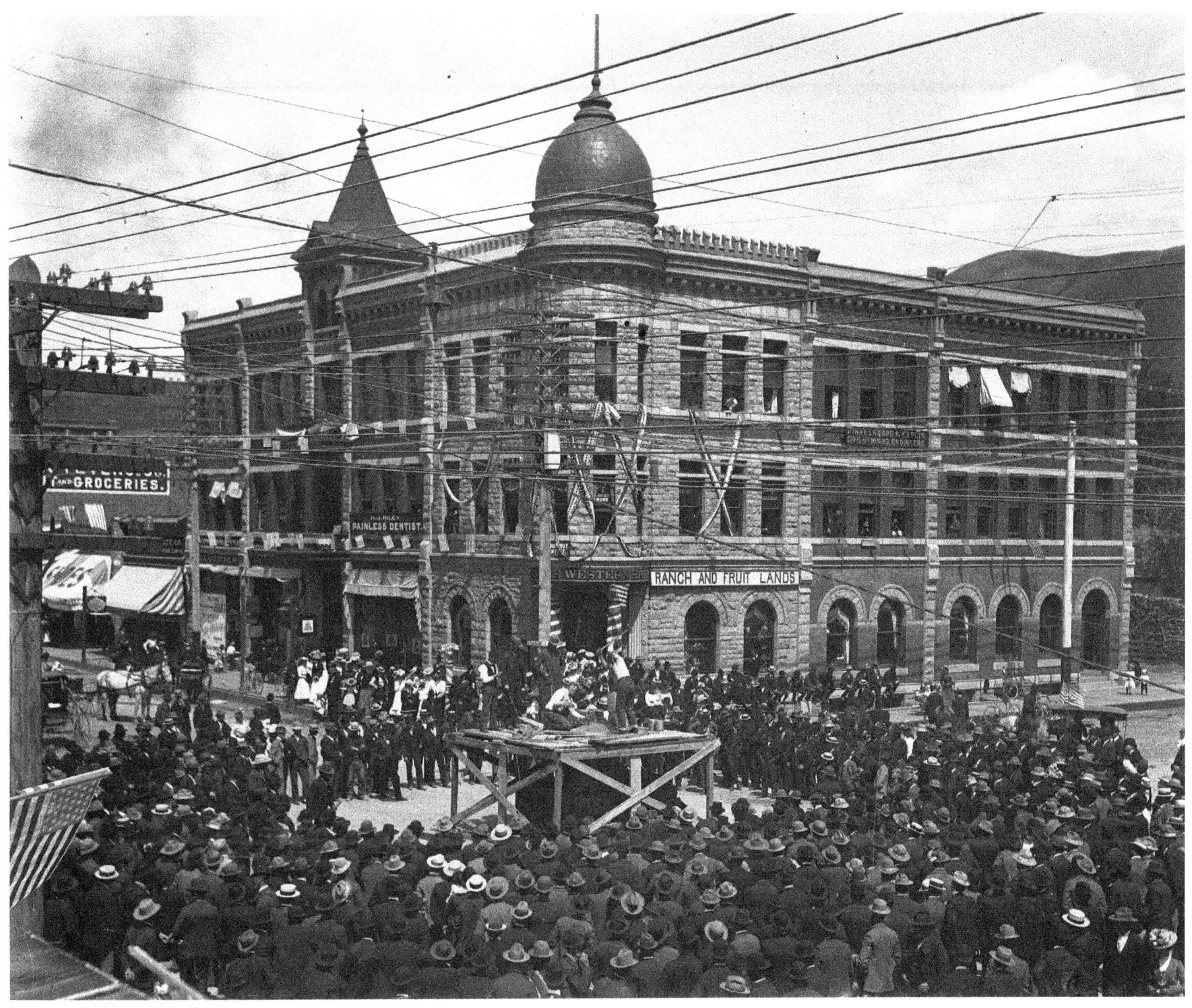

A crowd gathers at the corner of Higgins and Main in Missoula to watch miners compete in a drilling contest. Note that electrical lines proliferated by 1900.

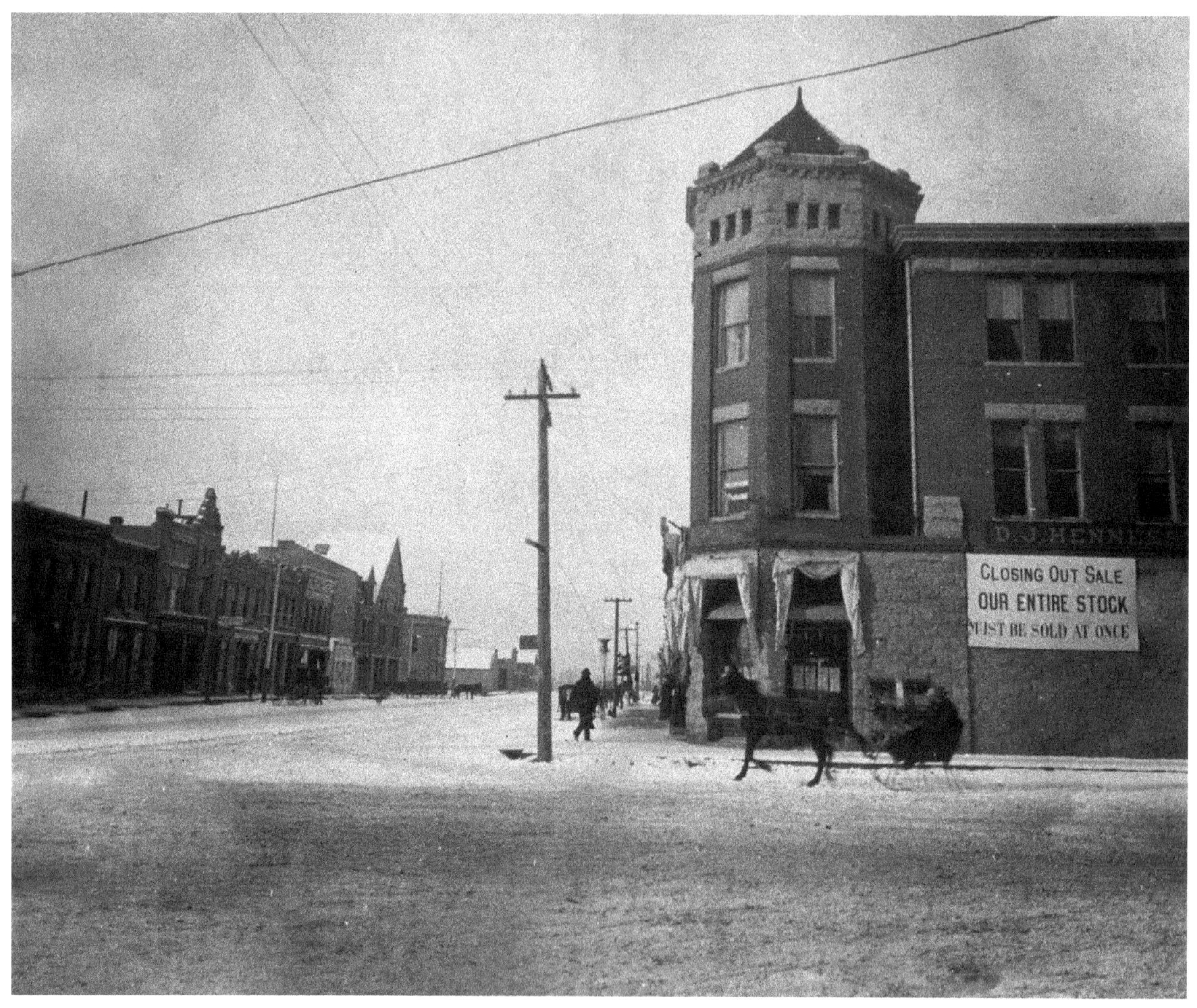

With financial backing from Marcus Daly, Butte businessman Daniel Hennessey opened a successful mercantile store in 1898, then rapidly expanded to Helena, Billings, and Missoula. This view is of his Missoula store during a closeout sale.

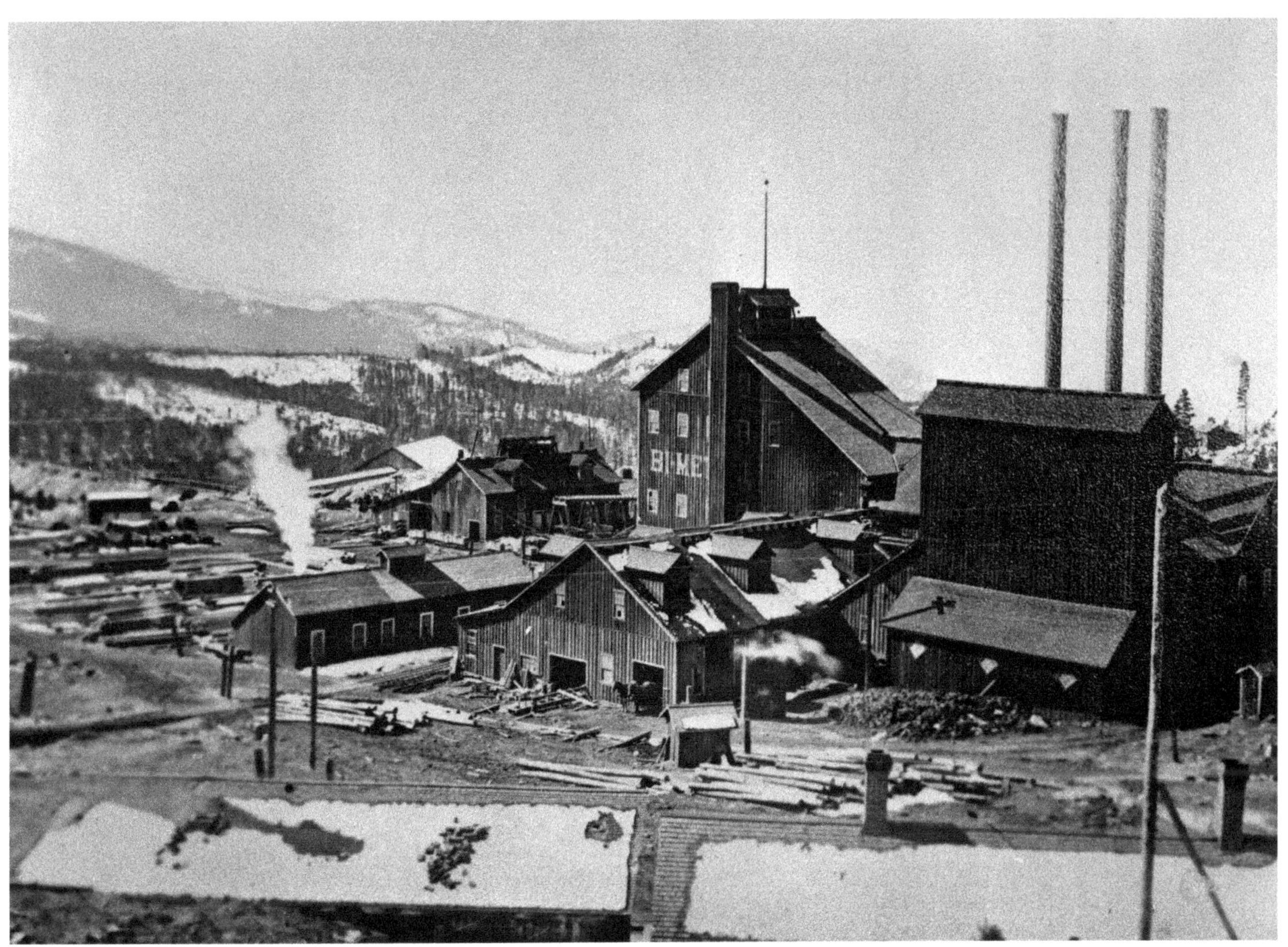

Seen here around the turn of the century, the Bi-Metallic Mine at Granite sat atop one of the richest silver deposits ever found. Between 1885 and 1892 almost $20 million in ore came from the mines of Granite. A fire in 1958 destroyed many of the above-ground buildings.

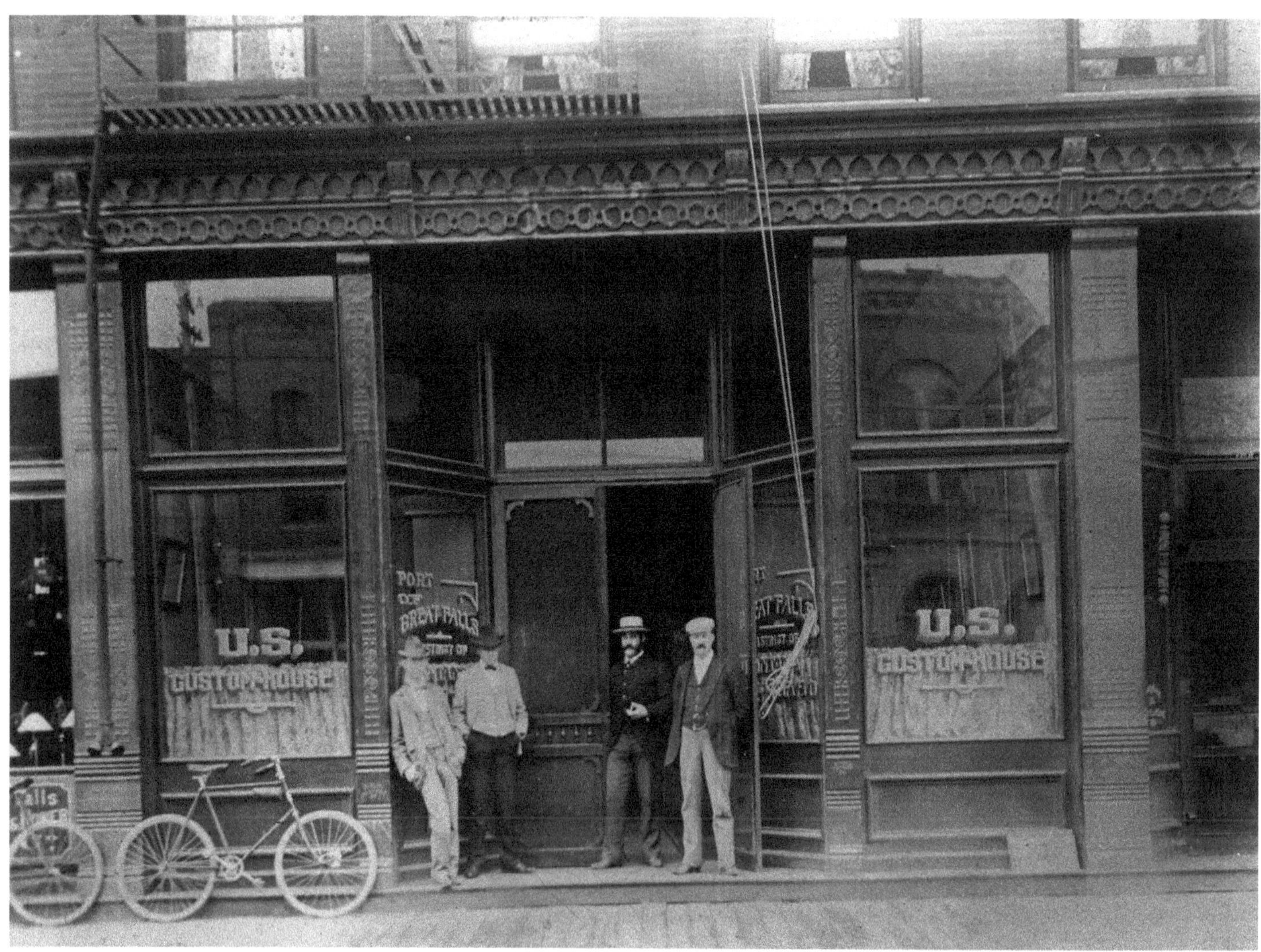

The U.S. Customs House, Port of Great Falls, handled trade and immigration issues that arose along Montana's 545-mile-long border with Canada. This view captures the building's ornate design details and a window reflection of the buildings across the street.

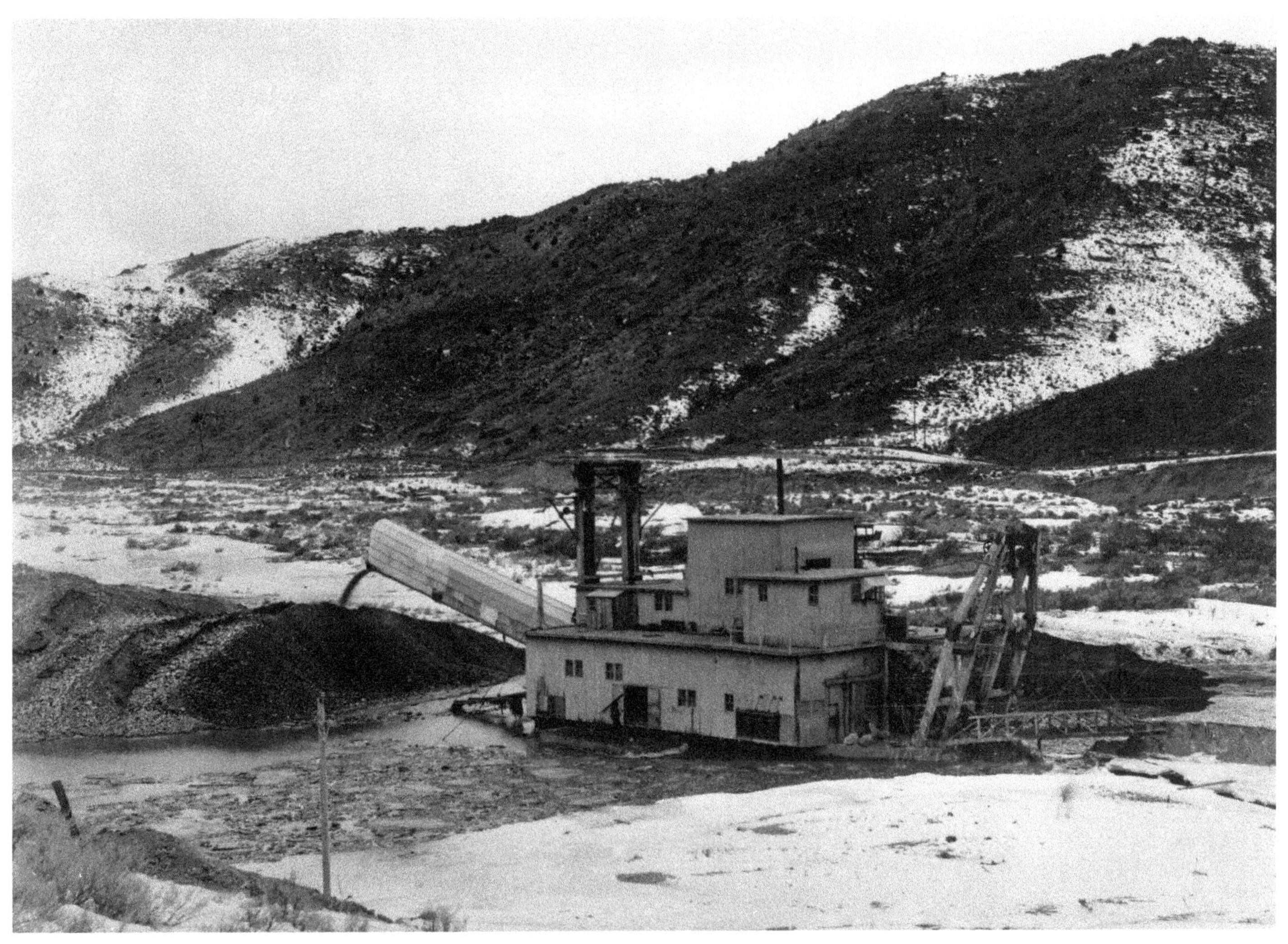

From 1898 to 1922, at least five floating dredges worked the gold-bearing gravel of Alder Gulch. This photo of the Cowrey Dredge No. 1 was taken several miles below Nevada City. Most of the city's buildings were eventually destroyed by dredges.

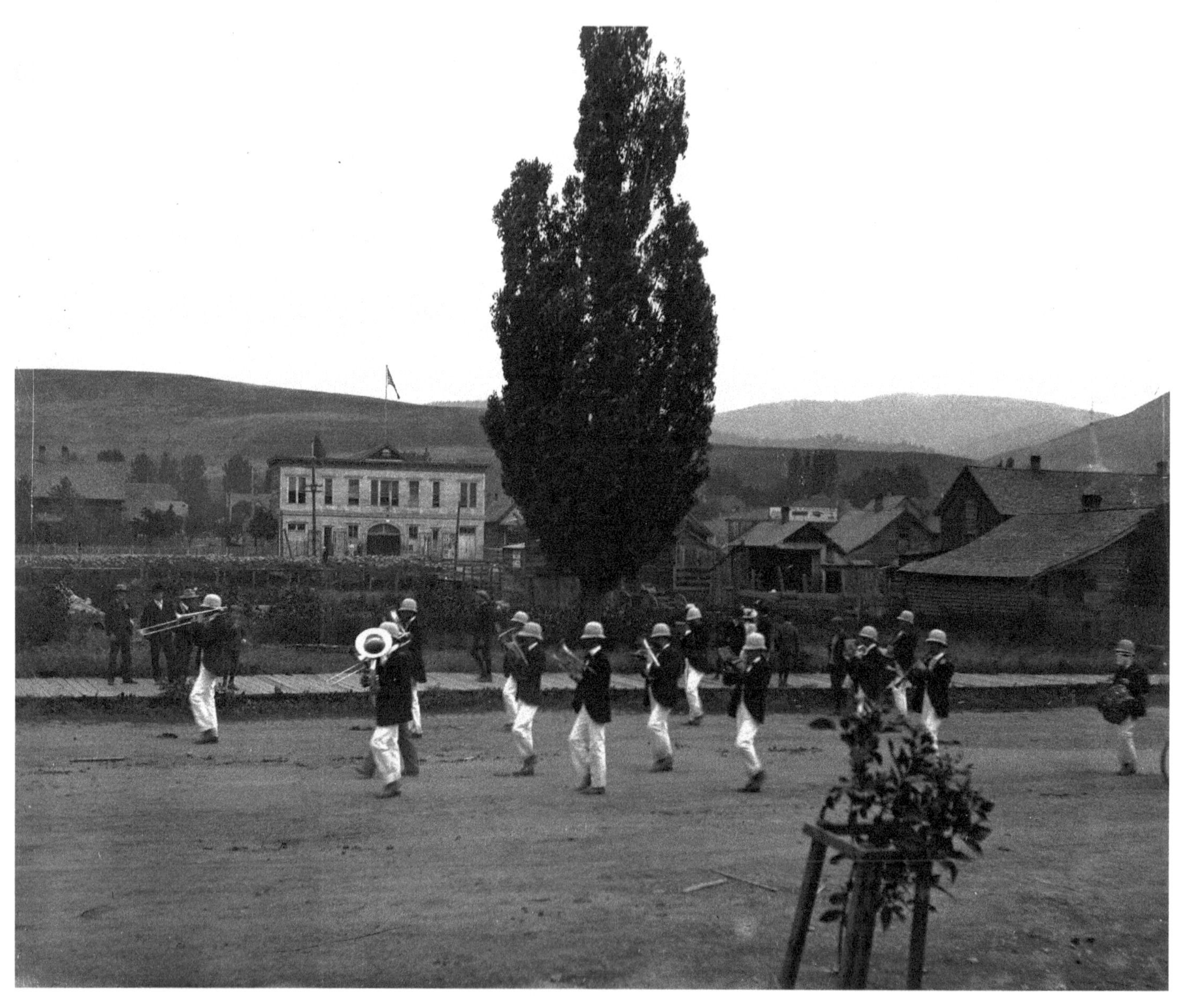

A marching band parades down East Front Street in Missoula around 1900. Marching bands originated from military bands and became popular in the late 1880s. Amateur photographer John Dunn snapped this photo.

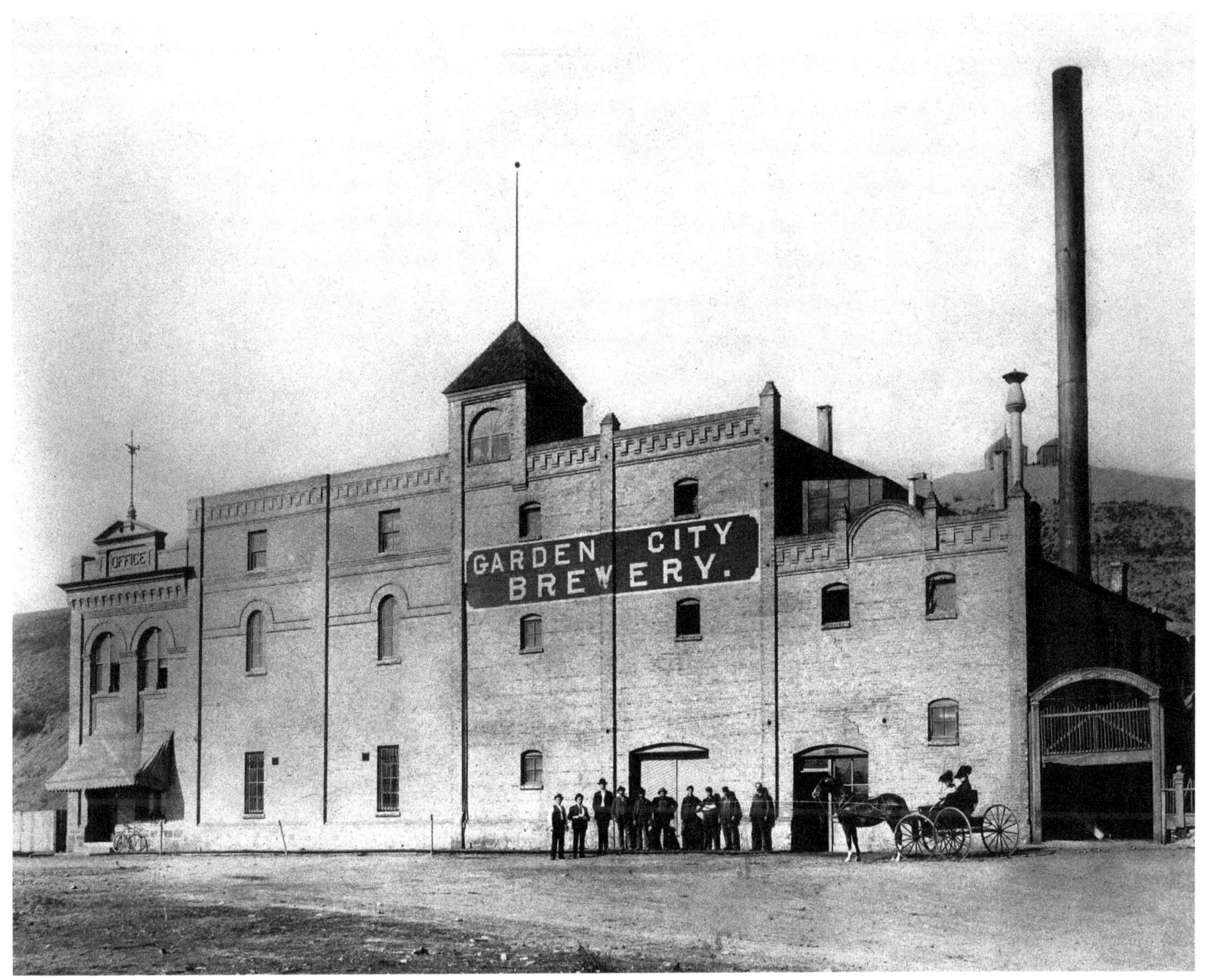

Photographed around 1902, this brewery was built near Missoula's Rattlesnake Creek in 1874 and by 1895 was known as the Garden City Brewery. By 1910 its signature brew was Highlander Beer. The brewery closed in 1964 and was torn down during construction of Interstate 90.

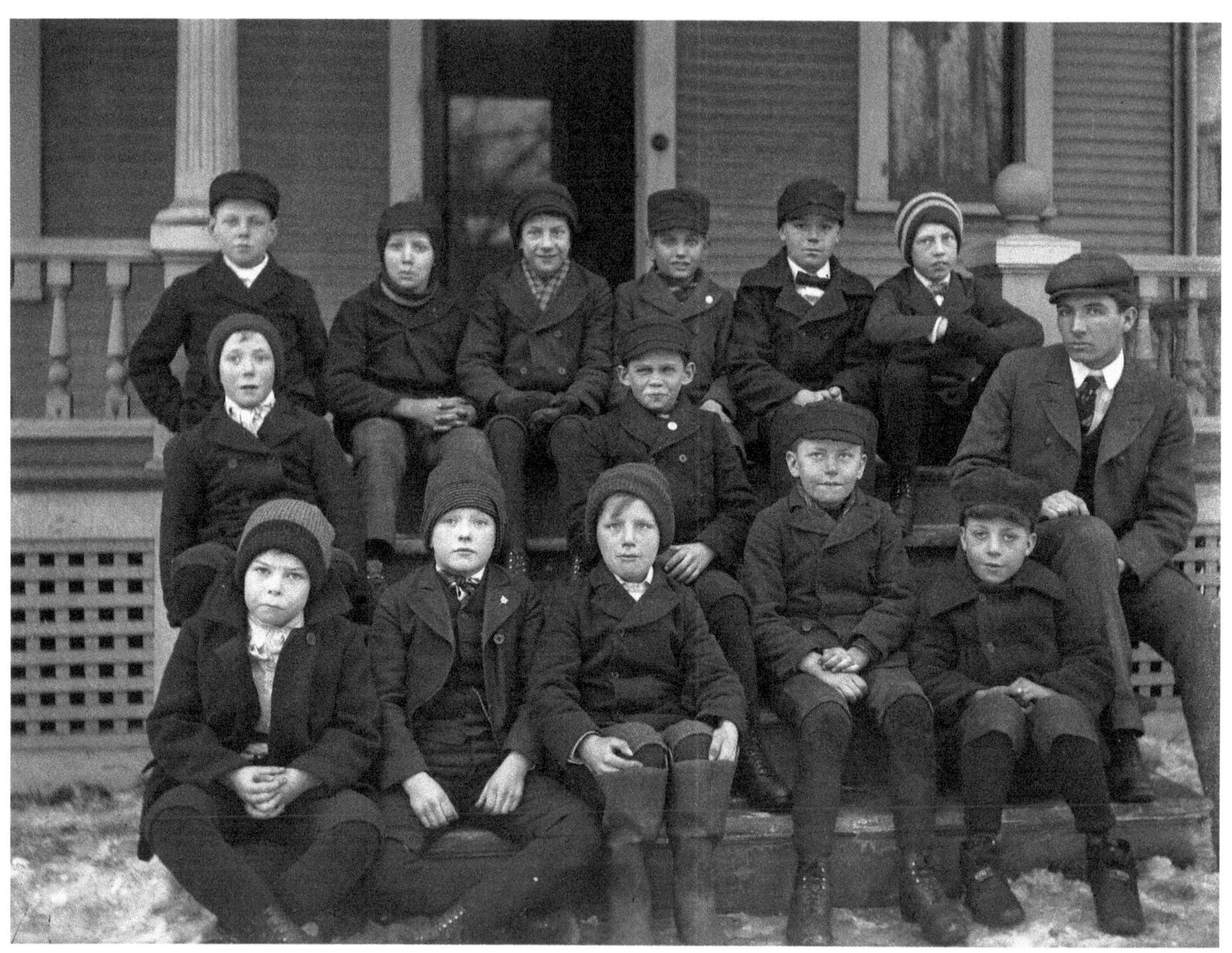

Located near the Two Medicine River on the Blackfeet Reservation, Holy Family Mission was built by Jesuits in 1886. Seen here in 1902, the vocational school served 100 boys and girls, primarily Blackfeet, who were forced to abandon their native customs and language.

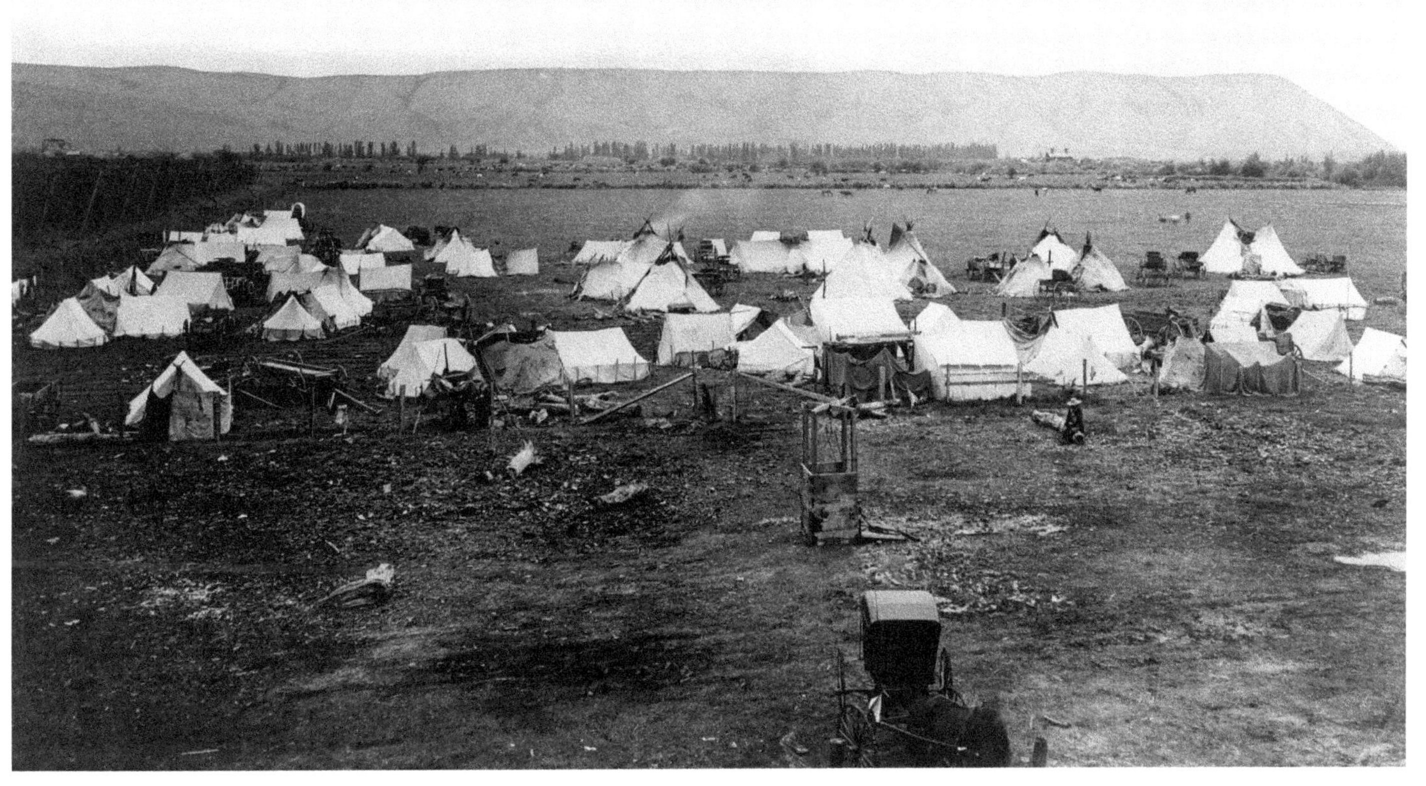

The near extinction of bison forced American Indians to replace their traditional hide tepees with canvas-wall tents. A water well and horse-drawn buggy can be seen in the foreground of this early-1900s view of a Crow village.

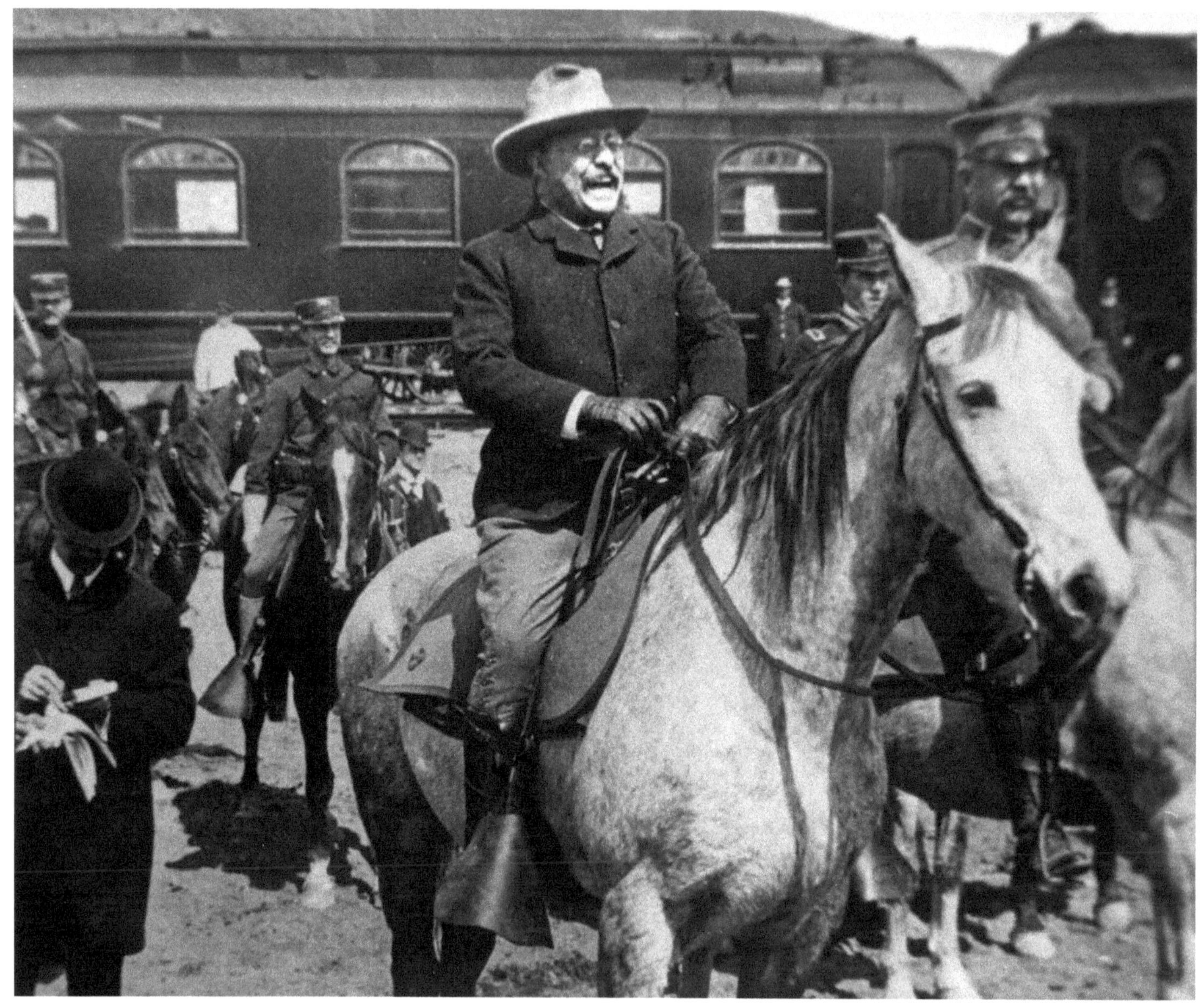

President Theodore Roosevelt dedicated the Roosevelt Arch, the northern entrance to Yellowstone National Park, at Gardiner on April 24, 1903. The arch became a major tourist destination once the Northern Pacific Railroad reached the area.

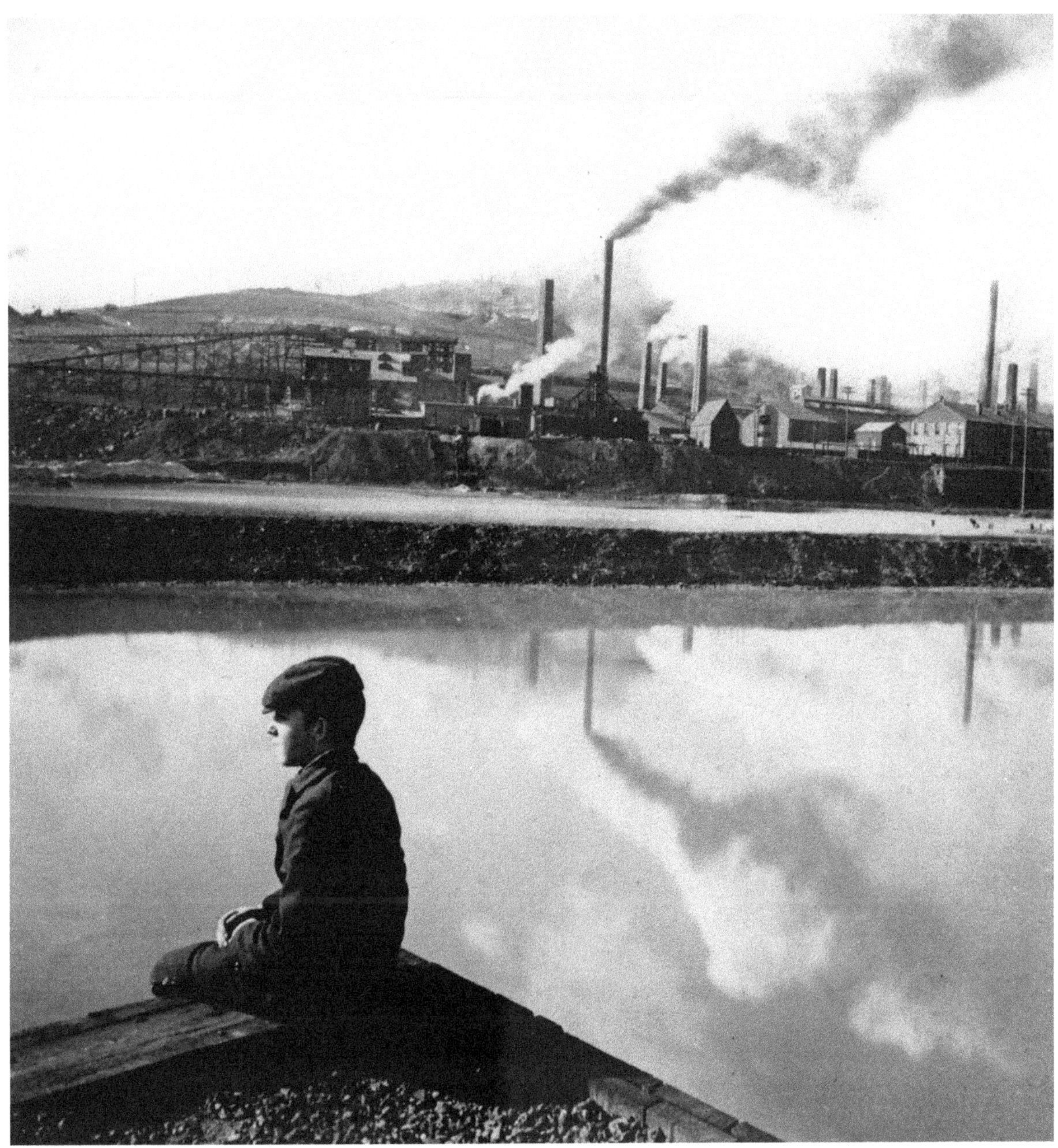

This 1904 image shows a boy posing in front of the belching smokestacks of the "Richest Hill on Earth." Mining operations contaminated Butte's air and water with arsenic and heavy metals for more than a century. In 1985 the Environmental Protection Agency declared Butte the center of the nation's largest Superfund site.

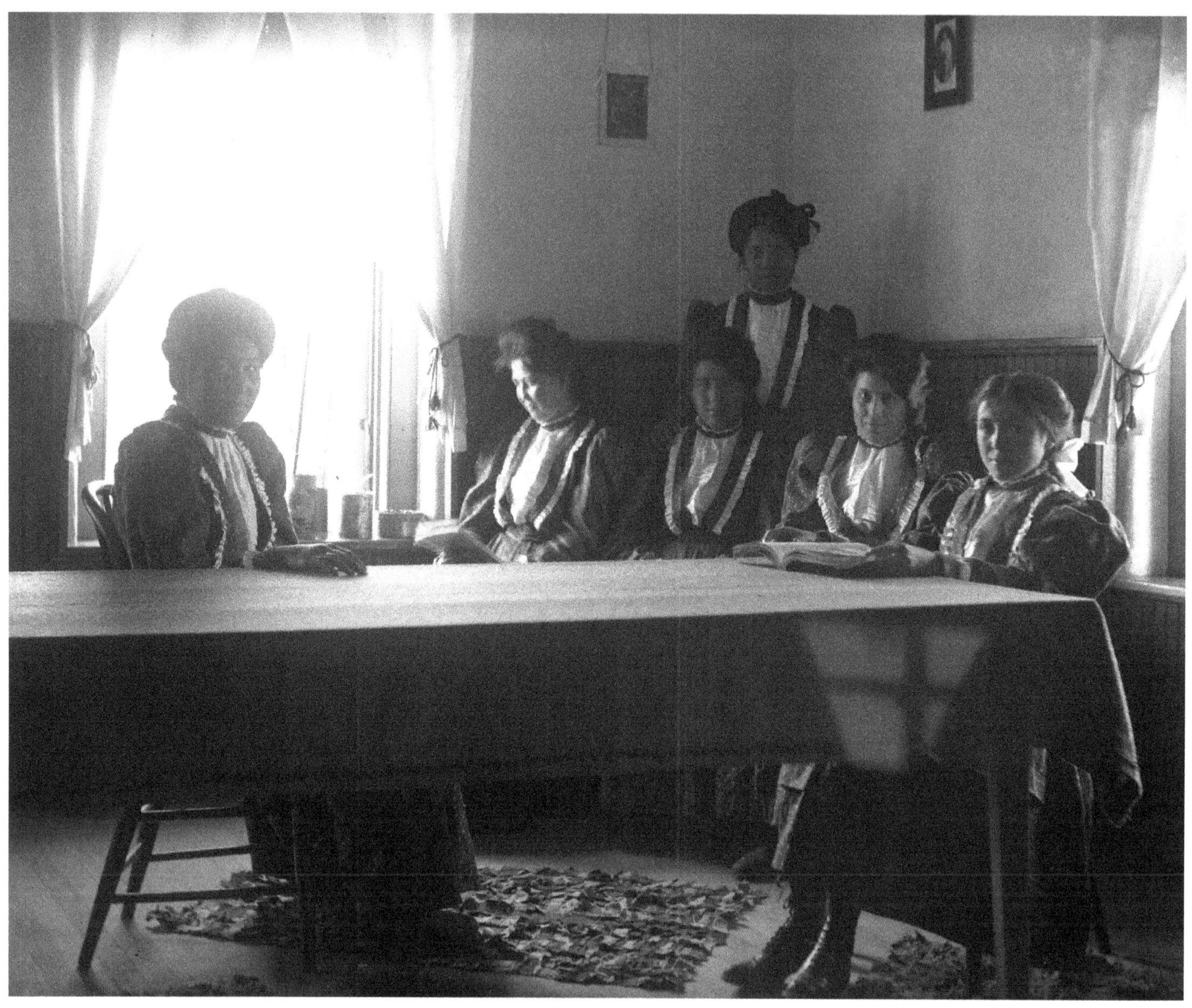

These young women were photographed in a sitting room at the Cut Bank Boarding School. Located northeast of Browning, the school was built in 1904 and operated for more than half a century. Native children were often taken from their families at a young age and sent to these boarding schools.

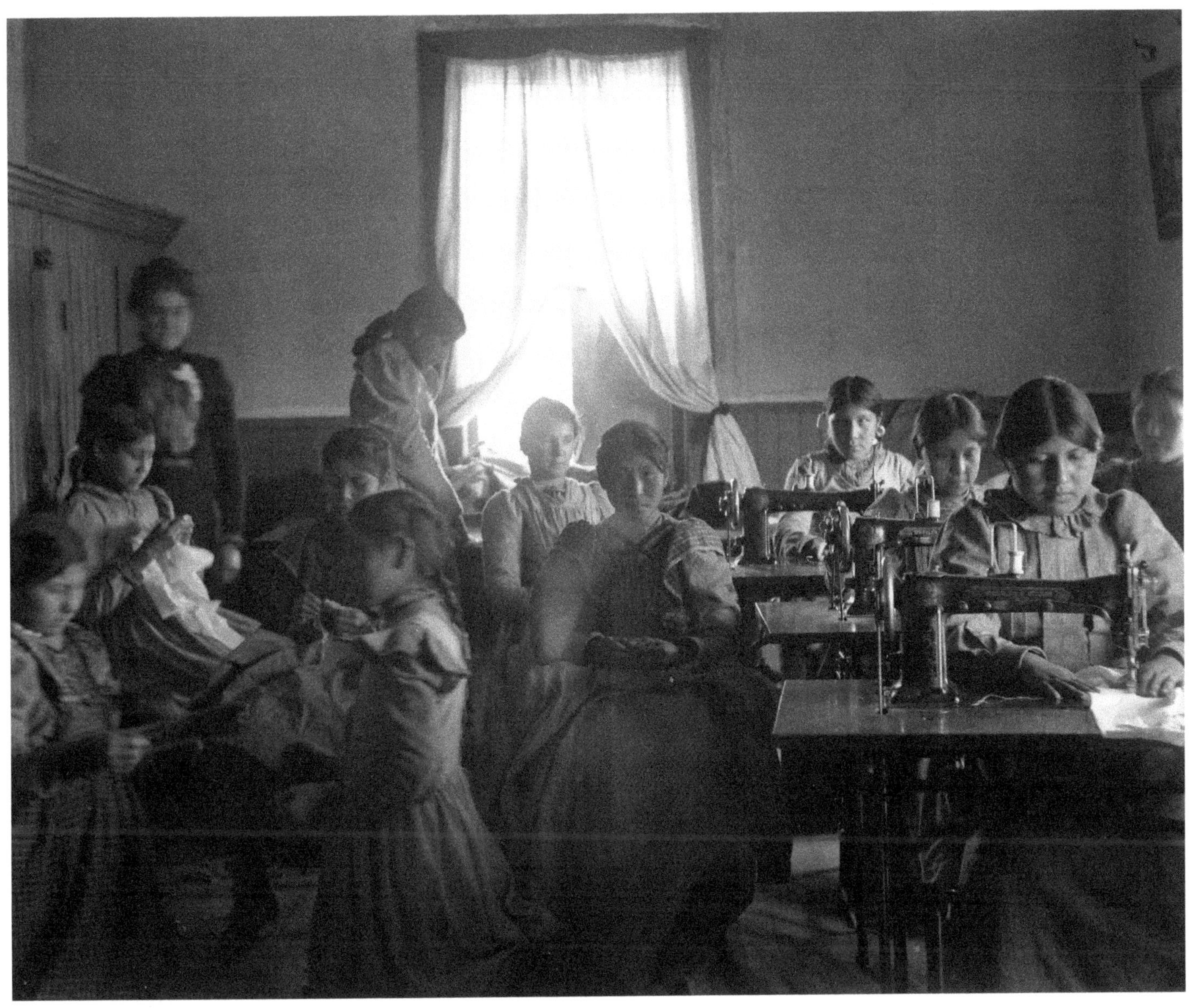

Female students at the Cut Bank Boarding School practice their sewing. The boarding schools taught both academic and vocational skills in an attempt to assimilate American Indians into Western culture. Native languages and traditional activities were discouraged.

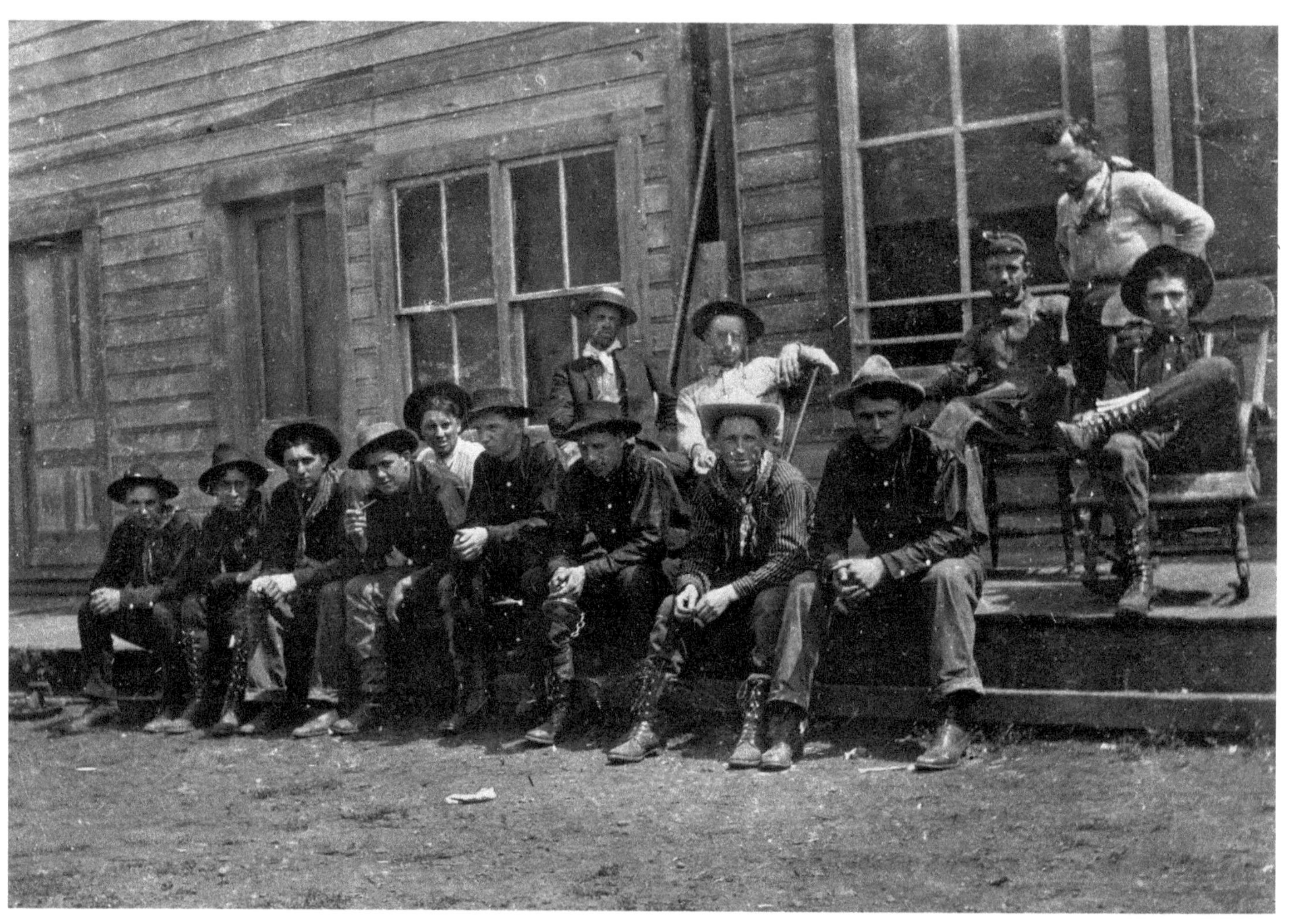

A dour crowd of miners, wranglers, and loggers pose for a photo on the front porch of the Quigley Hotel around 1905. Quigley was located on Rock Creek, a few miles from the junction with the Clark Fork River. The area today is a popular destination for fly fishermen.

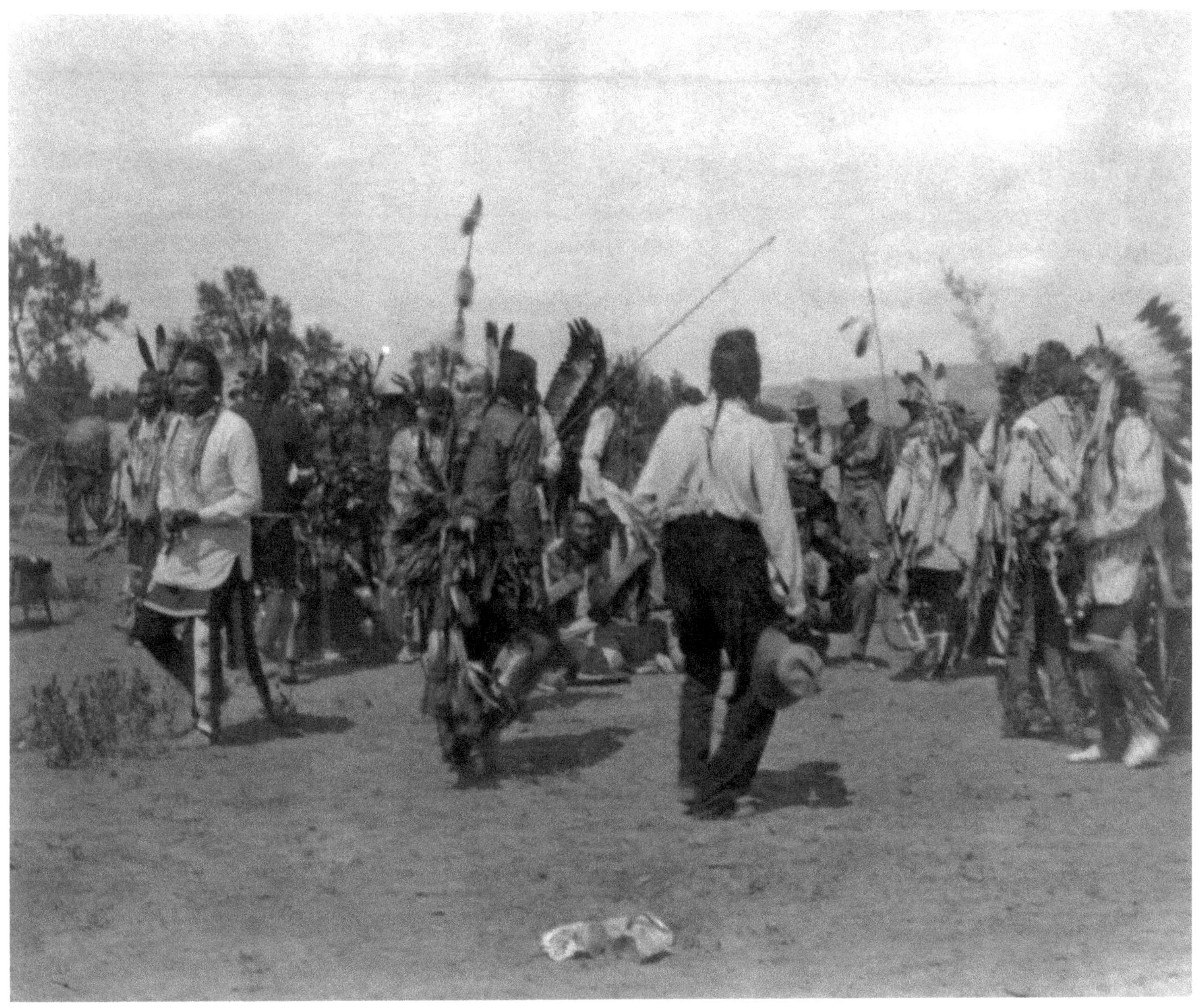

Warriors in traditional garb demonstrate a war dance at Crow Agency around 1905. Beginning in the 1880s, the Bureau of Indian Affairs discouraged many traditional tribal activities, including an outright ban on the sun dance. The ban was widely ignored by many tribes and was formally overturned by passage of the American Indian Religious Freedom Act of 1978.

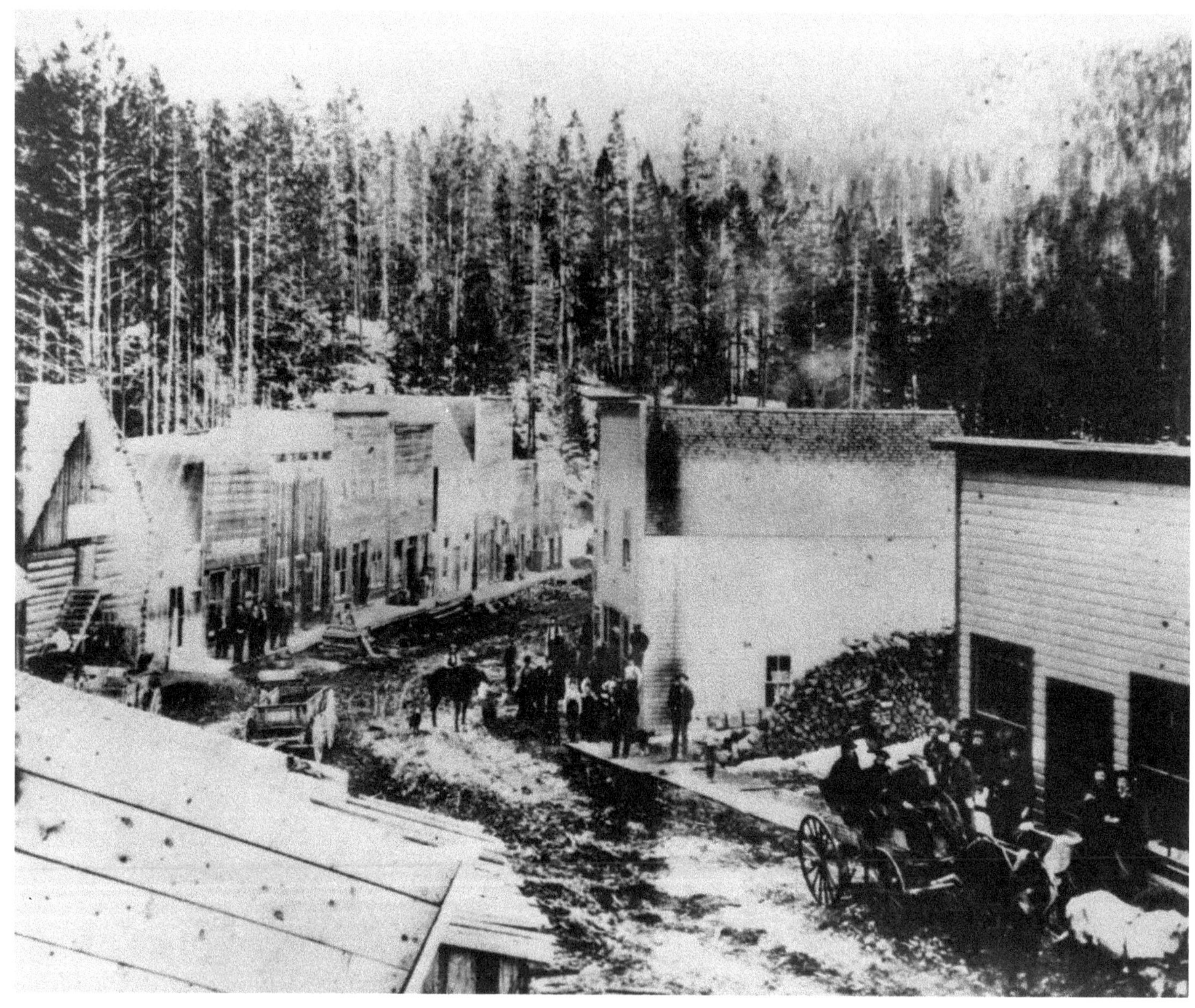

The bustling mining town of Garnet was named for a semiprecious stone found locally. Many of the buildings seen here remain, but Garnet today is a well-preserved ghost town. It is popular with tourists in the summer months and skiers in the winter.

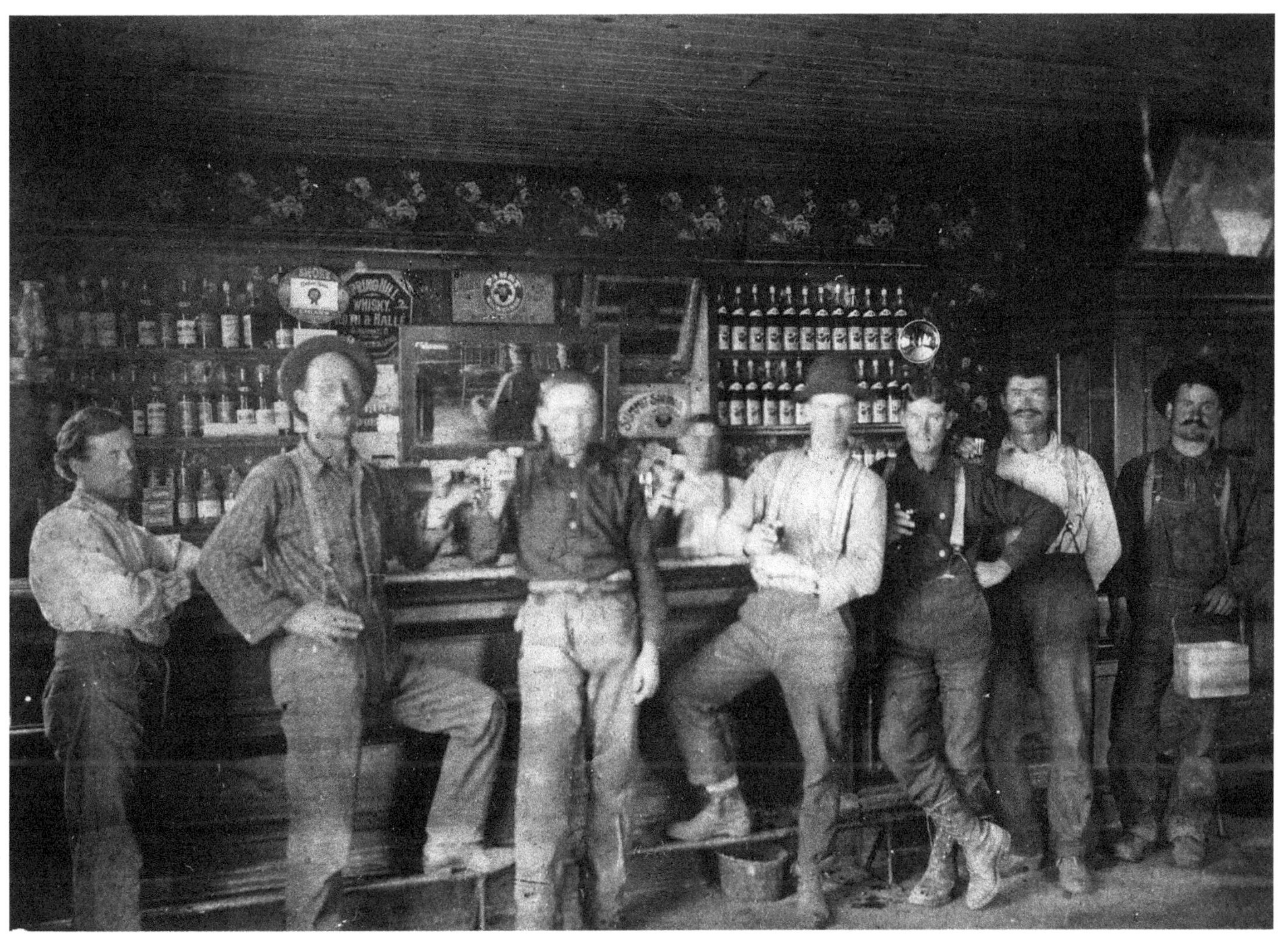

A group of local men enjoy refreshments at the Alex Ross Saloon in Huson. Located west of Frenchtown, Huson was named for H. S. Huson, an engineer with the Northern Pacific Railroad. Most of the town's residents worked in the Cherry Creek mines.

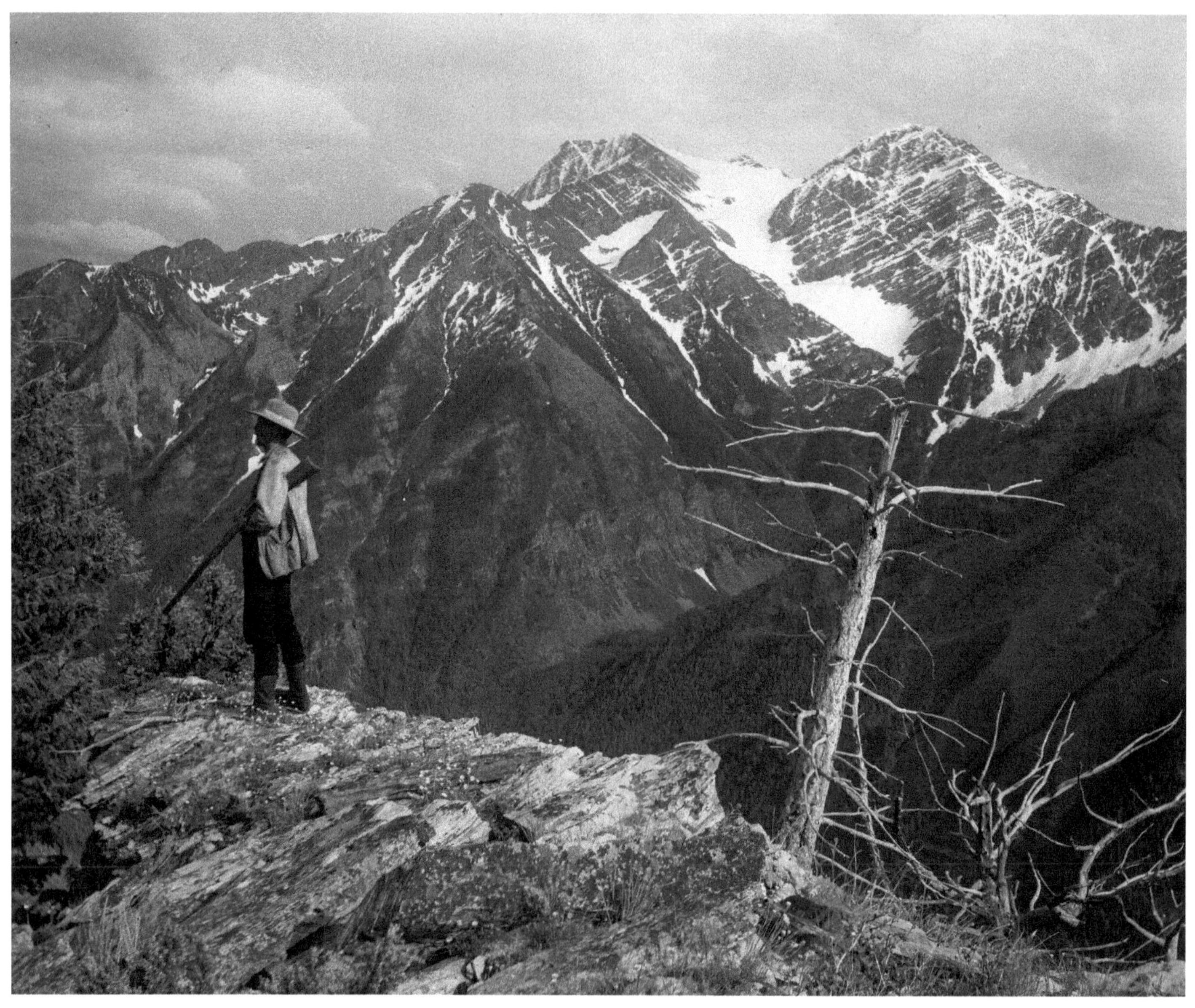

Professor Morton J. Elrod gazes on the Mission Mountains around 1905. A botanist, Elrod established the Flathead Lake Biological Station in 1899 and served as the first naturalist in Glacier National Park. He also wrote one of the first guidebooks on the park.

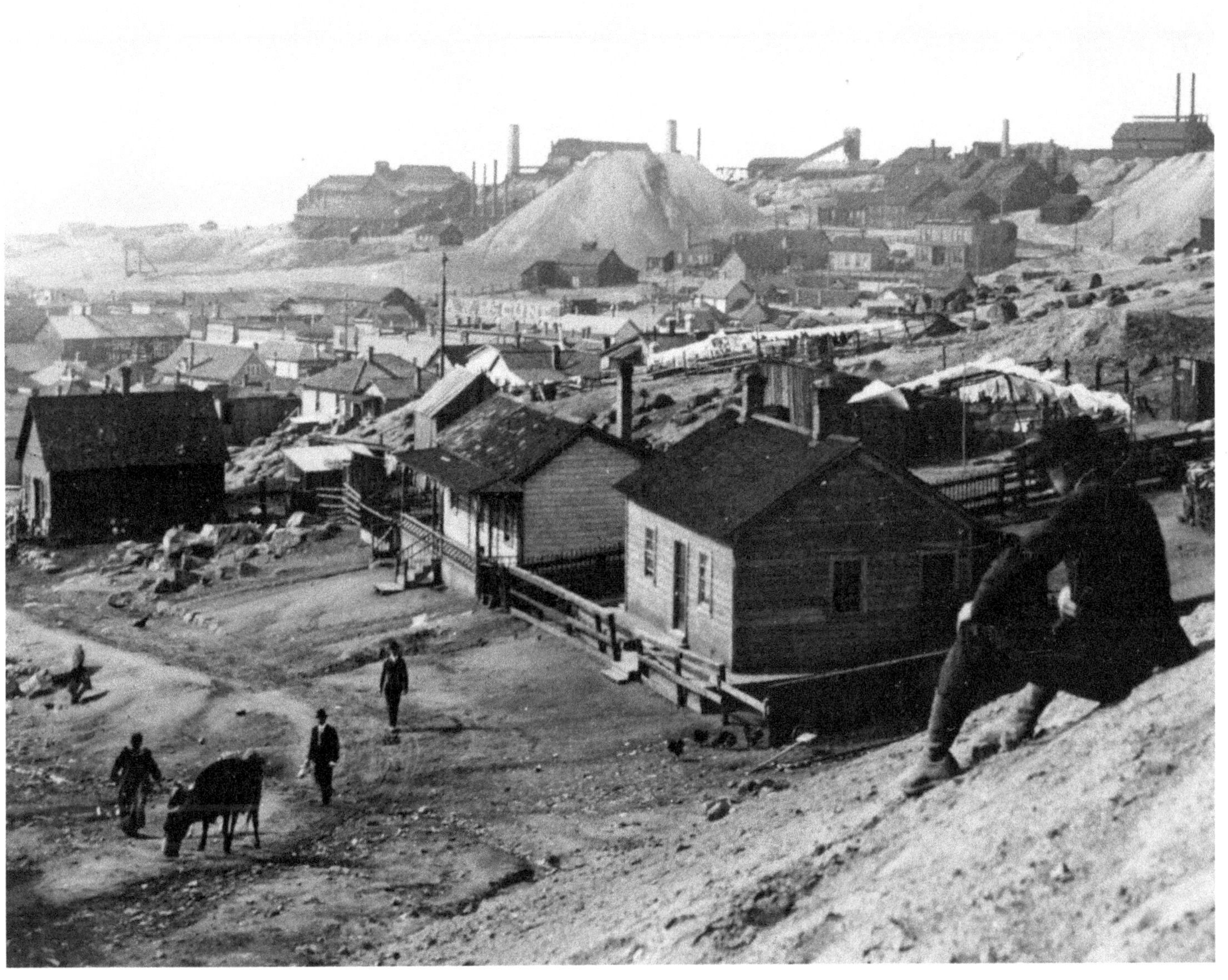

Located just north of Butte, Walkerville was named for the Walker brothers of Salt Lake City, owners of the famous Alice Mine in Butte. Seen here around 1905, Walkerville was primarily settled by Cornish miners who lived close to the mines, smelters, and tailing piles of the Richest Hill on Earth.

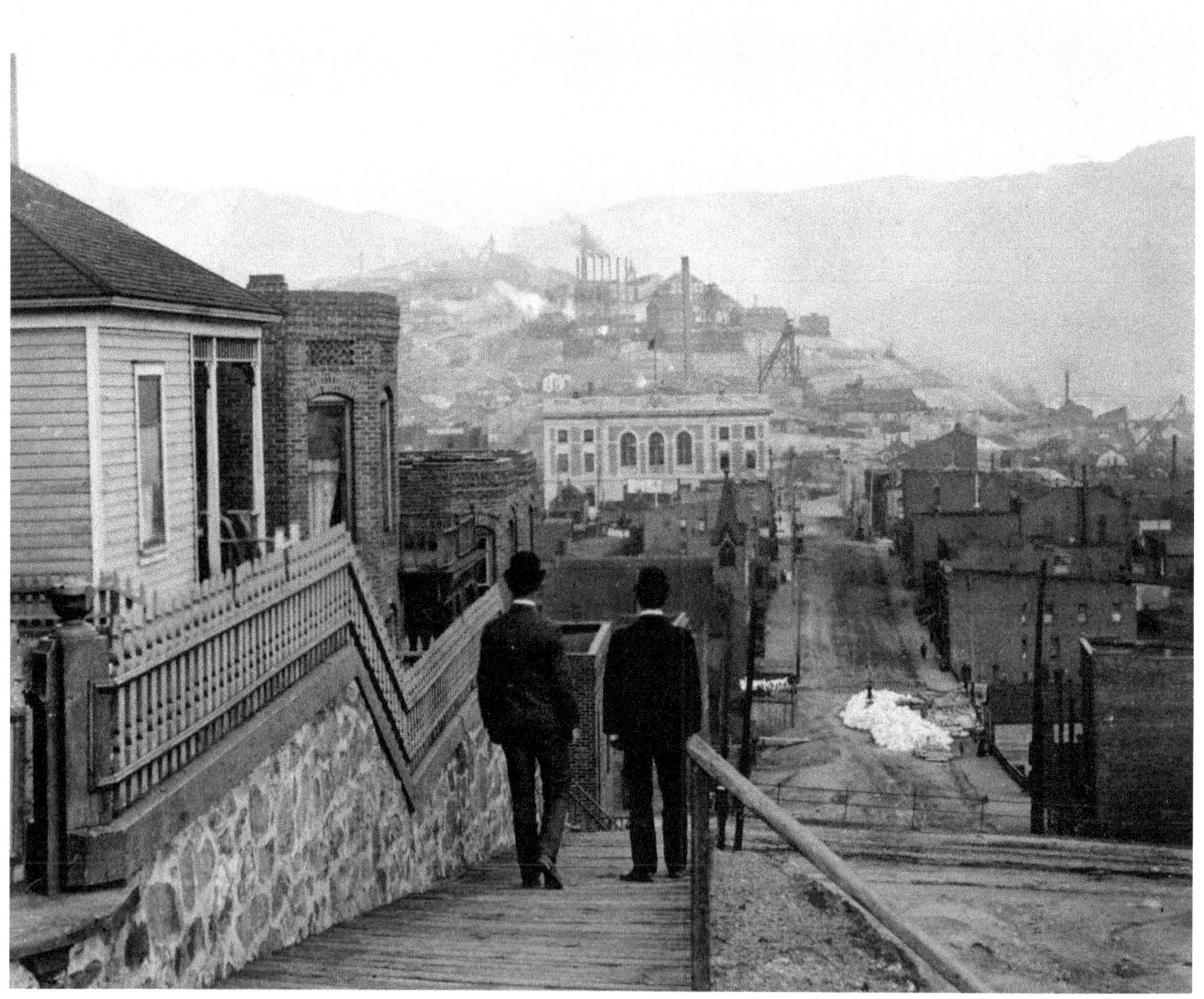

The Butte post office can be seen in this early twentieth century view of East Copper Street, better known as Dublin Gulch due to the many Irish miners who lived there. By 1916 Butte had a population of nearly 100,000. The city streets were built atop almost 2,000 miles of underground tunnels.

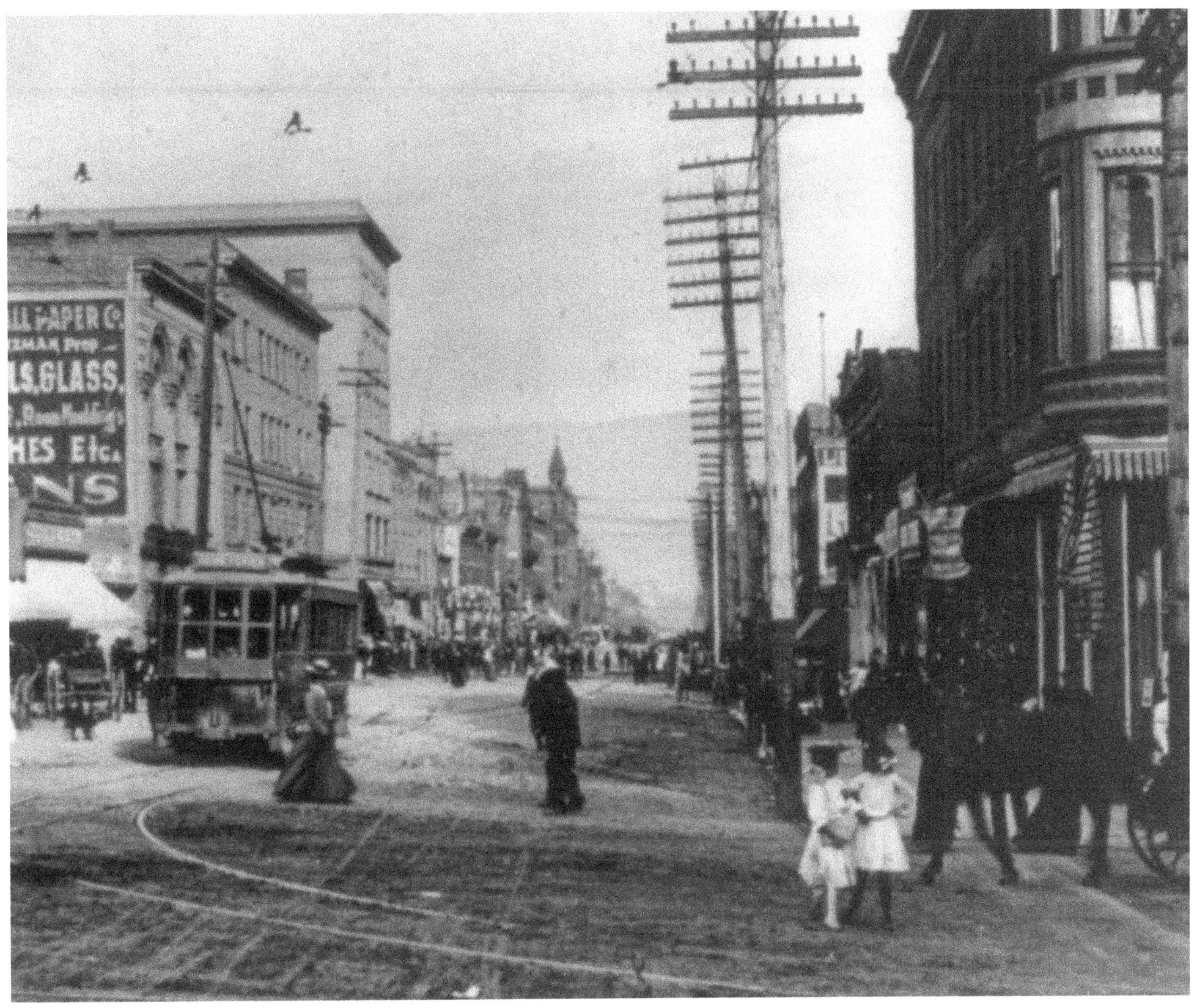

Pedestrians cross Main Street in Butte in this 1905 photo. The electric trolley was a popular form of mass transit in several Montana cities of the time. The prominent electrical lines required large amounts of copper, the source of Butte's wealth and industry.

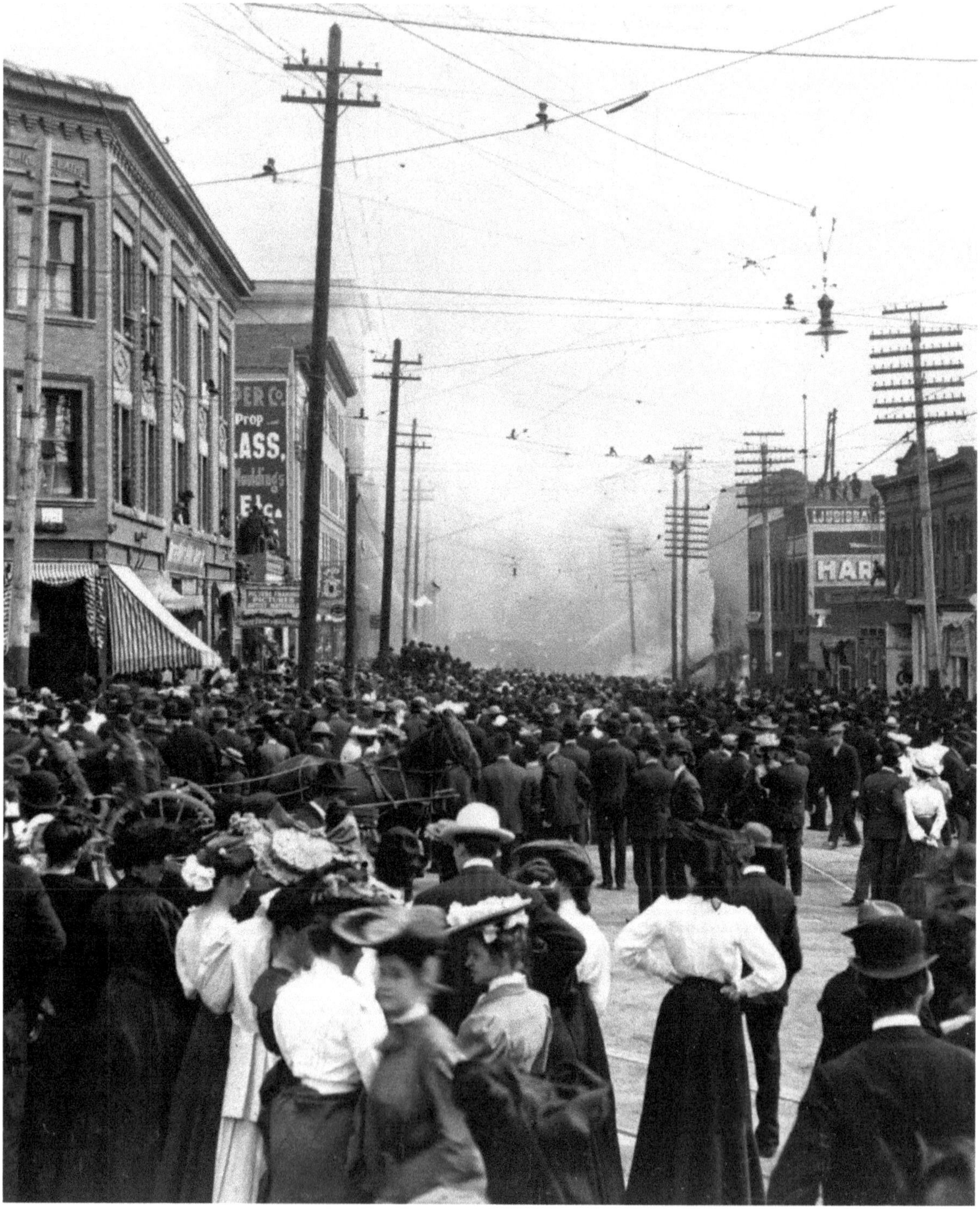

A crowd gathers at the corner of Broadway and Montana streets to watch smoke billowing from a fire in downtown Butte. This fire started in the basement of the Symons Dry Goods Company on September 24, 1905. The City Library and several commercial blocks were destroyed before a torrential rainstorm quenched the flames.

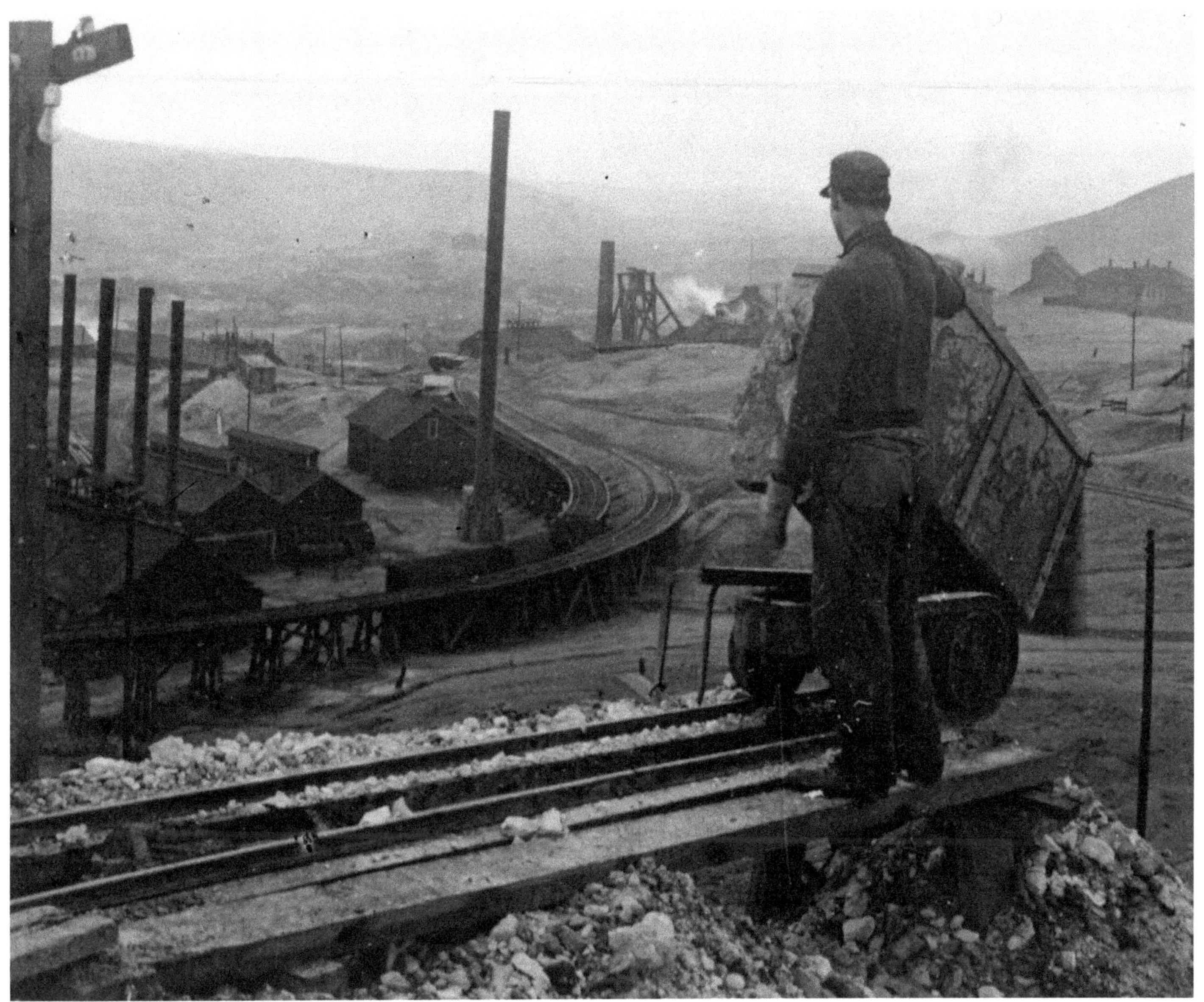

A mine worker gazes down on the city of Butte. Many residents lived close to the mines, smelters, and tailing piles of the Mining City. Wages were good, but working and living conditions were often deplorable, and life spans were short.

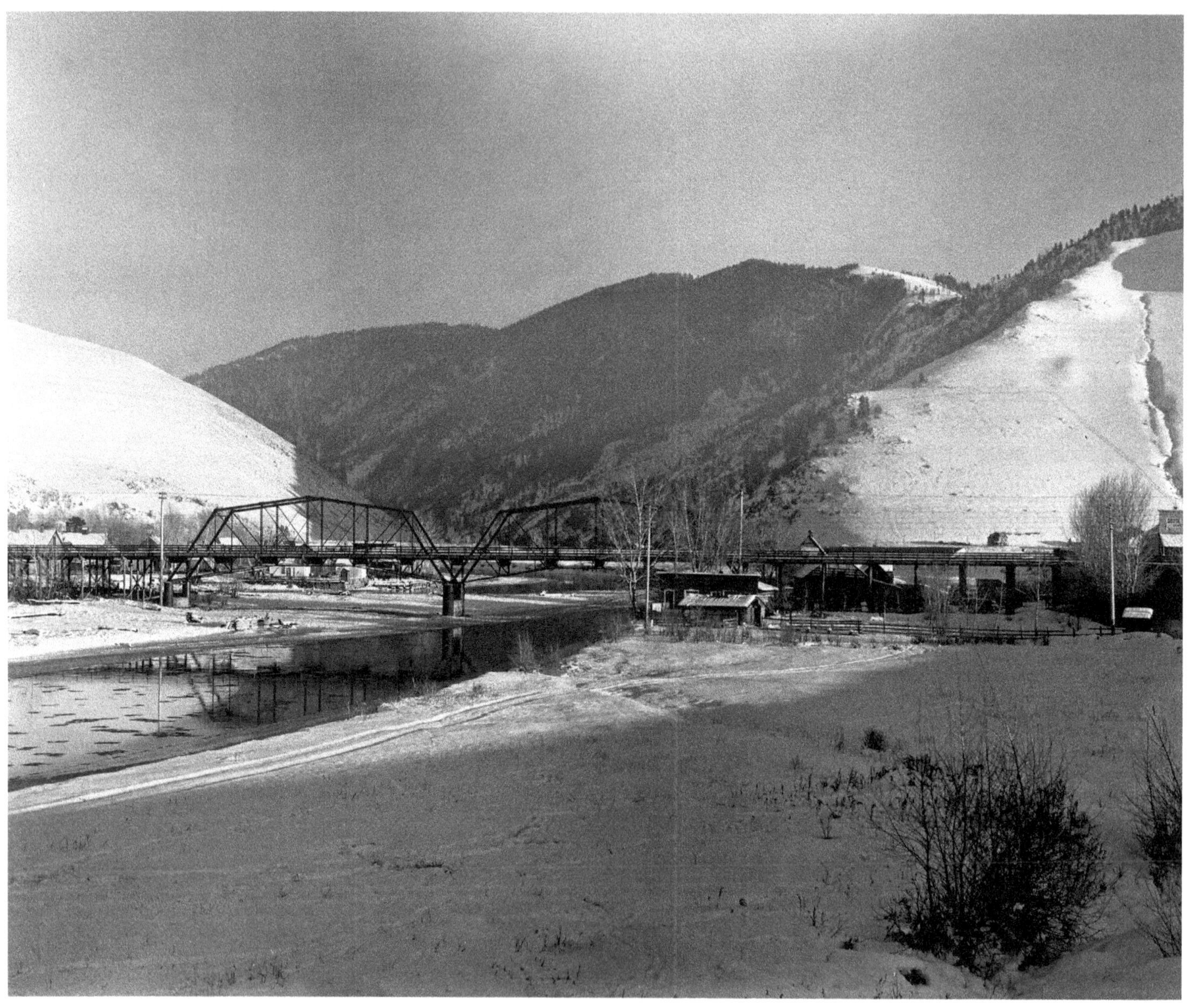

Morton Elrod took this photo of Mount Sentinel, the Hellgate Canyon, and the Higgins Avenue Bridge on a wintry Missoula day. This bridge collapsed during the 1908 flood of the Clark Fork River, then known as the Missoula River, cutting the city in half.

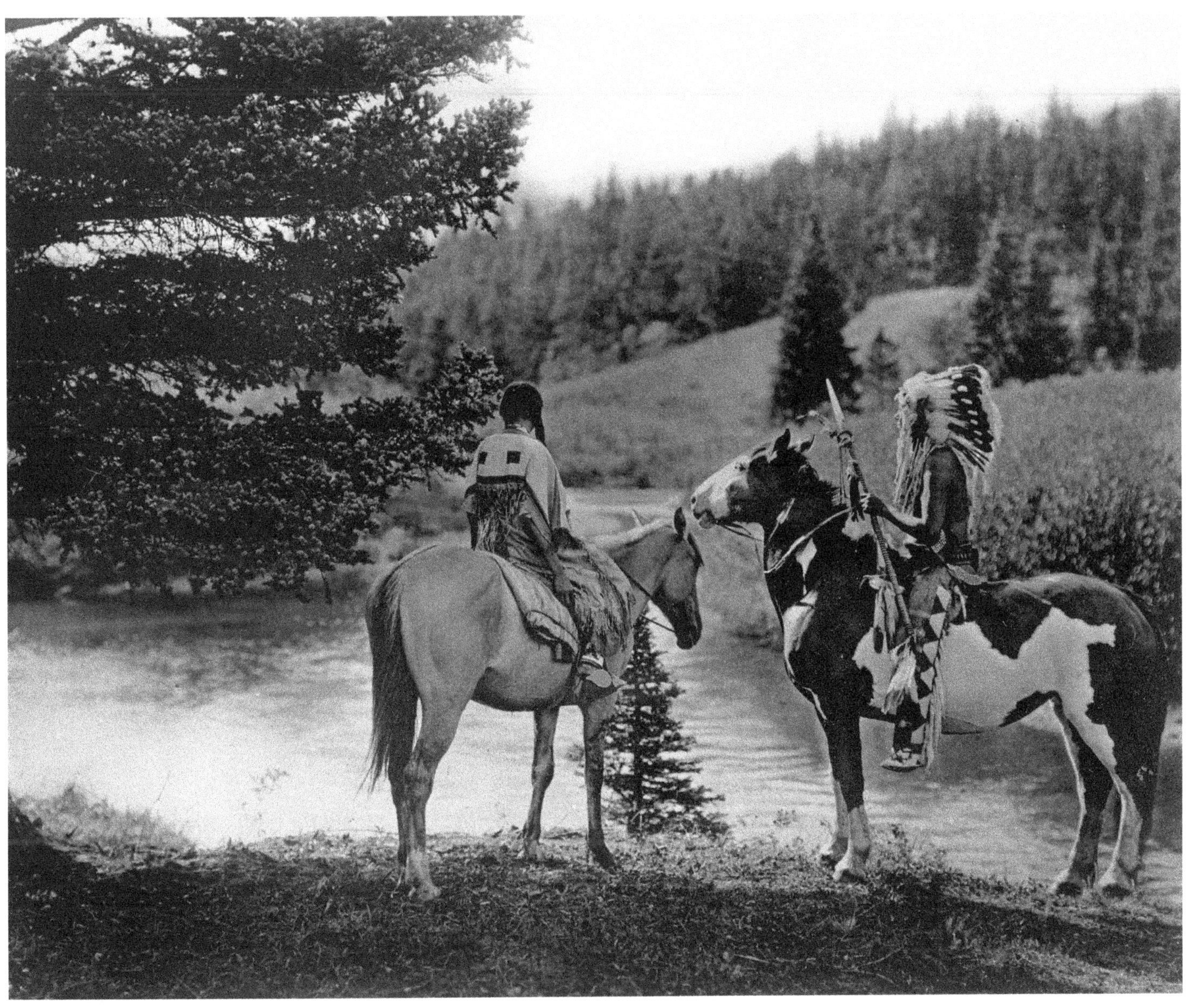

In this early twentieth century view, a Blackfeet man and woman pose on horseback in the mountains near Browning. Both are dressed in traditional garb, with the man wearing an eagle-feather warbonnet that signifies his acts of bravery. Several photographers helped document American Indian culture during this era.

Edward Curtis photographed these two Crow Indians at their winter camp on a river bottom around 1906. The Crows were nomads who traditionally occupied the areas around the Yellowstone, Big Horn, and Musselshell valleys and were known for their large horse herds.

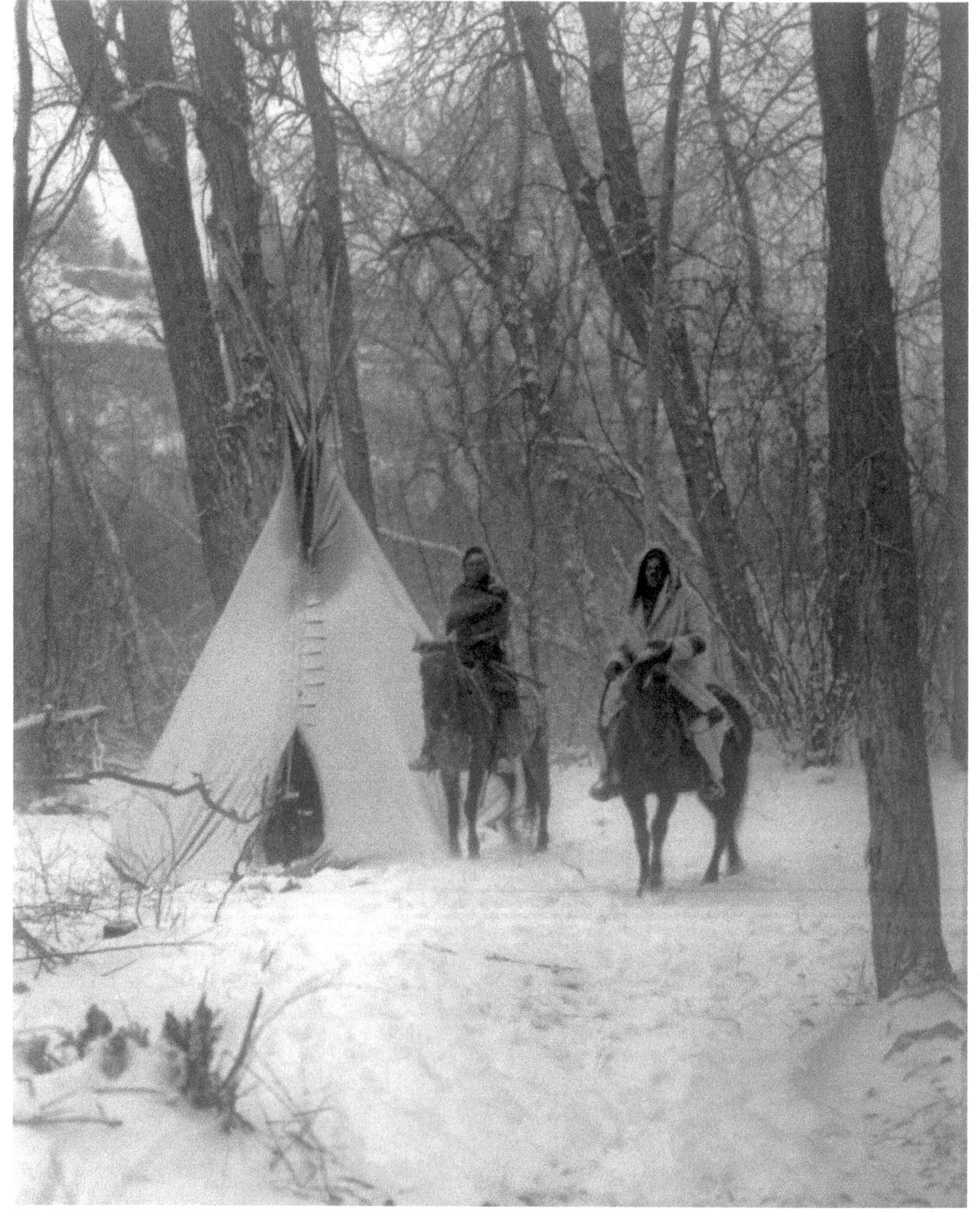

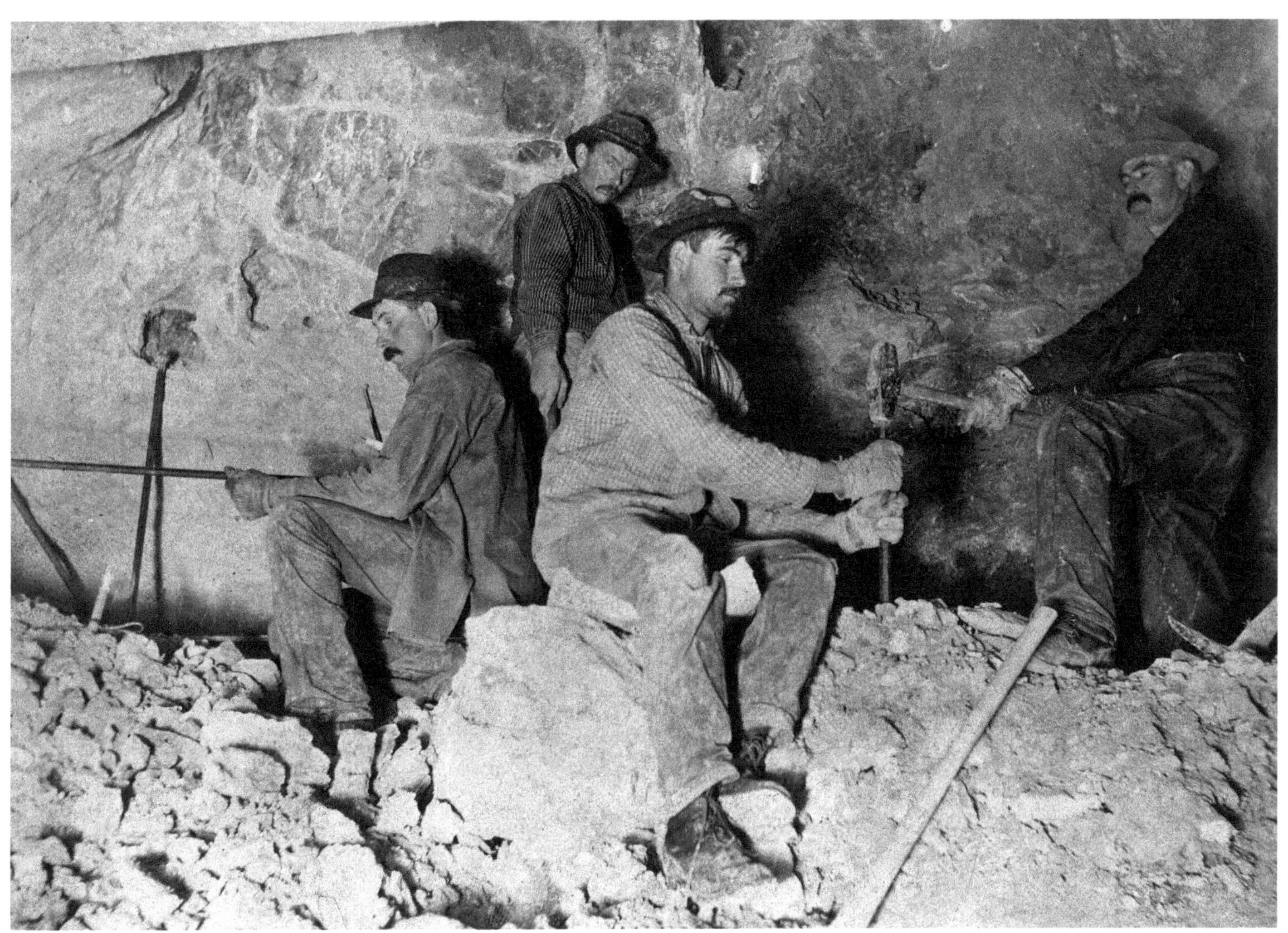

Prospector Jake Hoover was panning for gold in Yogo Gulch in the 1890s when he discovered small blue gemstones in his pan. They were later identified as sapphires of an unusually high quality, leading to the region's longtime renown as the source of a gem eventually designated the Montana state gemstone. Here miners search for sapphires in the underground workings of a Yogo mine.

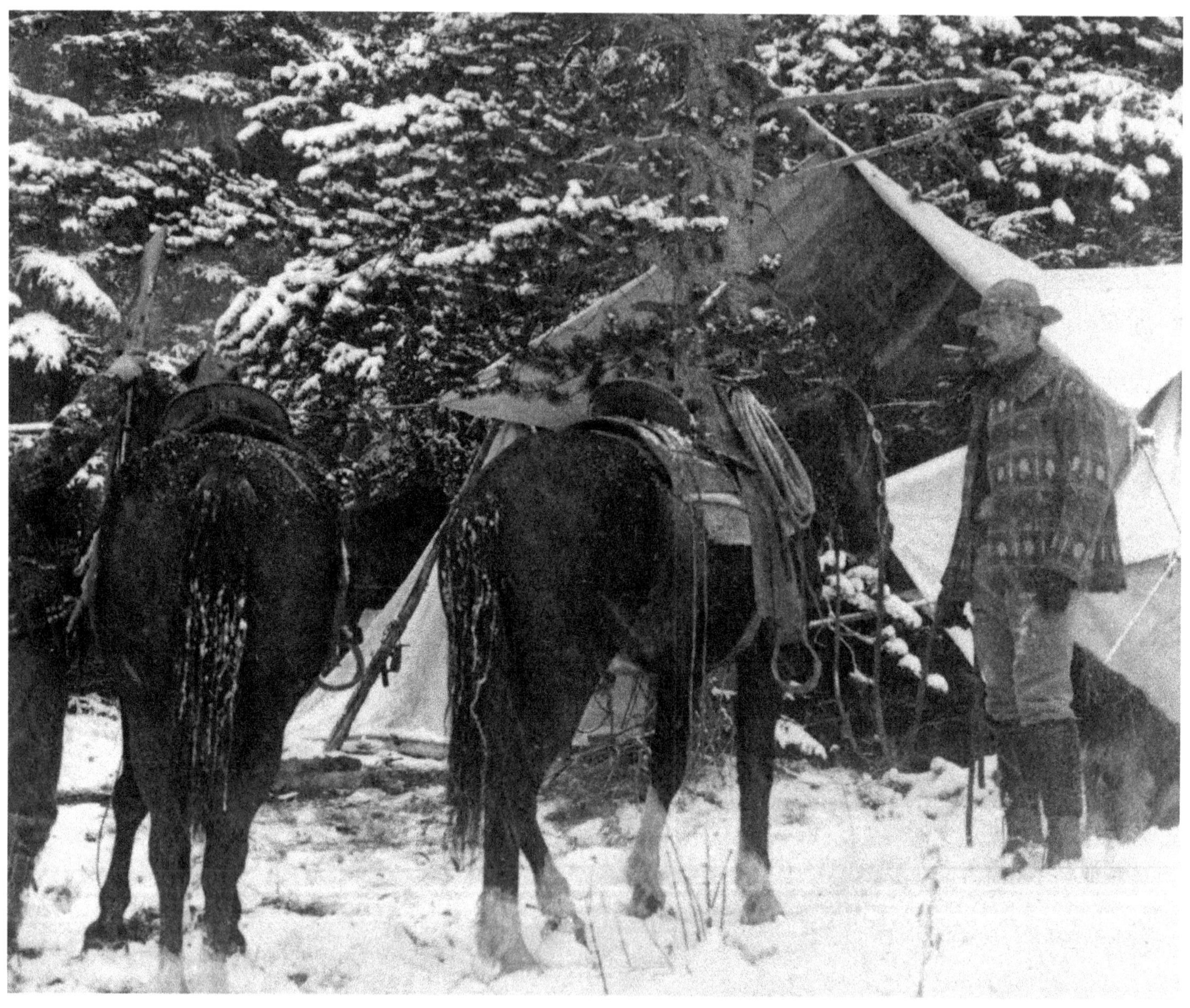

Two elk hunters tend their horses at a camp in the Gallatin Mountains around 1906. This scene is repeated every fall in the mountains of Montana, where big-game hunting is both a tradition and an important source of income for many guides and outfitters.

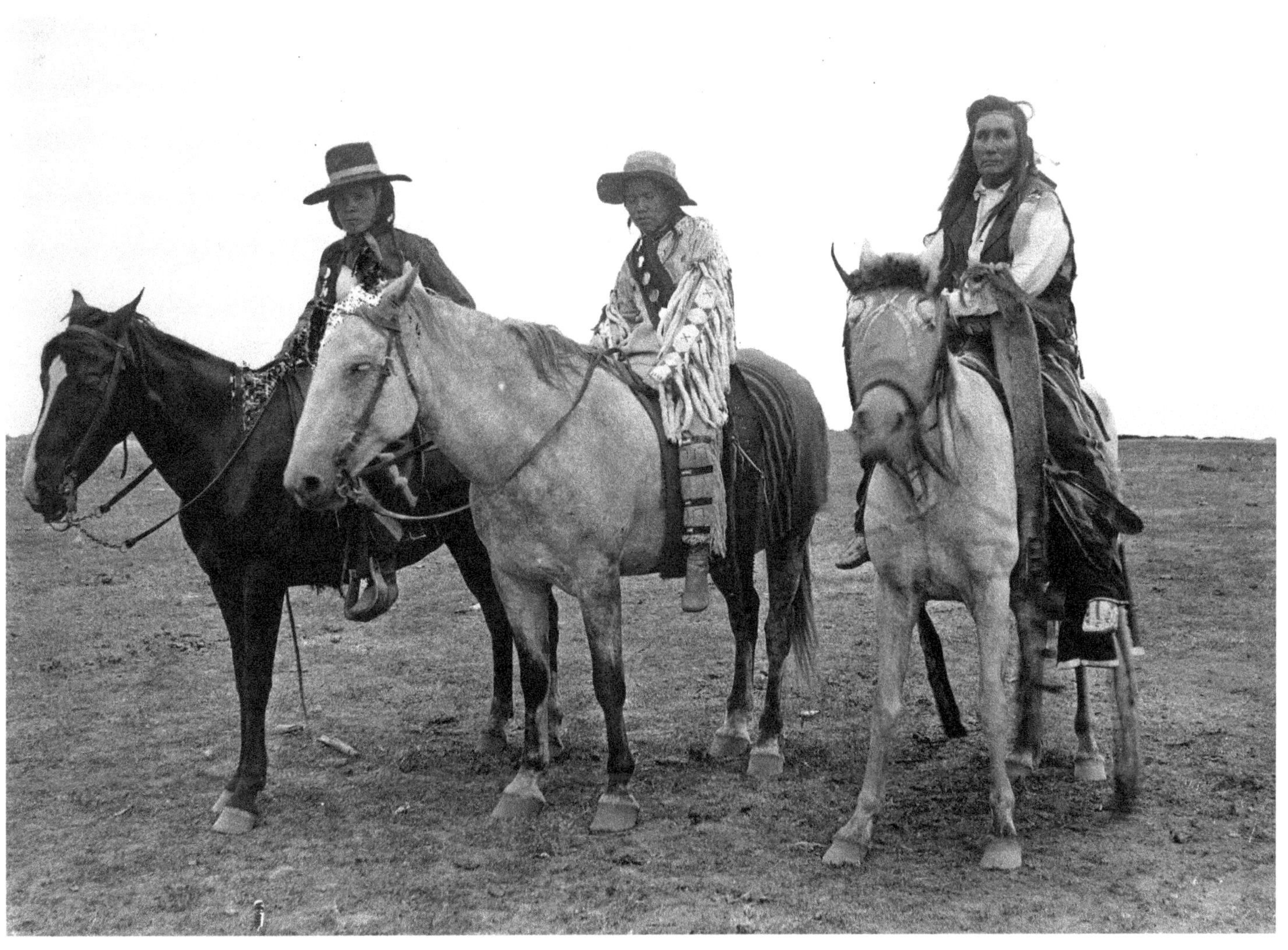

Joseph White Bull, at right, is seen with two acquaintances in this early twentieth century photograph. White Bull, a Sioux warrior and nephew of Sitting Bull, was a veteran of 19 battles by the age of 27. He is often credited with killing George A. Custer at the Battle of the Little Big Horn. White Bull lived to the age of 98.

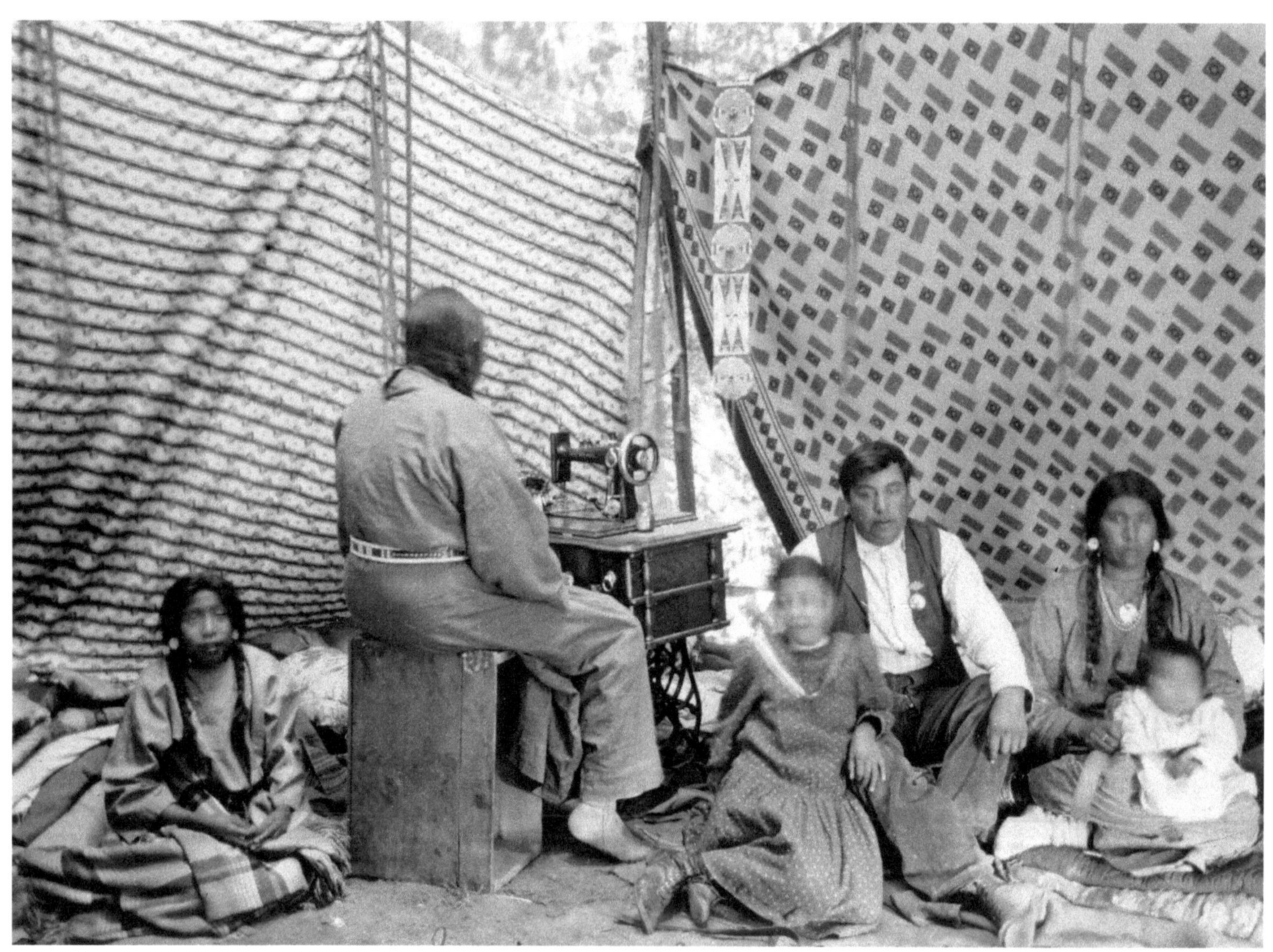

A Native American family is seen at home inside their tepee, with one member using a sewing machine, around 1906. This photo demonstrates the transition that occurred as traditional moccasins and buckskin clothing were replaced by leather shoes and garments made of fabric.

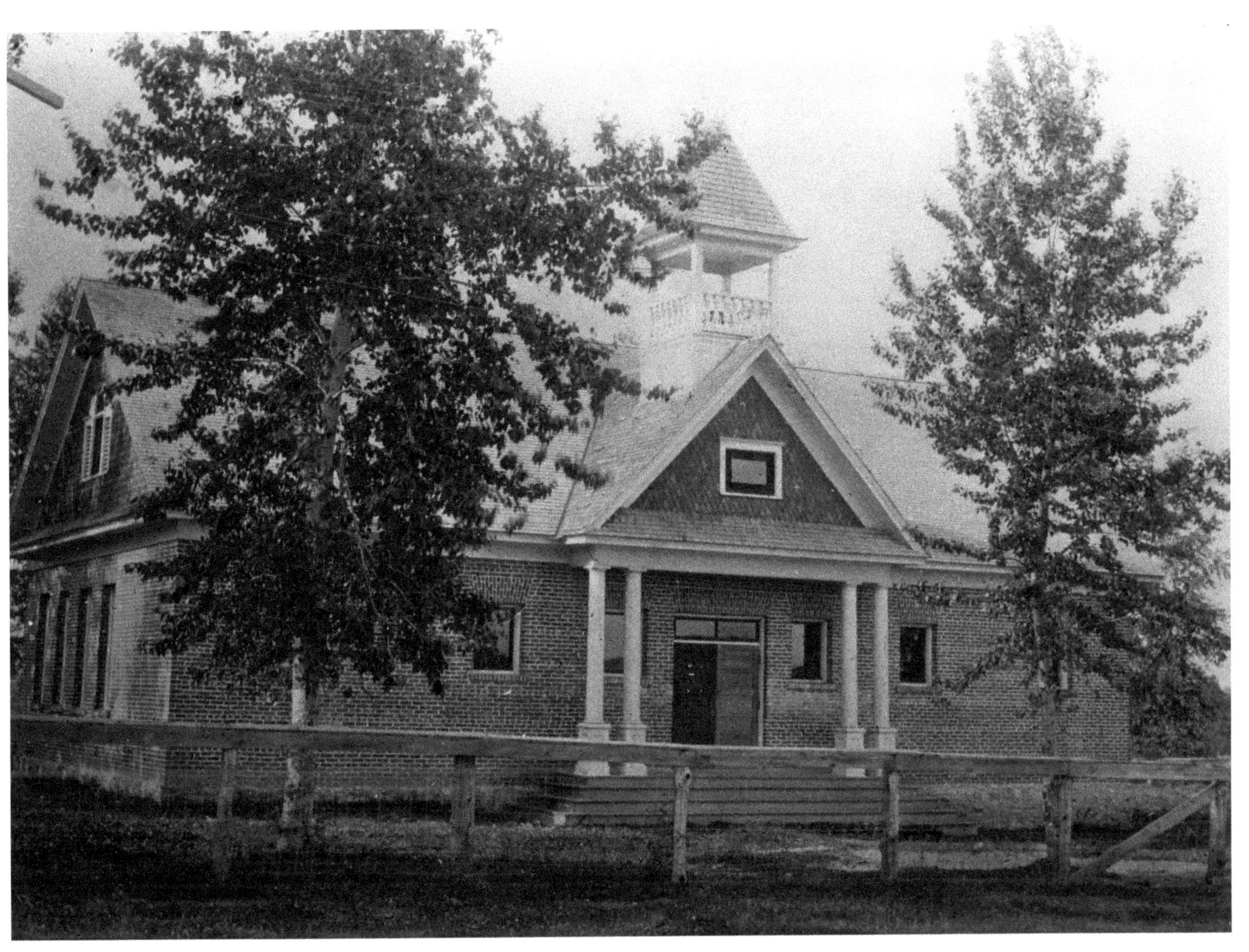

This tree-fronted schoolhouse was photographed in the Bitterroot Valley around 1907.

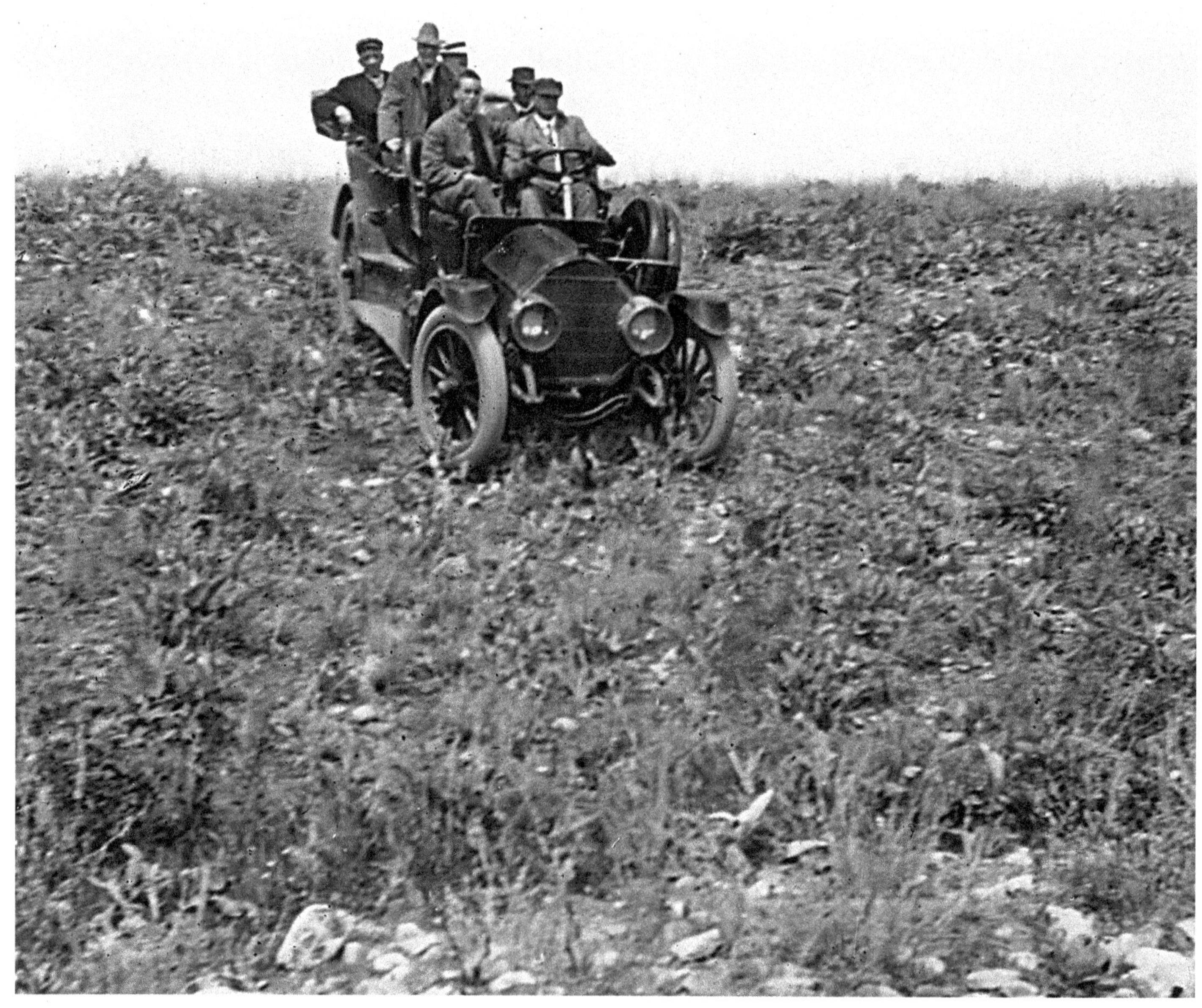

The Homestead Act encouraged Americans and immigrants alike to move west. The population of Montana increased by more than 50 percent from 1900 to 1910. This 1907 photo shows potential settlers touring the Bitterroot Valley by auto.

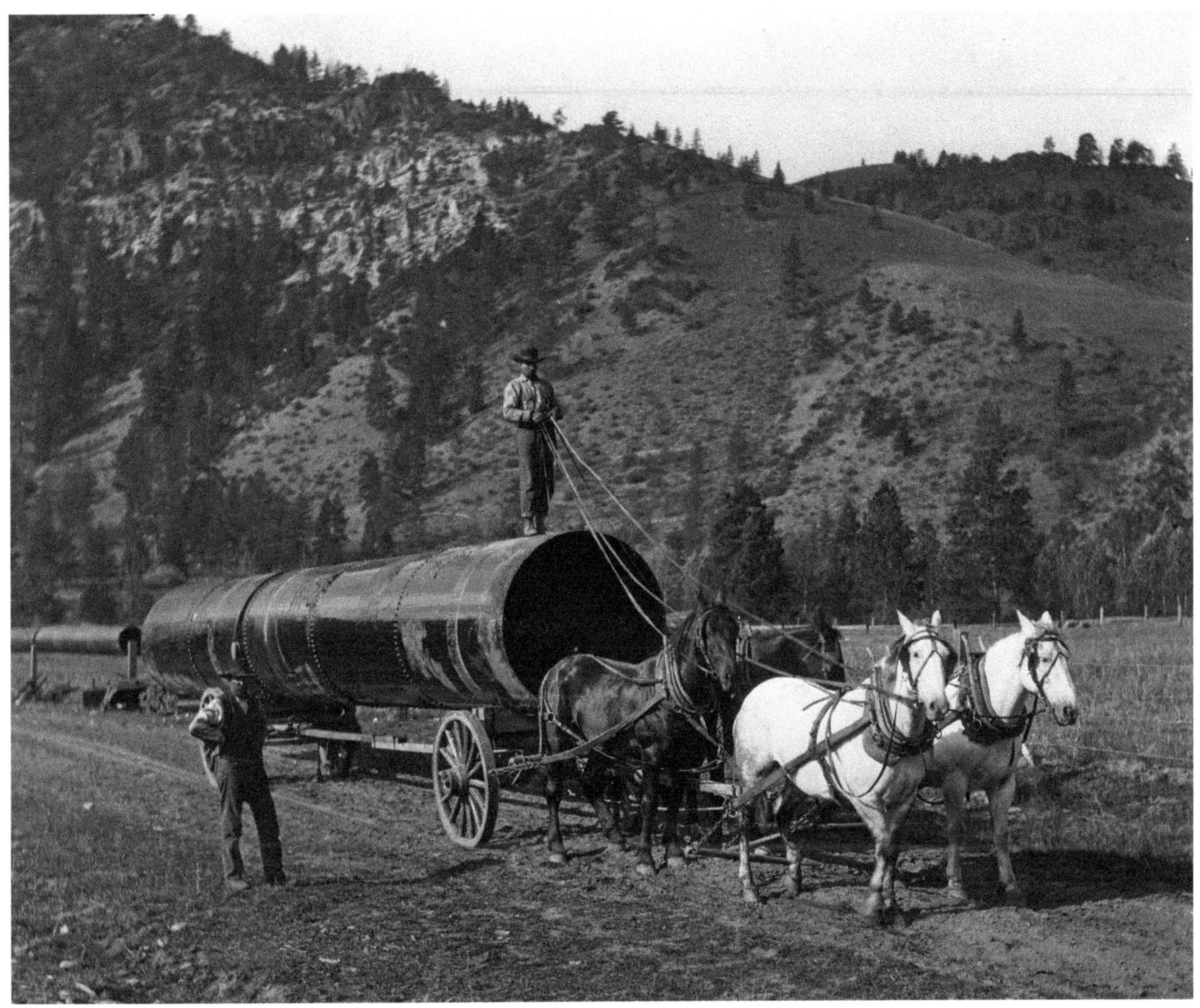

Millionaire Marcus Daly planned a major expansion of the irrigation system in the Bitterroot Valley before his death in 1900, but work on the project did not start until several years after he died. This 1907 photo shows a wagon loaded with pipe for the irrigation project.

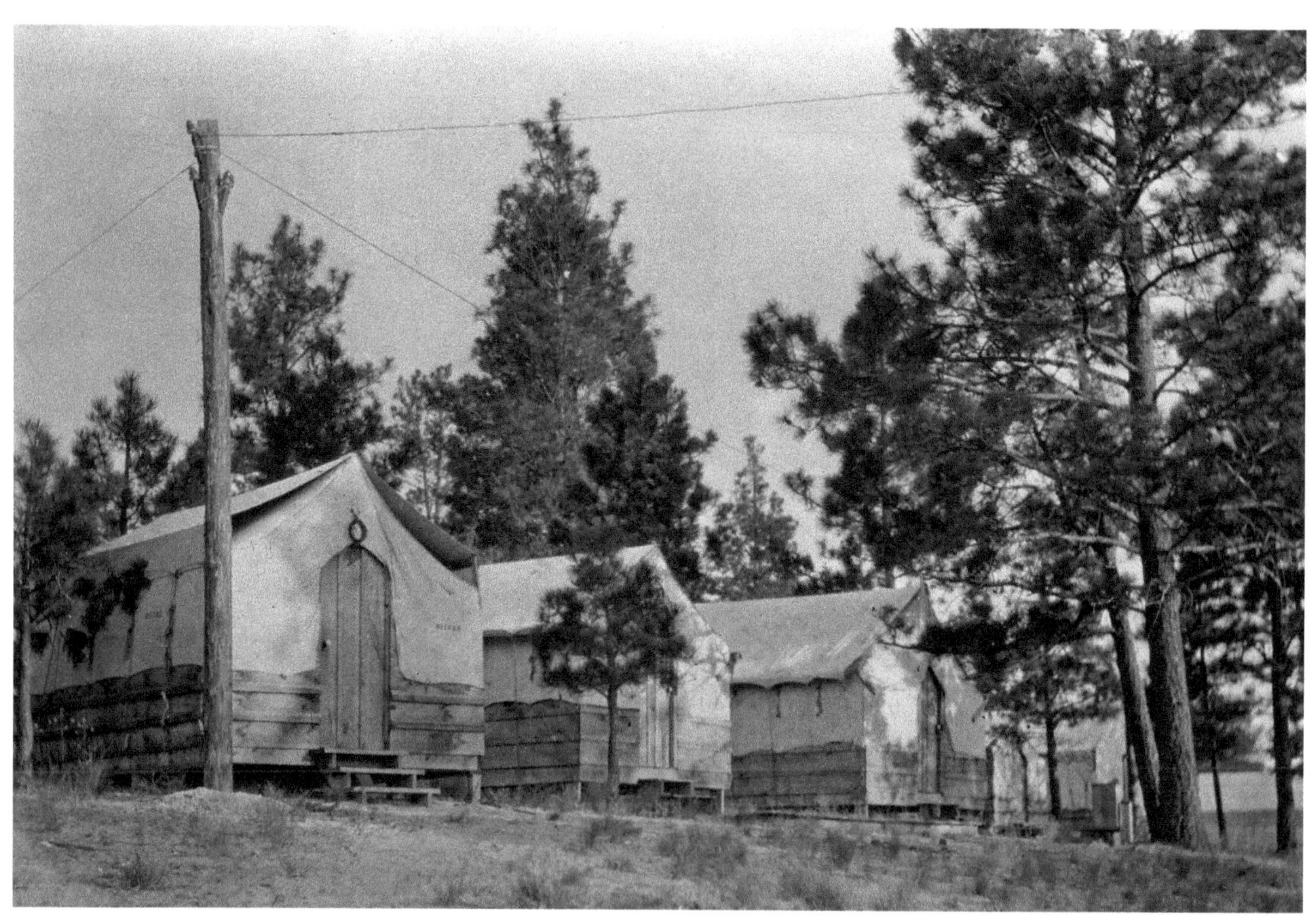

The fertile Bitterroot Valley was a perfect place for fruit orchards, a fact that farmers took advantage of after Chief Charlo and his Salish followers were finally forced to vacate the valley in 1891, 20 years after Charlo's name was reputedly forged on a treaty calling for the removal of his tribe. This photo shows a temporary camp established for fruit pickers around 1907.

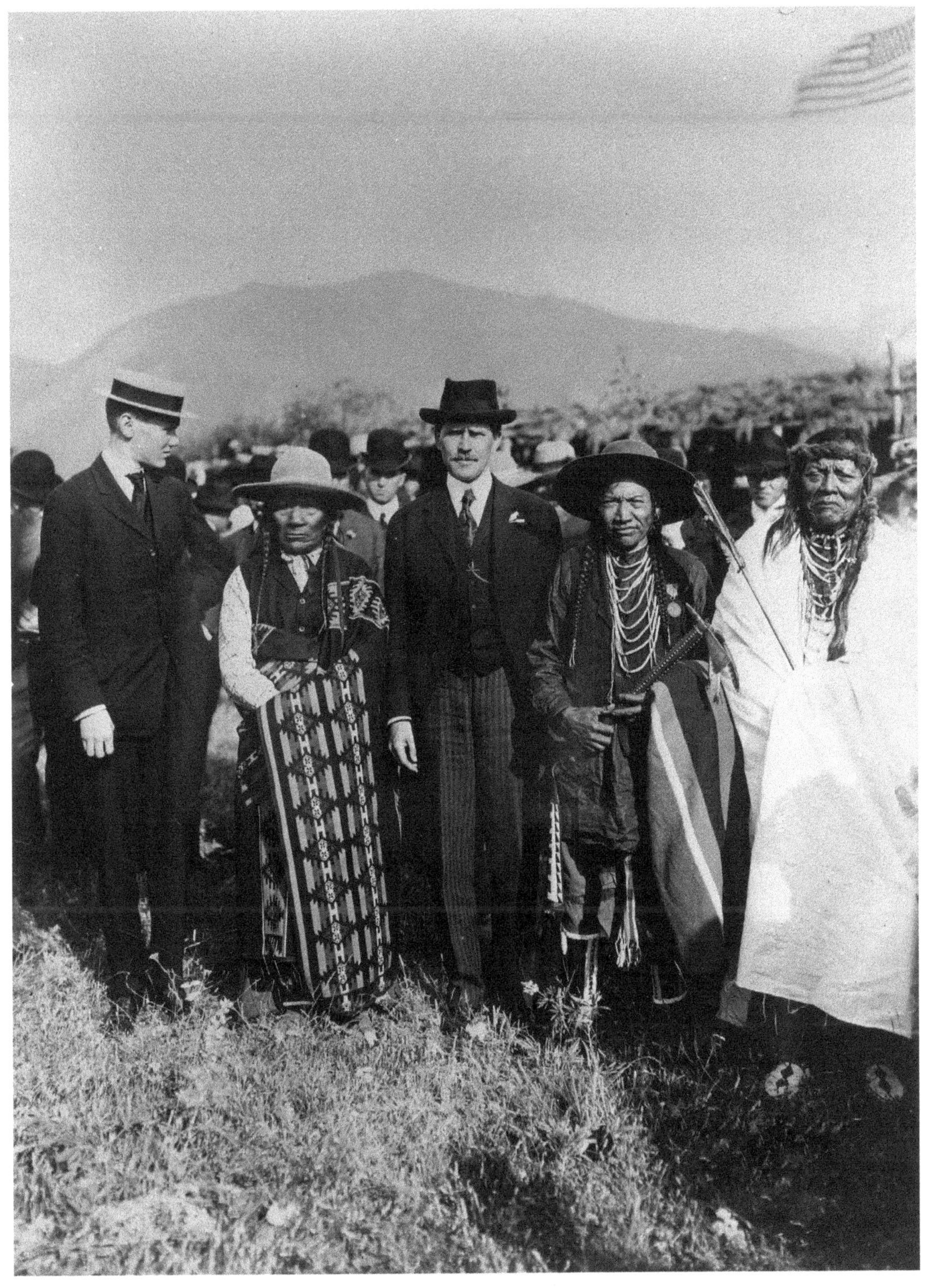

Secretary of the Interior James R. Garfield and his son met with Chief Charlo and his son on the Flathead Reservation in 1907. As a congressman from Ohio (and future president of the United States), Garfield's father, James A. Garfield, had been instrumental in negotiating the Salish removal from the Bitterroot Valley some 36 years earlier, over Chief Charlo's strenuous objections.

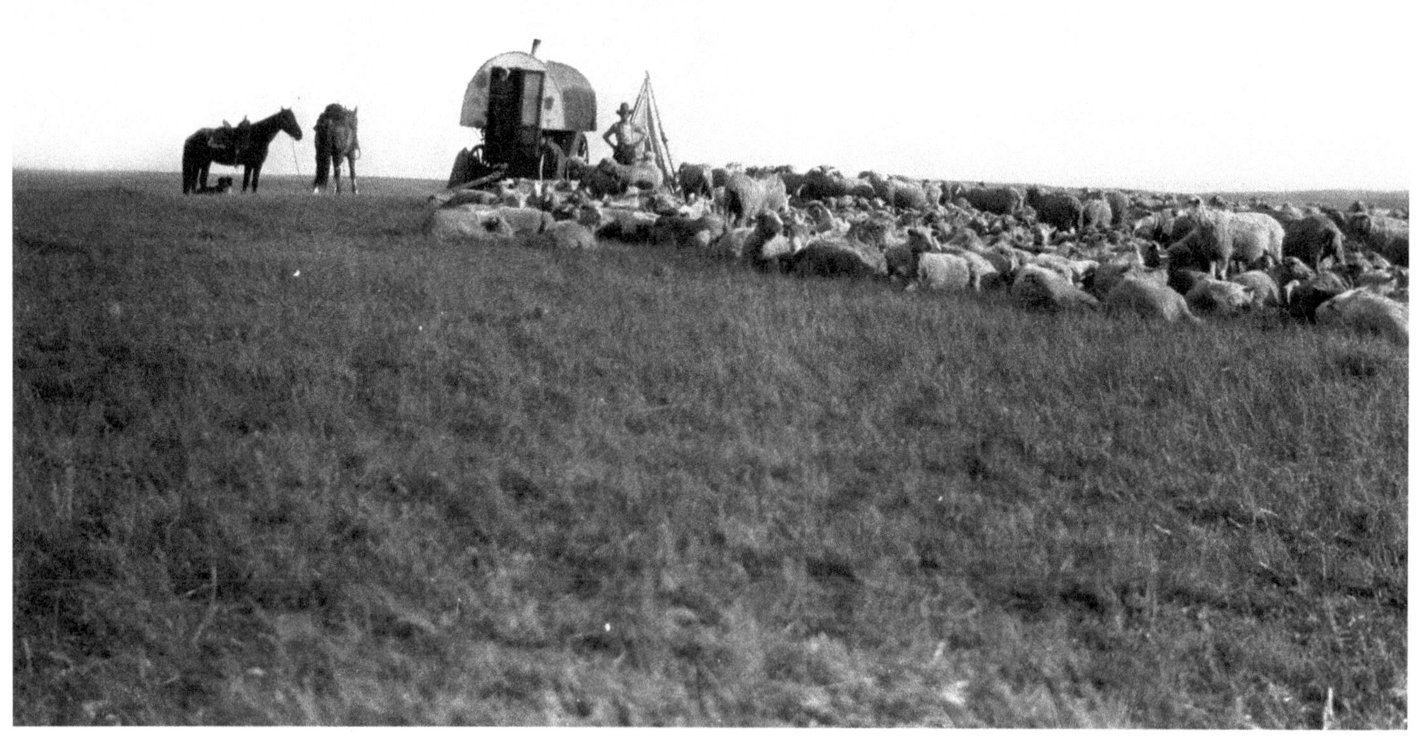

Sheep fared better than cattle during the hard winter of 1886, at least along the Smith and Musselshell rivers. By 1900 at least six million sheep ranged over Montana, making it the largest wool-growing state in the nation.

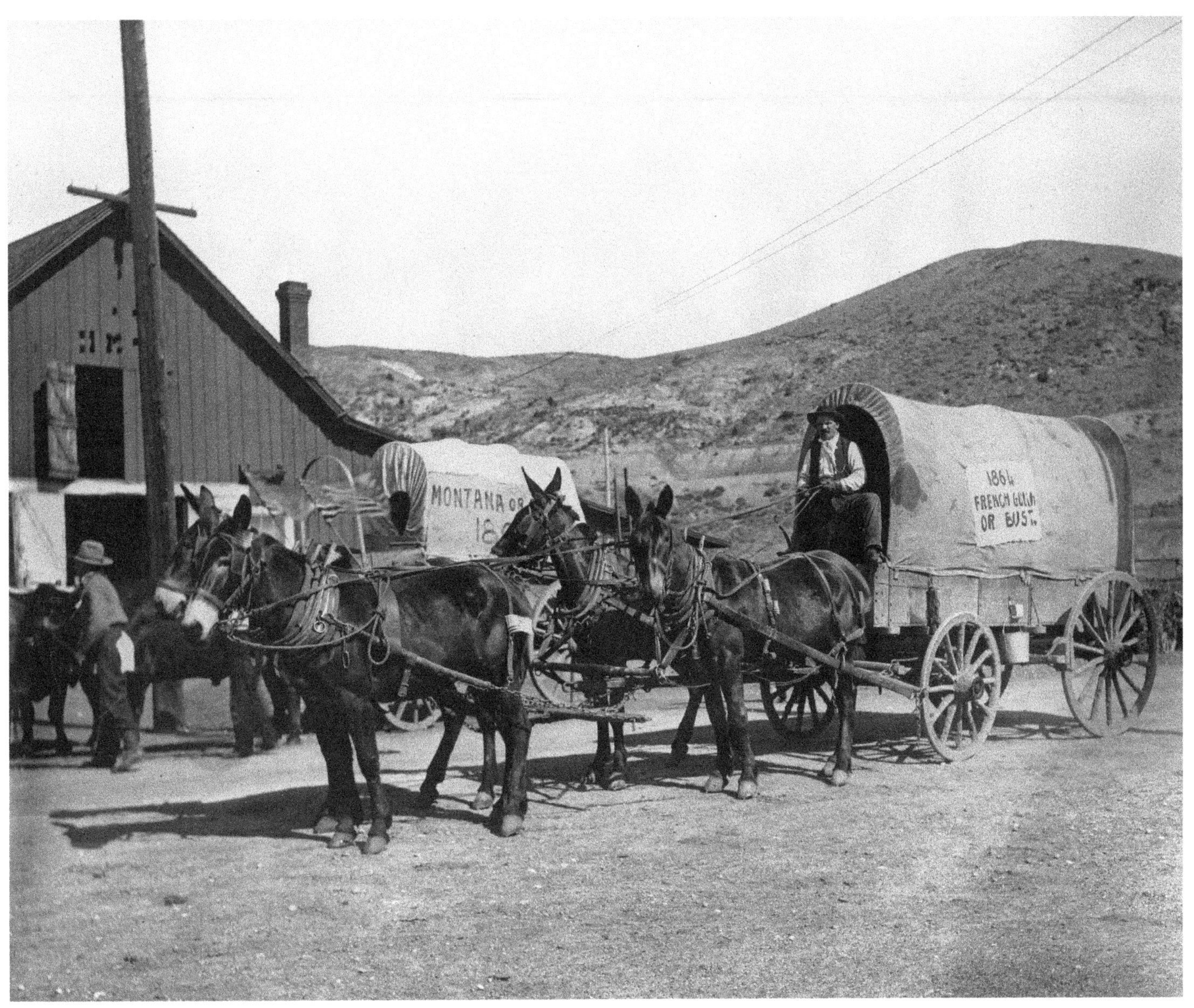

This Fourth of July photo from 1908 shows a wagon proclaiming "1864: French Gulch or Bust." Established in 1864, French Gulch was an early gold-mining camp that at one time boasted 30 houses, as well as an assortment of shops, saloons, and gambling houses. Large-scale hydraulic mining and dredging destroyed the last remnants of the camp by 1904.

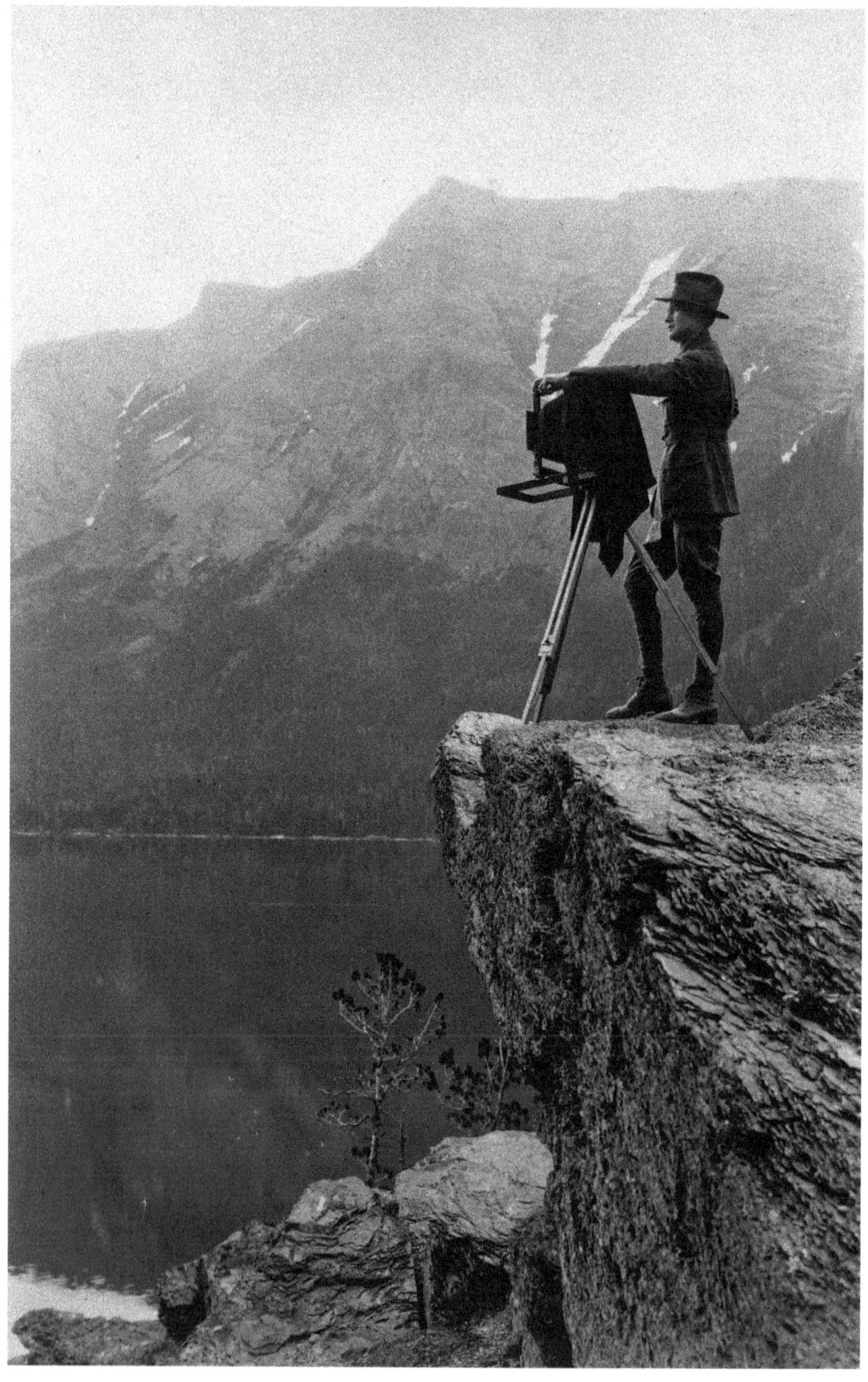

R. H. McKay, seen here with his camera, was one of western Montana's foremost photographers during the first half of the twentieth century. By 1911 he had opened his own commercial photo studio, and for the next 35 years he took thousands of images of the people and places of western Montana.

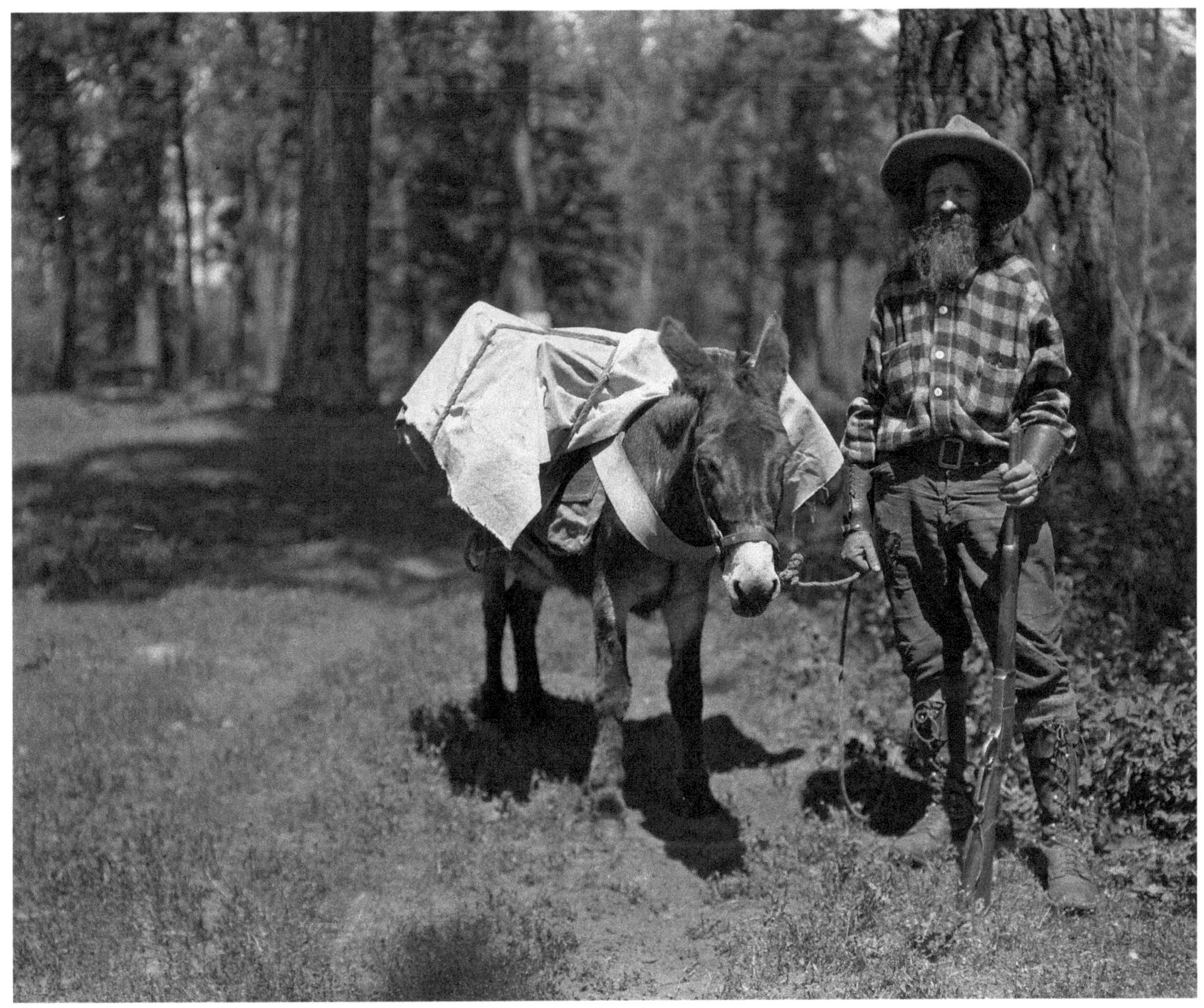

Some 50 years after the heyday of the gold rush in Montana, R. H. McKay snapped a series of photos of a local itinerant gold prospector, "Arizona Pete." In this photo, Arizona Pete and his burro pose in front of an old-growth ponderosa pine forest in western Montana.

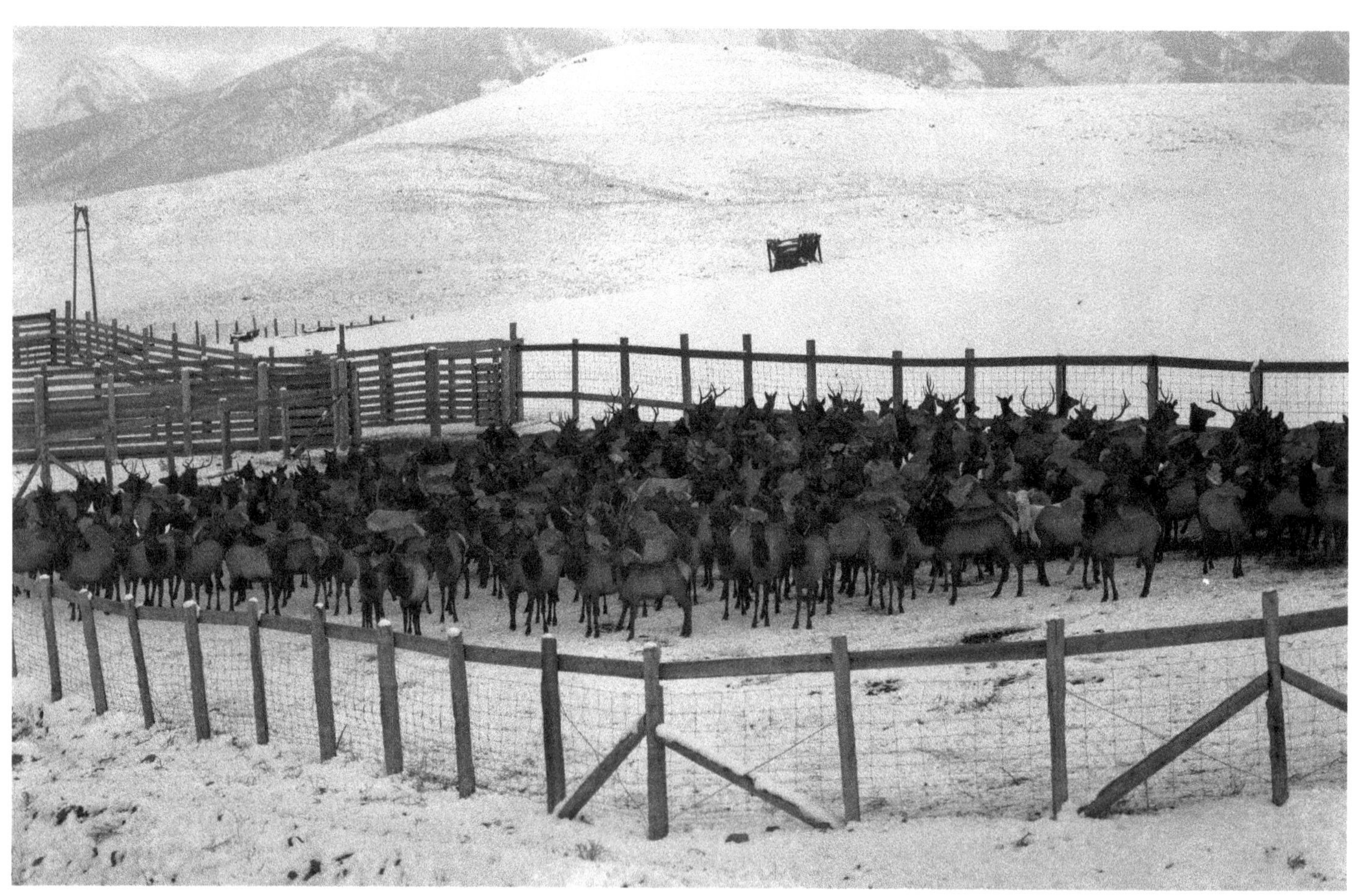

There were fewer than 50,000 elk left in North America by 1910. Over the next 30 years, more than 1,700 elk were transplanted from Yellowstone National Park and the National Bison Range to 31 locations across Montana. This herd of corralled elk boasts many large bulls.

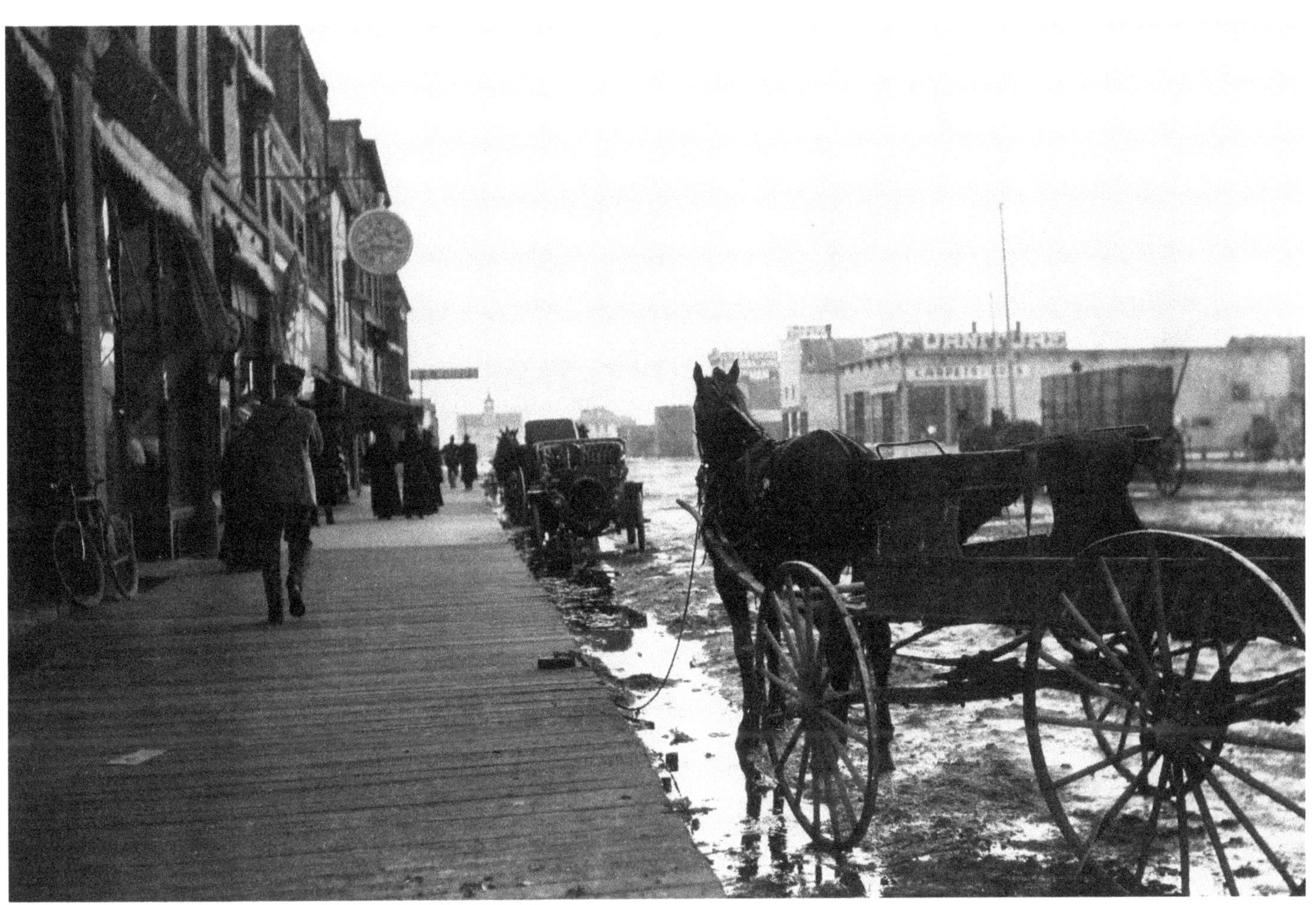

Hitched to a wagon, a horse stands patiently in the mud of Kalispell's Main Street around 1908. Charles Conrad founded Kalispell in 1891, and it soon grew into an important railroad and timber-industry center. Conrad's opulent mansion is now open to the public.

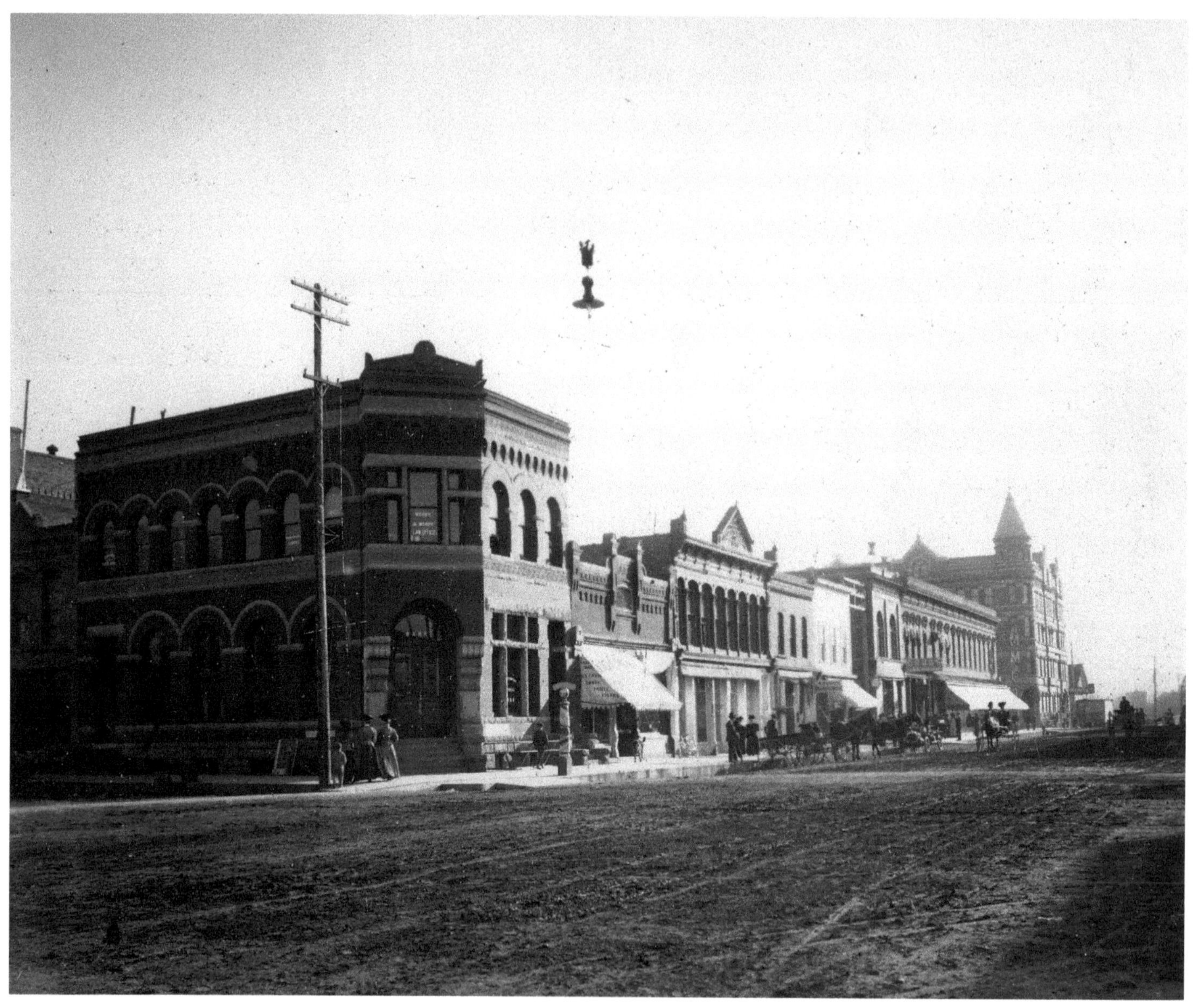

Missoula's Western Montana Bank Building is seen here at the corner of Broadway and Higgins in 1908. Missoula founder C. P. Higgins began construction of the building in 1888 but died before it was finished. His son Frank oversaw completion of the "Higgins Block" and later was elected mayor of Missoula.

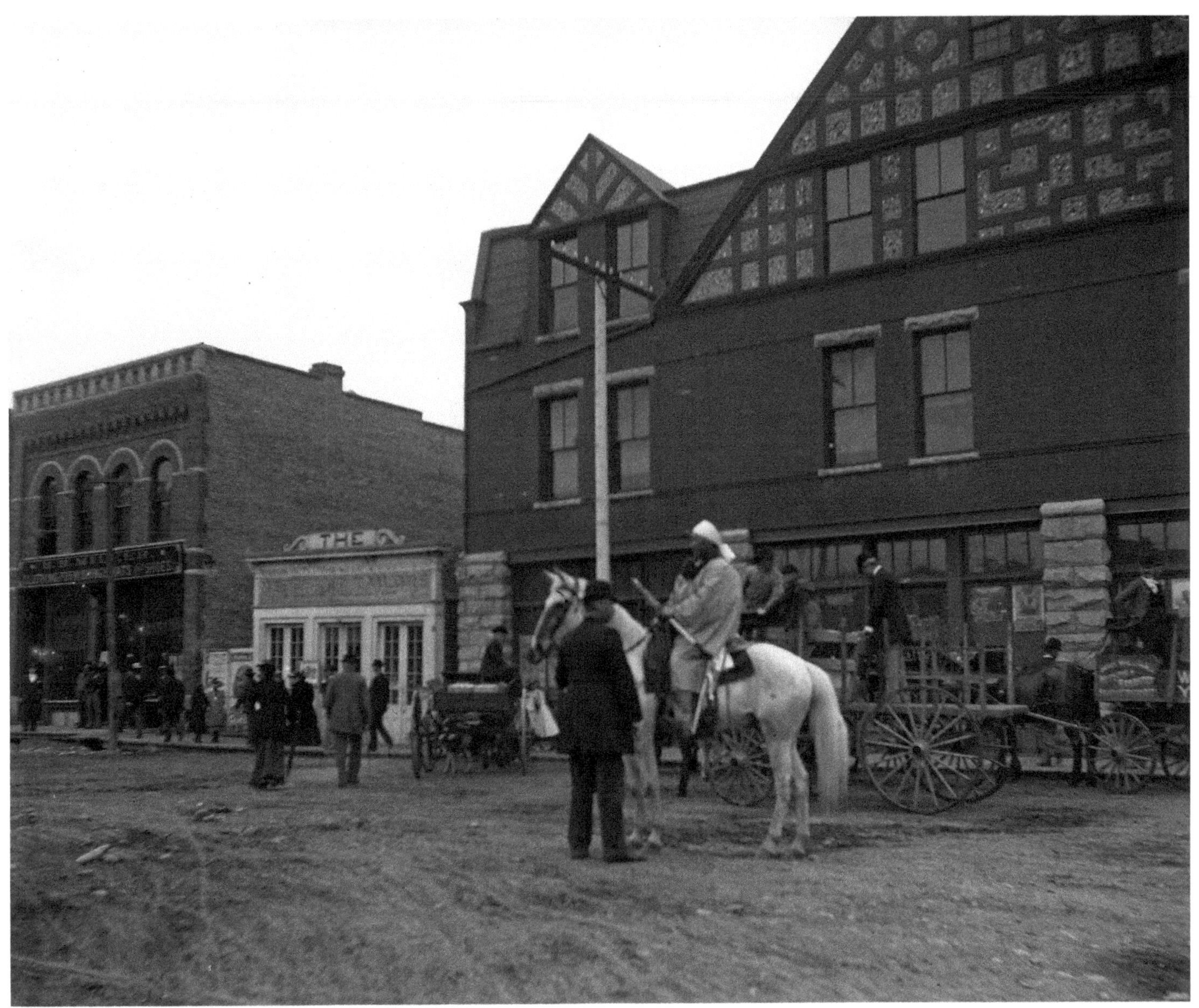

The Tudor styling of the Missoula Hotel is evident in this street scene from 1908. Located at the corner of Main and Ryman, this building served as regional headquarters of the Northern Pacific Railroad for a time. It was converted into apartments in the 1950s.

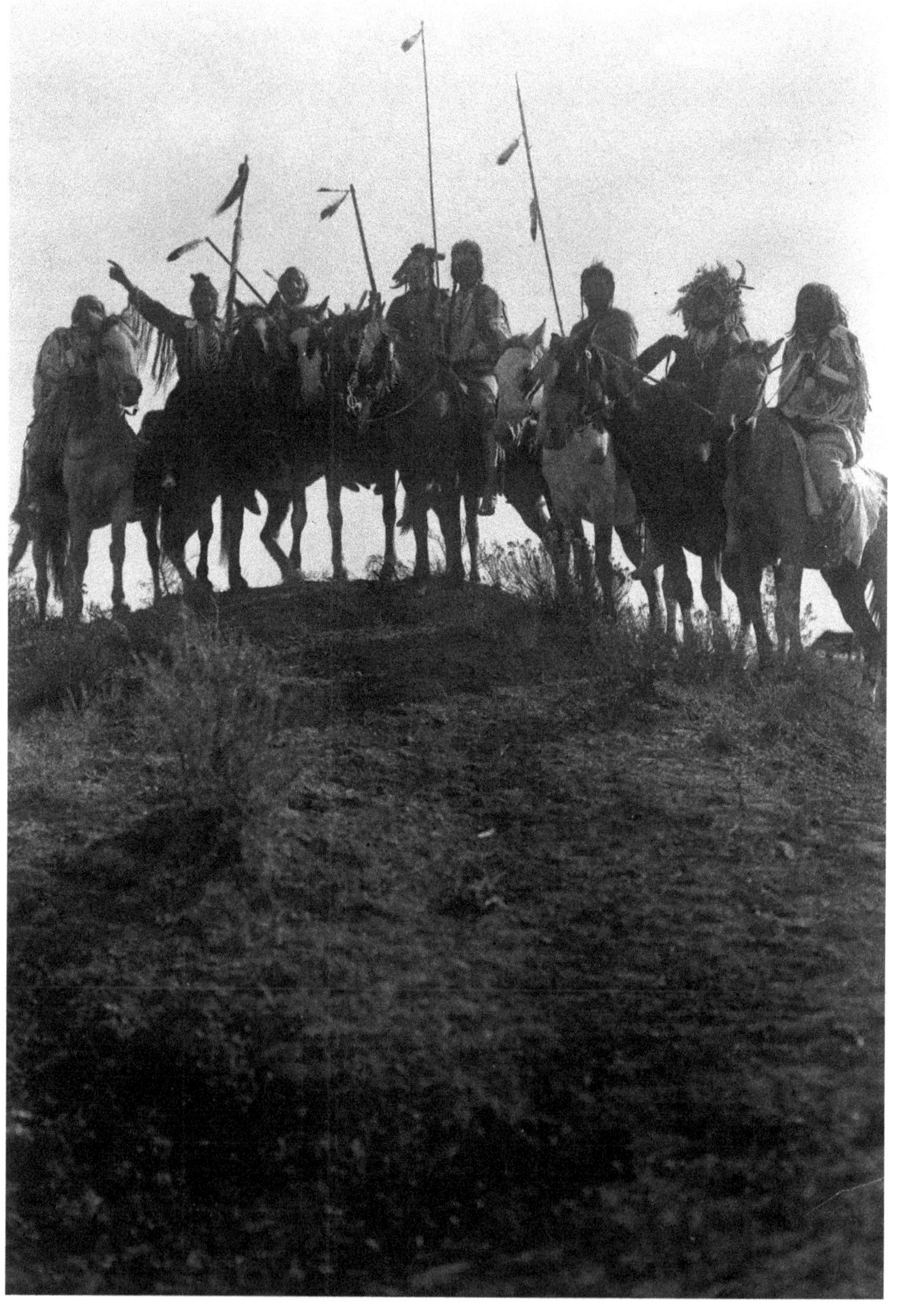

Crow Indians reenact a war party for photographer Edward Curtis, who became enamored of Native American traditions after witnessing a Piegan sun dance. Curtis spent years compiling an ambitious, 20-volume photographic study of the North American Indian.

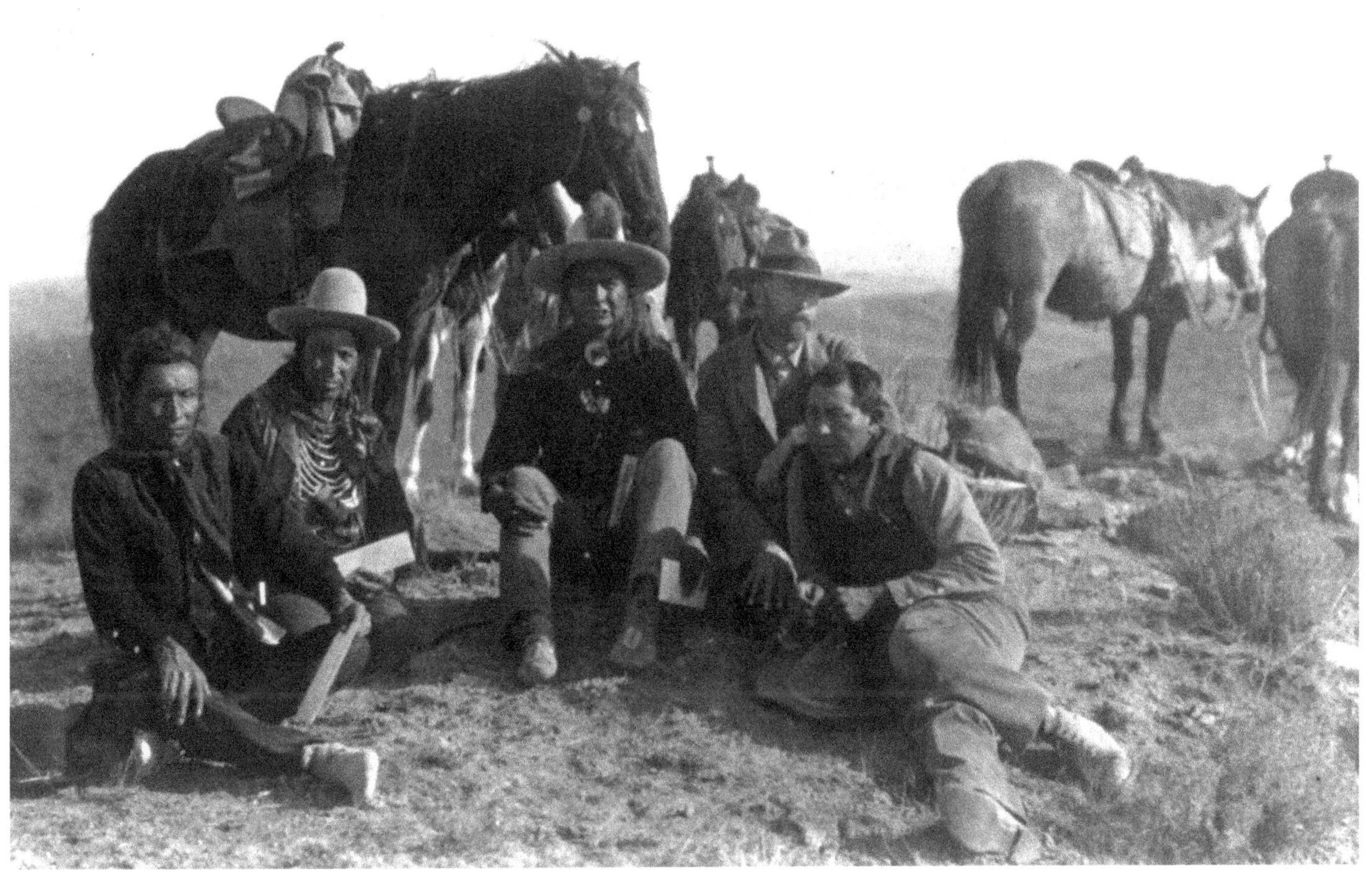

Edward Curtis spent much of 1908 photographing Montana's various American Indian tribes. After touring the Little Big Horn battlefield in the company of several of the Crow scouts who had ridden with Custer's 7th Cavalry, Curtis, second from right, sits with four of the Apsáalooke elders at a point overlooking the battlefield known as the Crow's nest.

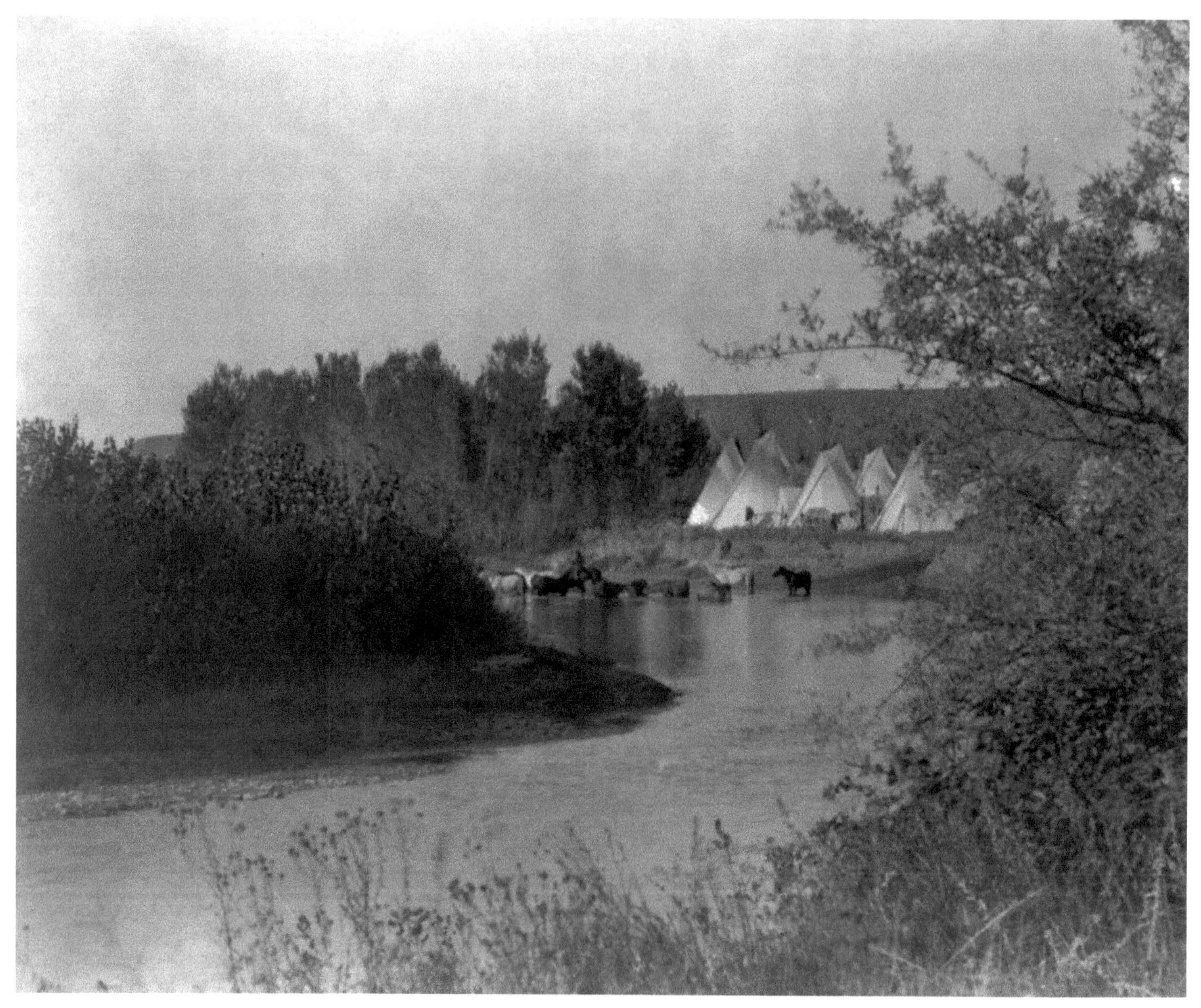

Crow tepees line the banks of the Little Big Horn River, while the horse herd frolics in the water. The Crow Indian Reservation, which was created in 1851, is more than 2 million acres in size, yet that represents only a fraction of the traditional range of the Apsáalooke.

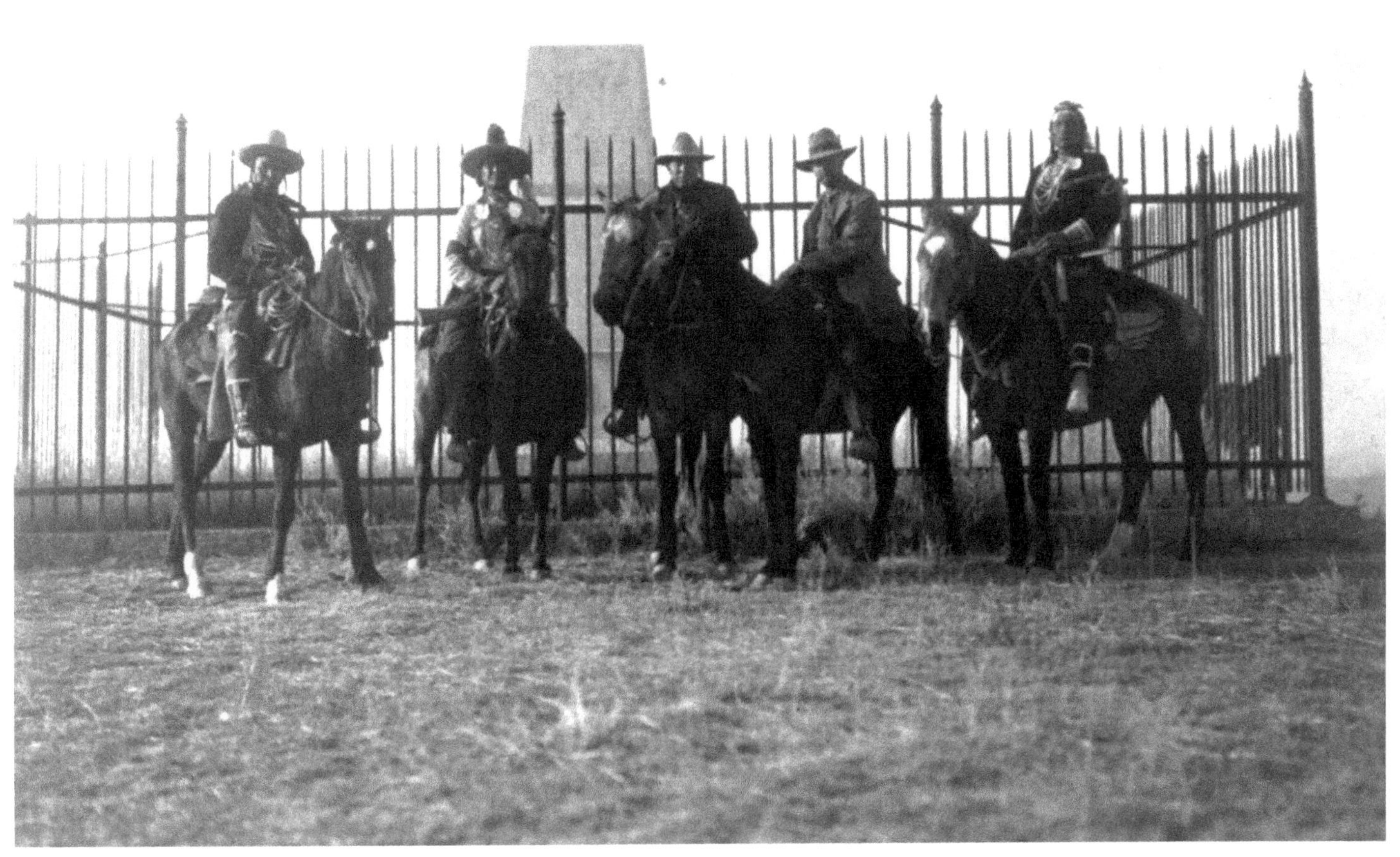

Photographer Edward Curtis, second from right, and four Crow scouts pose in front of the Custer Monument. The Indians are likely Goes Ahead, Hairy Moccasin, White Man Runs Him, and Curly. Curtis had already published two popular volumes of Indian photographs by 1908.

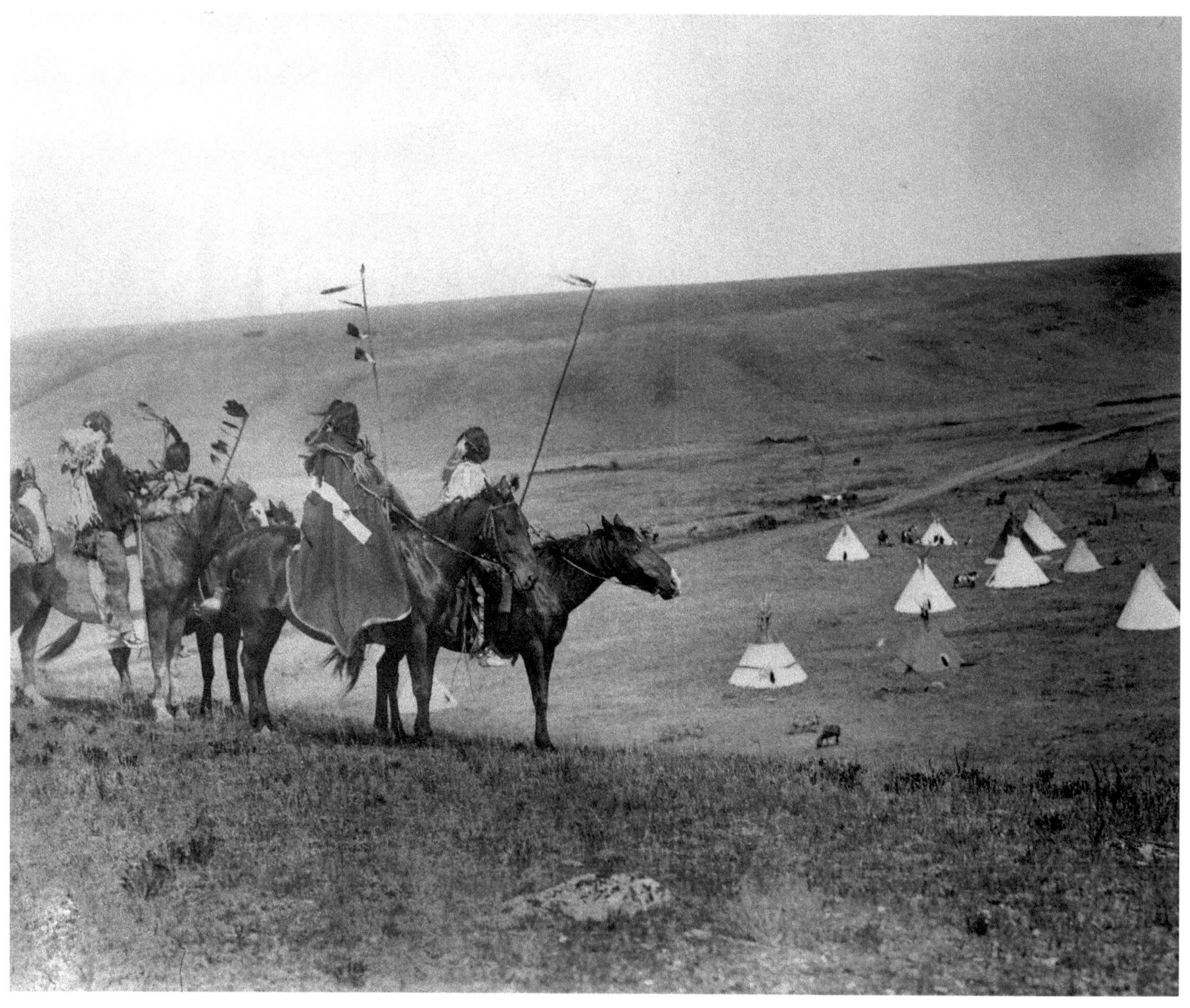

The Gros Ventre tribe has shared the Fort Belknap Reservation with the Assiniboine tribe since 1887. Named the Gros Ventre (or Big Bellies) by the French, they prefer the name A'aninin (People of the White Clay). They are related to the Arapaho and Cheyenne tribes. Edward Curtis photographed this group of A'aninin in 1908.

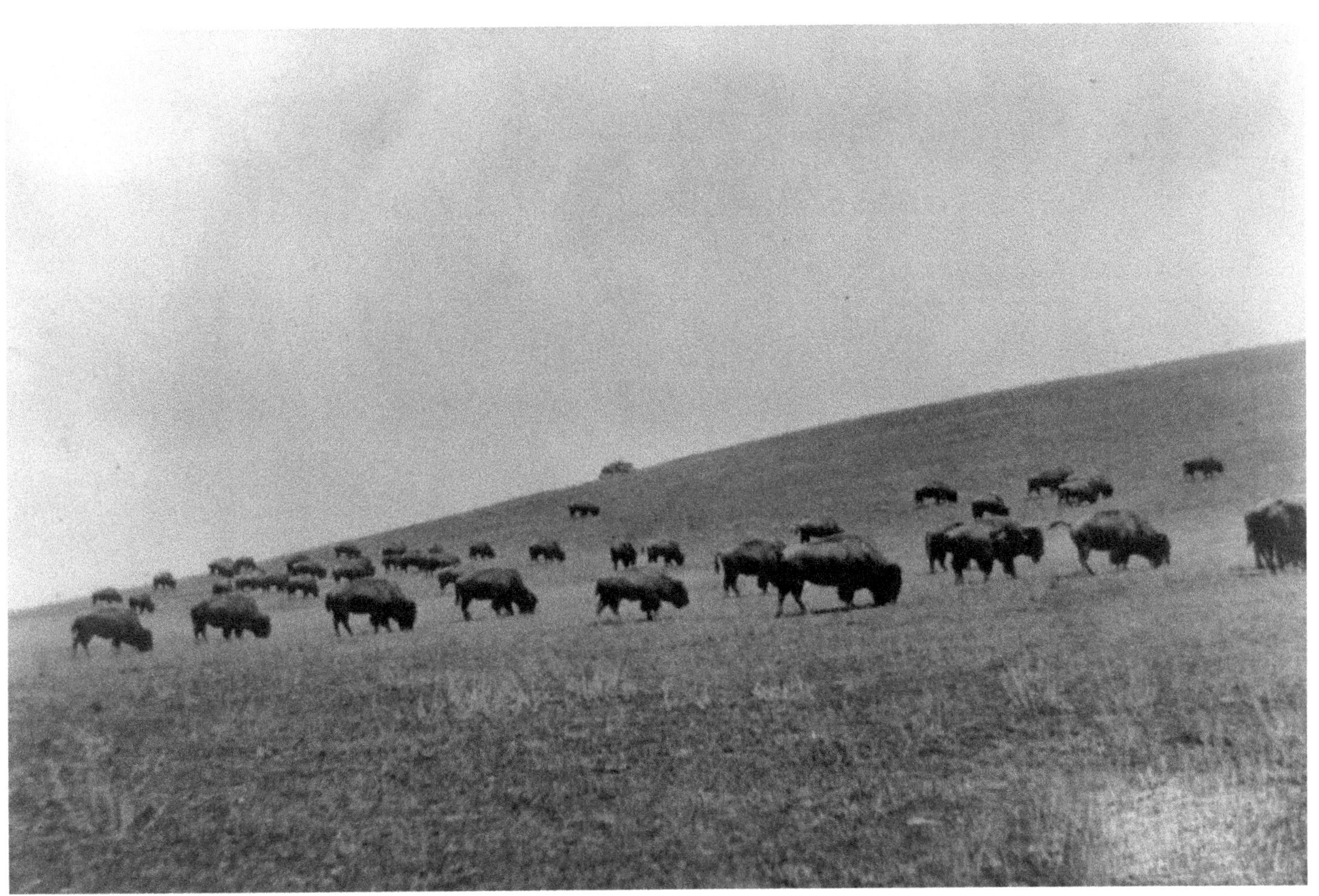

Hide-hunters nearly exterminated the estimated 10 million bison that once wandered the Great Plains. By the end of the nineteenth century there were only a few hundred left, and the National Bison Range at Moiese was established in 1908 to help protect them.

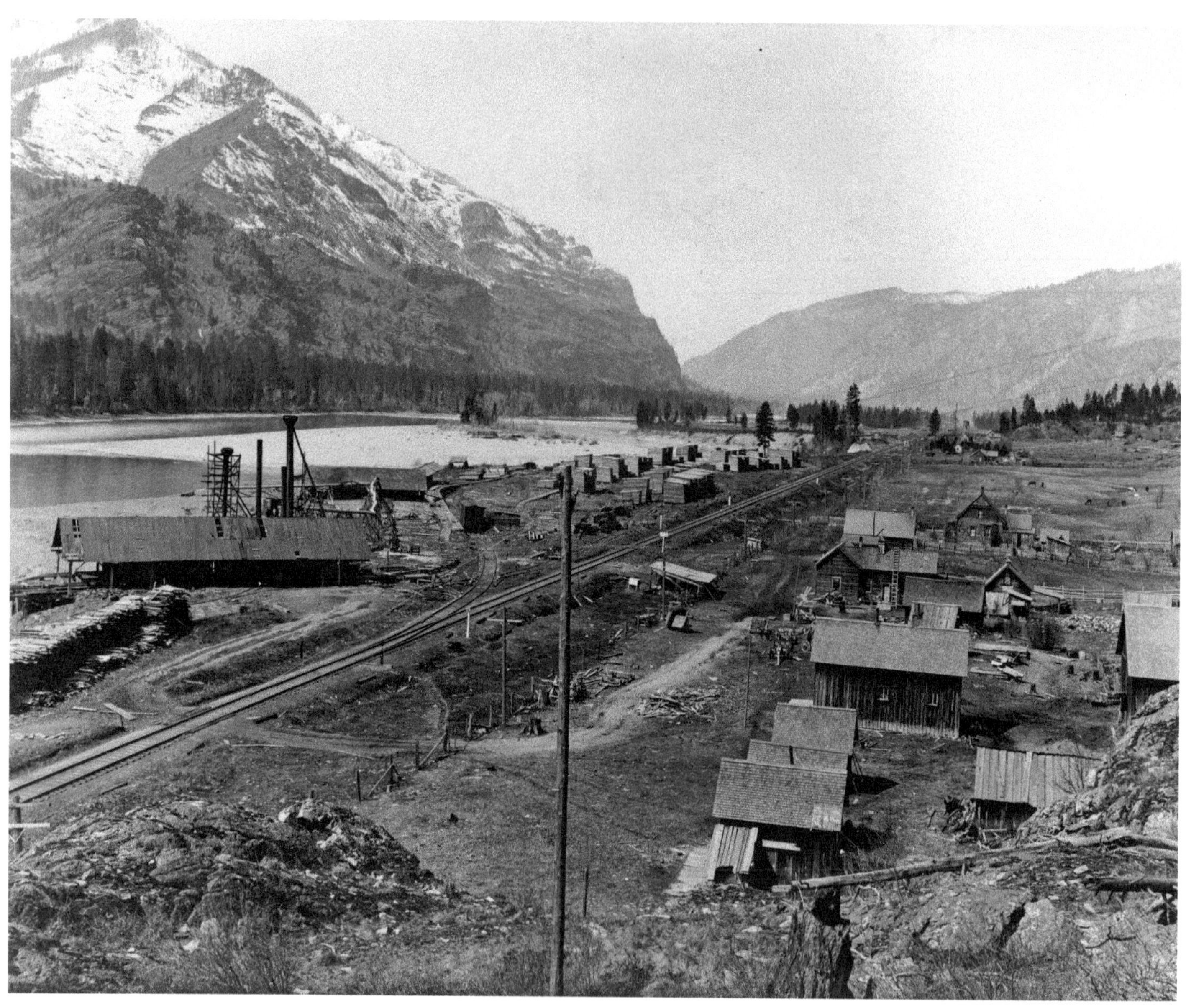

This cliff-top view shows the town of Eddy, located on the banks of the Clark Fork River a few miles upstream of Thompson Falls. Snow covers the upper slopes of nearby Eddy Mountain. Salish Post, the first Hudson's Bay Company trading post in Montana, was located nearby.

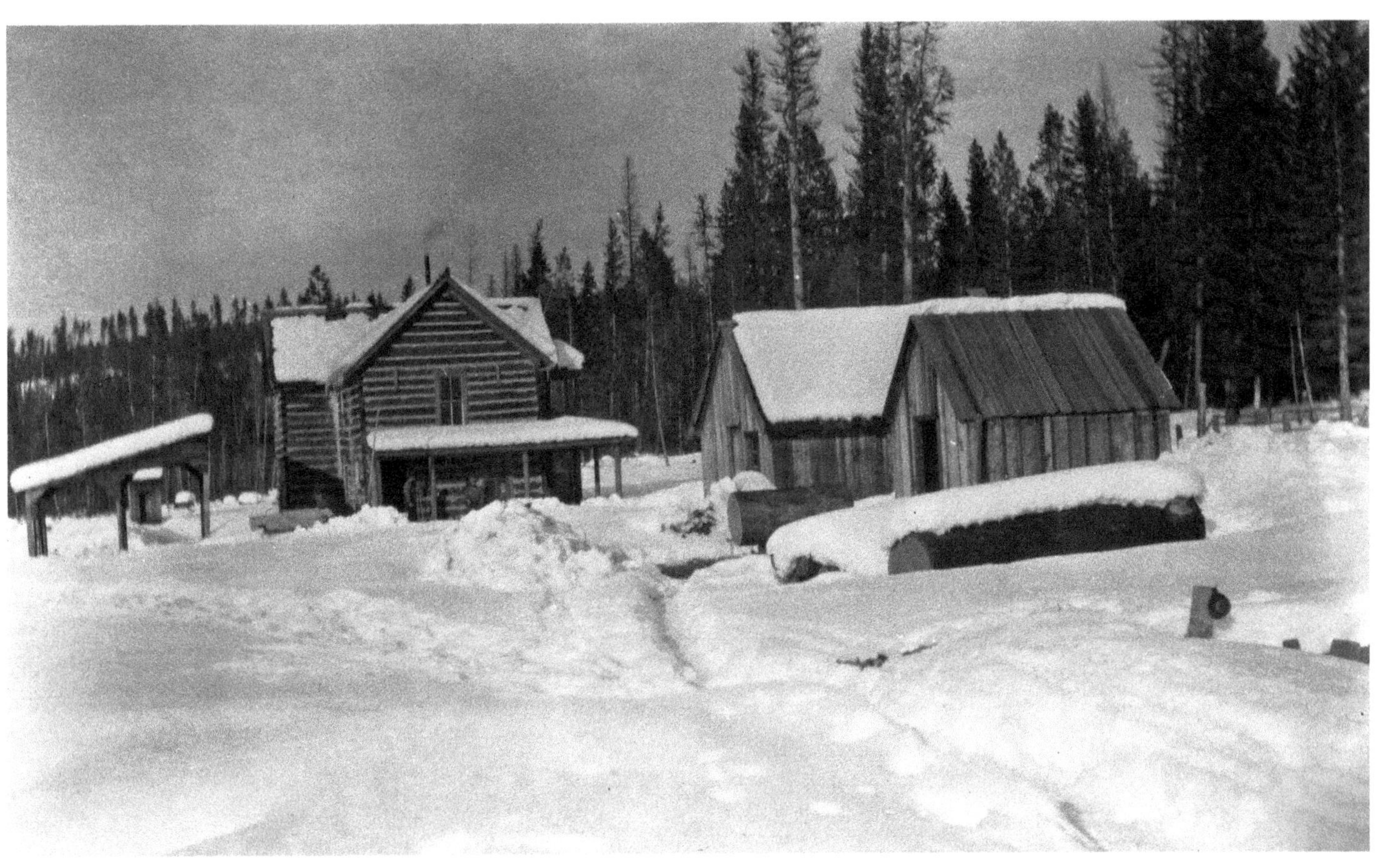

The headquarters of the Seeley Lake lumber camp, with the foreman's shack nearby, are shown here in 1909. Beginning in 1906, the Anaconda Mining Company logged 10 million board feet per year from this area. Logs were floated down the Clearwater and Blackfoot rivers to the company mill in Bonner.

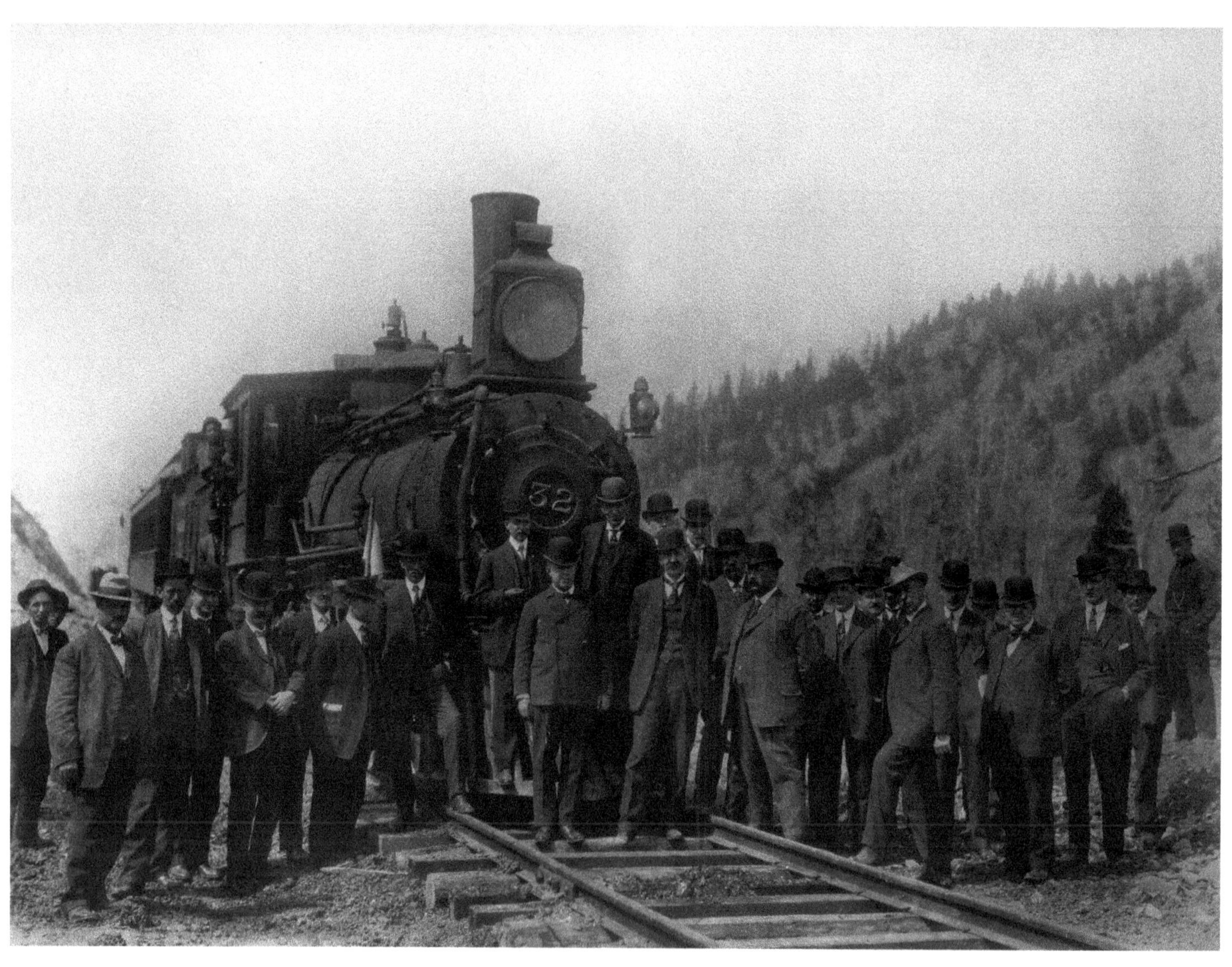

Local dignitaries and railroad officials celebrate the completion of the Pacific Coast extension of the Chicago, Milwaukee, and St. Paul Railroad at the "Last Spike" ceremony, held at Garrison on May 19, 1909. Passenger service started a year later.

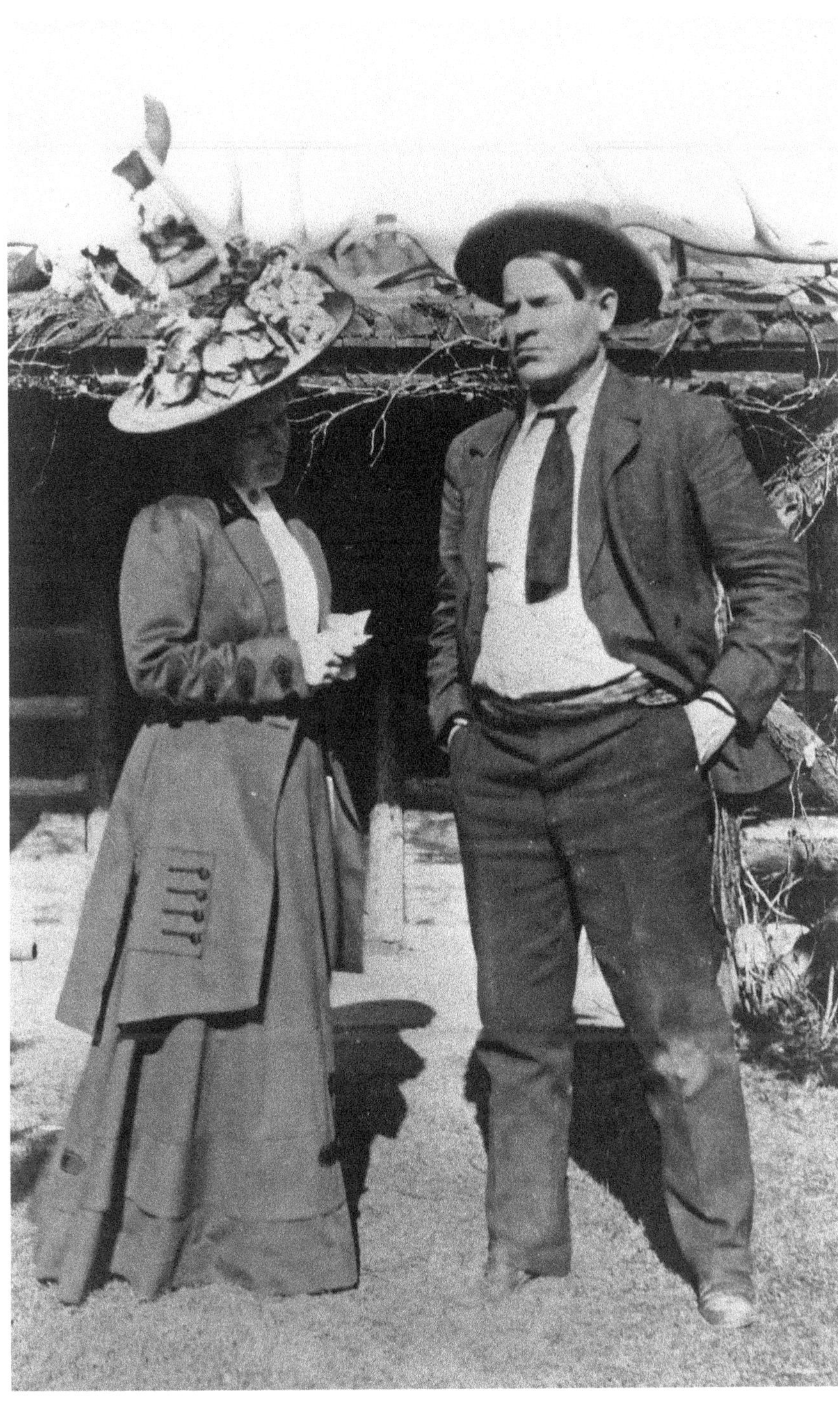

Painter Charles M. Russell, famous for his western imagery, and his wife Nancy are seen here at their home in Great Falls in February 1909. Although Nancy was just 17 when she married the much older Charles in 1896, she was instrumental in promoting his paintings and career.

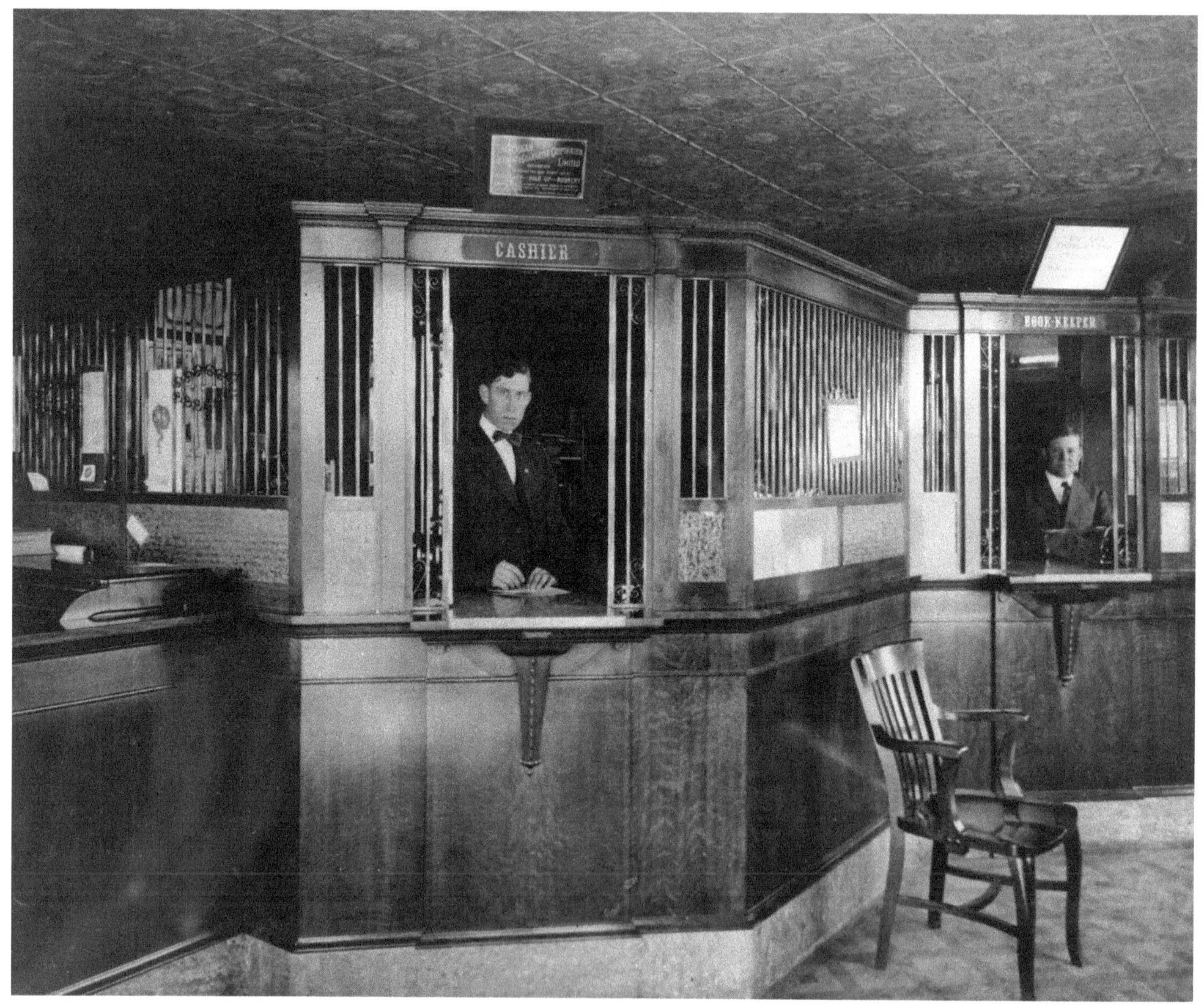

Metal cages offered the tellers of the Security State Bank and Trust Company in Polson some protection from bank robbers. A Polson institution, seen here around 1910, the bank was purchased by First Interstate Bank in 1999.

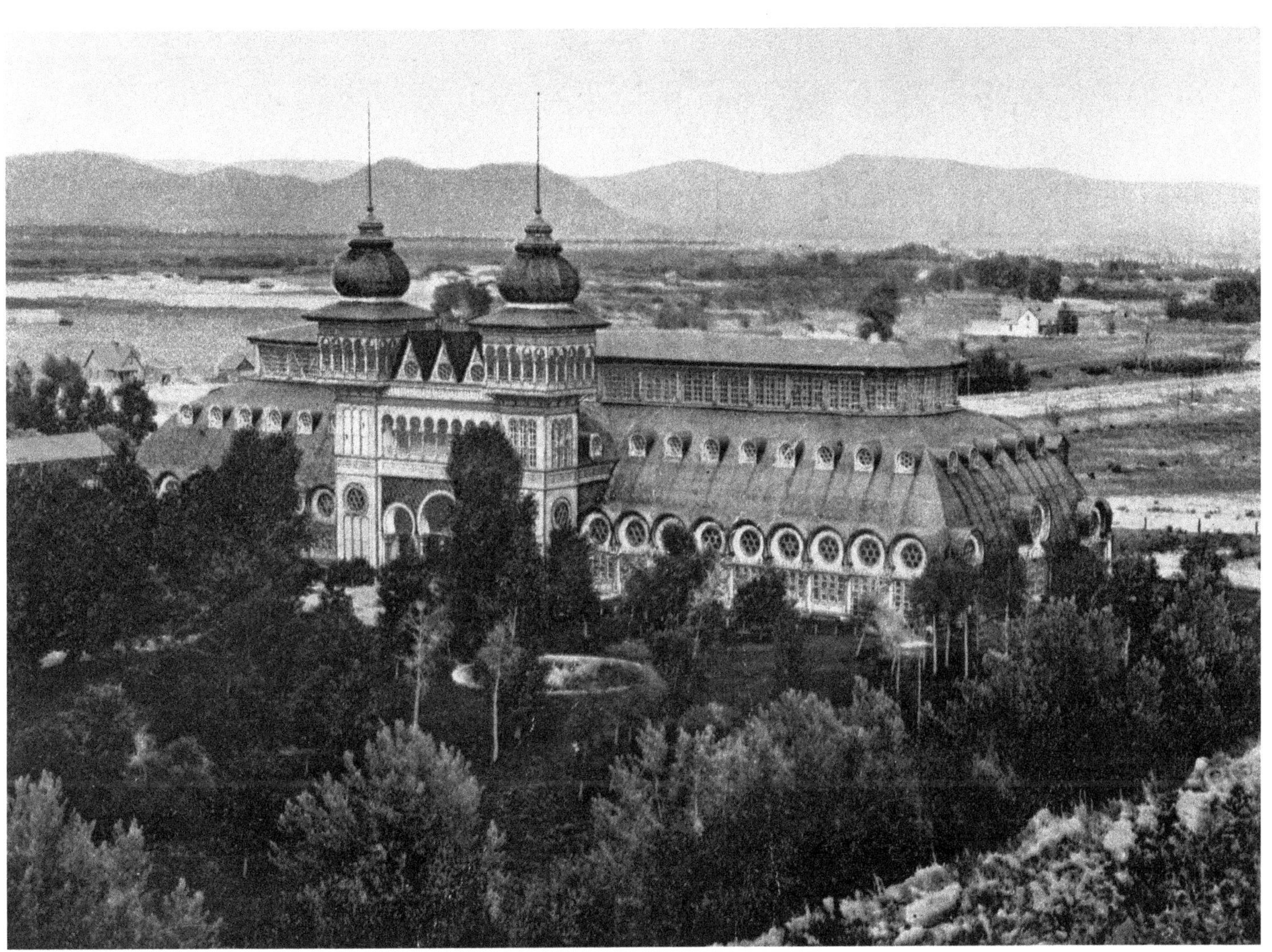

Charles Broadwater spent $500,000 to build the Moorish-design Broadwater Natatorium, a combination hotel and indoor swimming pool, west of Helena in 1888. His untimely death doomed the resort to a slow decline. Seen here around 1910, the hotel closed in 1941, and the natatorium was demolished five years later.

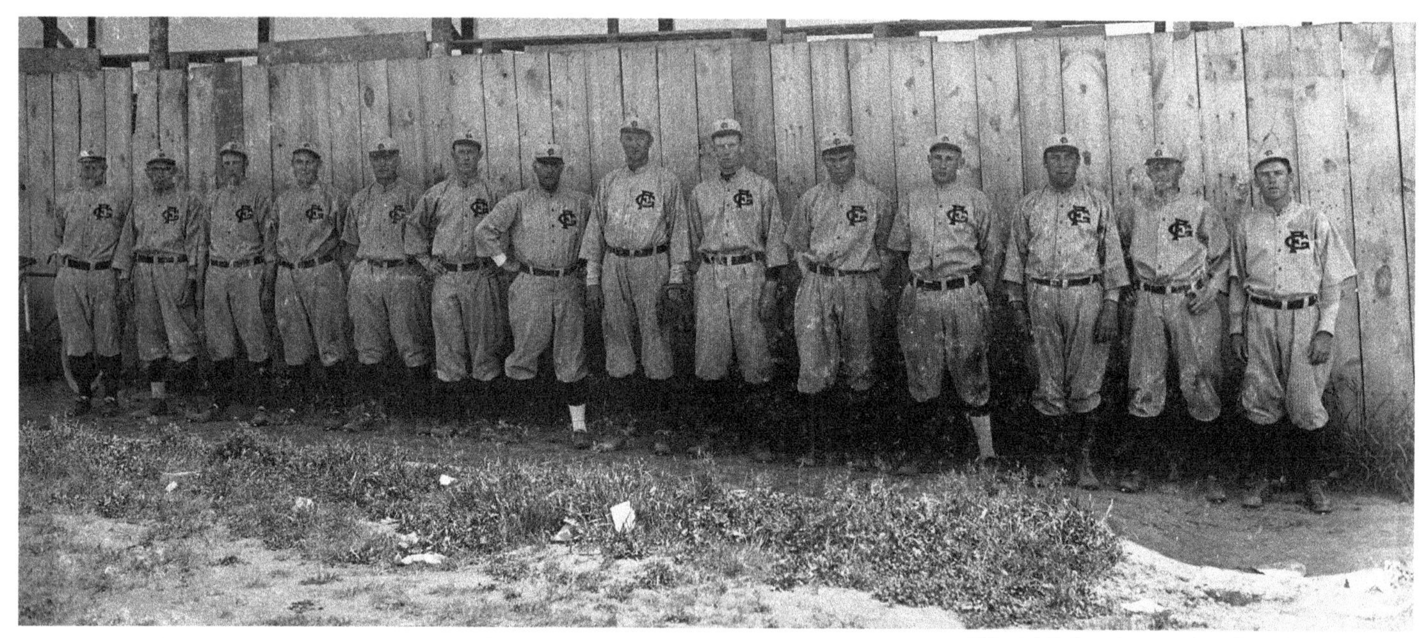

The Great Falls Electrics baseball team was formed in 1911 as part of the Union Association League. They were league champs in 1911 and 1913, but disbanded in 1917. The team returned to the field in 1948 and became an affiliate of the Brooklyn Dodgers in 1952.

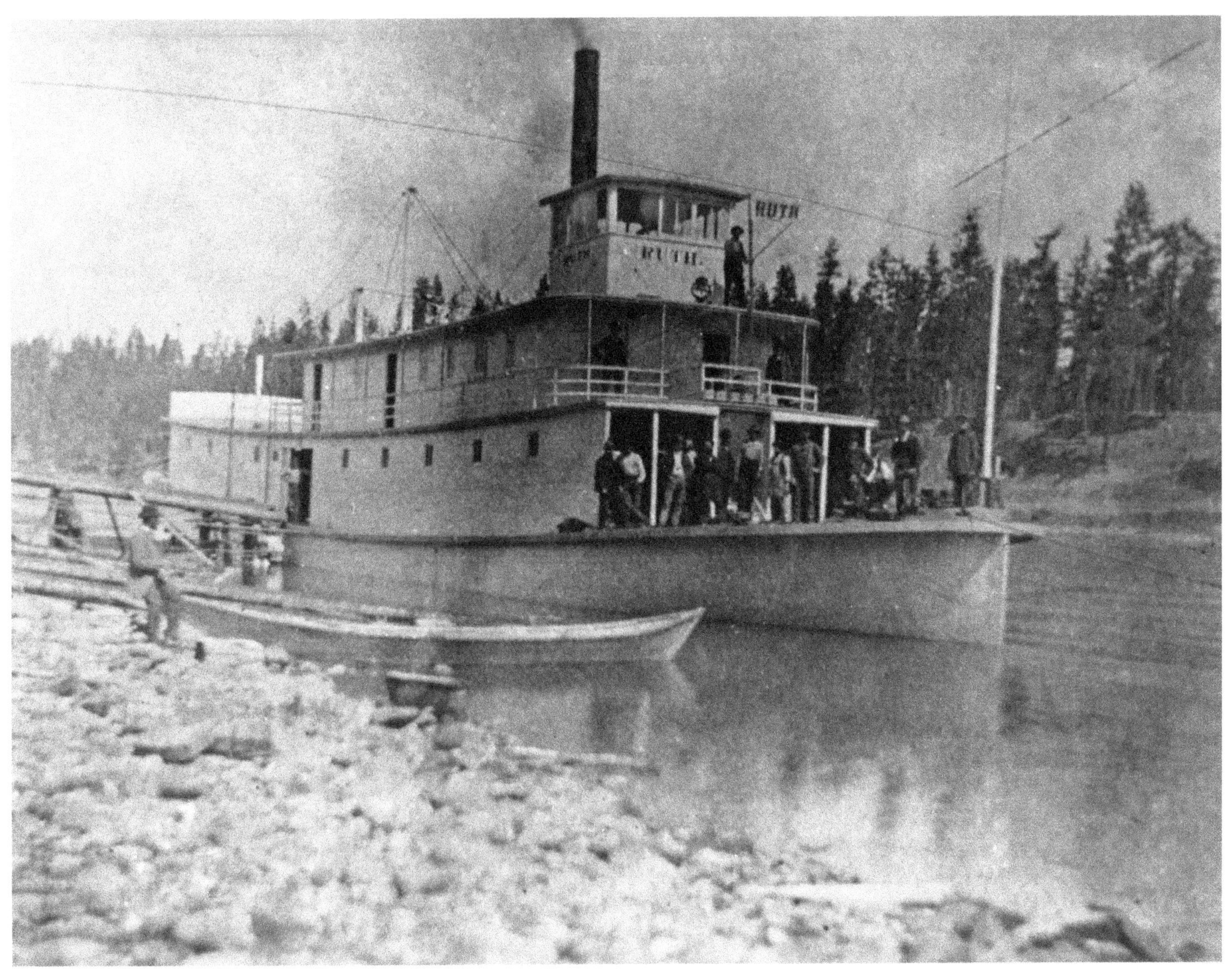

The steamboat *Ruth*, which offered travelers a dining room and individual cabins, was launched in 1896 on the Kootenai River. It carried ore from the Canadian mines at Fort Steele on its southbound journey and returned north with cargo from the U.S. railroads.

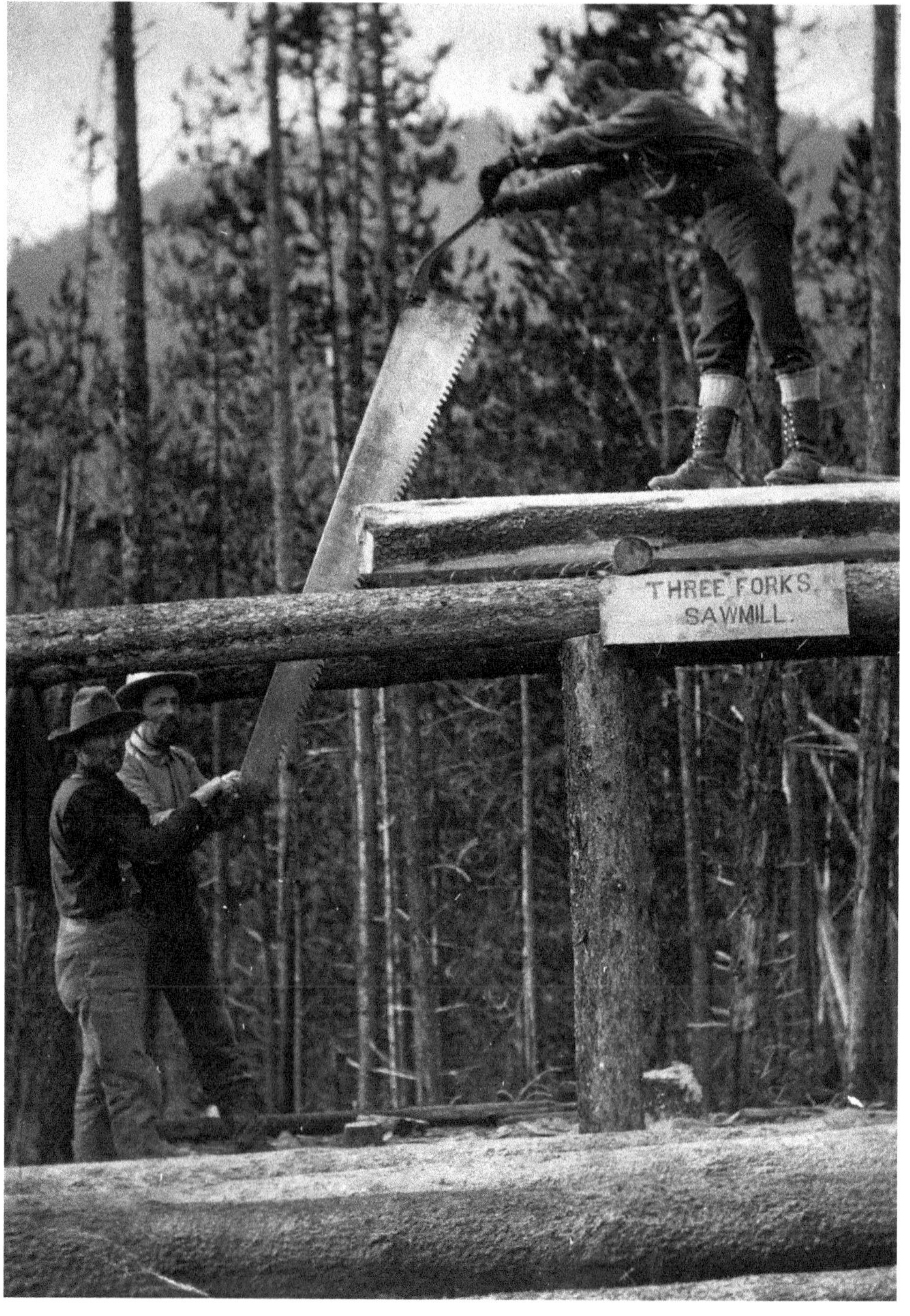

This simple pit sawmill at Three Forks in 1910 utilized a principle developed by the early Egyptians—a "top man" pulled the saw up, and the "pit man" pulled it down. The saw cut only on the downstroke.

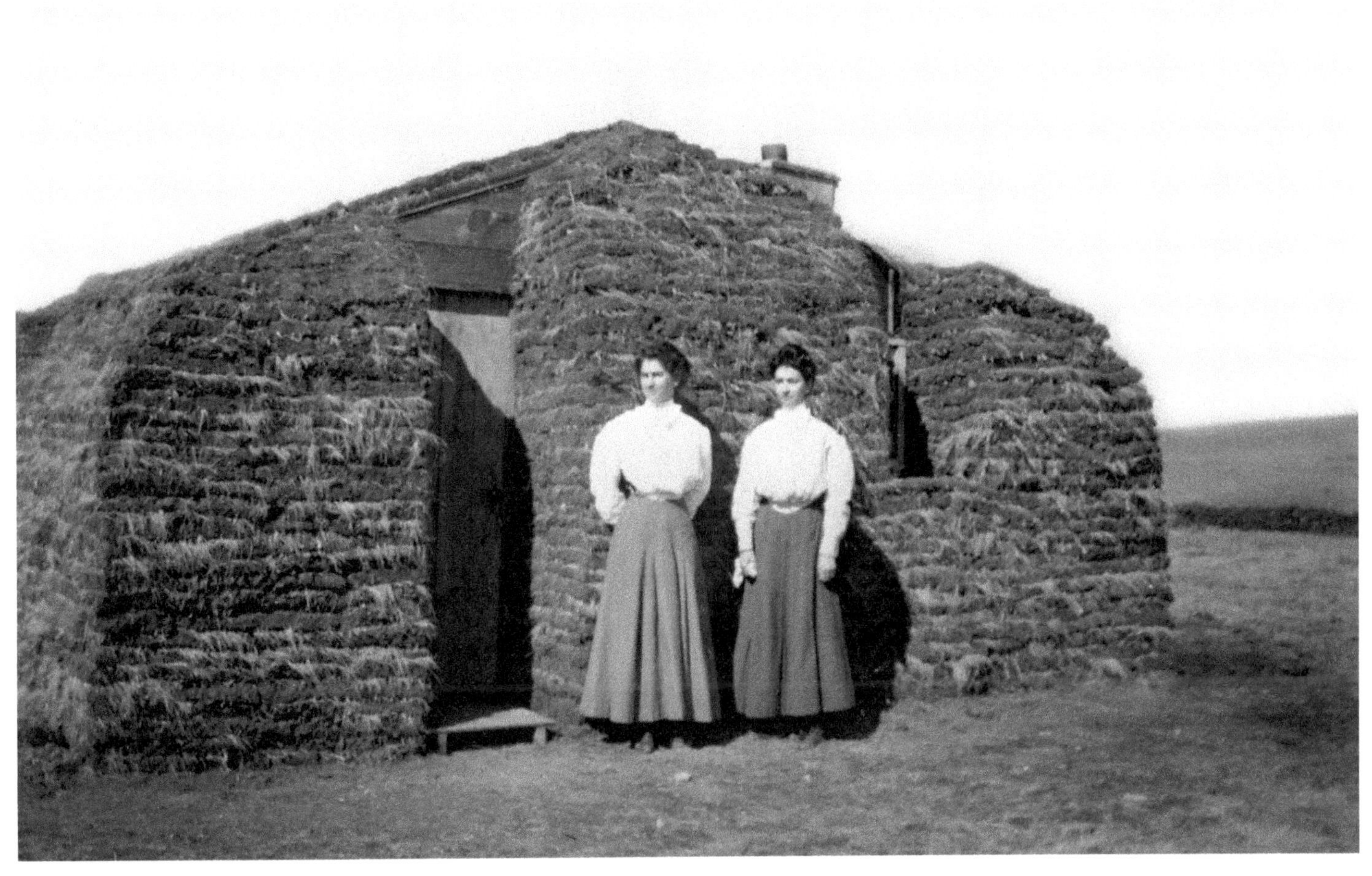

Two women pose in front of their sod house on a homestead east of Judith Gap. Constructed of chunks of prairie grass, a "soddy" was both well insulated and cheap to build.

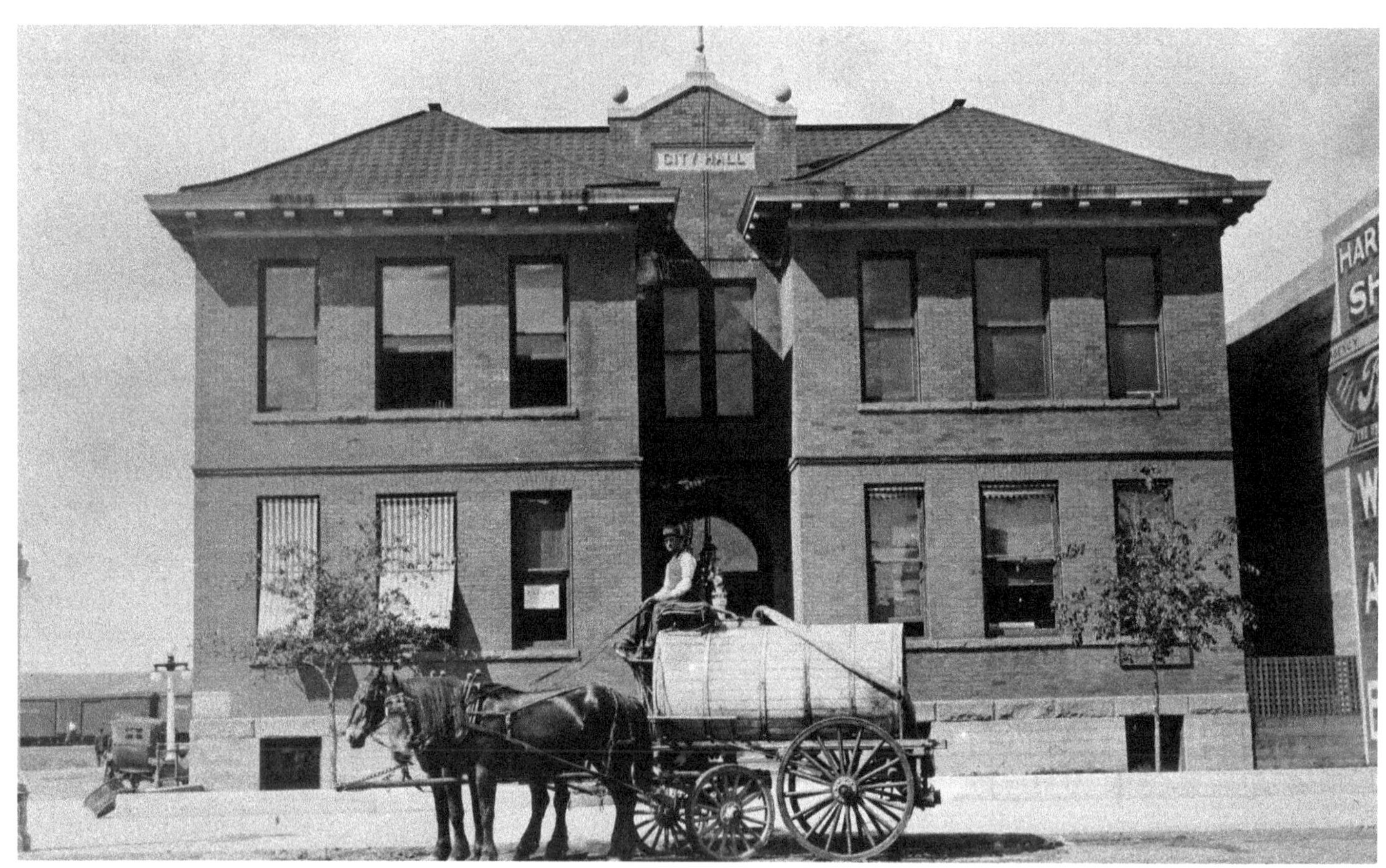

A water wagon waits in front of the City Hall in Havre around 1912. Havre grew up on the outskirts of the Fort Assiniboine Military Reservation, and like other towns along the Hi-Line, benefited greatly when the Great Northern Railroad brought an influx of homesteaders to the area.

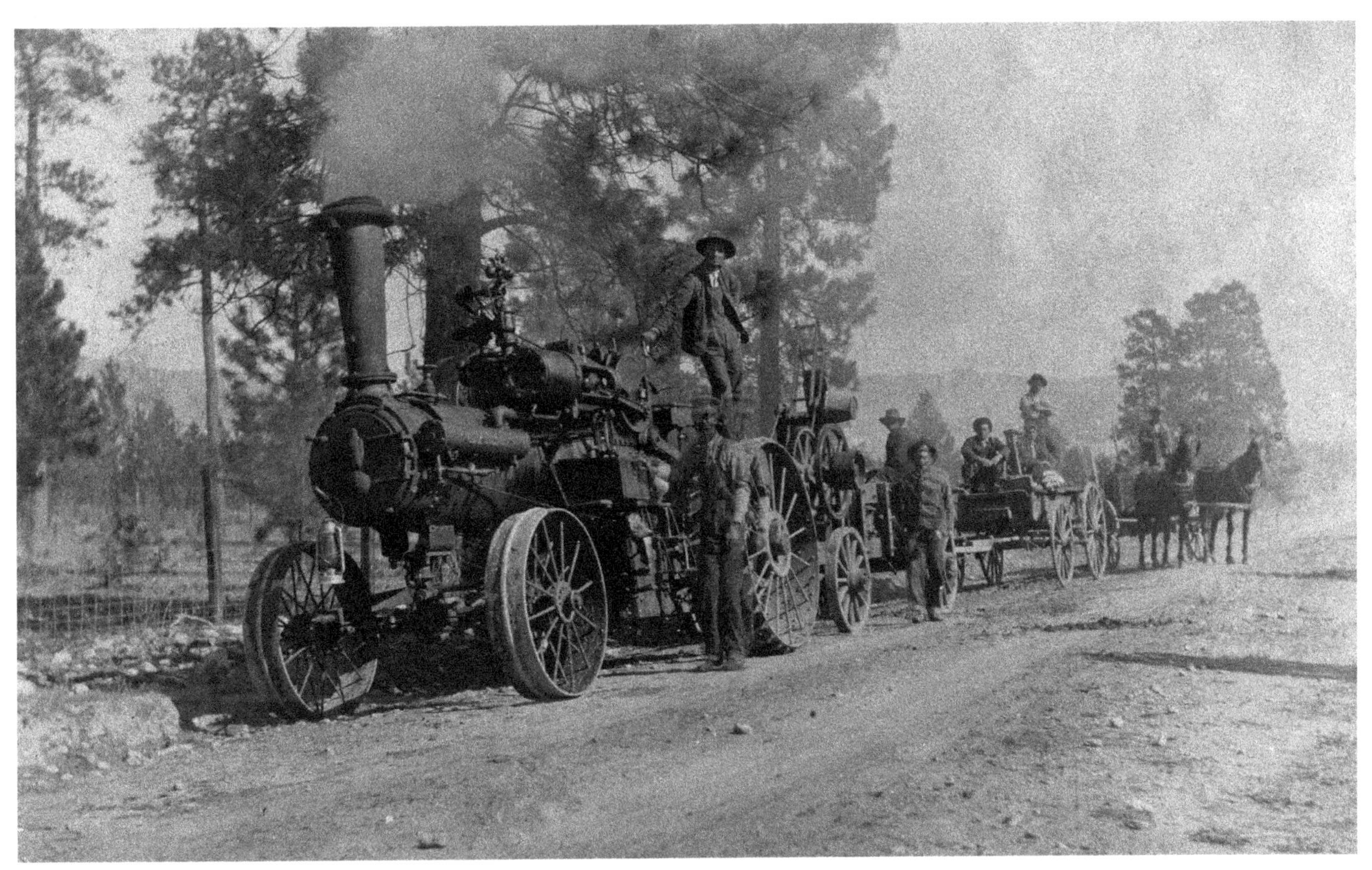

Florence men use a steam tractor and horse-drawn wagons to bale hay. After the winter of 1886, stockmen realized the value of putting up hay, and by 1900 there were 700,000 acres of hay fields in the state.

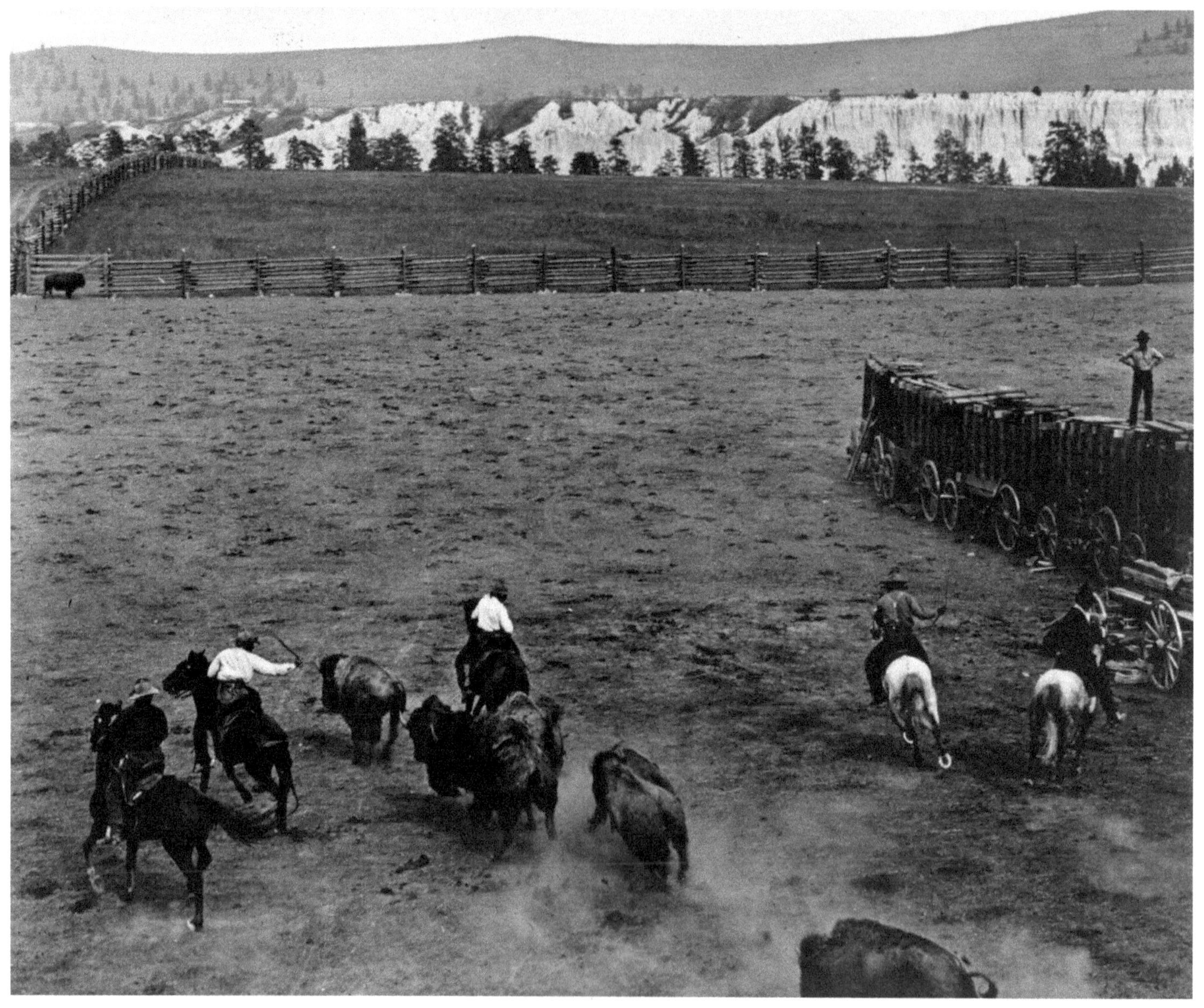

A stock wagon waits as a cowboy learns that herding bison is a little different from herding cattle. An angry bull is chasing the center horse, while the stout fence in the background is testament to the difficulty of holding bison. This photo was taken near Butte around 1909.

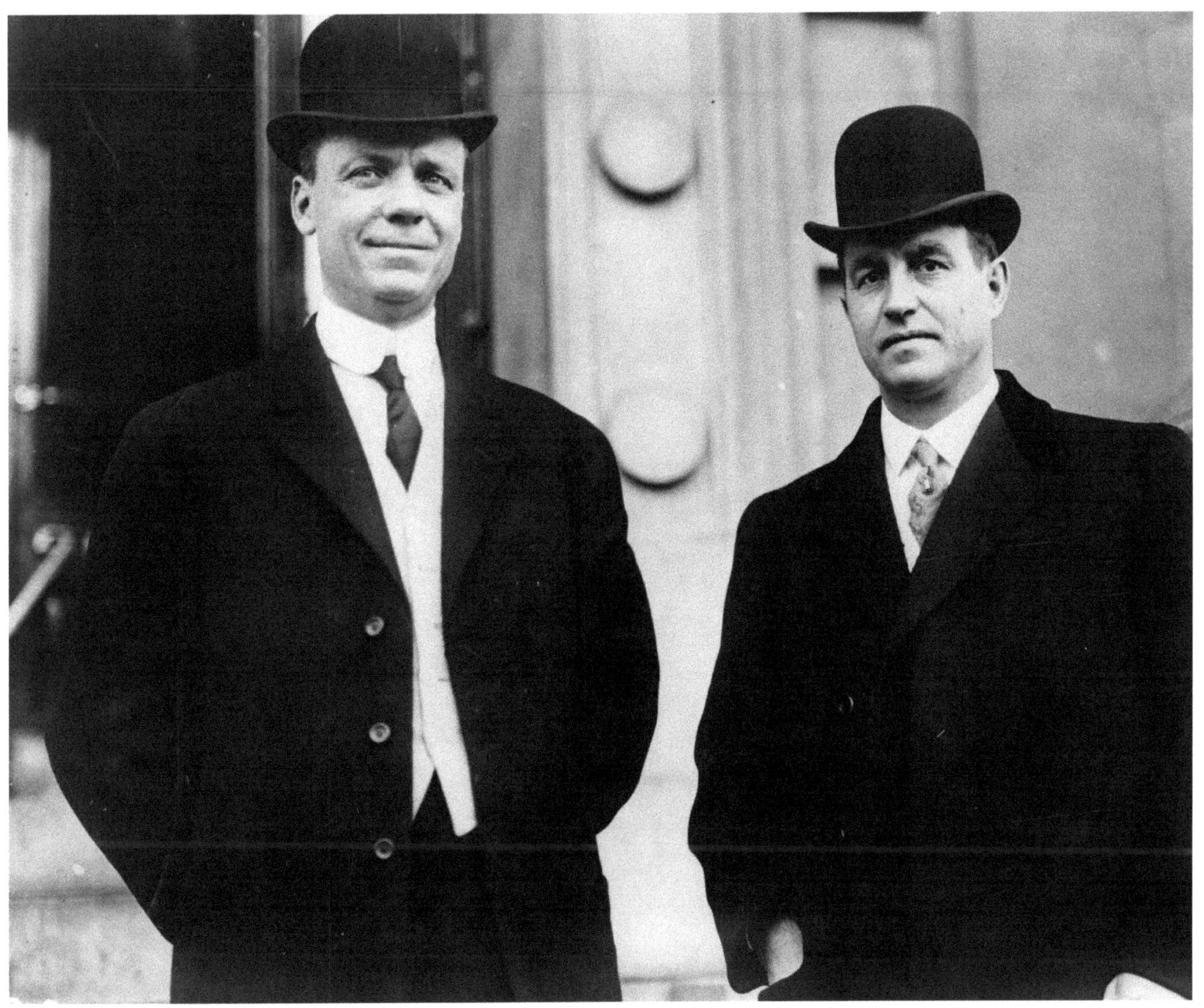

A Dillon lawyer, Lieutenant Governor Edwin L. Norris, at left, became Montana's chief executive when Governor Joseph Toole resigned for health reasons in 1908. Norris then won reelection on his own, serving until 1913. He is seen here with John Mitchell, president of the United Mine Workers.

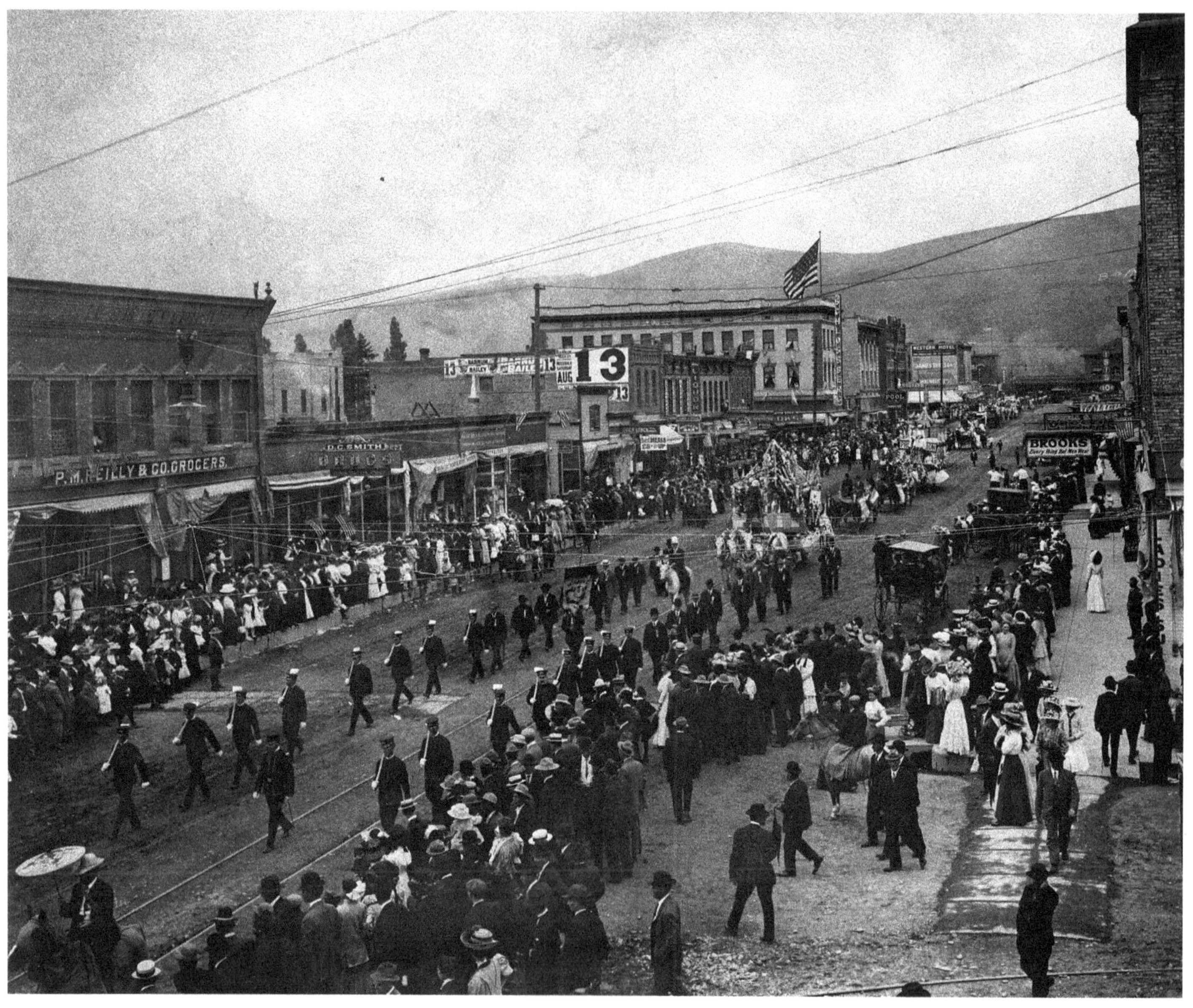

In this Missoula scene, around 1910, a large crowd lines Higgins Avenue as a parade passes by. Taken from the corner of Higgins and Broadway, the view is to the north. Smoke from Missoula's numerous lumber mills hangs behind the downtown buildings.

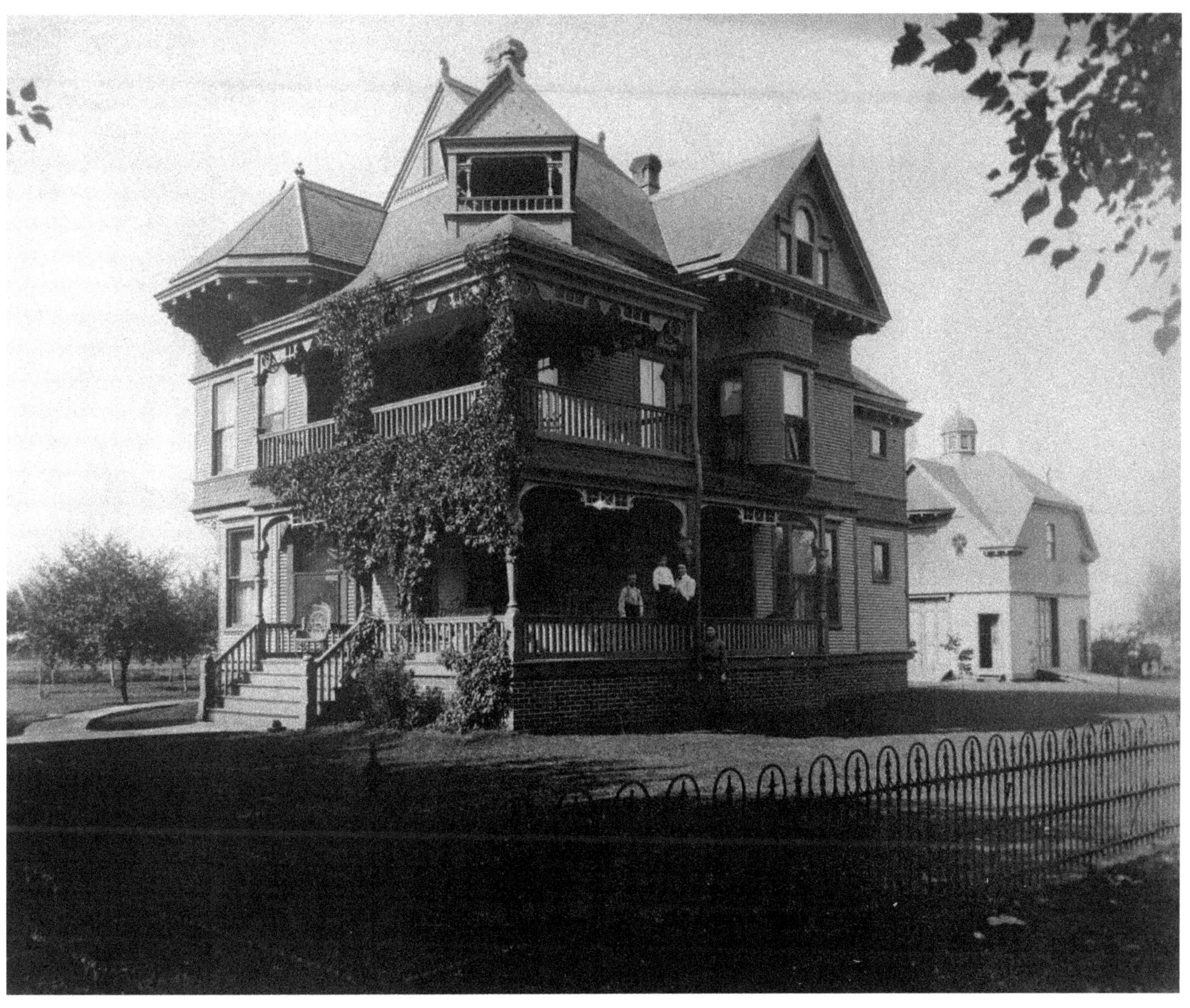

Kenneth Ross went to work for the A. B. Hammond Company in the early 1880s and later worked for the timber division of the Anaconda Company at Bonner. Marcus Daly personally presented Ross with this house on Gerald Avenue in Missoula in 1893, and it is seen here a decade or two later.

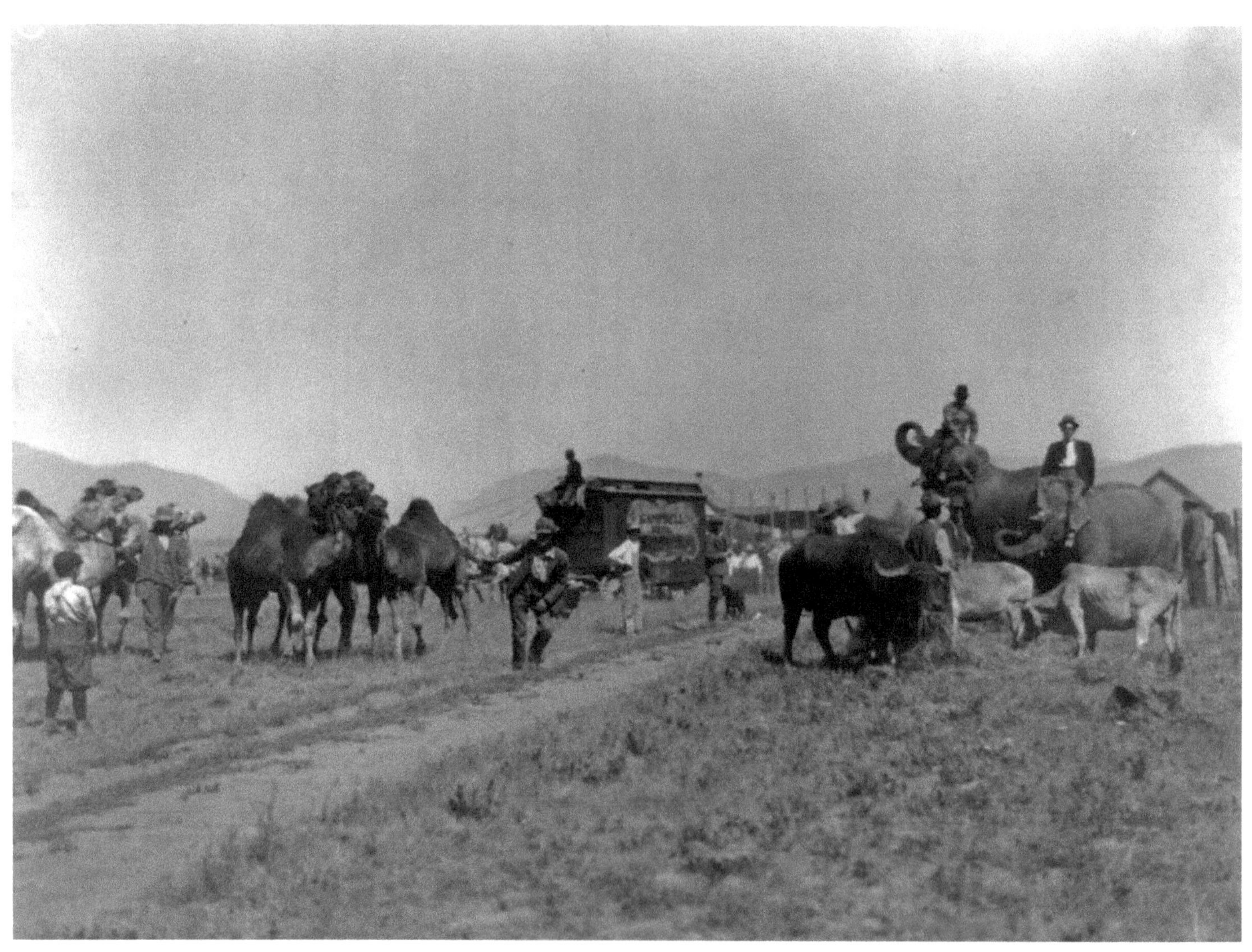

The Campbell Brothers Circus prepares for a performance at Plains under a threatening sky around 1910. Based in Nebraska, the circus had its own railroad train and operated from 1889 to 1912. An admission ticket in 1896 cost 20¢ for adults and 10¢ for children.

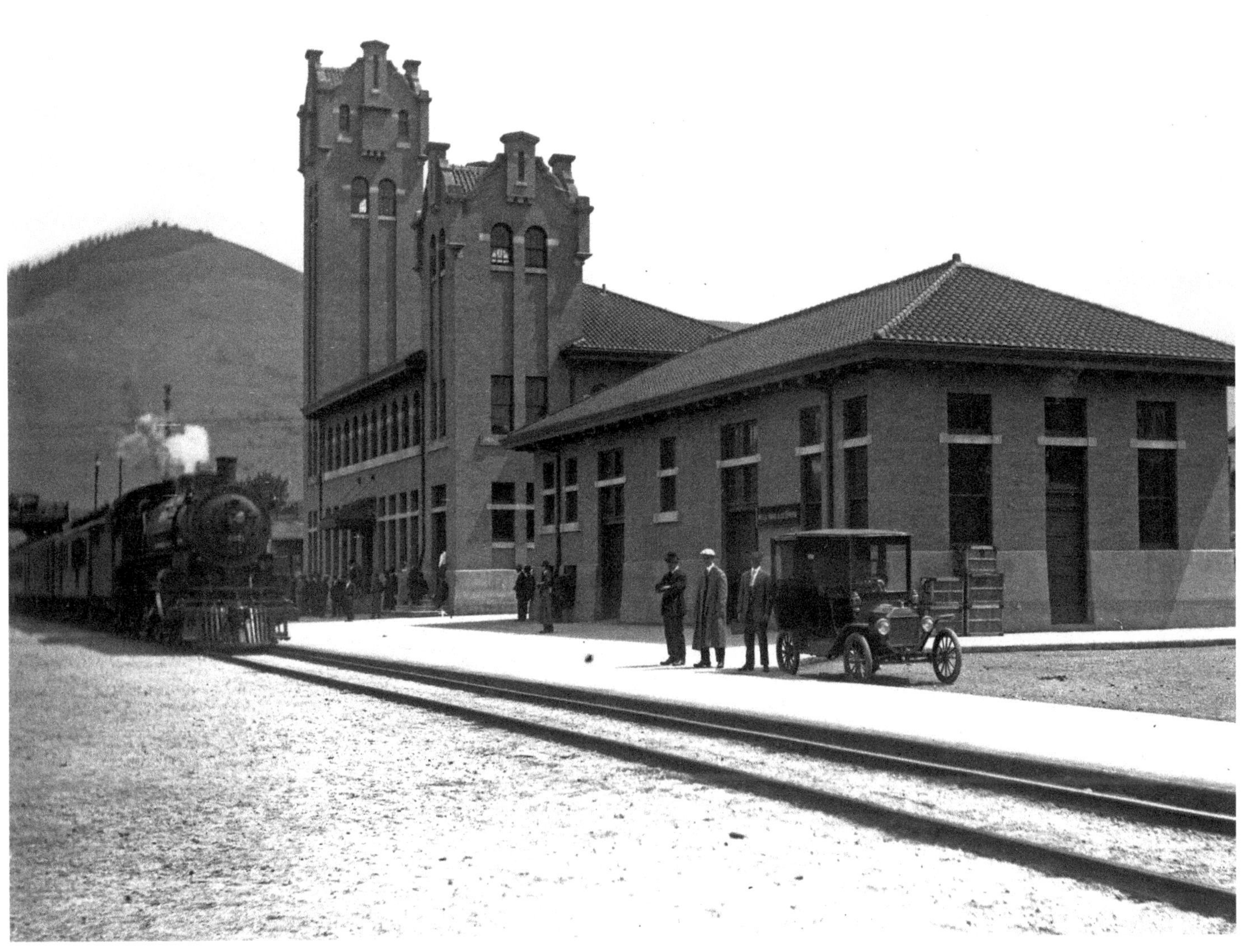

This well-composed photo shows a locomotive pulling into the Milwaukee Railroad Depot in Missoula, with Mount Sentinel rising in the background. The depot building was purchased and restored by the Boone and Crockett Club in the 1990s.

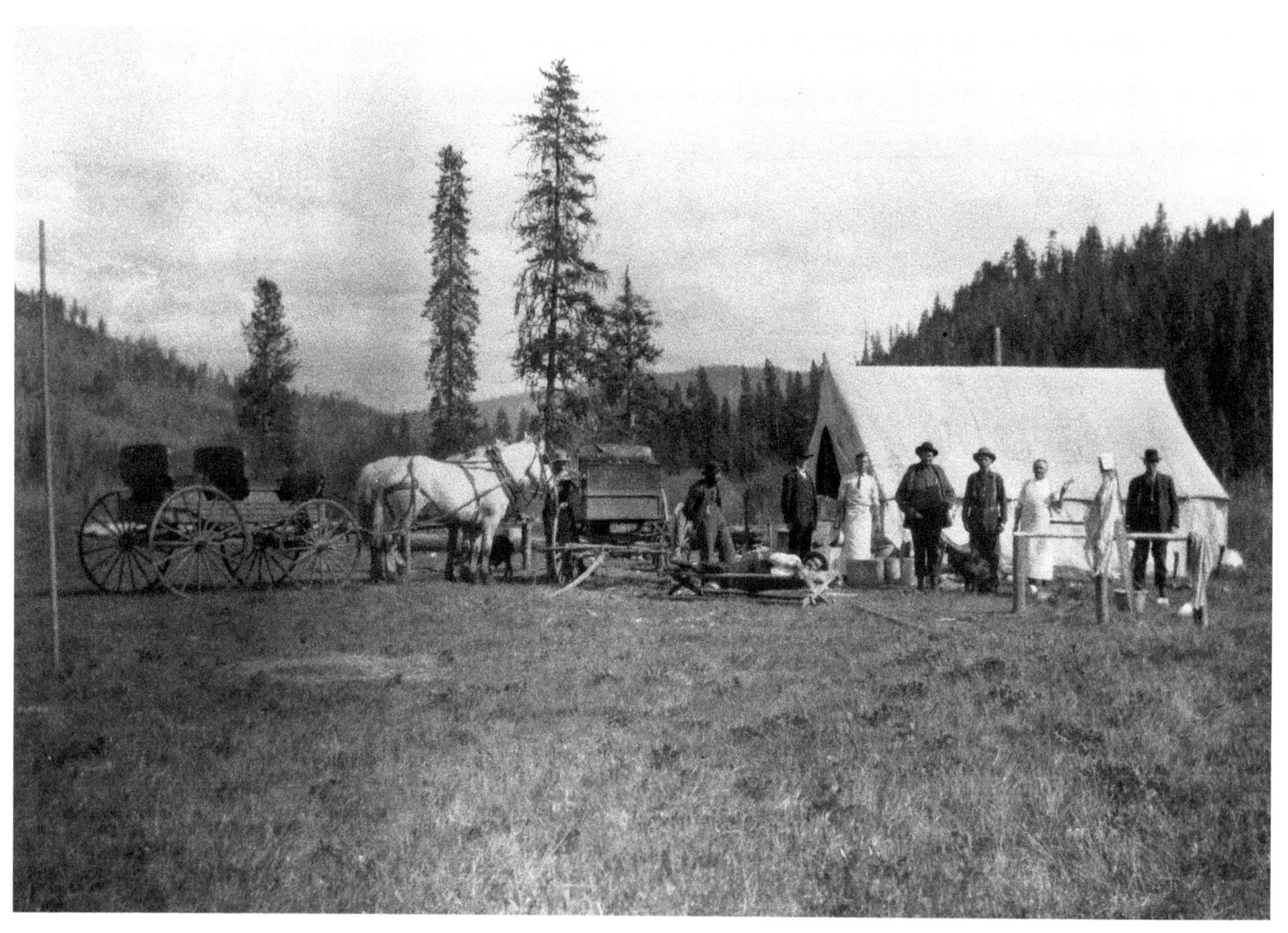

Cooks, teamsters, a U.S. Forest Service employee, and two foremen pose in front of a logging camp on Morell Flat, near Seeley Lake, in 1910. A carriage and a lunch wagon wait nearby. Massive forest fires swept the Northern Rockies in 1910, the year this photo was taken.

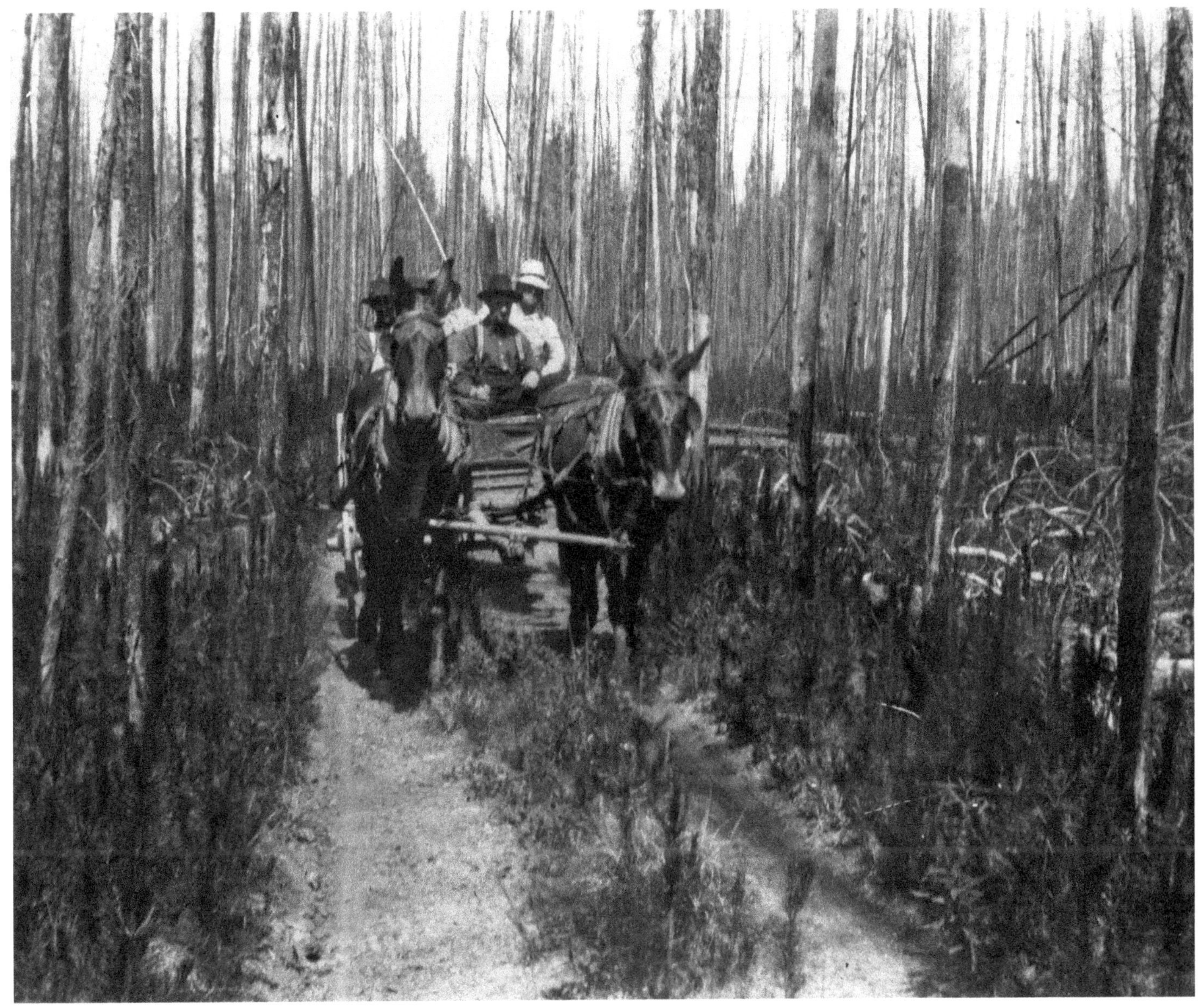

The fires of 1910 consumed 3 million acres in Montana and Idaho, including this lodgepole pine thicket near Seeley Lake. The U.S. Forest Service, not realizing the natural role that fire plays in the forests of the Northern Rockies, responded by aggressively suppressing all fires, which eventually resulted in more frequent and intense fires.

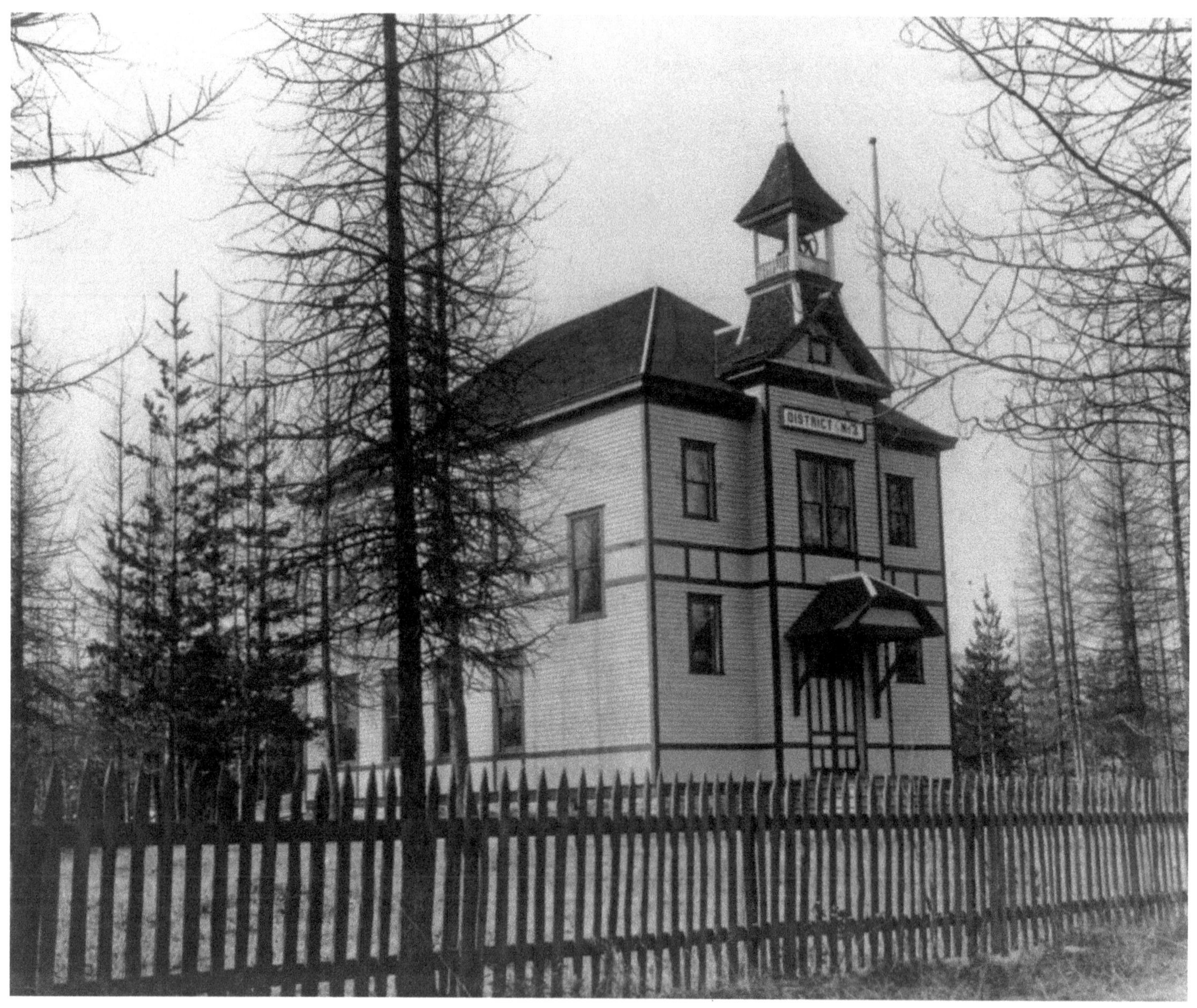

Seen here around 1910, the Heron School (District No. 3) is located just east of Heron in northwestern Montana. A logging community, Heron depended for its economy on the large cedar trees located nearby. The school is now a community center, home to the local library and the Heron Players theatrical troupe.

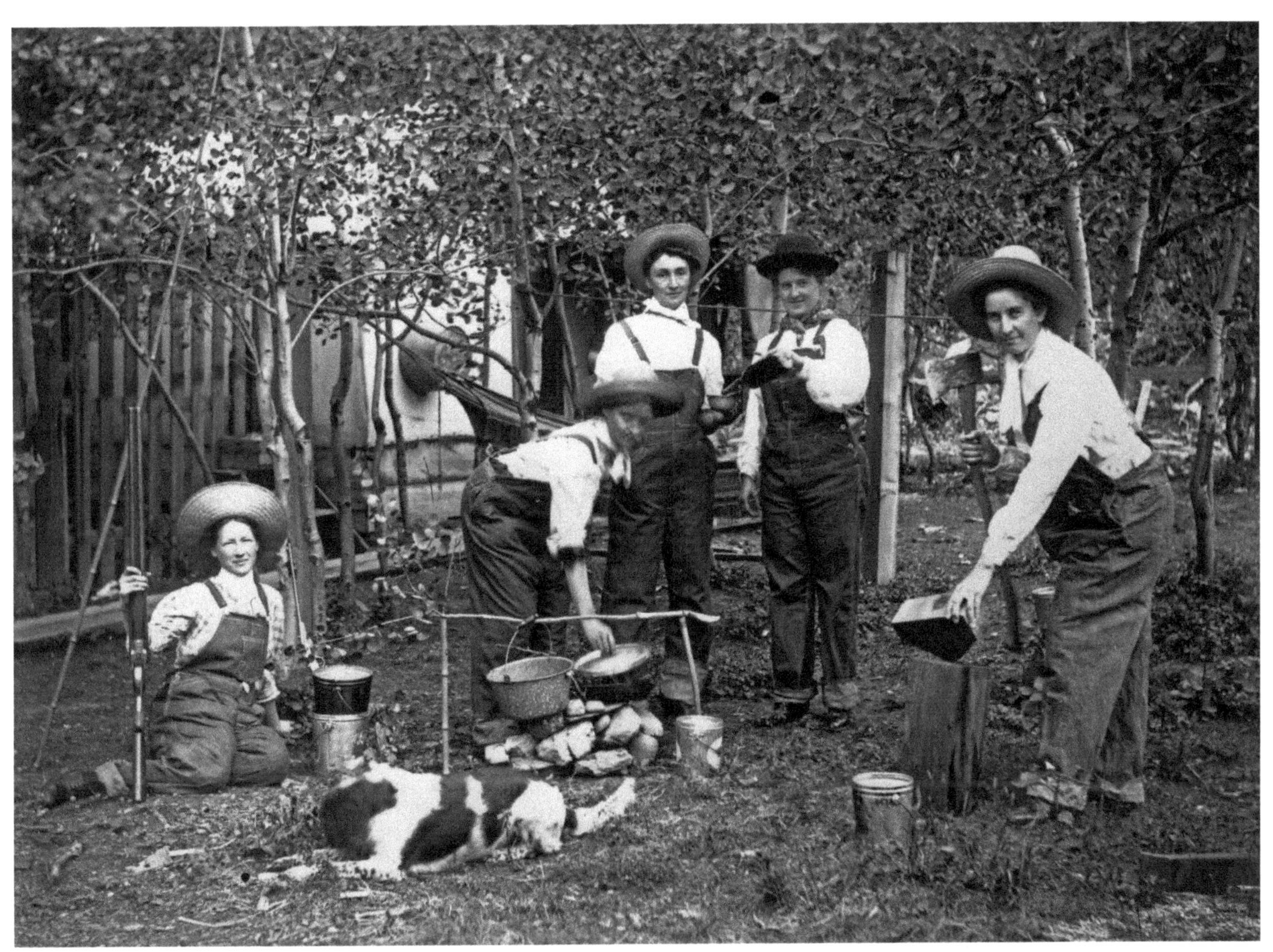

Dressed in overalls, five women pose as if they are camping. The lady on the left wields a shotgun while the one on the right has an ax. This photo was taken around 1910, probably in or near Bonner.

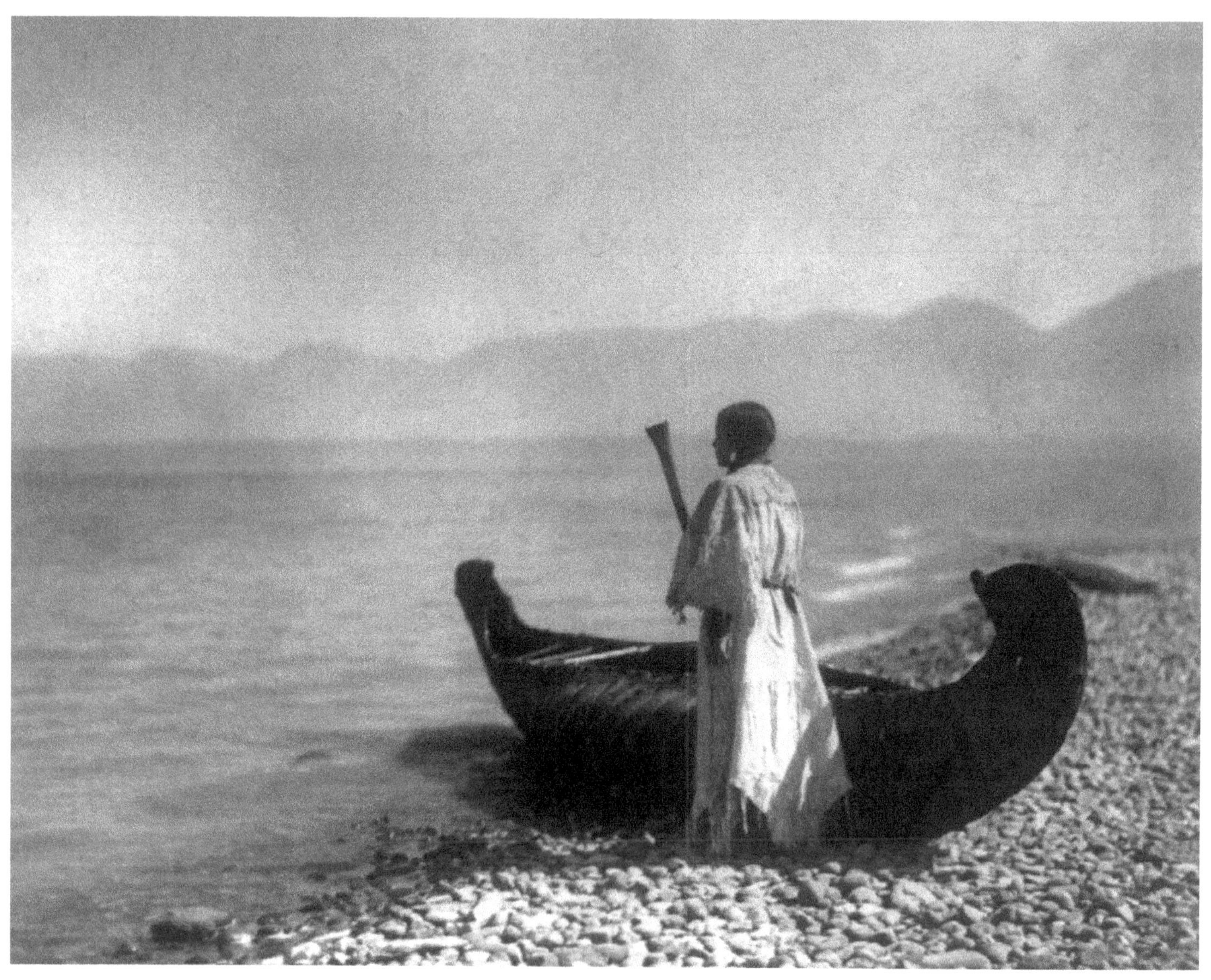

A Kootenai woman holding a paddle stands next to a traditional canoe on the shores of a lake, probably Flathead. Edward Curtis took this photo in 1910 as part of his 20-volume series on the North American Indian.

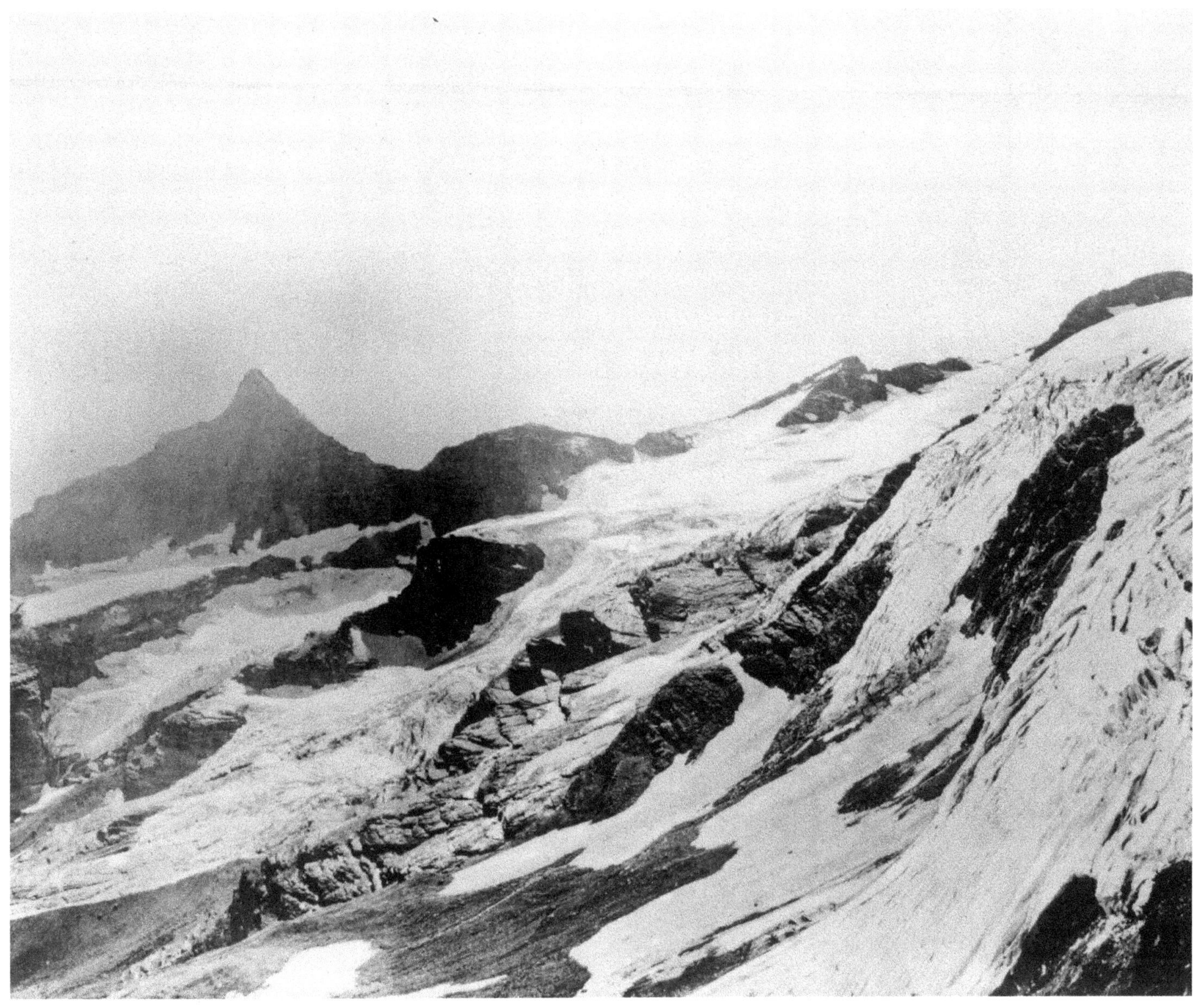

Harrison Glacier, viewed from the Continental Divide near the southern end of Glacier National Park, has shrunk considerably since this photo was taken in 1913. Scientists estimate that all of the park's glaciers will melt away by 2035.

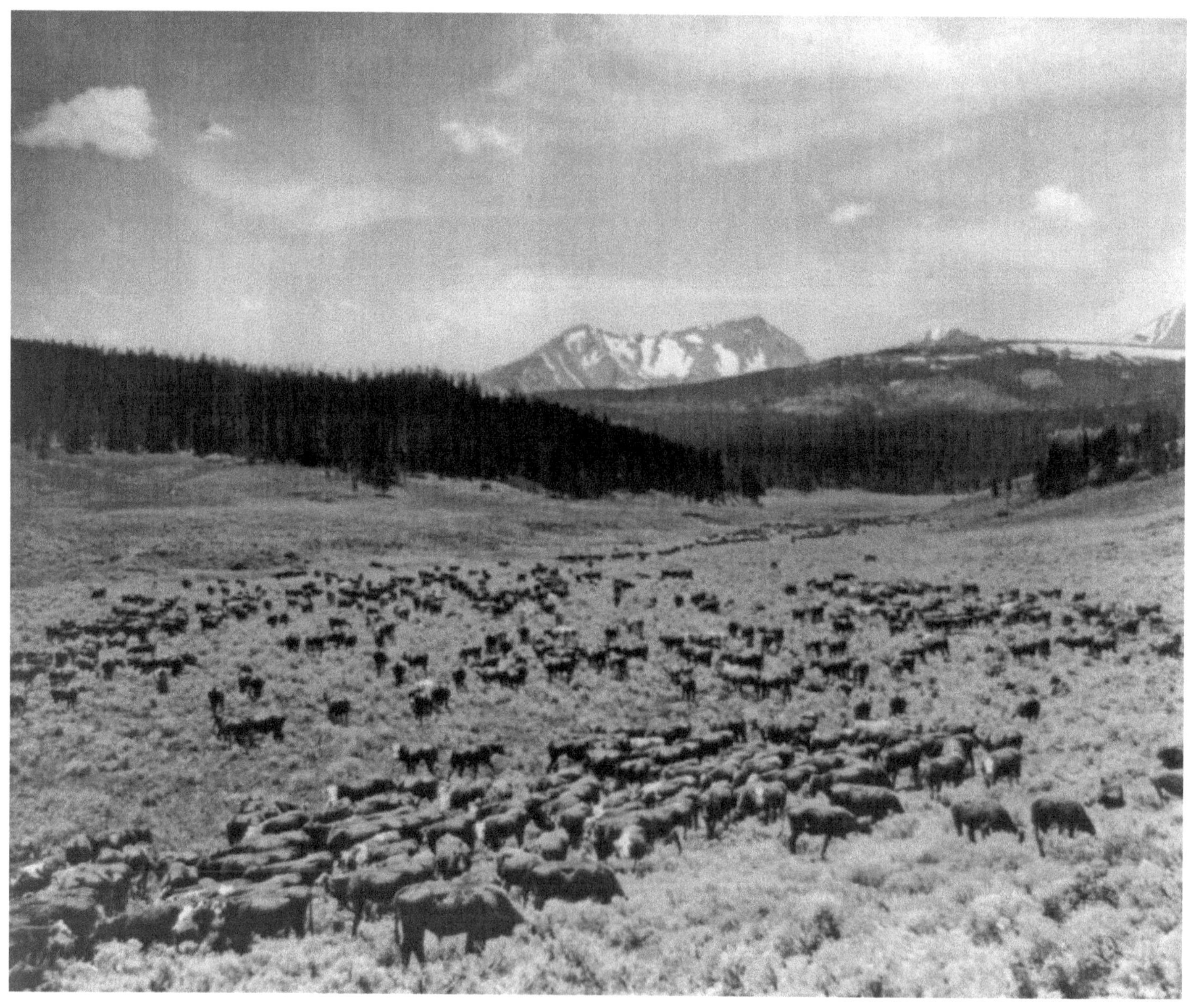

A large cattle herd grazes on the Nine Quarter Circle Ranch around 1911. Sitting at an altitude of 7,000 feet, the ranch is just a few miles from Yellowstone National Park and is now a family-owned guest ranch.

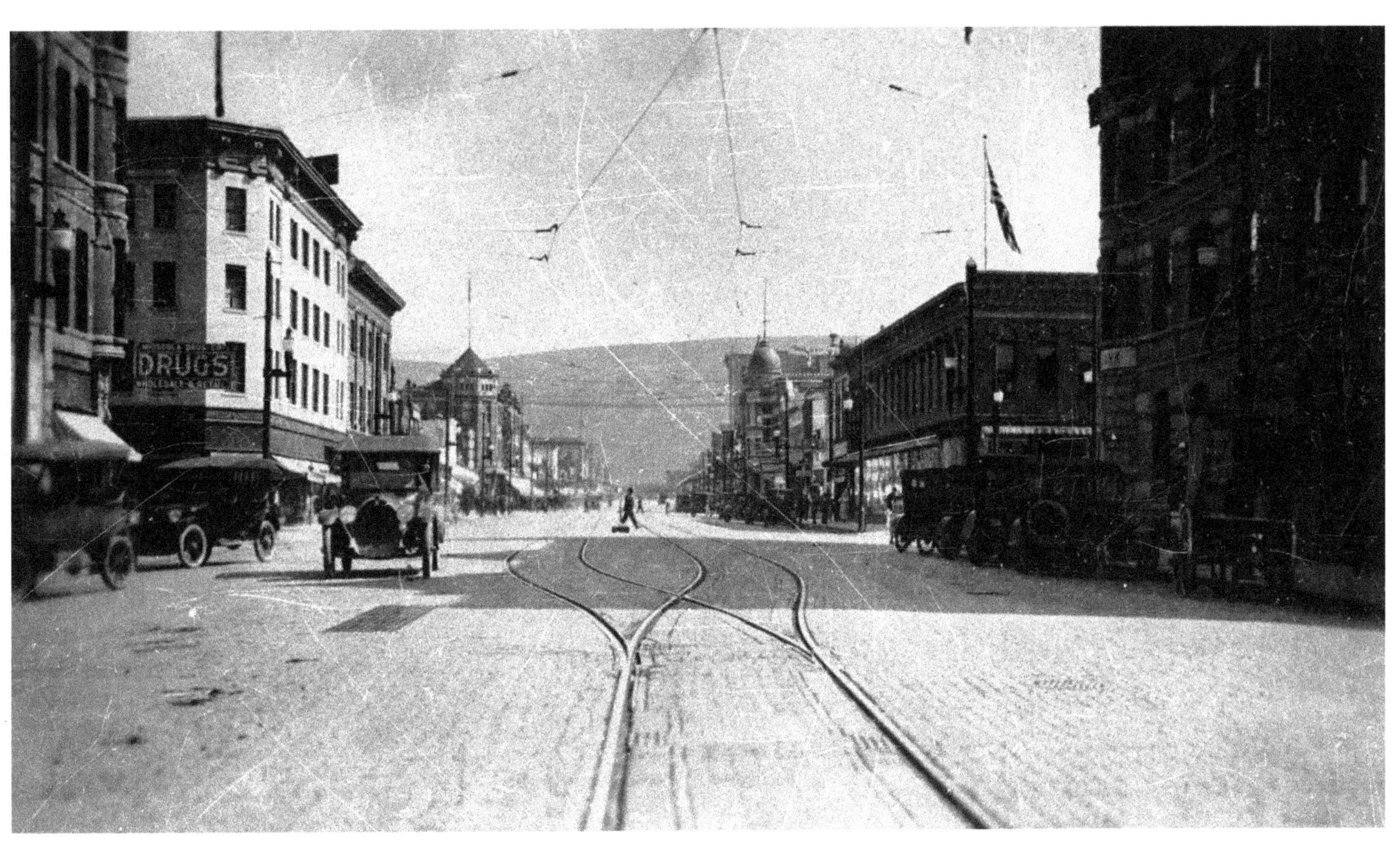

This photo of Missoula focuses on the electric trolley tracks on Higgins Avenue. Every major city in Montana had an electric trolley system in the early years of the twentieth century, but they lost popularity with the rise of ownership of private autos.

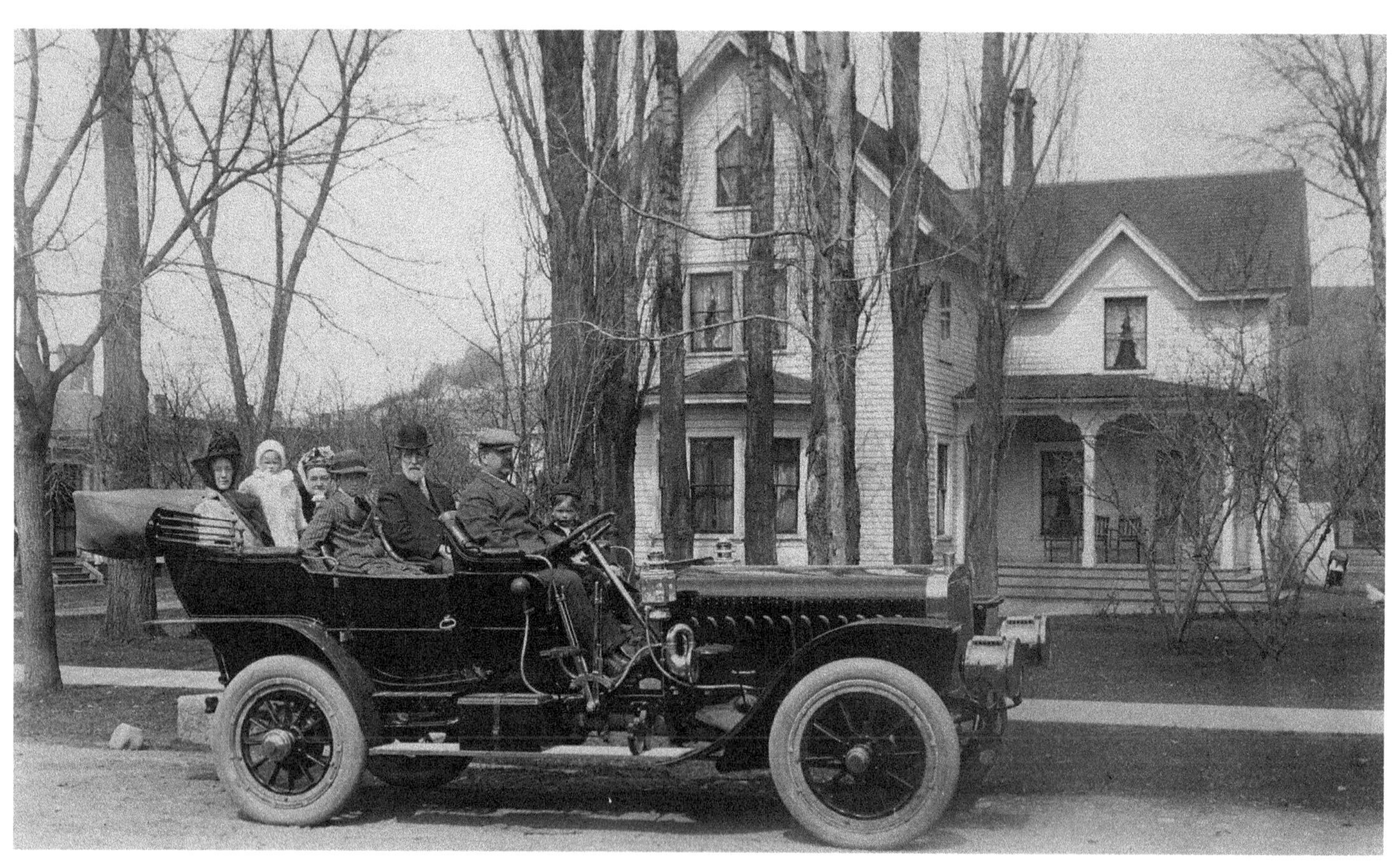

A loaded passenger car sits in front of the F. L. Worden House in Missoula. Built in 1874, this is the oldest residence in the city and is listed on the National Register of Historic Places. Worden's family owned the home for portions of three centuries. It is now a gift shop.

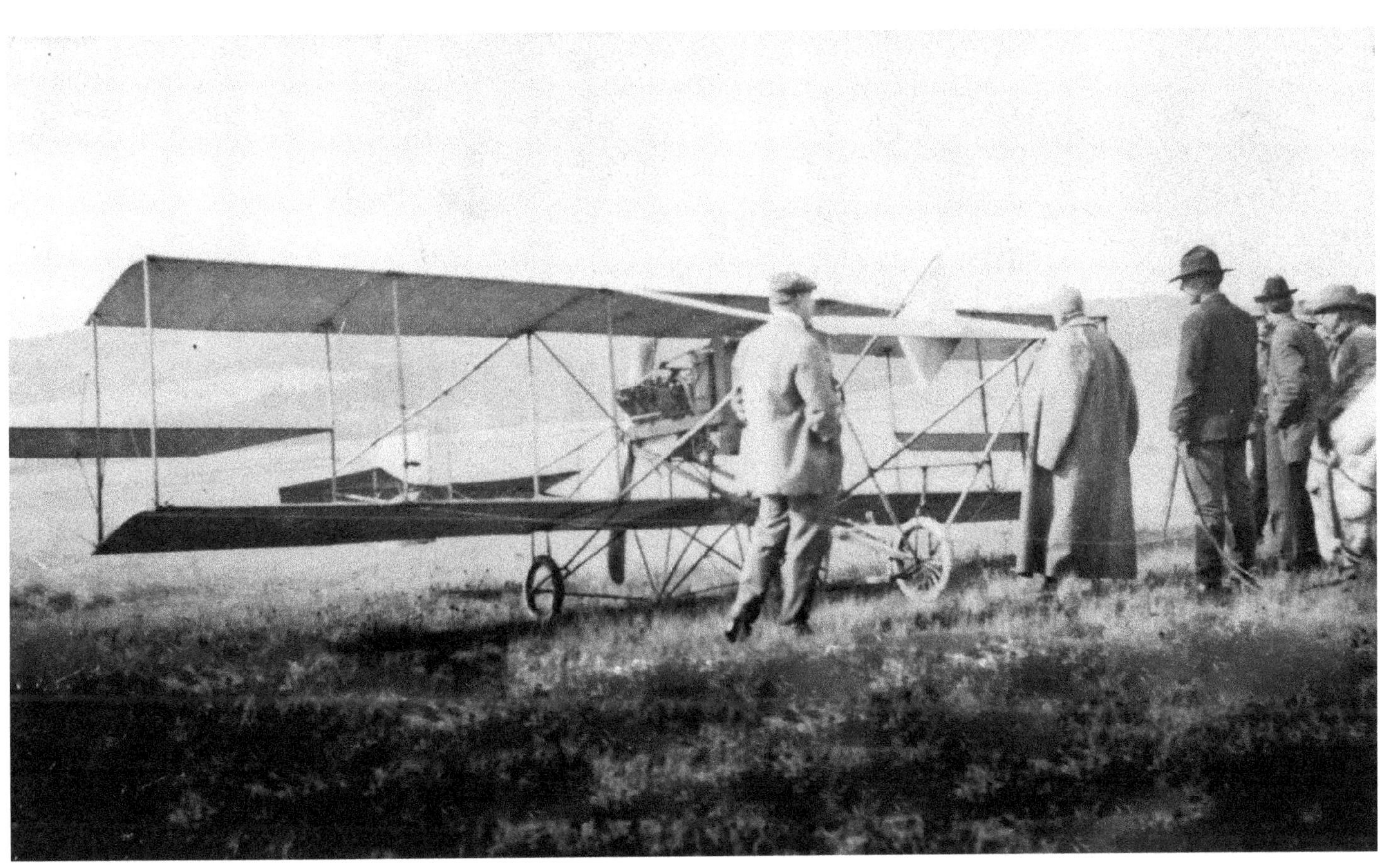

At age 19, stunt flier Cromwell Dixon became the first aviator to cross the Continental Divide. On September 30, 1911, he took off from Helena and flew 16 miles to Blossburg, just over the divide, where he and his Curtiss biplane were photographed after landing. He was killed two days later while performing in Spokane.

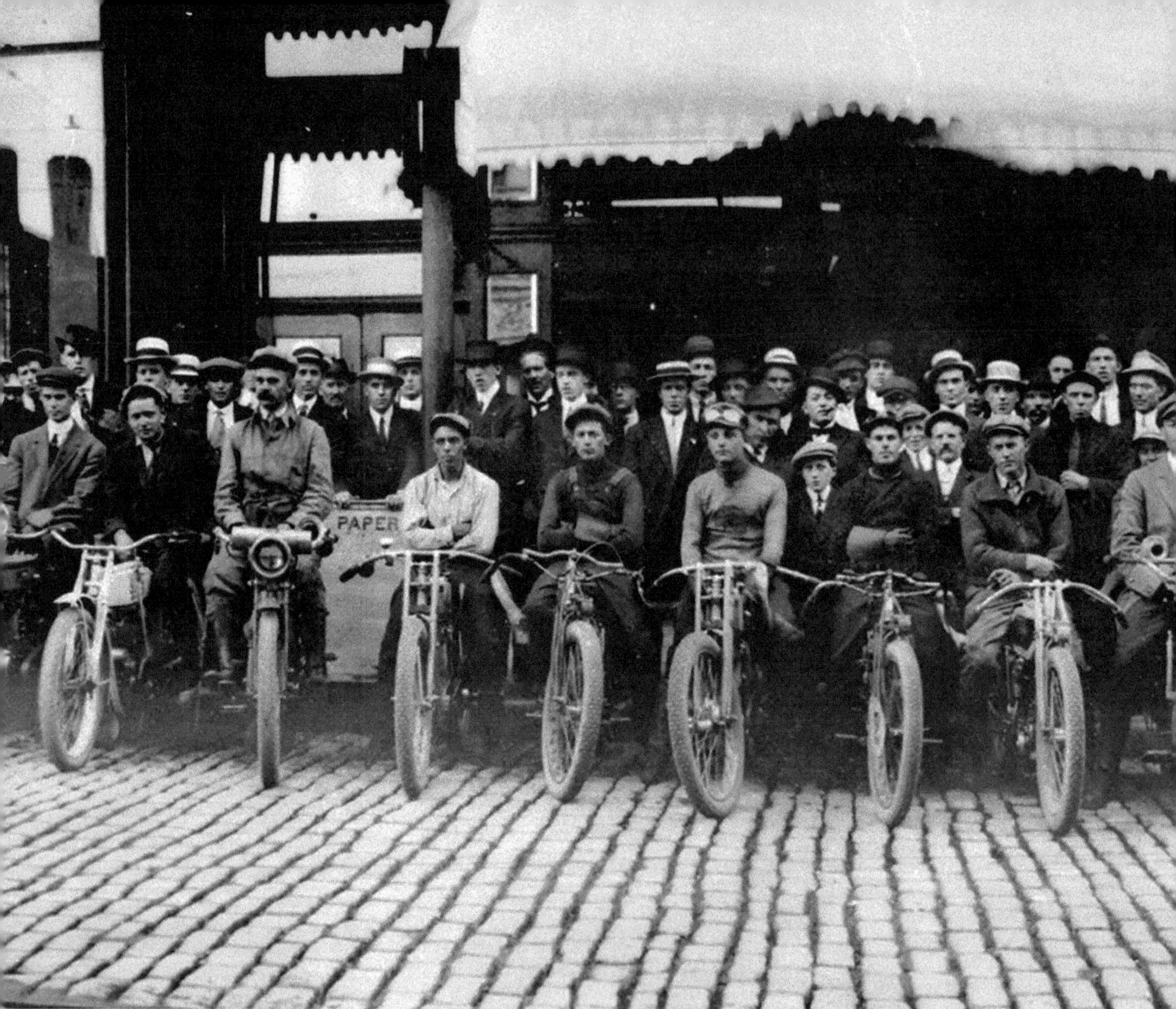

This photo of the Butte Motorcycle Club was taken on the 100 block of West Park Street in 1914. Obviously, motorcycling was already very popular. The Billings Motorcycle Club was founded in 1914 and still exists today.

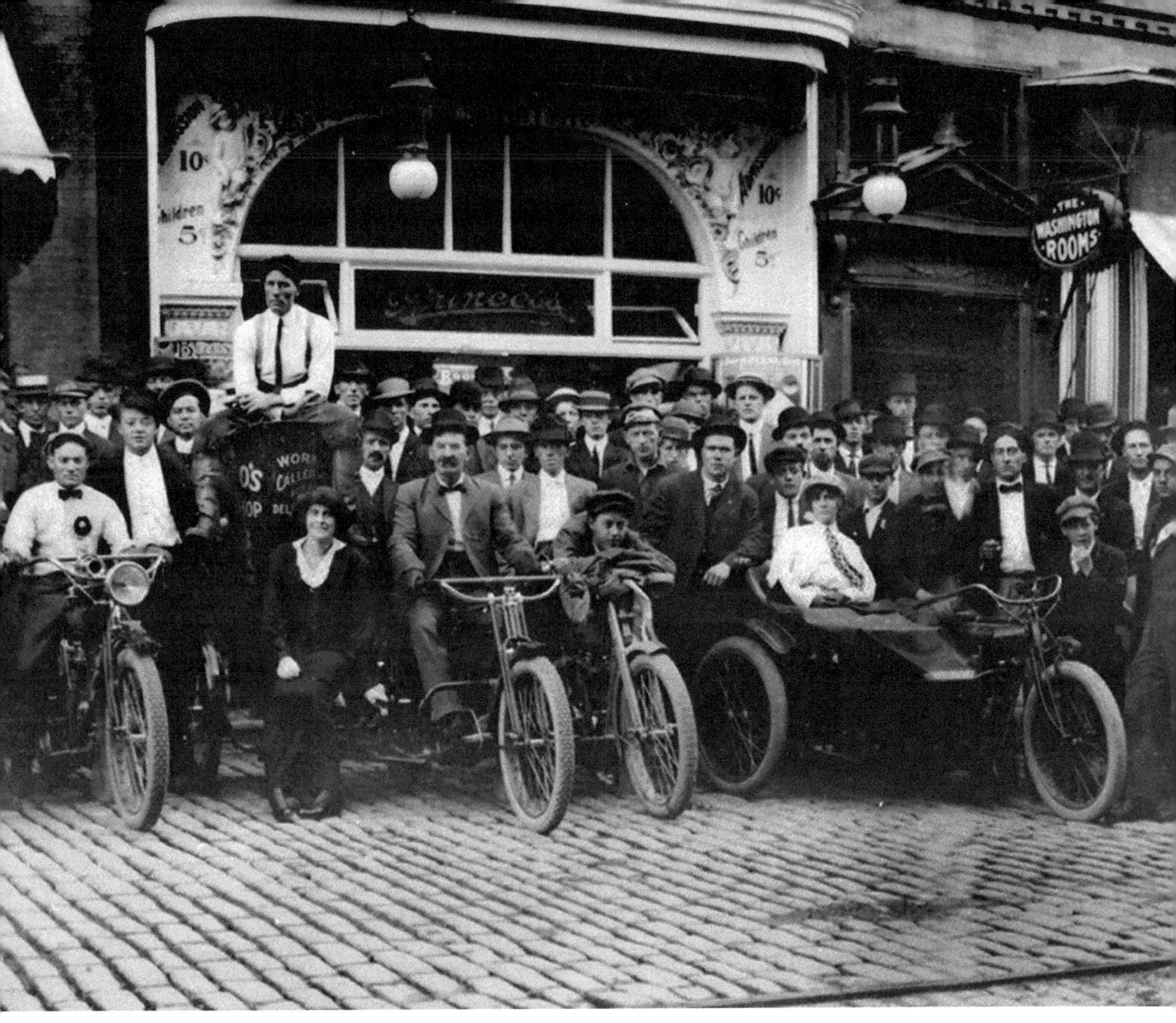

10¢
Children 5¢
10¢
Children 5¢
THE WASHINGTON ROOMS

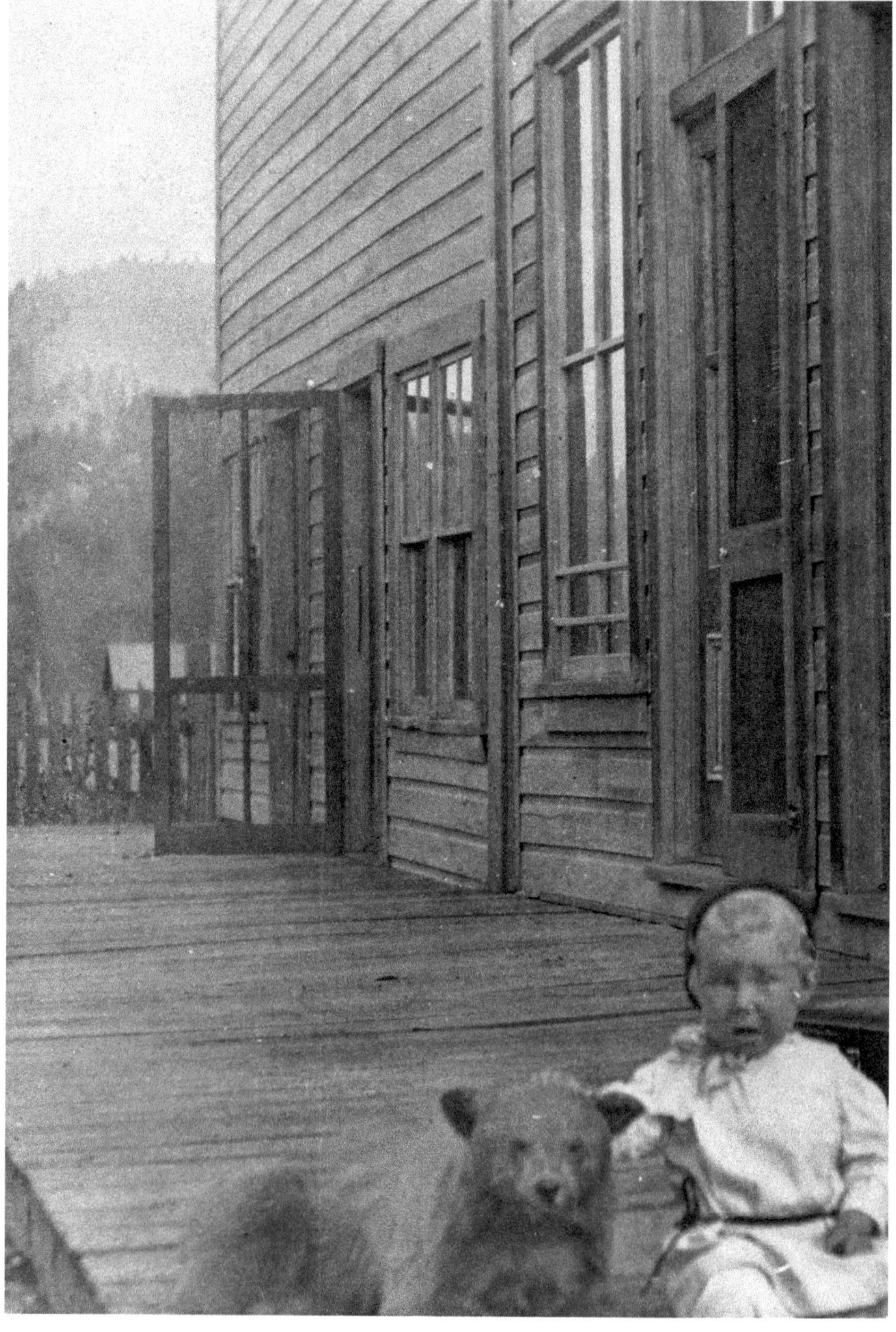

Toddler Edgar Daigle pets a tame bear cub on the porch of the Quigley Hotel on Rock Creek in 1911. Daigle not only survived this experience, he was still alive and living in Polson some 65 years after this photo was taken.

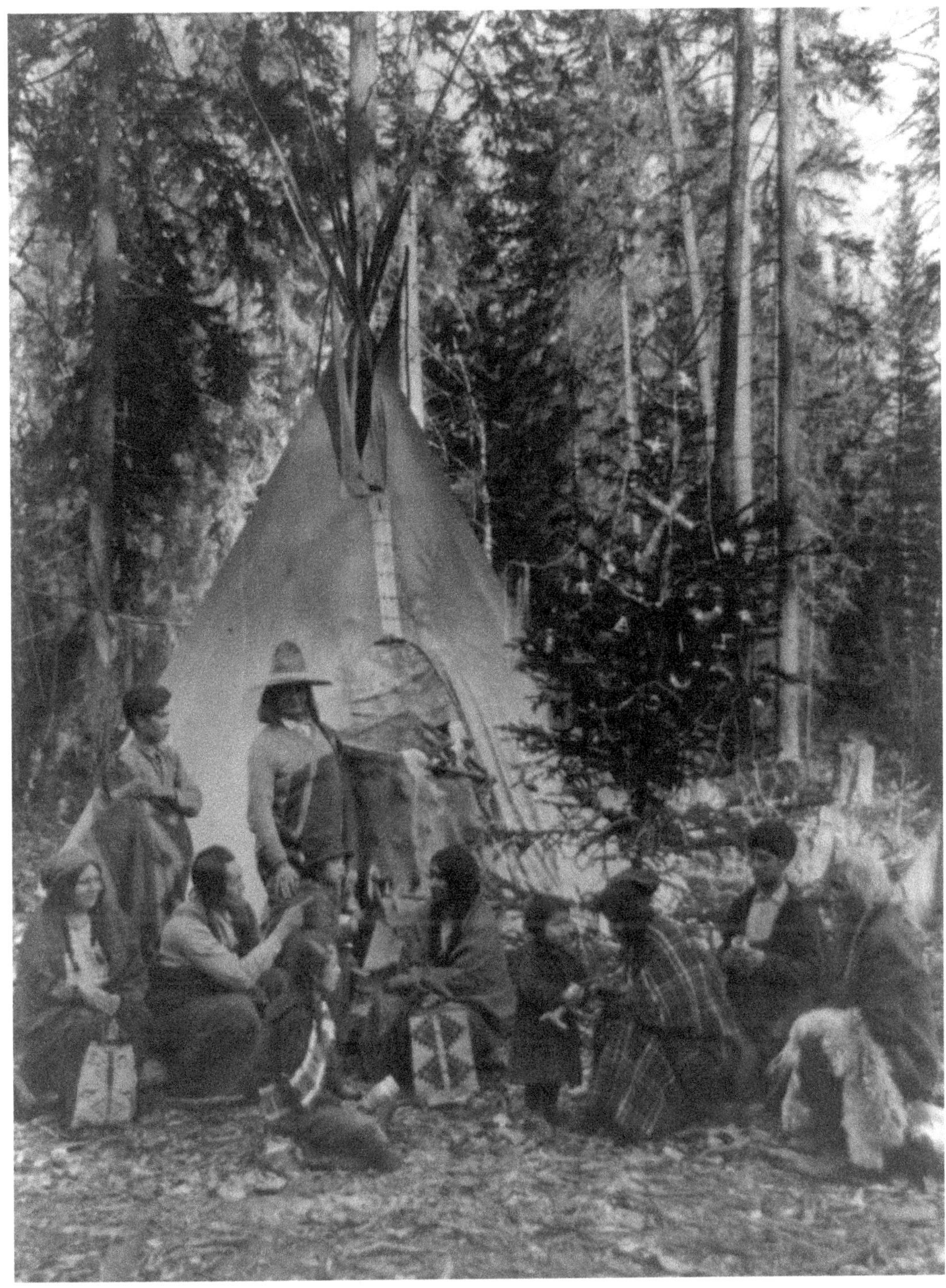

Eleven members of a Salish family stand around a decorated Christmas tree outside of their tepee on the west side of Glacier National Park.

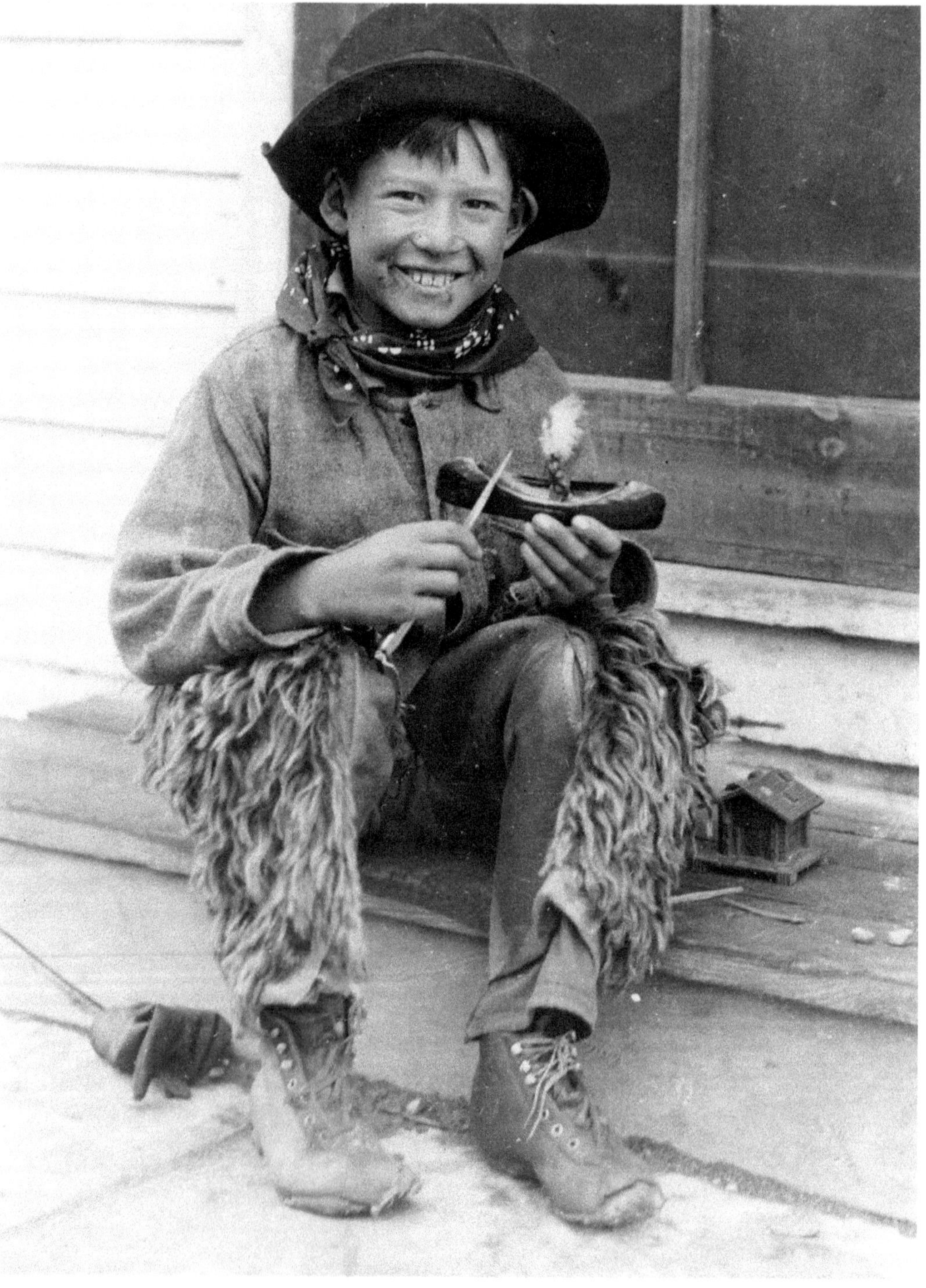

A young Eagle Aims Back skillfully carves a toy canoe on the Blackfeet Indian Reservation.

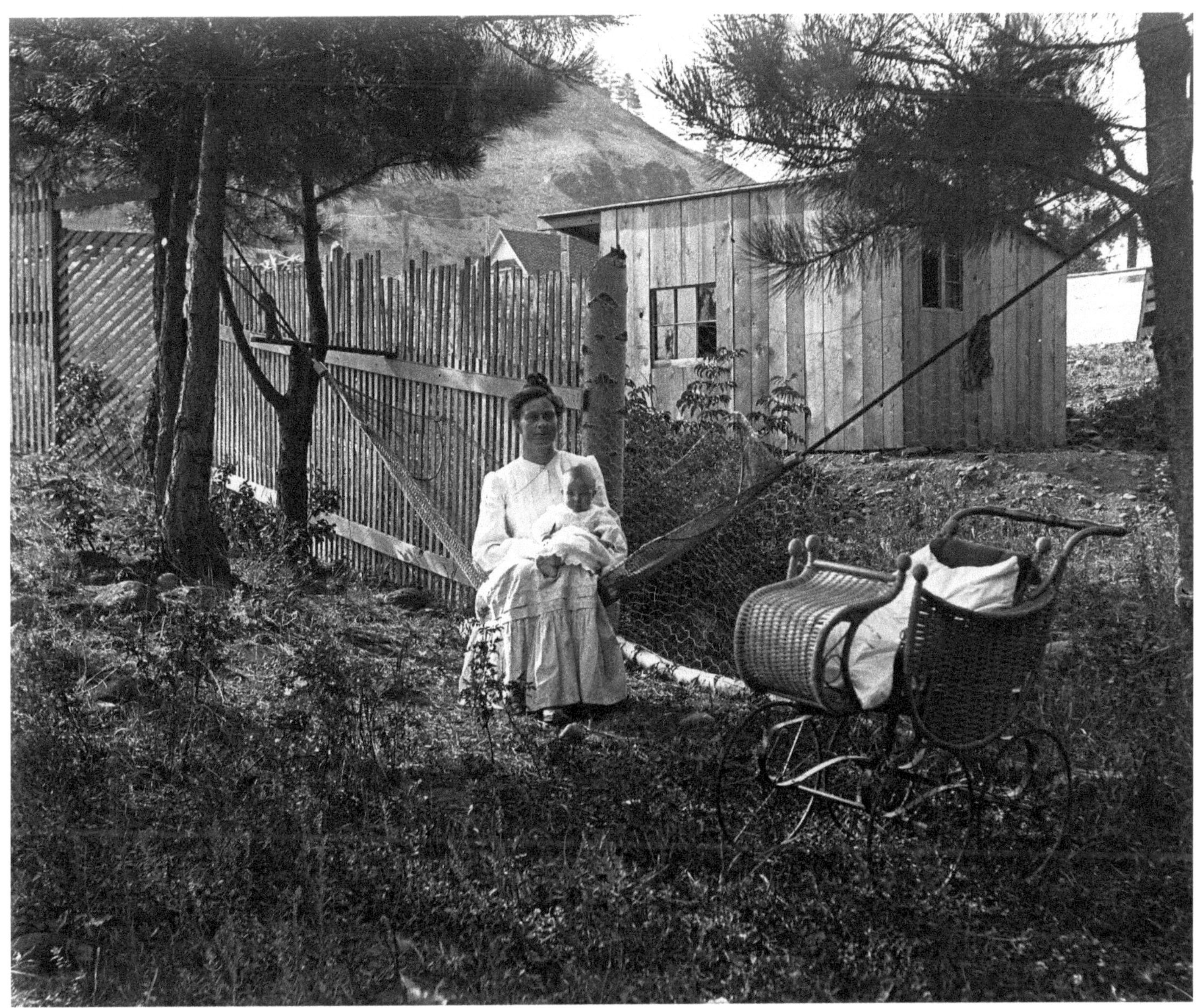

Missoula carpenter John Dunn spent much of his leisure time as an avid amateur photographer. Two of his favorite subjects were wife Edith and son Jack, both seen here around 1912. Dunn helped build Main Hall at the University of Montana and many of the university-area homes.

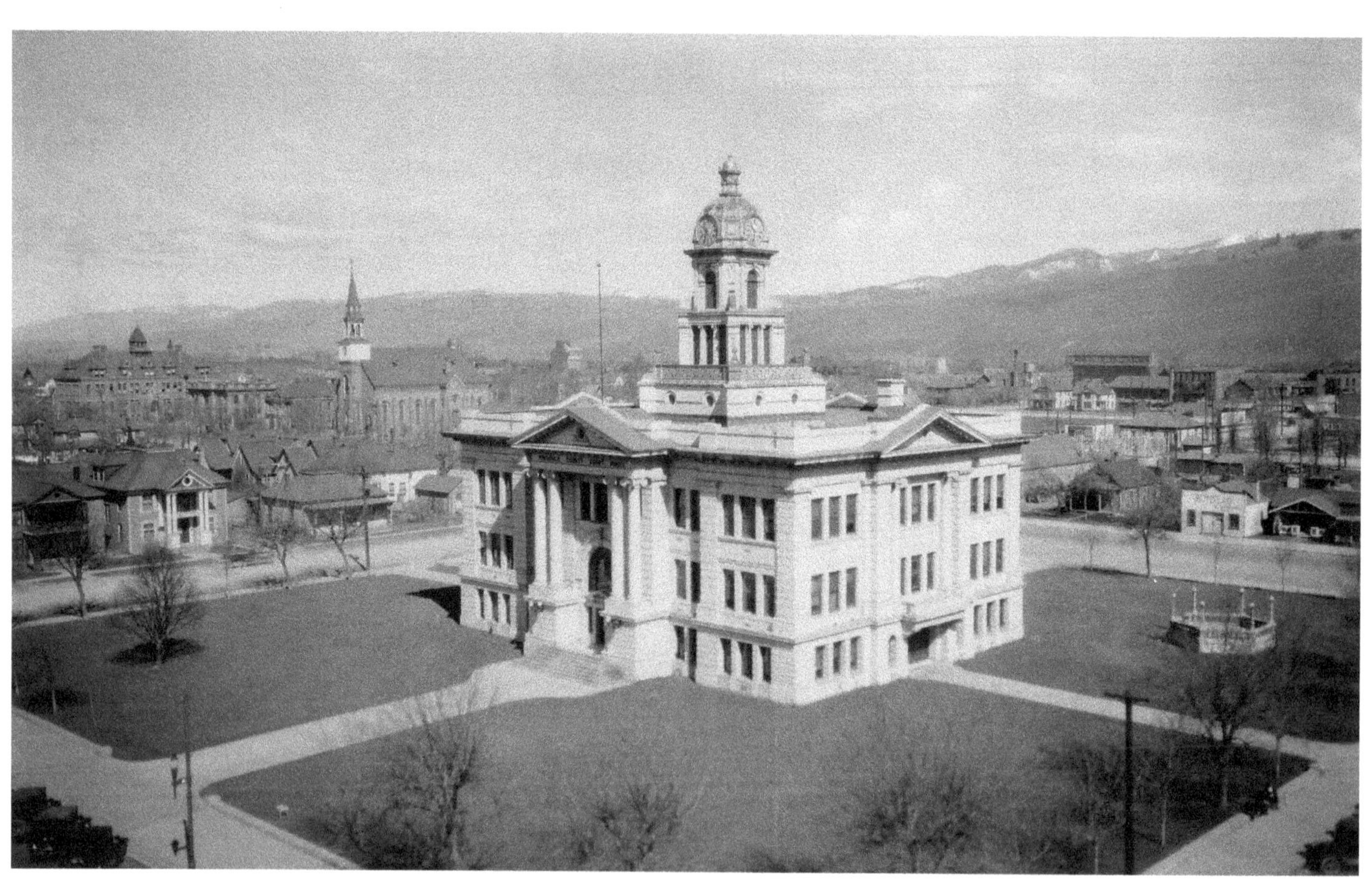

In 1908 architect A. J. Gibson was hired to design a new courthouse for Missoula County. This was a controversial decision, since Gibson was both an alderman and friends with members of the County Commission. Artist E. S. Paxson painted the eight murals that hang inside the building.

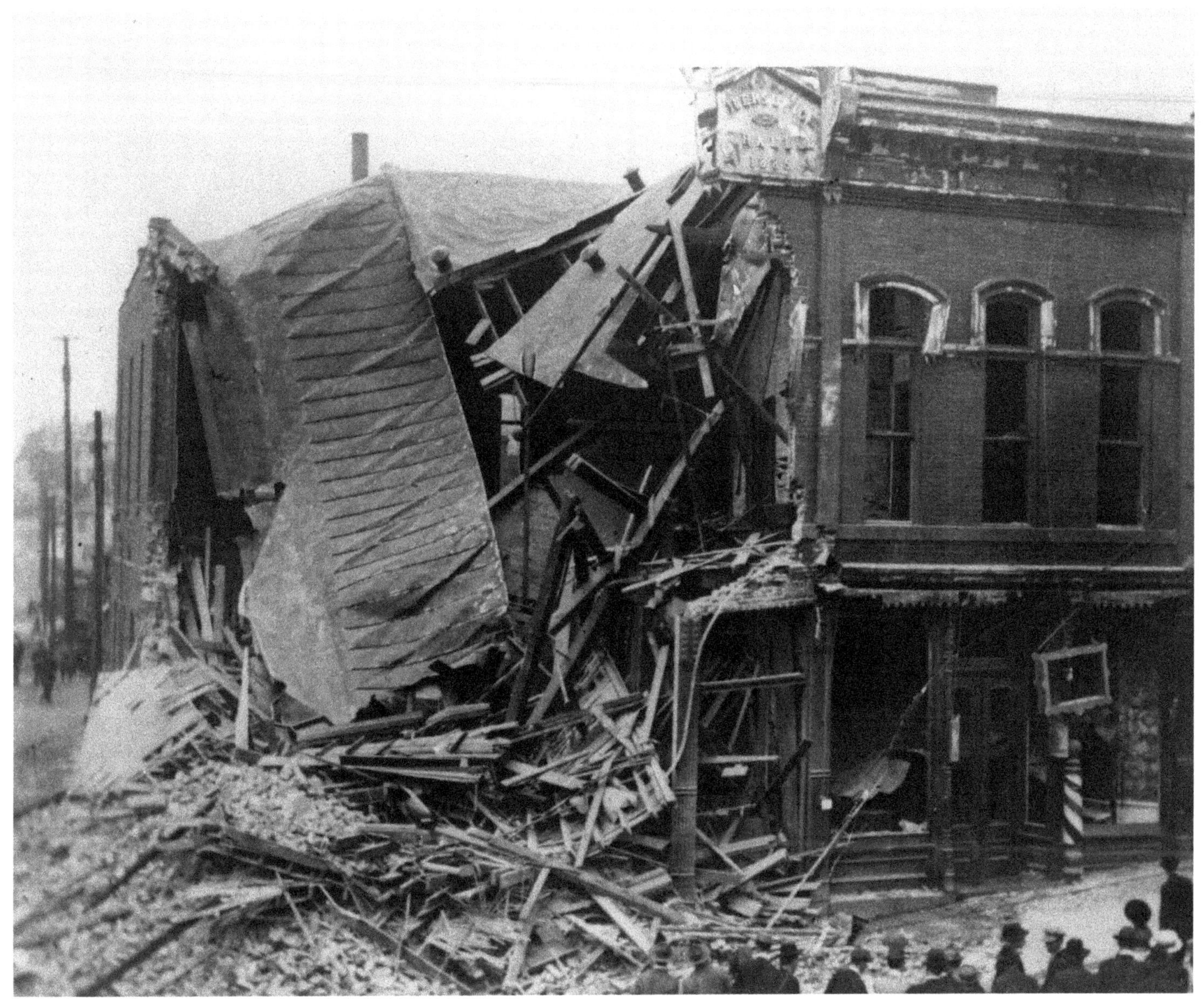

In 1914 the once-powerful Butte Miners' Union split into two rival factions. On June 23 two men were killed by gunfire at a union meeting. Fearing for their lives, officials of the Butte Miners' Union and several Butte police officers fled the scene, leaving the Miner's Hall in the hands of dissident union members, who promptly blew it up with several cases of dynamite. The wreckage is seen here.

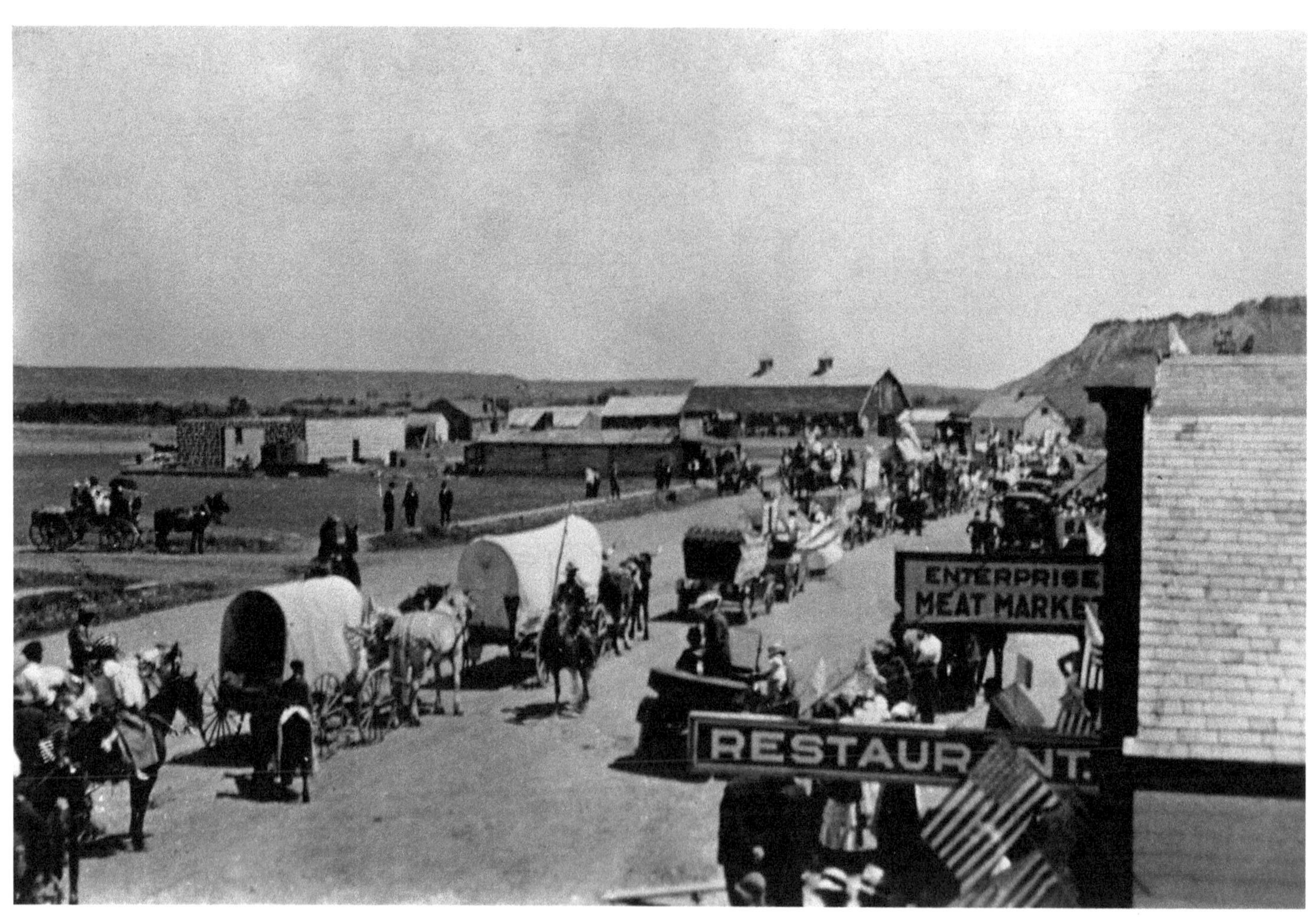

Many communities held an annual Fourth of July parade, including the tiny farming and ranching community of Winnett, where this photo was taken in 1916. Three years later a rich deposit of oil was located at the Cat Creek field, and Winnett became a boomtown.

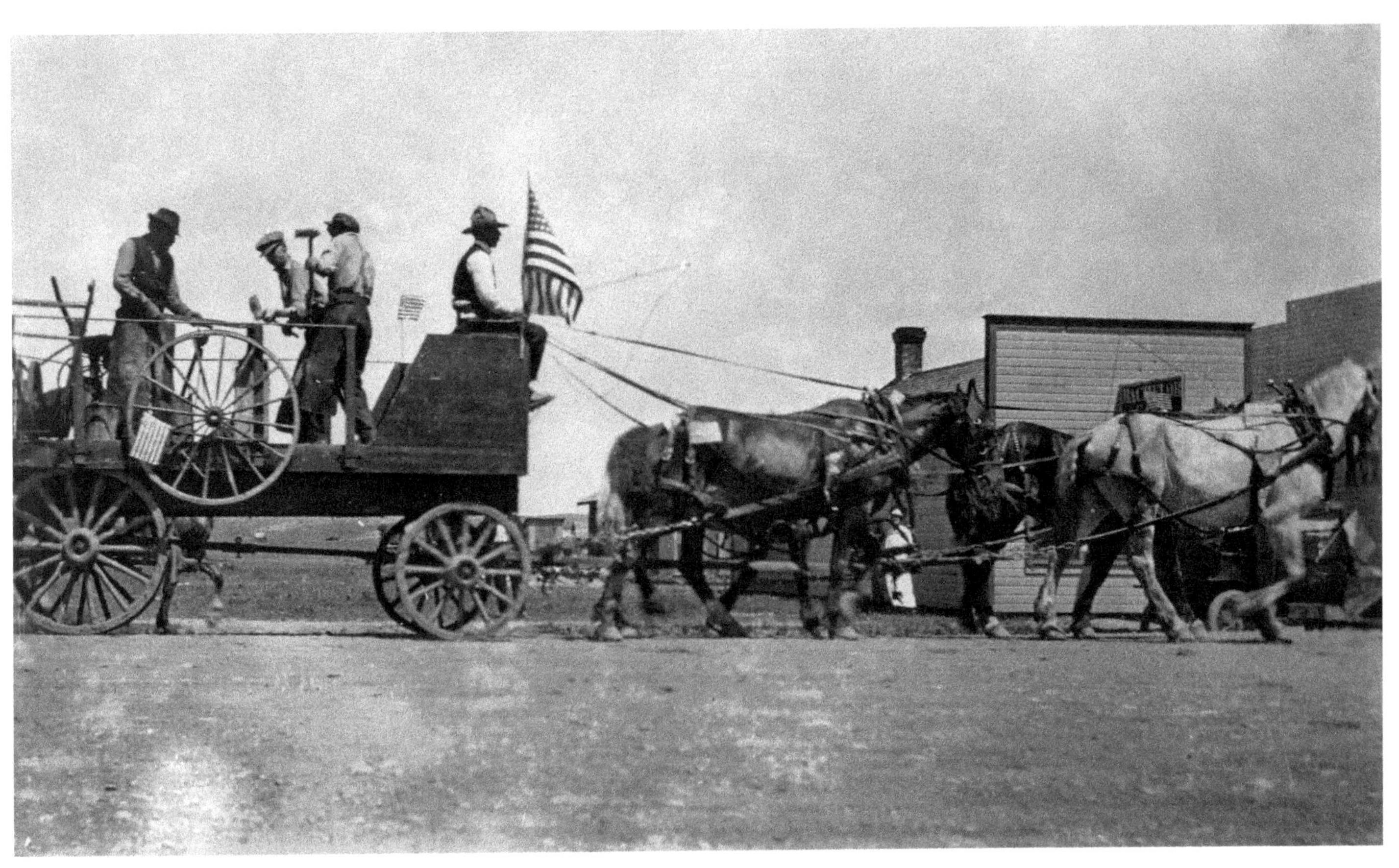

Patriotism was on full display during the Fourth of July 1916 festivities in Winnett, which was named for a local rancher. The oil boomtown became the seat of newly formed Petroleum County in 1925, but a fire four years later destroyed much of the business district of the town.

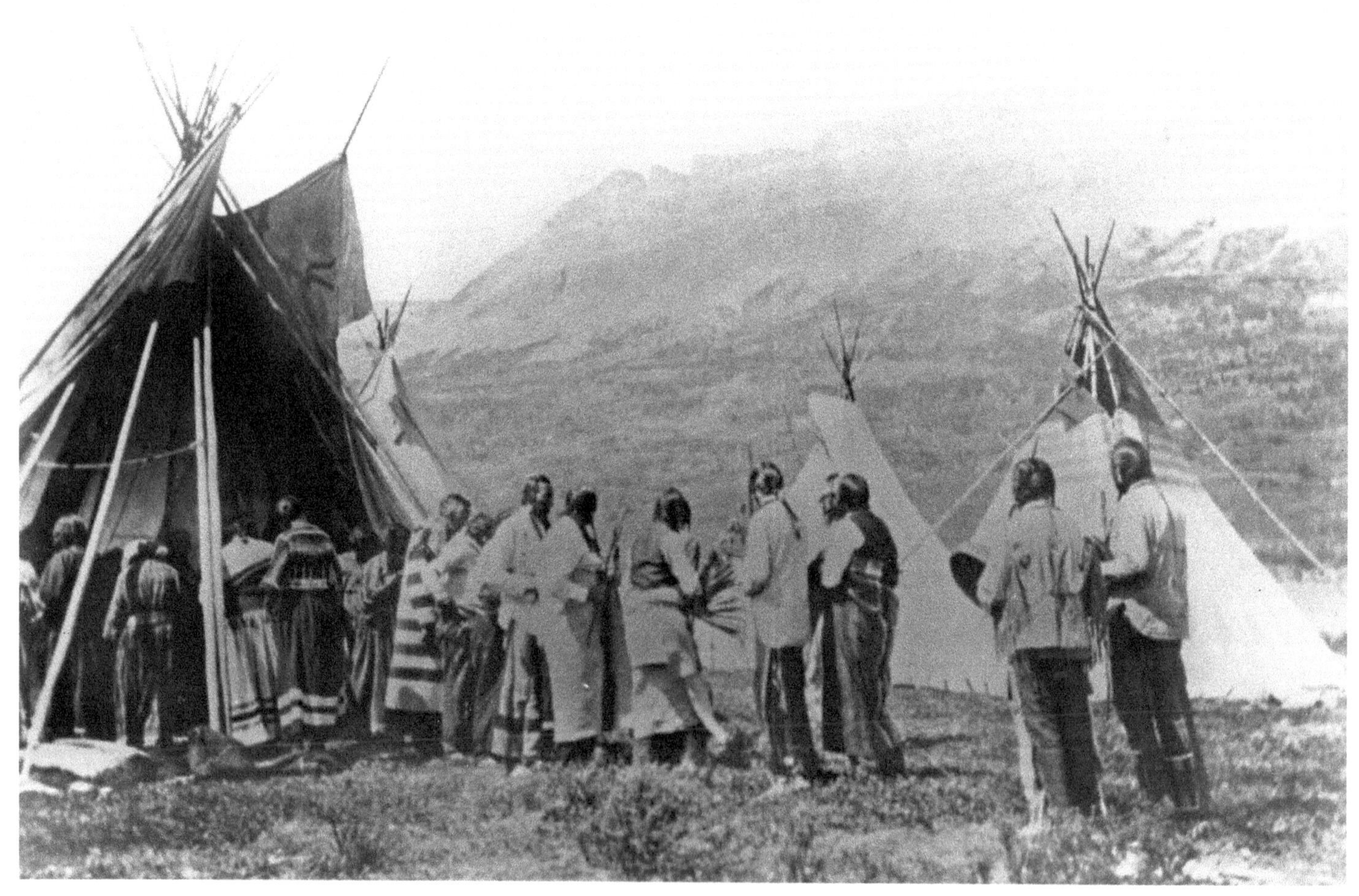

This Blackfeet medicine ceremony was held at the southern end of upper St. Mary's Lake around 1915.

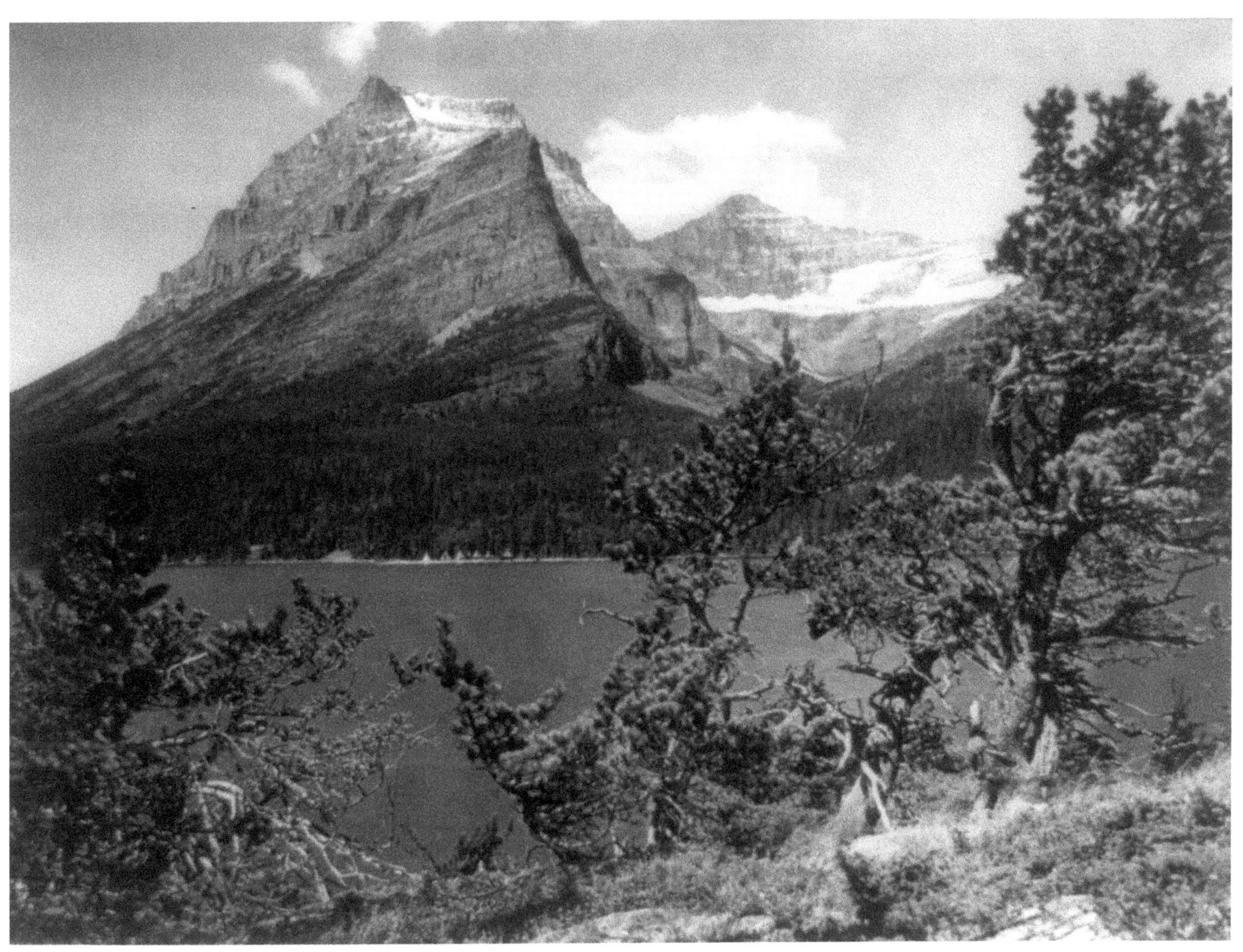

Author George B. Grinnell is considered the father of Glacier National Park. In 1901 he wrote, "Far away in northwestern Montana, hidden from view by clustering mountain-peaks, lies an unmapped corner—the Crown of the Continent." This view of the park around 1917 shows Going-to-the-Sun Mountain.

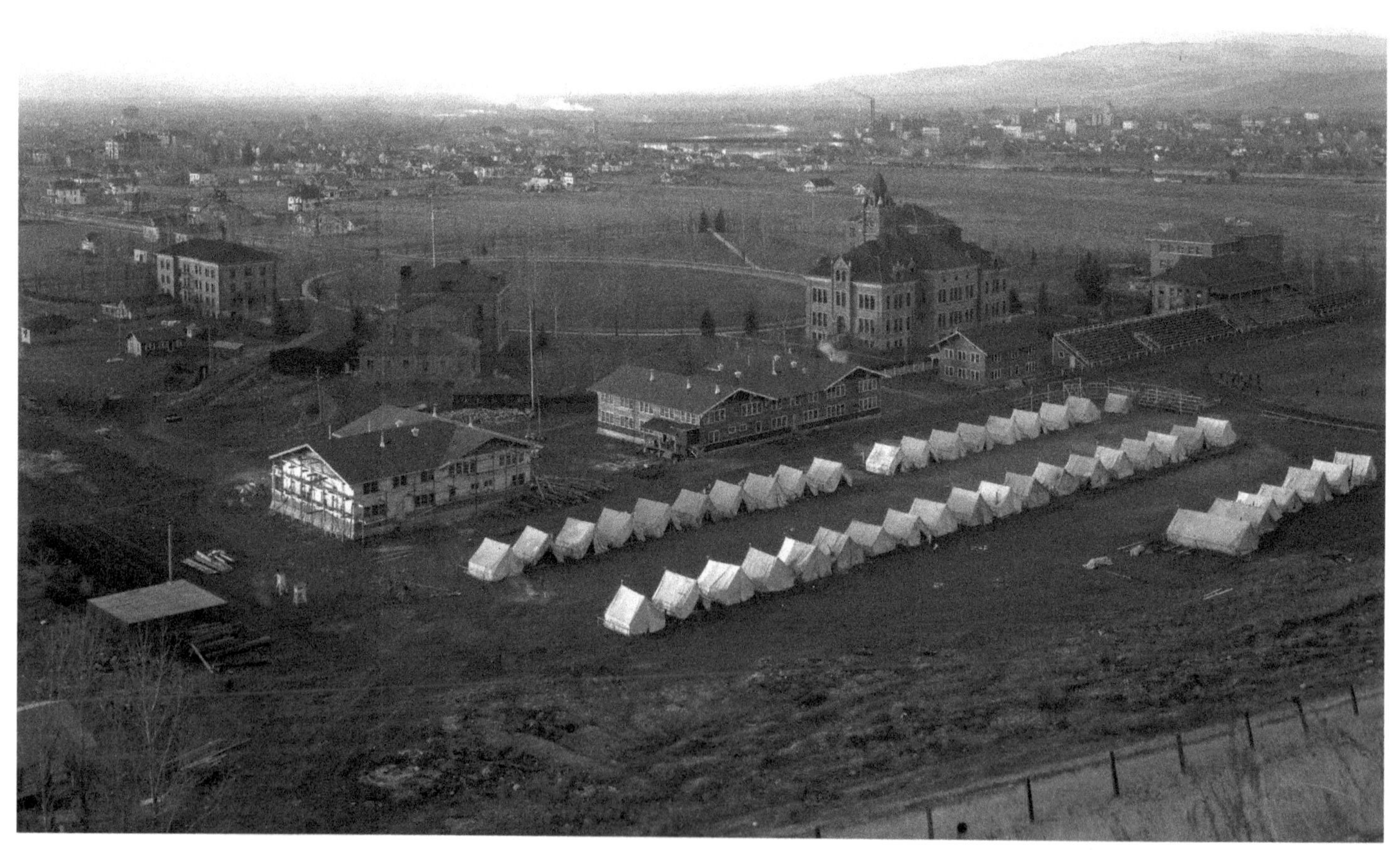

During World War I, the University of Montana campus hosted an Army camp just east of Main Hall. The Montana National Guard was mustered into federal service on April 7, 1917, and was ultimately designated the 163rd Infantry Regiment, of the 41st Division.

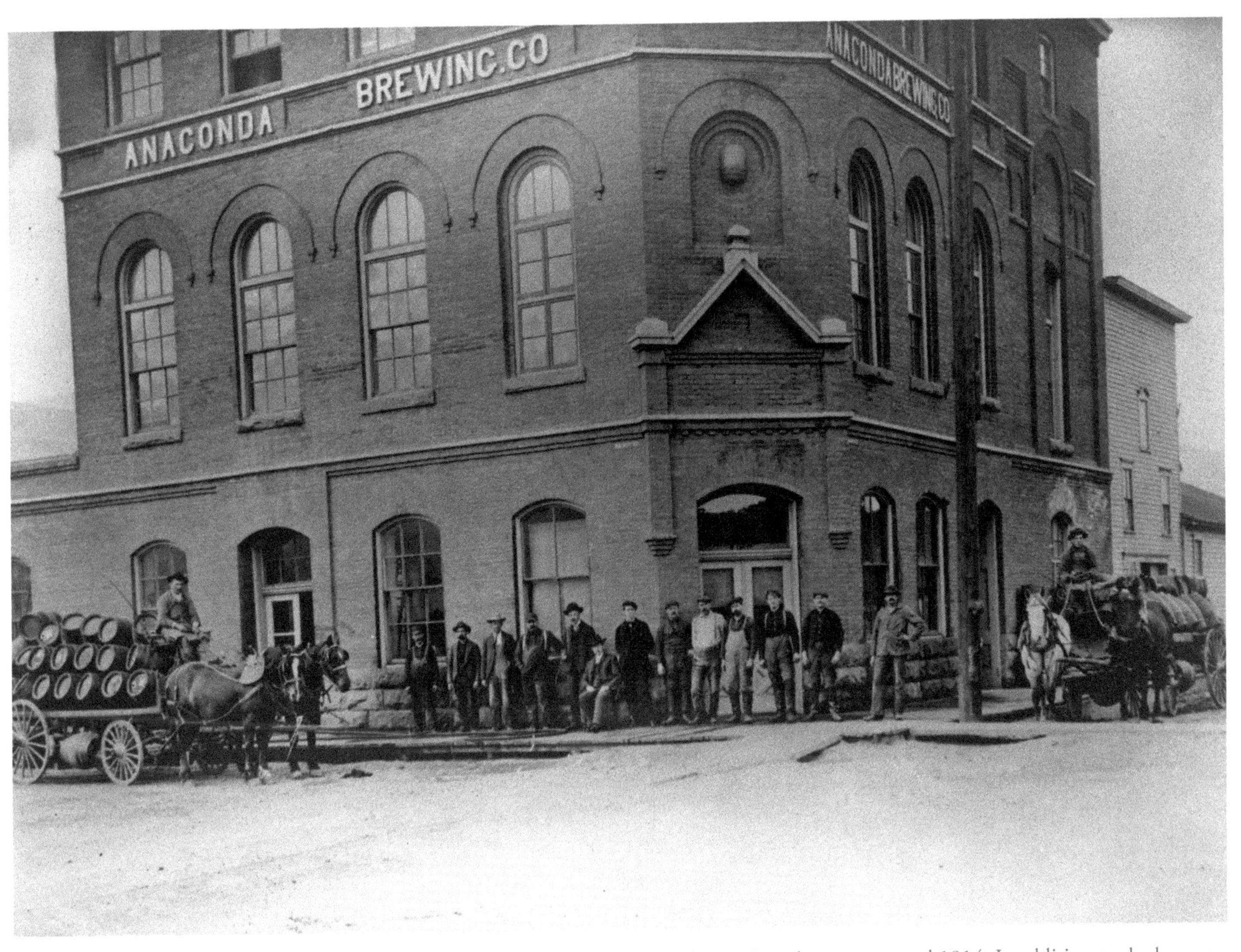

Employees pose in front of the Anaconda Brewing Company at Walnut and West Fourth streets around 1914. In addition to the brewery, the building had a saloon, a beer garden, and a bowling alley. Prohibition closed the brewery in 1918, and the company switched to producing soda until Prohibition was lifted.

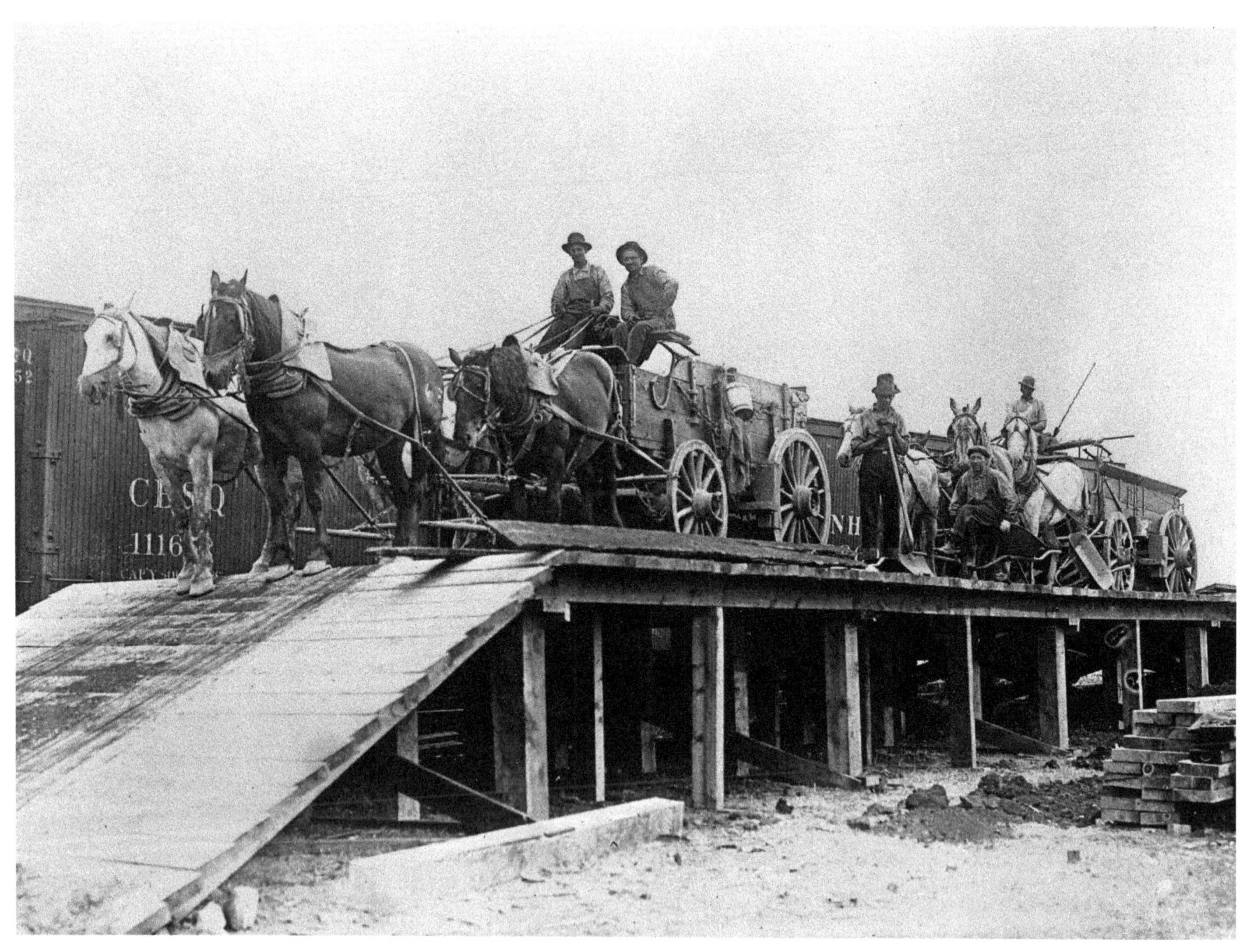

Teamsters unload manganese ore at Philipsburg, the town that had grown up around the Flint Creek Mines. The area was best known for its silver mines but also had some of the richest manganese ore found in the United States, as well as outcrops of lead and zinc.

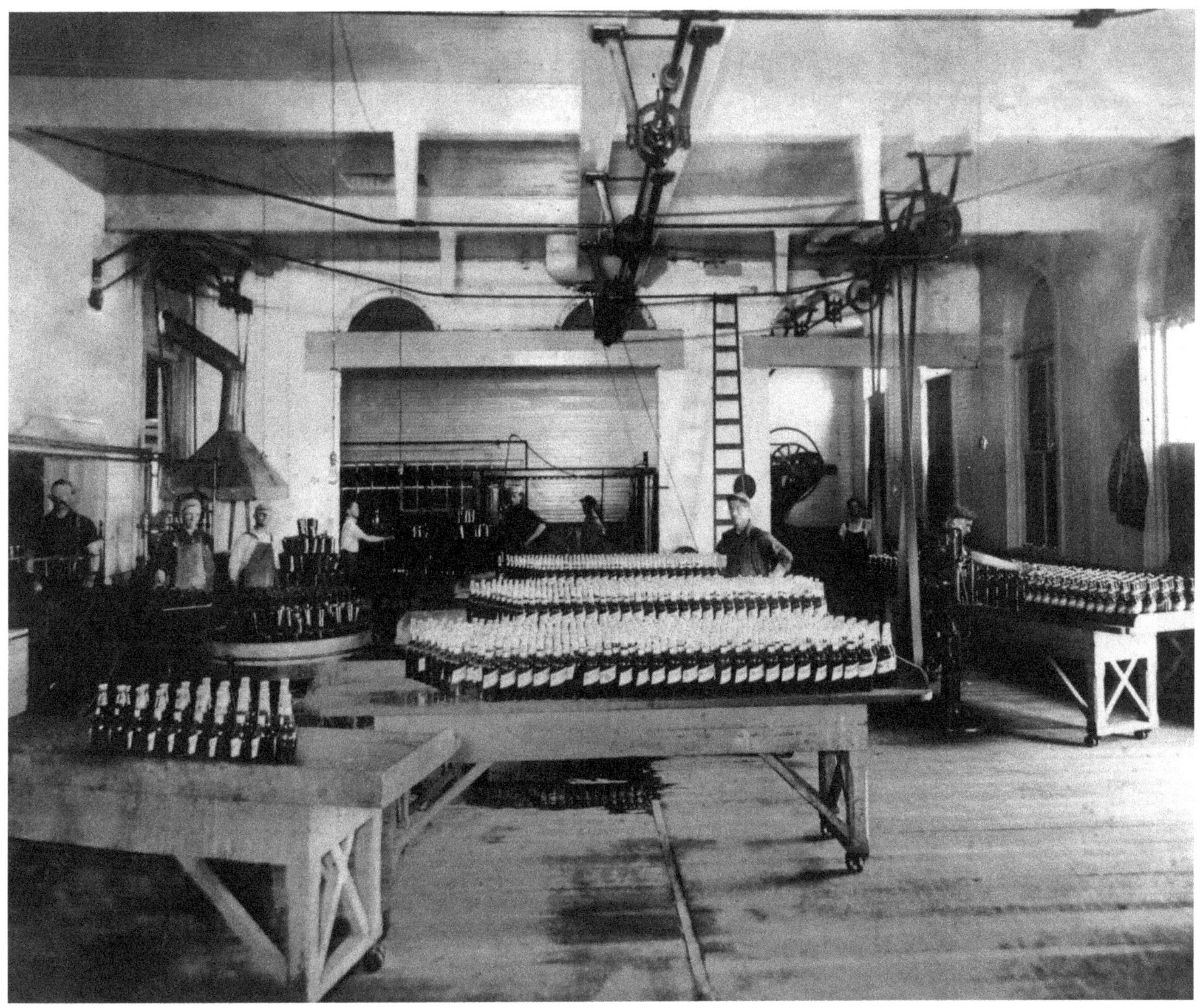

Loaded bottling tables at the Billings Brewing Company. This photo was taken in 1918, when the enactment of Prohibition in the state forced the company to dump hundreds of gallons of beer. During Prohibition, Tip Top Soda was produced in this facility.

Grinnell Point looms over a waterfall in Glacier National Park around 1919. The 7,890-foot mountain was once known as Stark Peak, after a miner who had a claim on it. The mountain was renamed for George B. Grinnell.

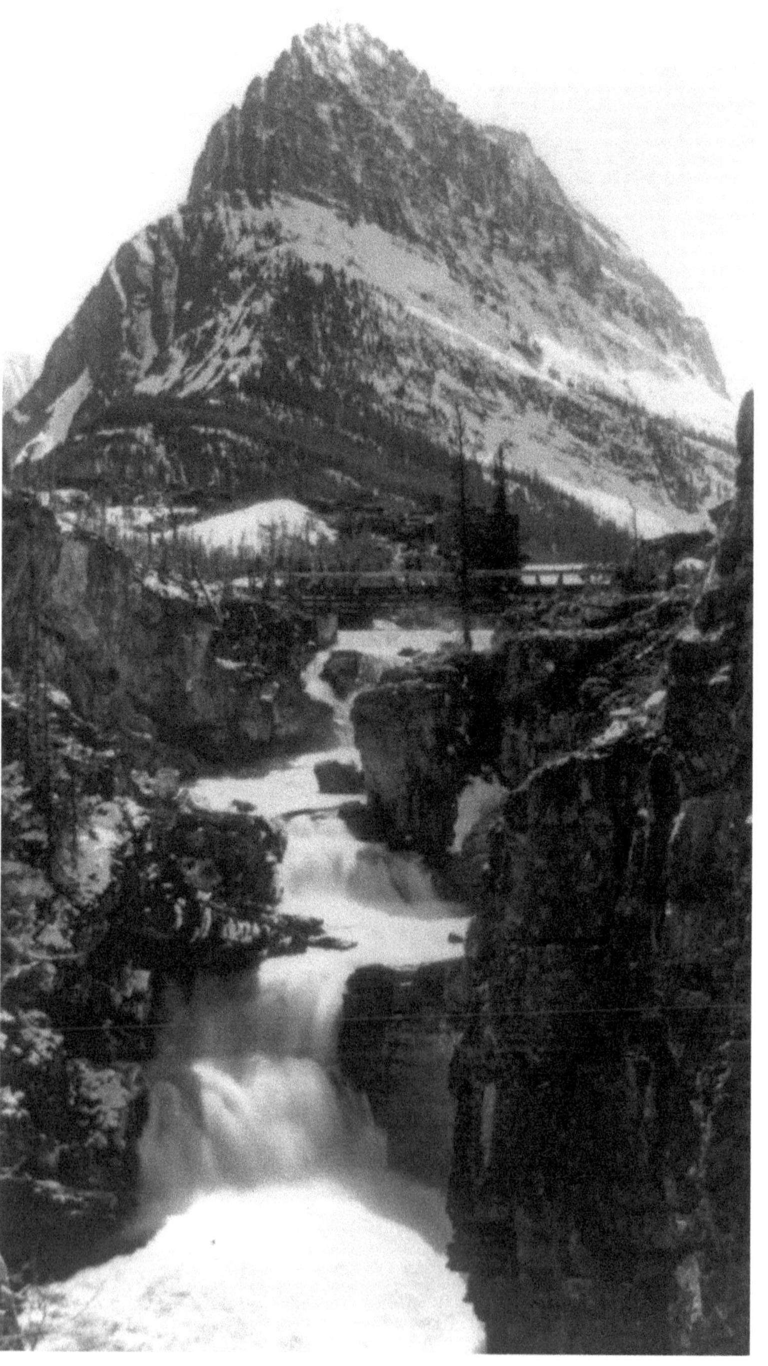

A Time of Drought and Depression

(1920–1939)

The Roaring Twenties never quite reached the homesteaders on the plains of Montana. A drought that began in 1919 devastated those trying to make a living on small, dryland farms. Not enough rain fell on the plowed fields, and the wind carried the thin topsoil away. Failed crop followed failed crop, while prices for agricultural products and for commodities such as copper and lumber dropped sharply at the end of World War I. Tens of thousands of homesteaders held on for as long as they could before eventually abandoning their farms. The homestead boom of a decade before had given birth to numerous small towns along the railroad lines, and each town had a local bank. In a period of a few years, more than half the banks in the state went bust, often dooming the small towns in which they were located.

Despite a few bright spots like the discovery of oil at the Cat Creek field near Winnett, Montana's economy suffered greatly throughout the 1920s, and it became the only state in the Union to lose population during that period.

After a few years of adequate rainfall in the mid-1920s, another long-lasting drought returned in 1929. By 1931 Montana's economy had reached rock bottom, thanks to the combined effects of the drought and the Great Depression, which drove prices for agricultural products and commodities into the cellar. As copper prices fell, the Anaconda Copper Mining Company laid off thousands of workers in Butte, Anaconda, Great Falls, and East Helena.

In 1933, President Franklin Roosevelt introduced a variety of New Deal programs designed to help Americans suffering from the effects of the Depression. The Rural Electrification Administration brought power to Montana's farms and ranches. Workers with the Civilian Conservation Corps helped improve campgrounds, trails, and forests. The Works Progress Administration employed 14,000 people in a wide variety of projects, from building highways to writing books about the state. Construction of the federally authorized Fort Peck Dam employed 11,000 workers by the end of the decade, and the project was featured on the cover of the very first issue of *Life* magazine, November 23, 1936. President Roosevelt himself showed up for the dedication of the massive, earth-filled dam the following year.

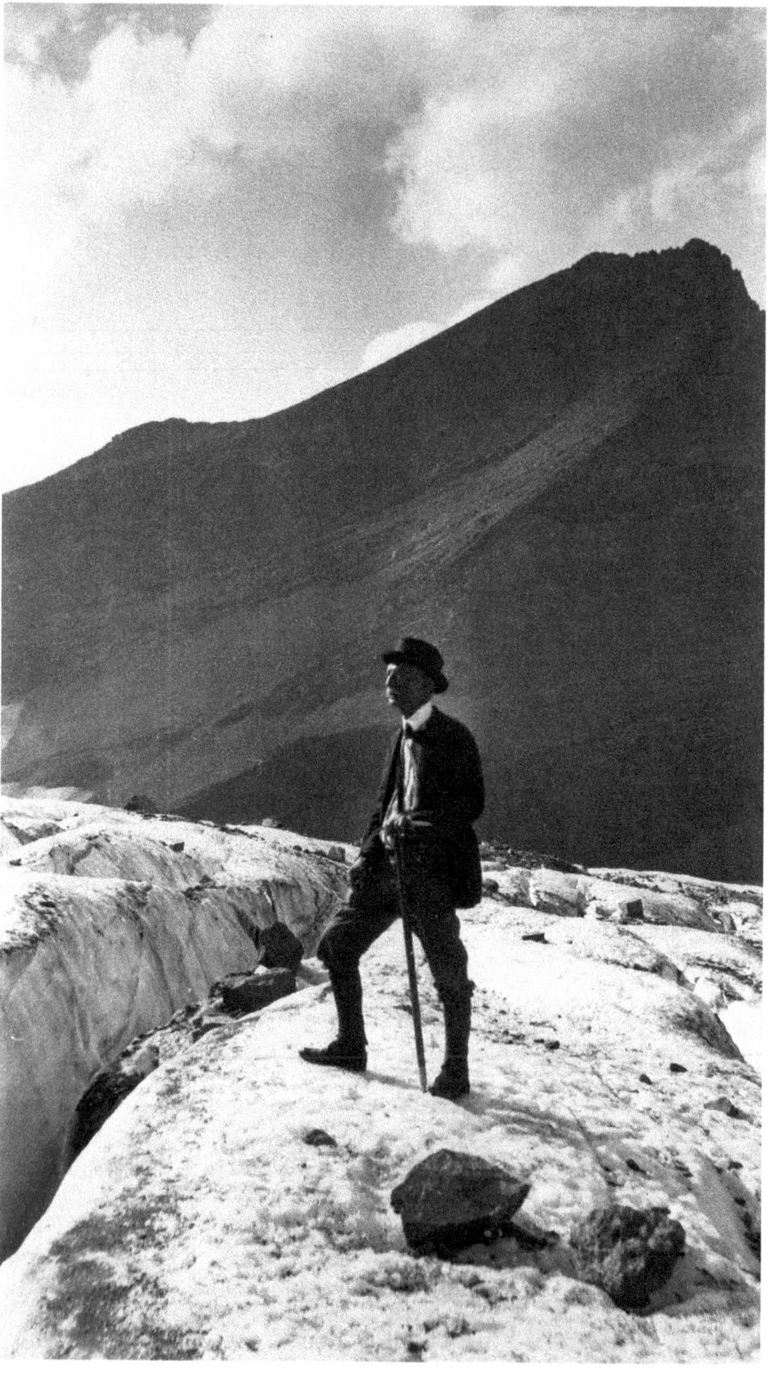

George B. Grinnell stands on Grinnell Glacier in 1920. The prominent editor of *Forest and Stream* magazine, Grinnell was a founding member of the Audubon Society and the Boone and Crockett Club, and was instrumental in the protection of Glacier National Park.

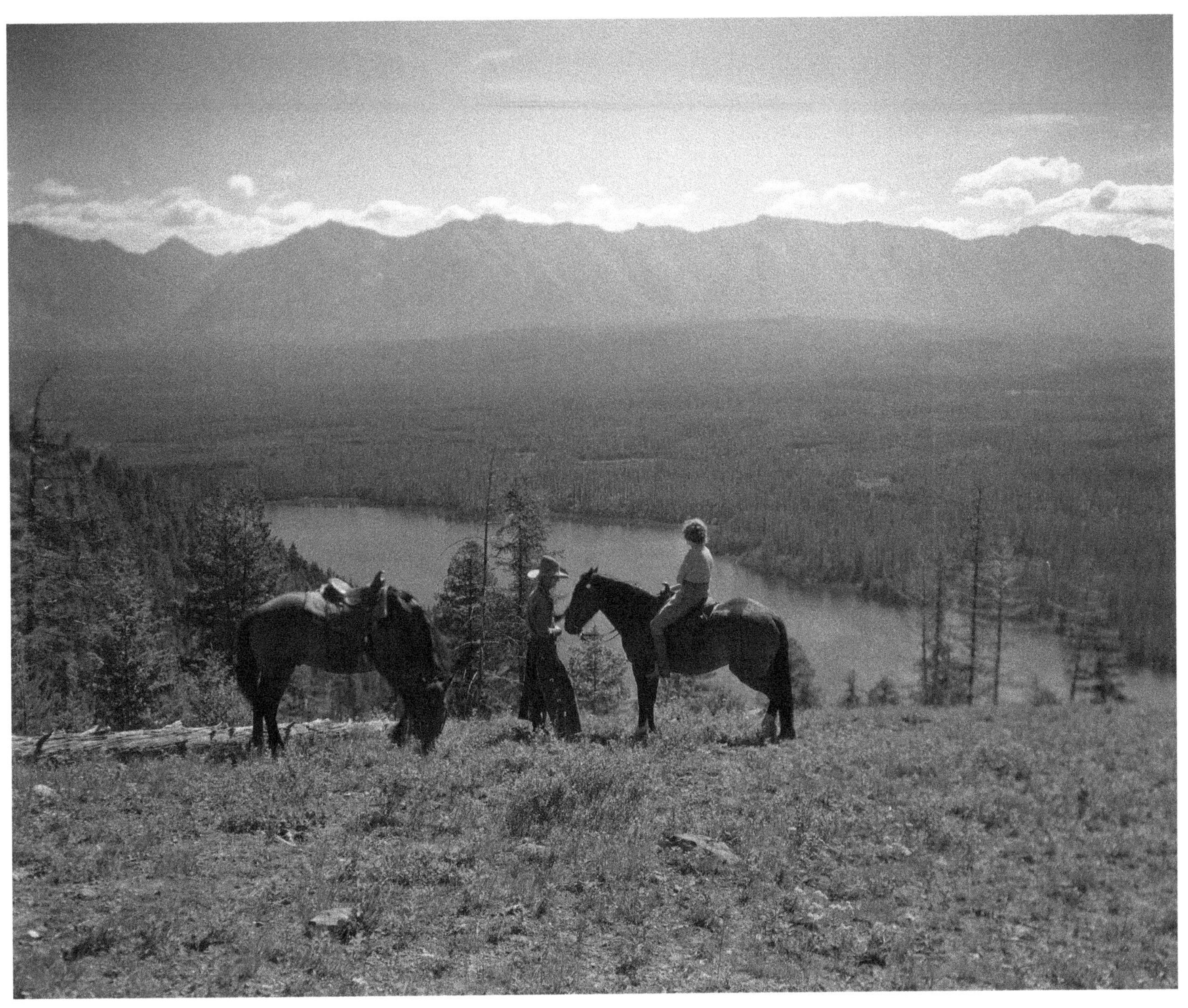

Horseback riders gaze toward Lindbergh Lake, a six-mile-long, glacially carved lake that lies between the Mission Mountains and the Swan Range. The Swan River flows north from Lindbergh Lake some 70 miles before it empties into Flathead Lake near Bigfork.

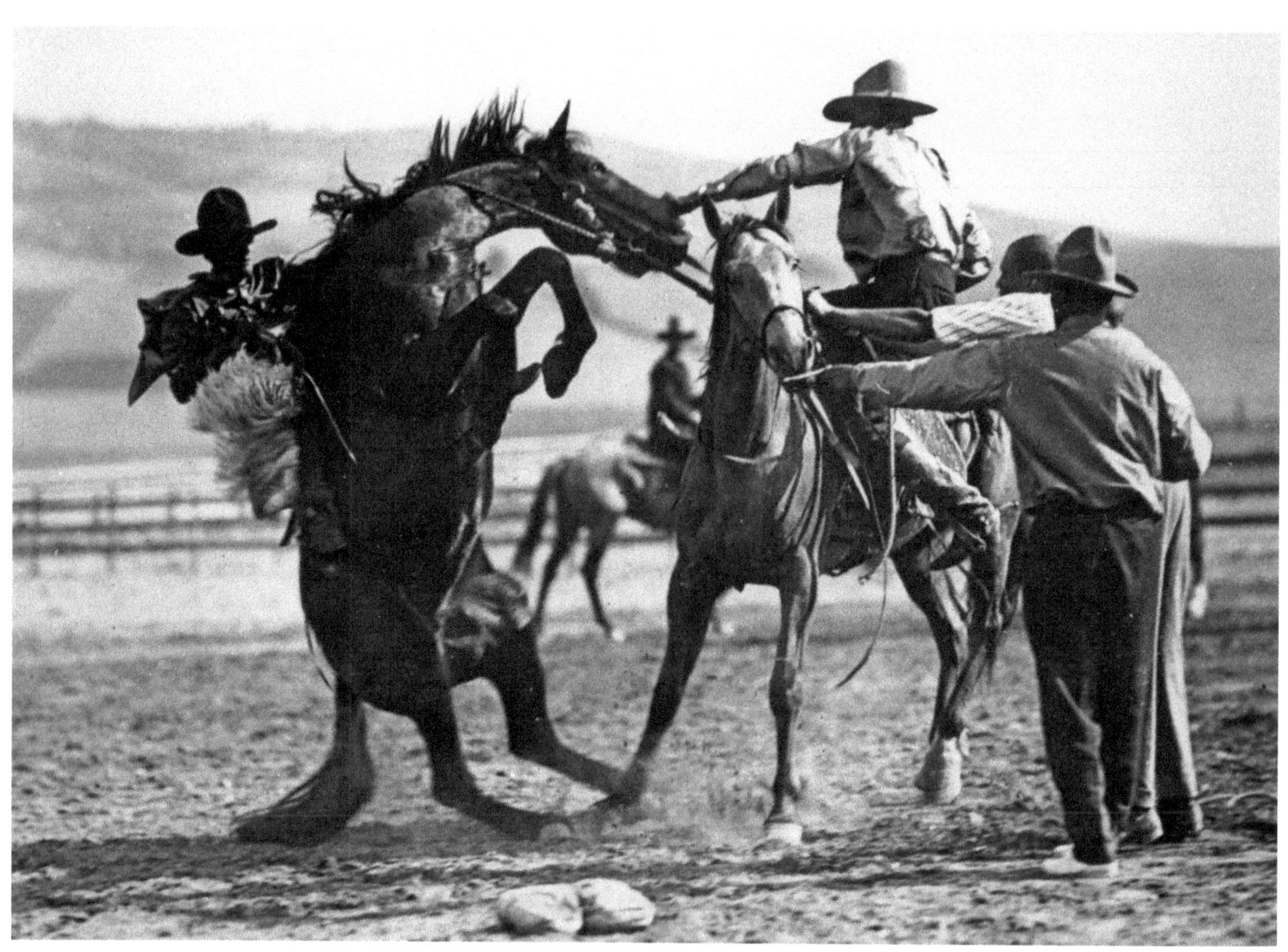

A bronc rider finds trouble at the Missoula Stampede. A pickup man on horseback tries to control the bronco, while others circle nearby, waiting for a chance to help. The Missoula Stampede was one of the largest western shows in the United States and was often held on the Fourth of July.

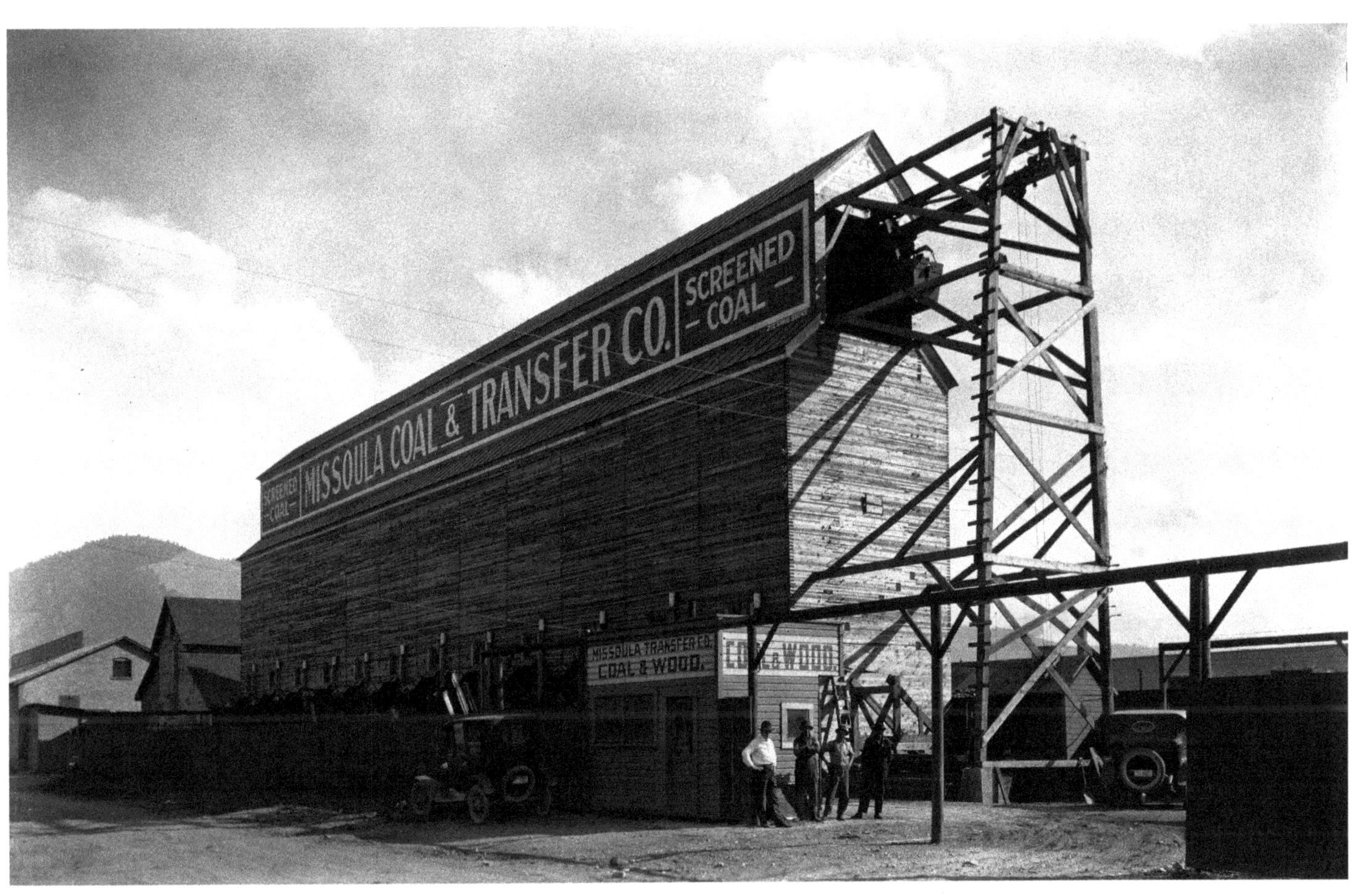

Coal was an important source of heat in many communities, and Montana had the largest coal reserves in the nation. This photo taken by R. H. McKay shows the Missoula Coal and Transfer Company during the 1920s. The company also sold firewood.

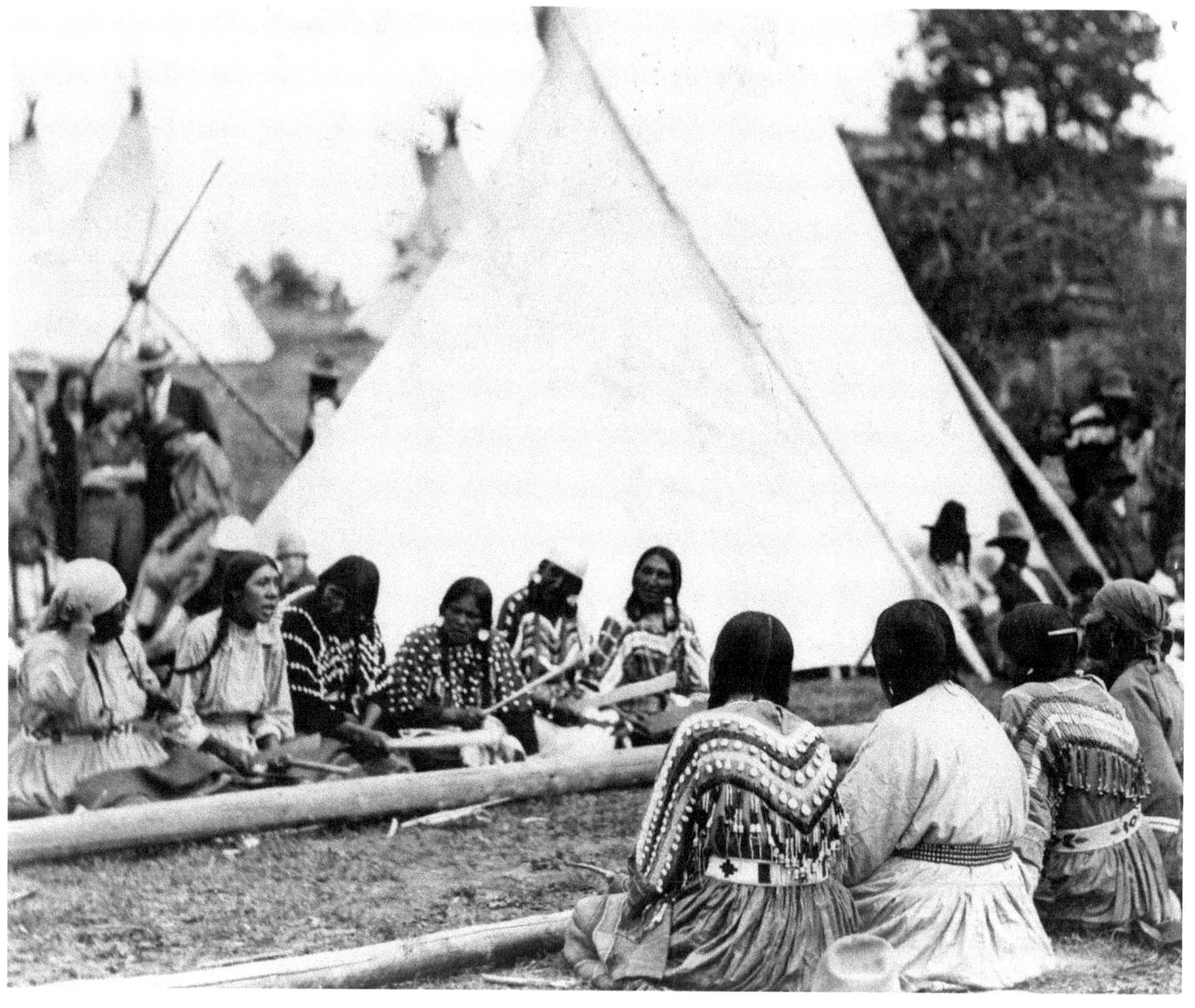

Piegan women play the stick game on the Blackfeet Indian Reservation. The stick game was very popular among many of the Plains Indian tribes. The Piegans are the southern branch of the Blackfeet tribe, with a reservation adjacent to Glacier National Park.

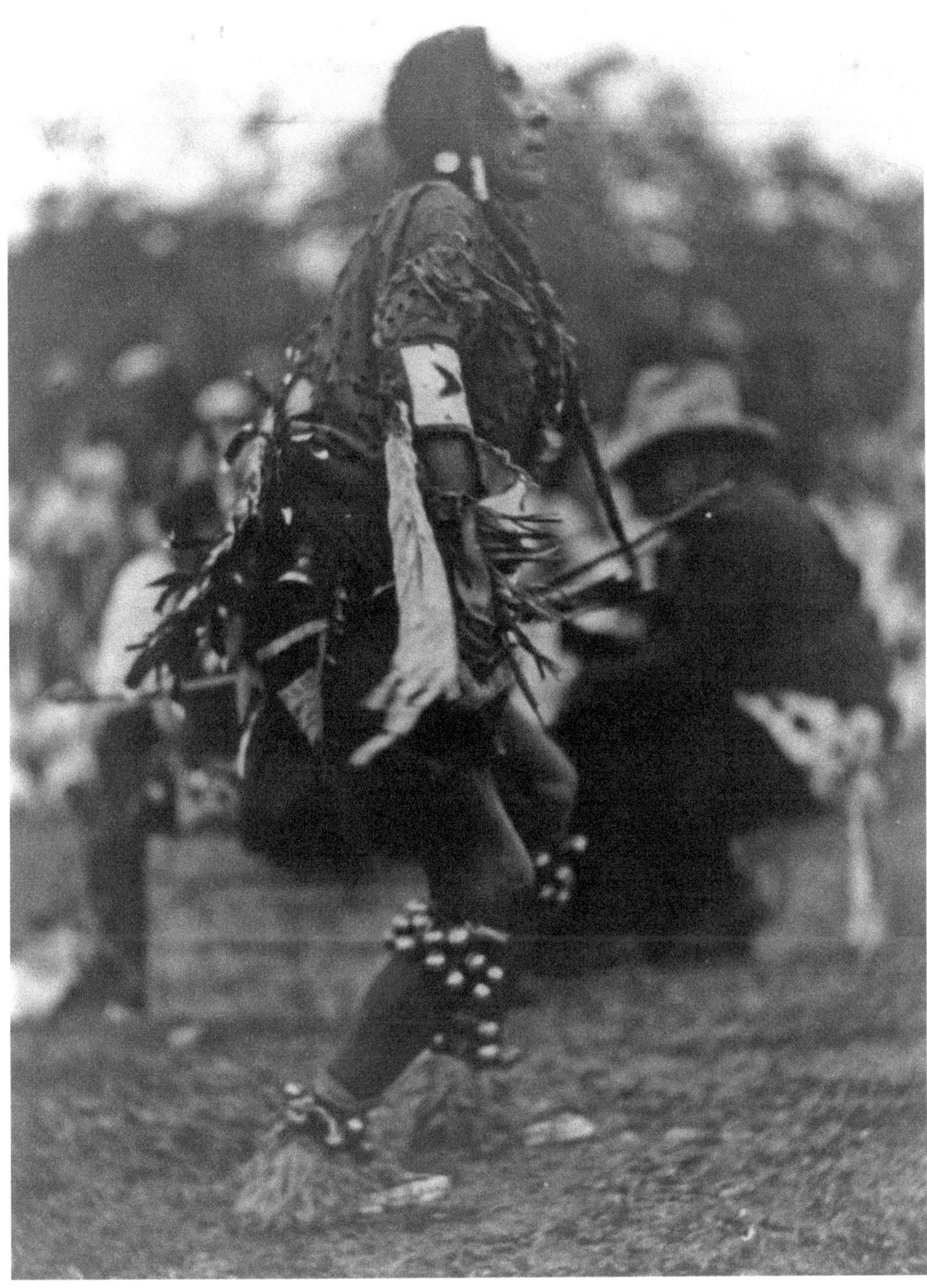

Chief Turtle demonstrates the storm dance at a Blackfeet celebration in Two Medicine Valley, Glacier National Park. Just after the chief finished his interpretation of the storm dance, a torrential rain struck the valley.

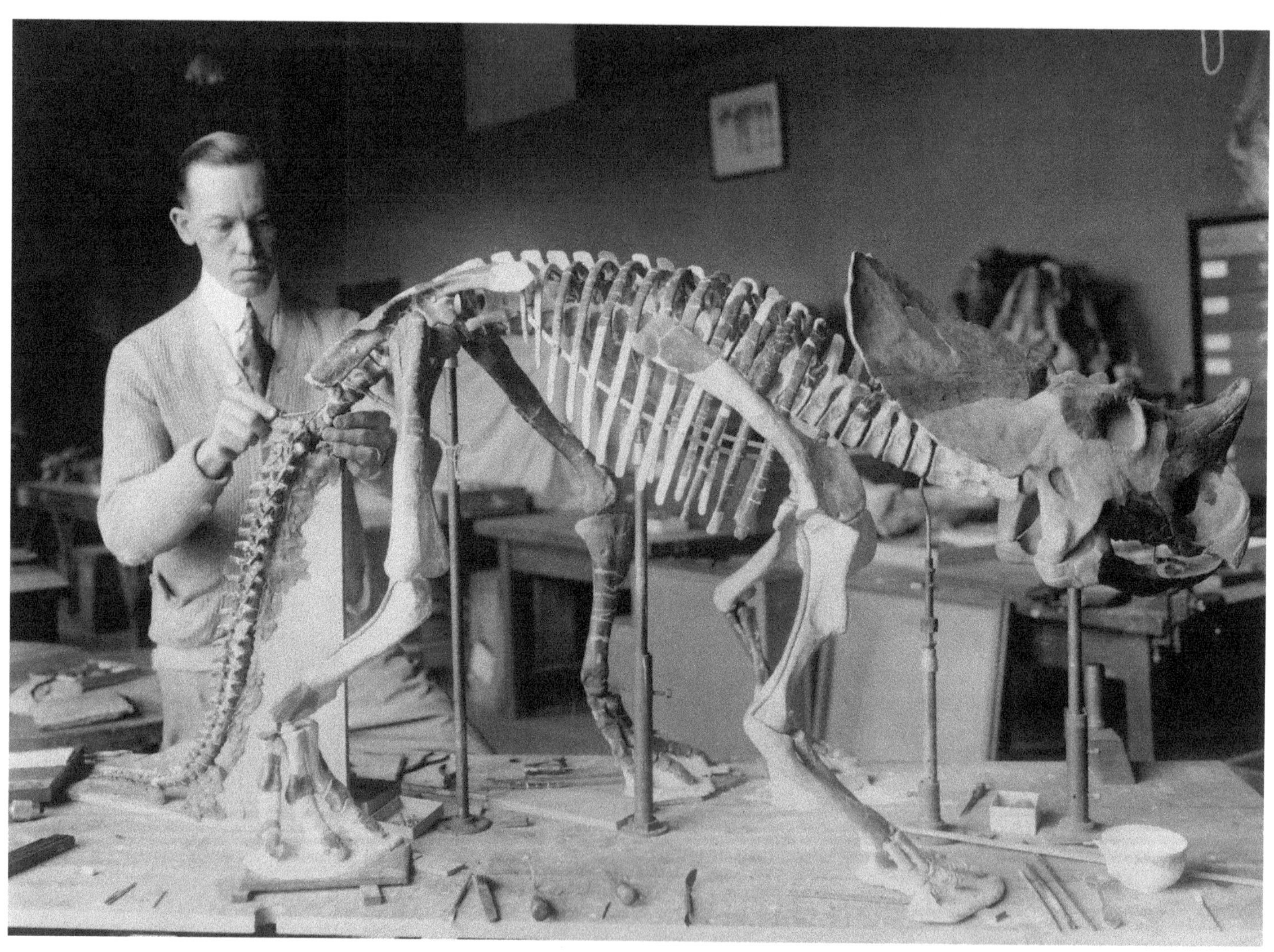

This 1921 photo depicts Norman Ross of the Smithsonian's National Museum of Natural History examining the skeleton of a baby dinosaur found in Montana. The skeletons of numerous baby dinosaurs, along with nests and fossilized eggs, have been found in the state.

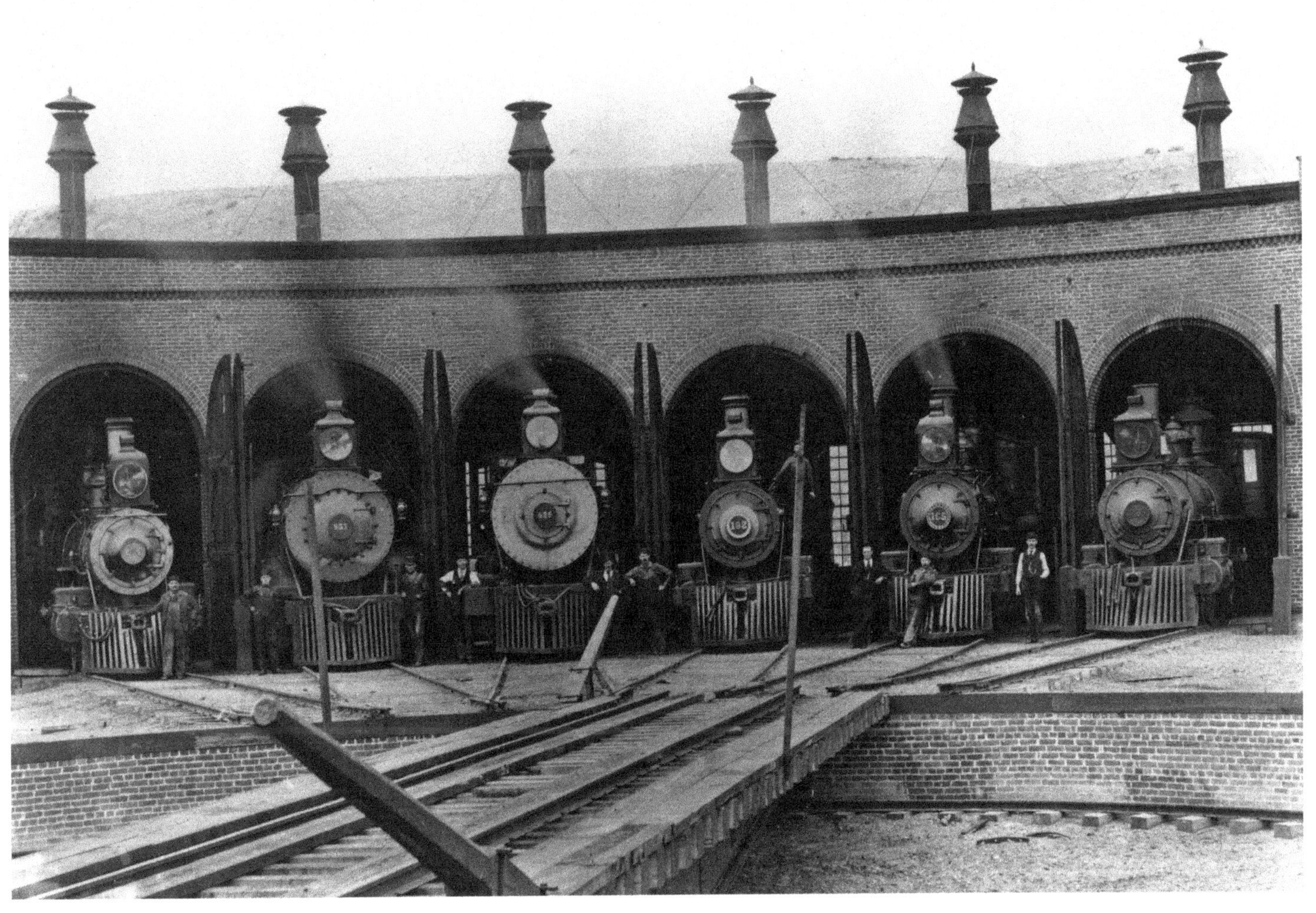

Steam locomotives fill the bays of the Northern Pacific Railway Roundhouse in Missoula, built in 1923. Beginning in the mid-1950s, the roundhouse would blow a whistle at 7:30 A.M. and 4:30 P.M. each day. The roundhouse and machine shops were torn down after the interstate highway was built in the mid-1960s.

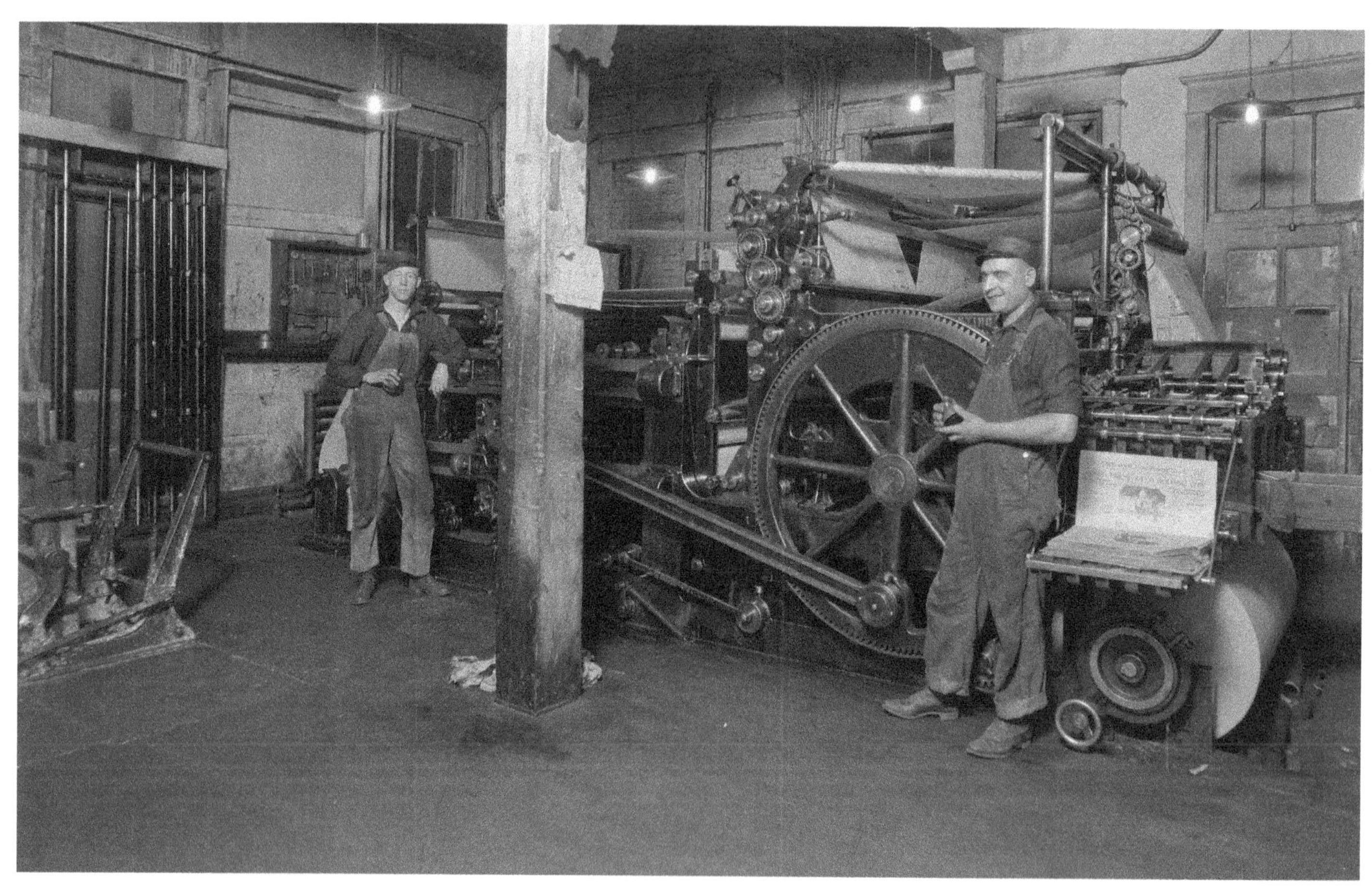

The pressroom of the *Daily Missoulian* is shown here in 1923. Originally called the *Missoula and Cedar Creek Pioneer,* the newspaper has been published continuously since 1870. The Anaconda Copper Mining Company owned the *Missoulian* (and numerous other papers) for 42 years.

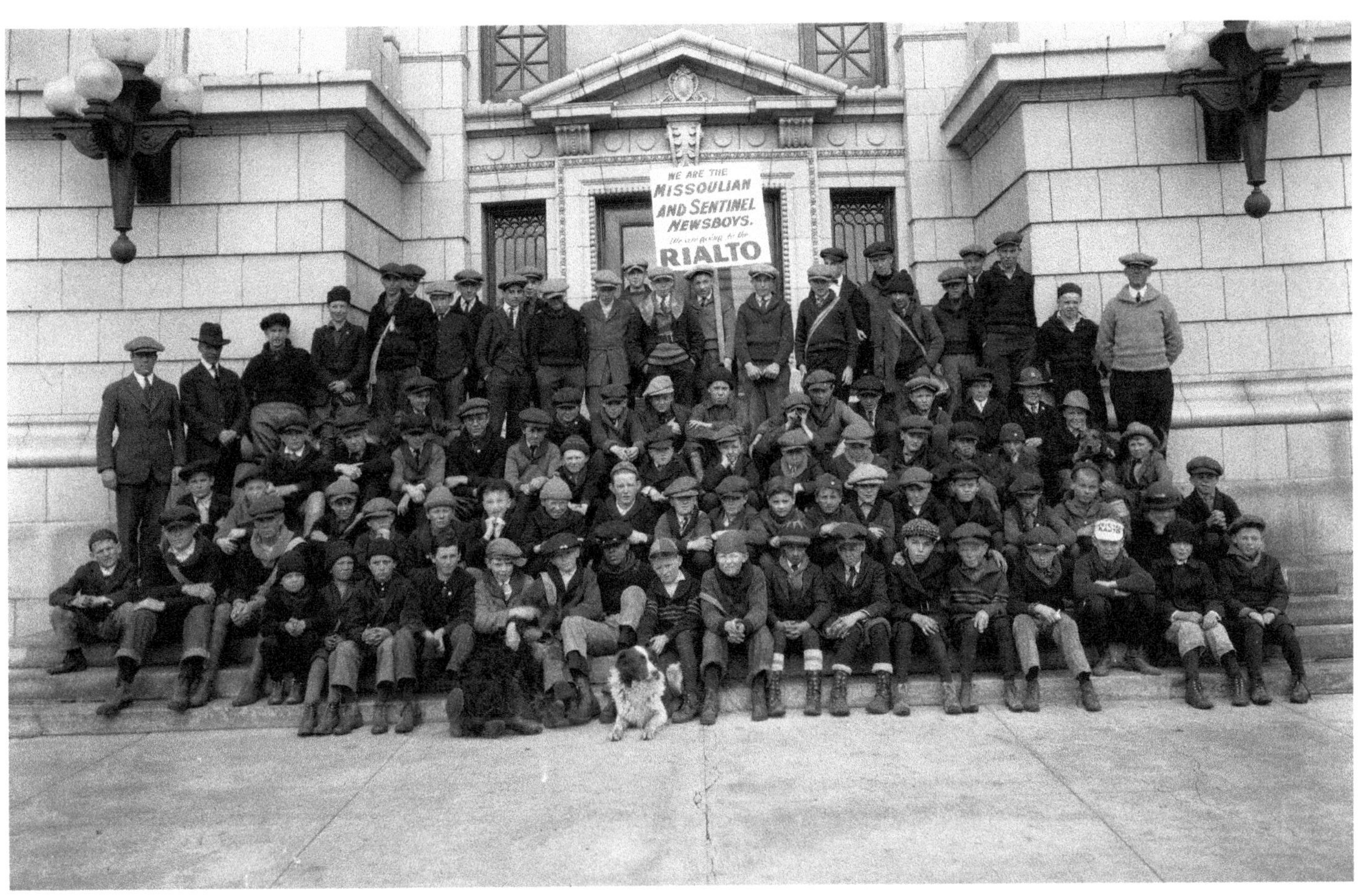

Newsboys for the *Missoulian* and *Sentinel* newspapers pose for a photo on the steps of the Missoula County Courthouse in 1923. These boys could be found hawking newspapers all over downtown, from the Northern Pacific Depot to the Higgins Bridge.

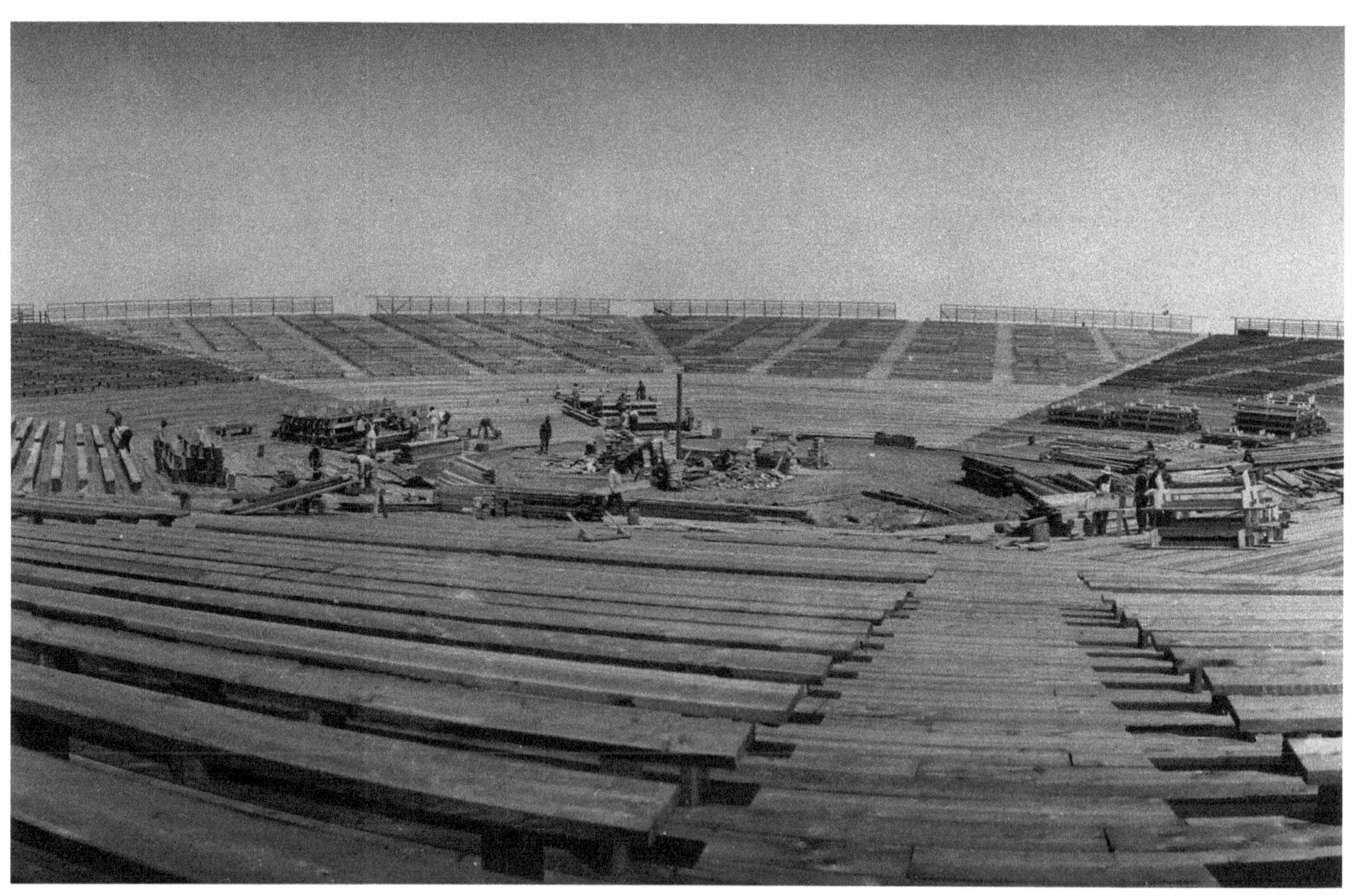

In 1923 boosters in the Shelby area promoted a boxing match starring heavyweight fighters Jack Dempsey and Tommy Gibbons, and this arena was constructed just for the fight. But only 7,000 paying customers showed up for the July 4 bout, and four local banks were ruined.

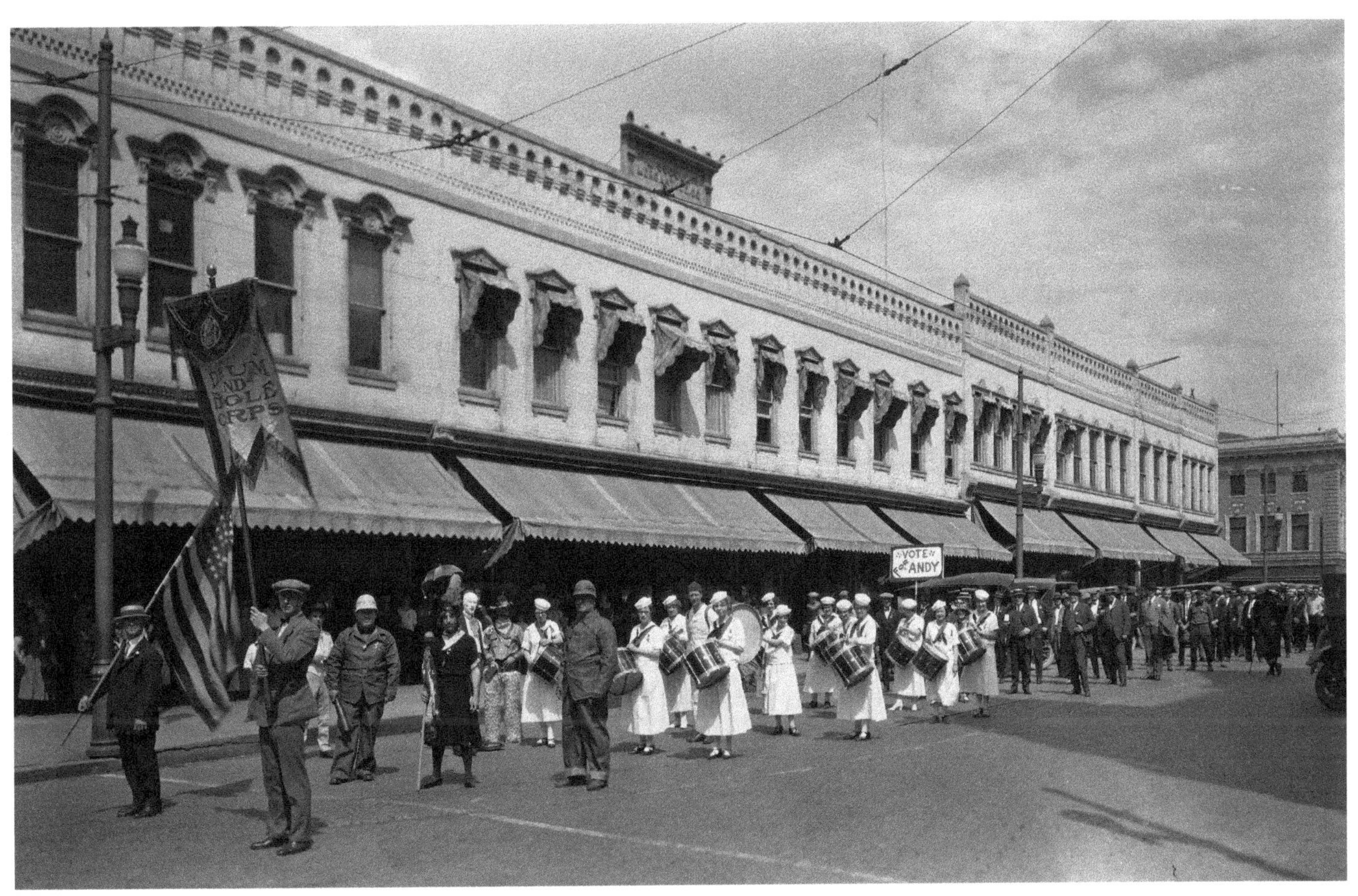

On the day of the annual Missoula Mercantile company picnic in 1924, employees parade past the company store on Higgins Avenue. Founded in 1865, the "Merc" is believed to be the oldest continuously operating retail store west of the Mississippi. It is now owned by Macy's.

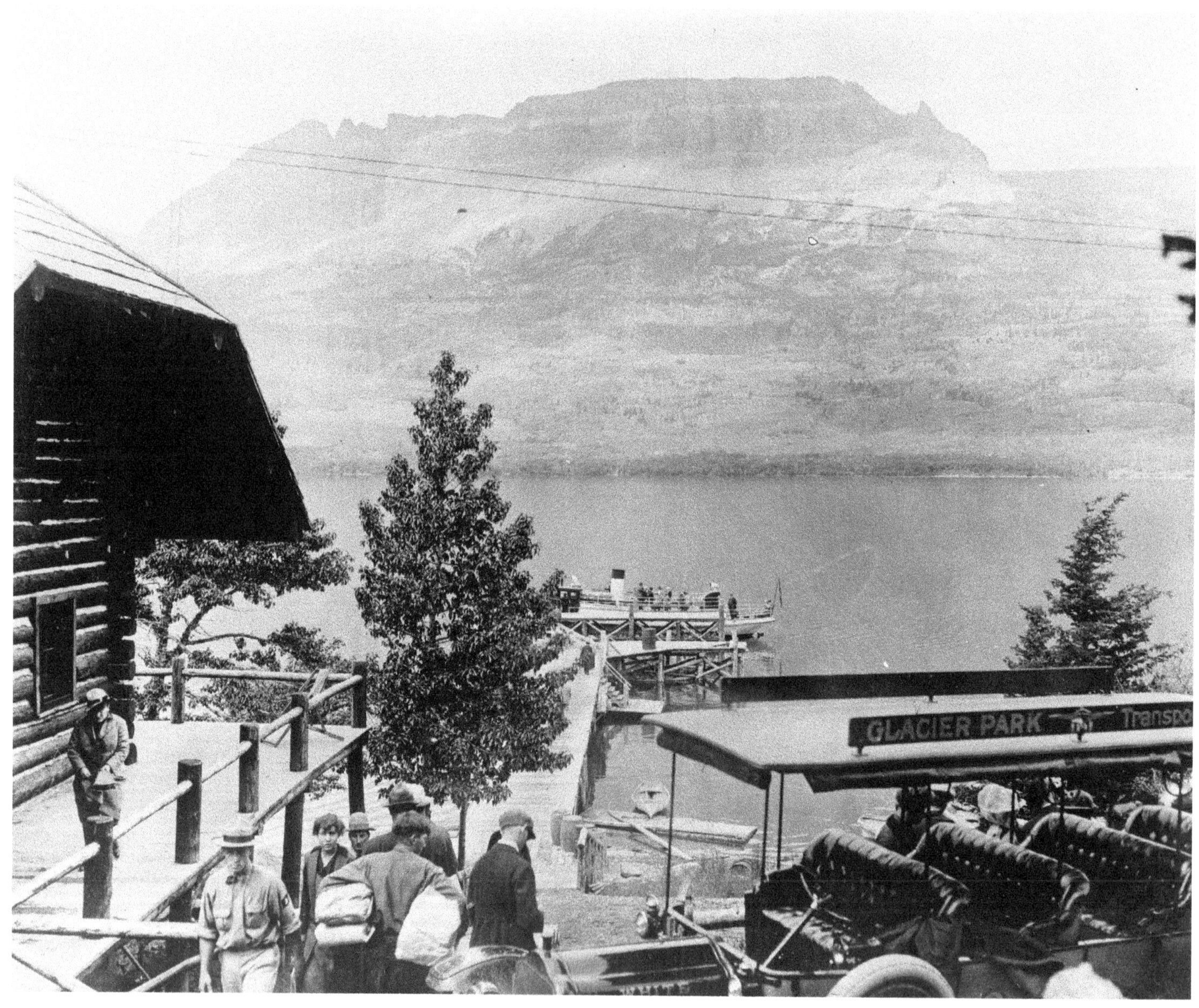

Tourists prepare for a boat tour of one of the many lakes in Glacier National Park. In the foreground sits a forerunner of the "jammers," the buses that ferried tourists over the spectacular roads of the park.

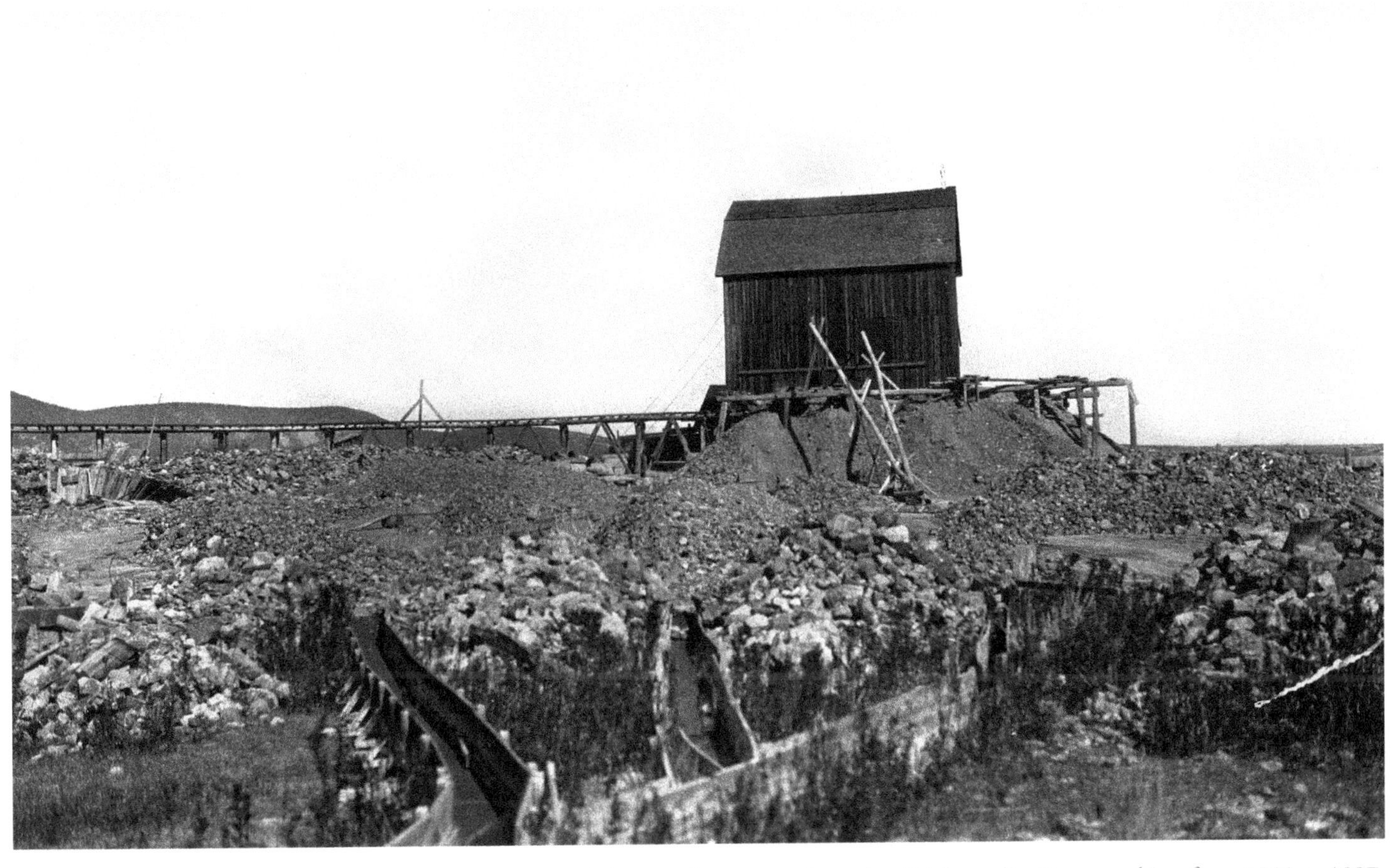

The New Mine Sapphire Syndicate was an English-owned company that mined high-quality Yogo sapphires from 1899 to 1927. Known for their unique color as well as their quality, Yogo sapphires are found along a five-mile-long dike of volcanic rock near Utica. This site was photographed in September 1924.

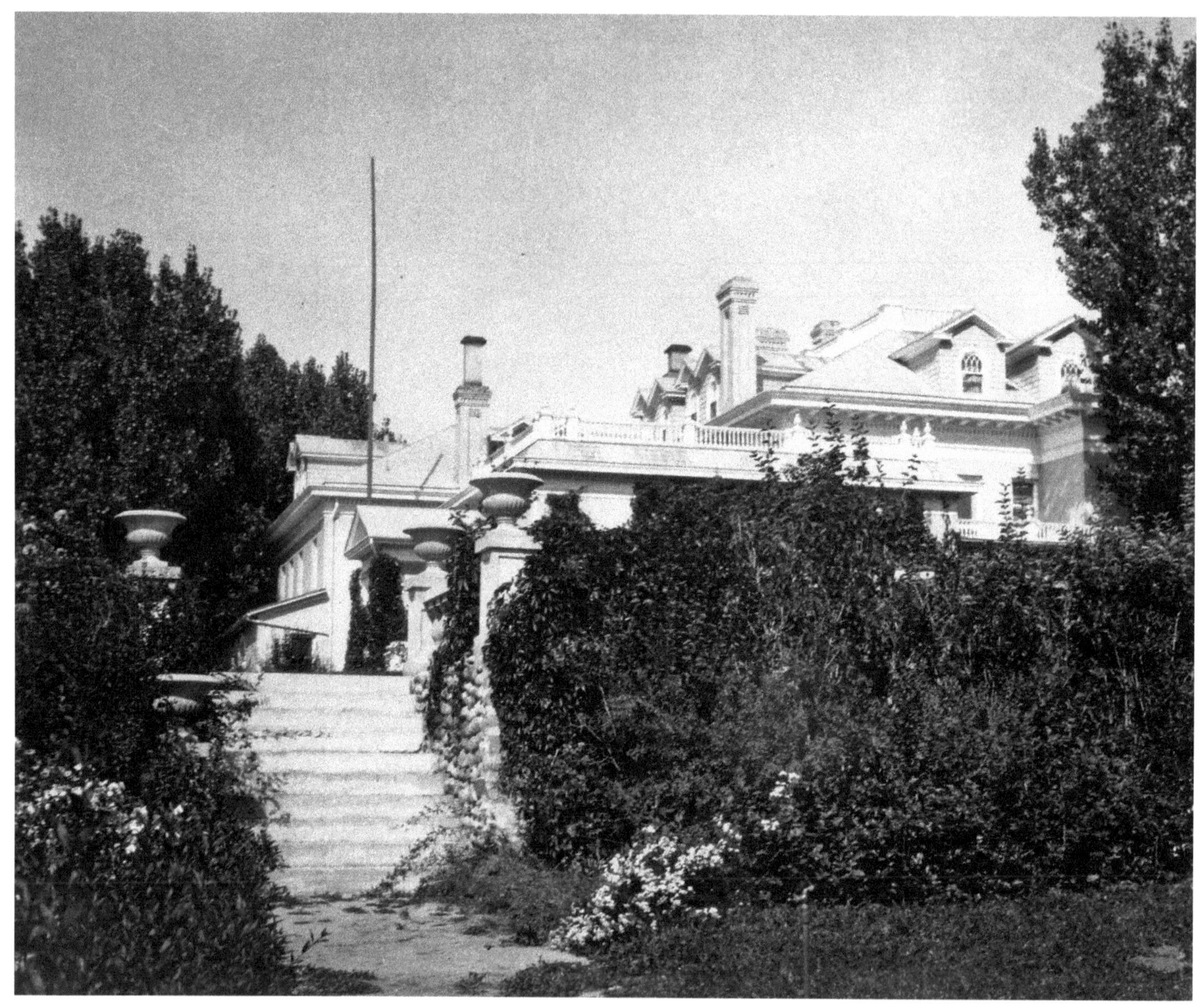

In 1886 copper king Marcus Daly bought a large stock farm near Hamilton. Over the next several decades he undertook an extensive remodeling of the existing farmhouse, and his widow continued with the improvements after Daly's death in 1900. The Daly Mansion, seen here in 1925, is now owned by the state of Montana.

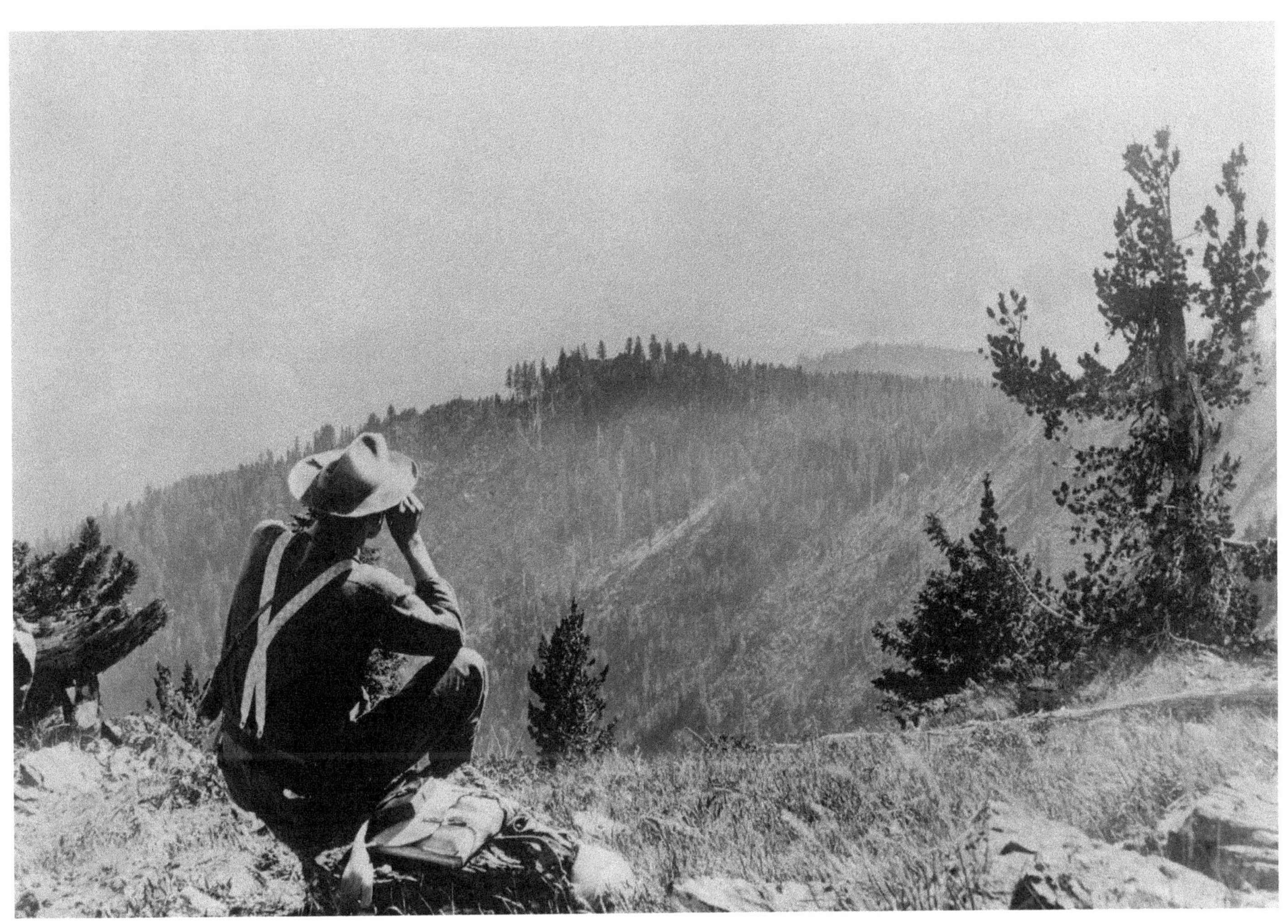

A U.S. Forest Service ranger scans the Clark Fork Valley from the heights of the Mount Silcox lookout, near Thompson Falls.
The Bitterroot Range rises on the far side of the river.

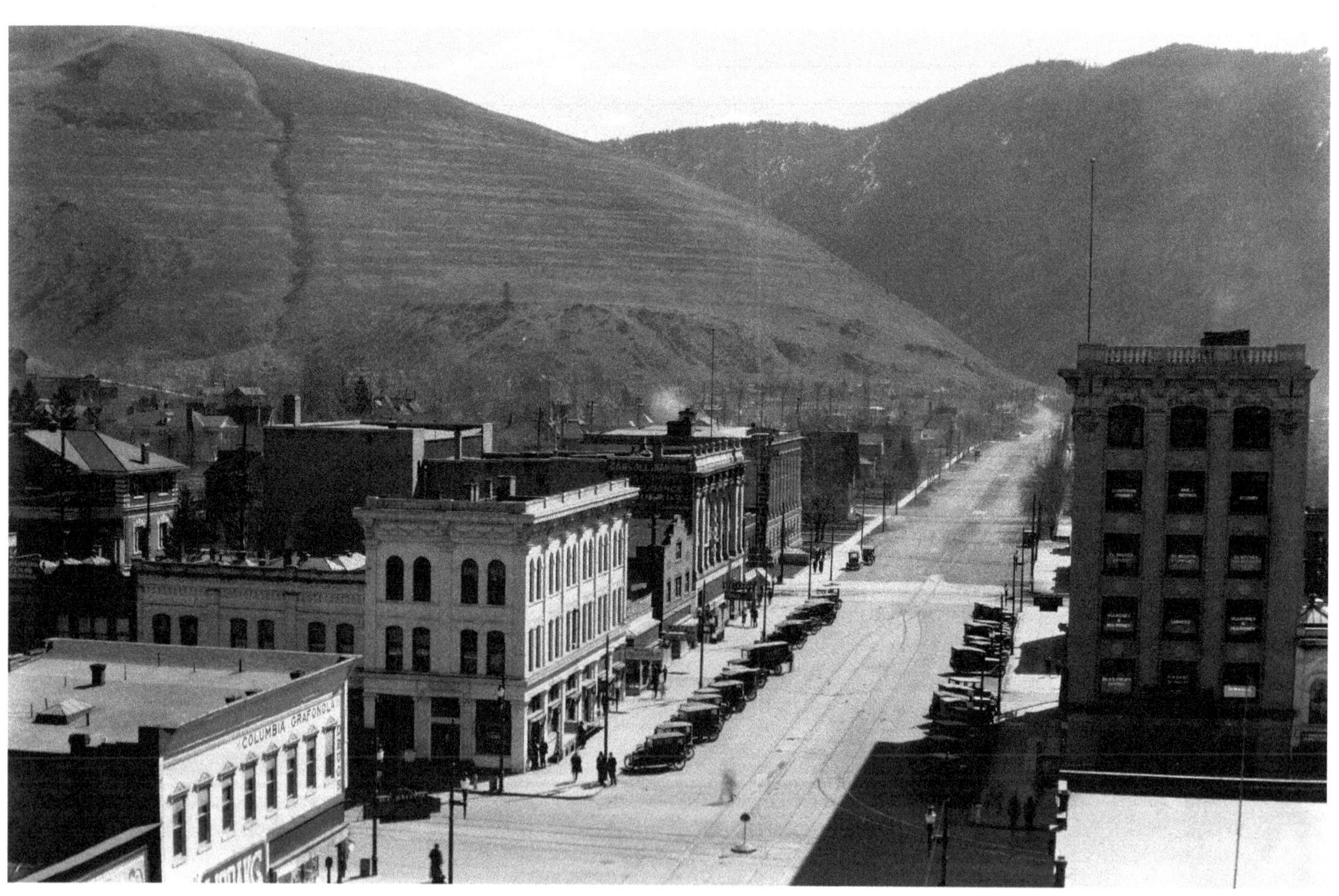

Taken from the roof of the Palace Hotel in Missoula around 1925, this photo shows East Broadway. In the background is Hellgate Canyon, so named because of the frequent Blackfeet ambushes on Salish and Nez Perce that once took place there. Mount Jumbo is on the left, with Mount Sentinel on the right.

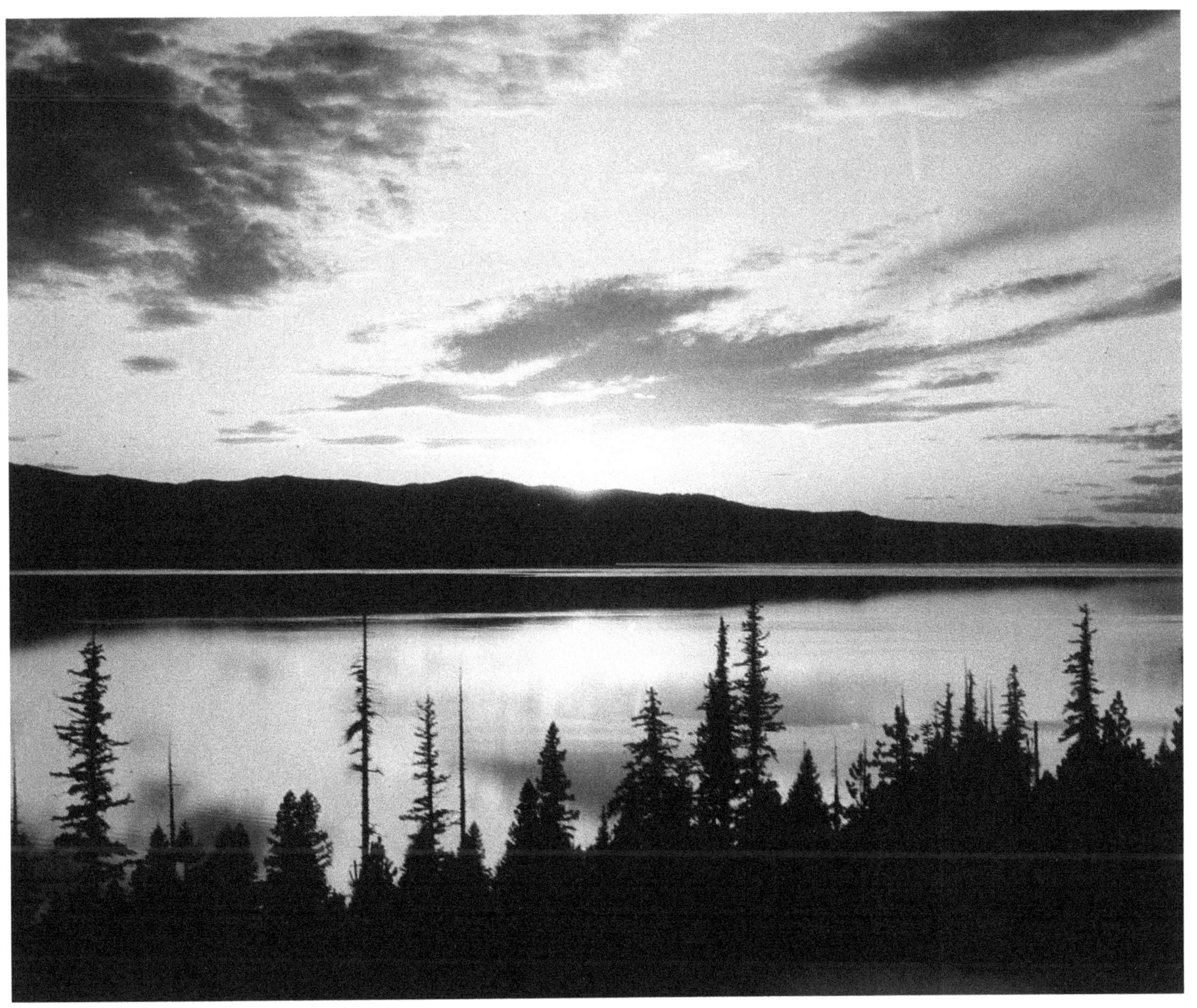

R. H. McKay took this photo of a spectacular sunset over Flathead Lake as viewed from the east shore in June 1927.

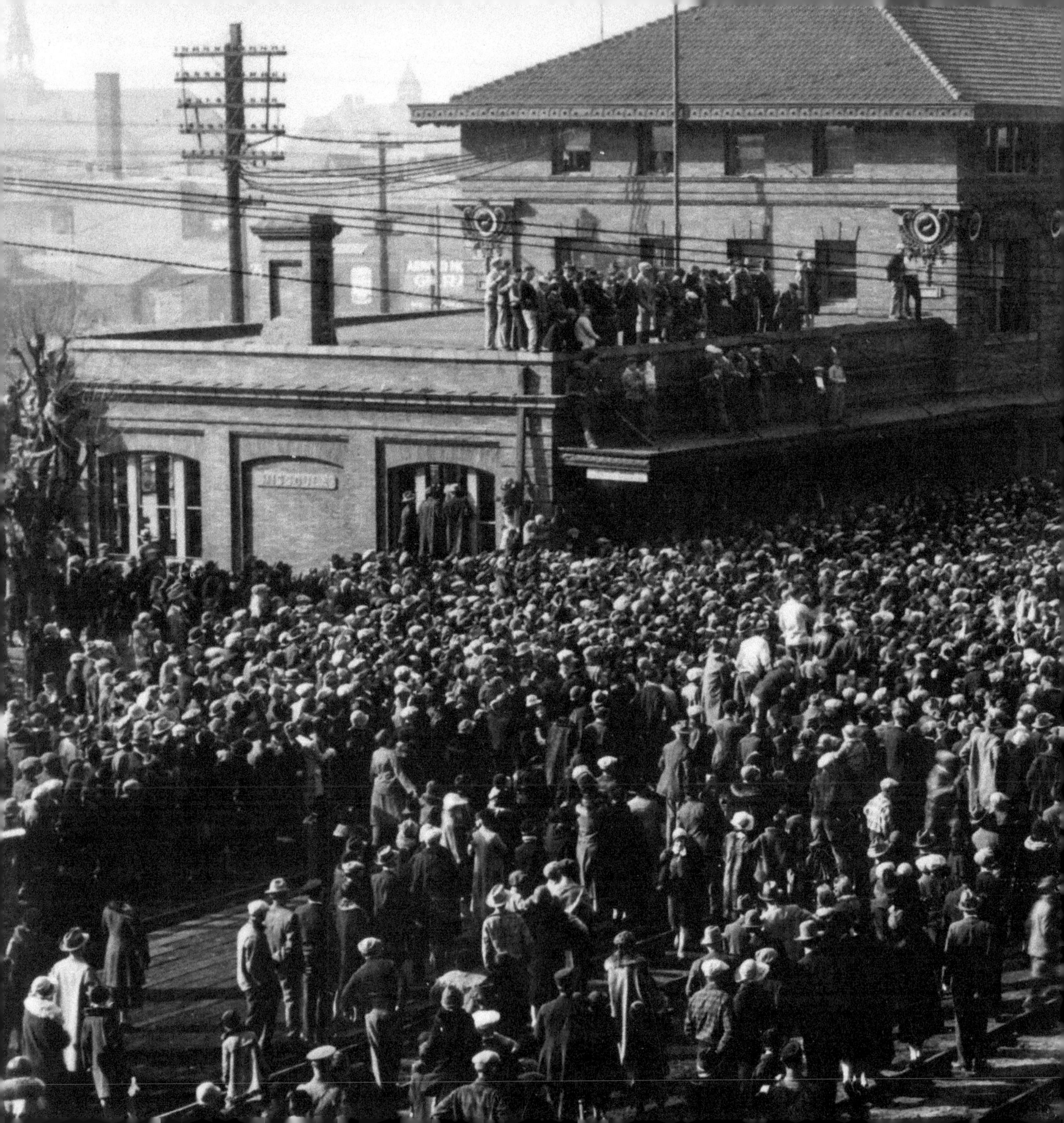
MISSOURI

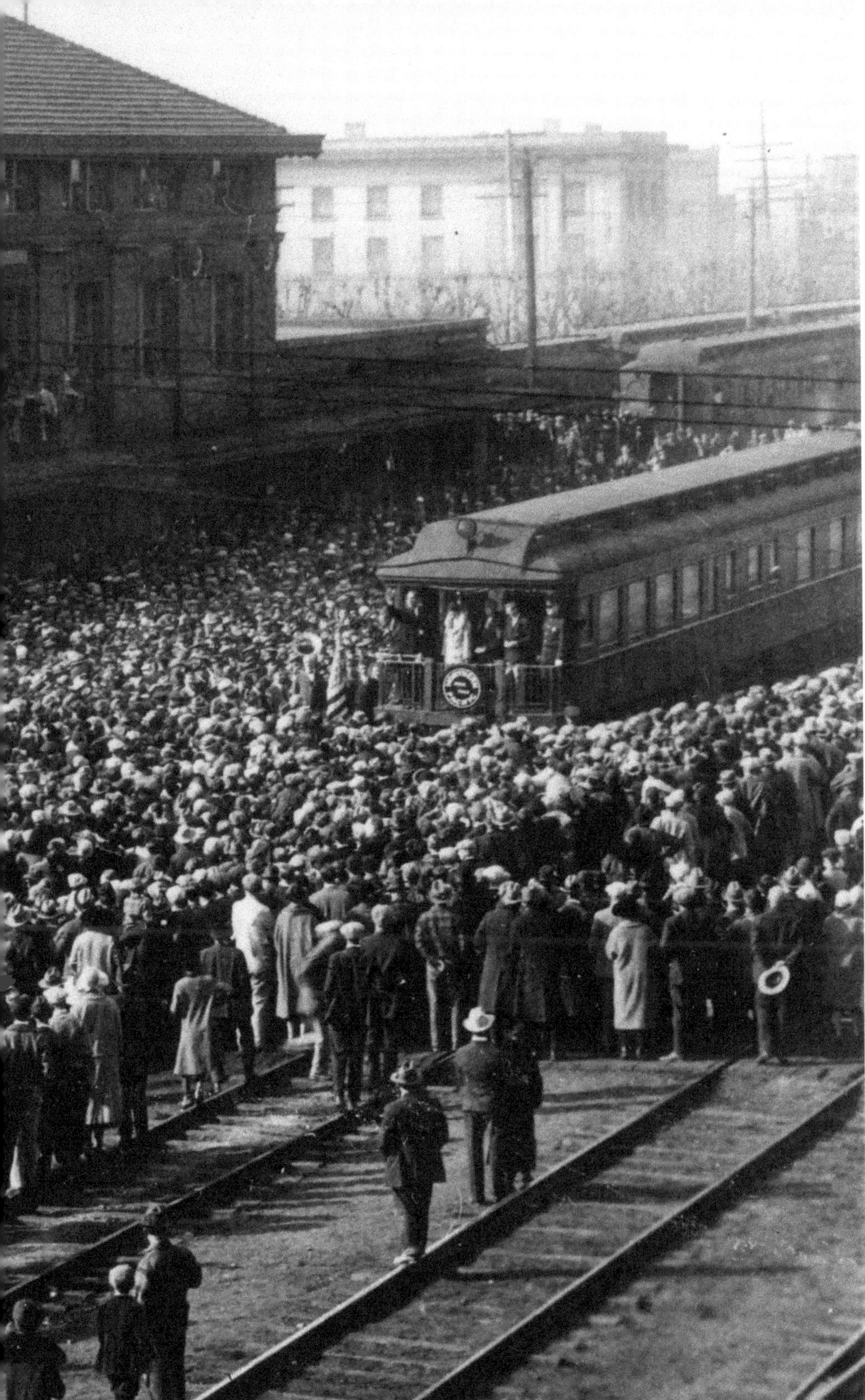

Queen Marie of Romania arrives at Missoula's Northern Pacific Depot in 1926. A granddaughter of Queen Victoria on her father's side and of Czar Alexander II on her mother's side, the English-born princess married the Crown Prince of Romania when she was 17. She authored numerous books during her lifetime.

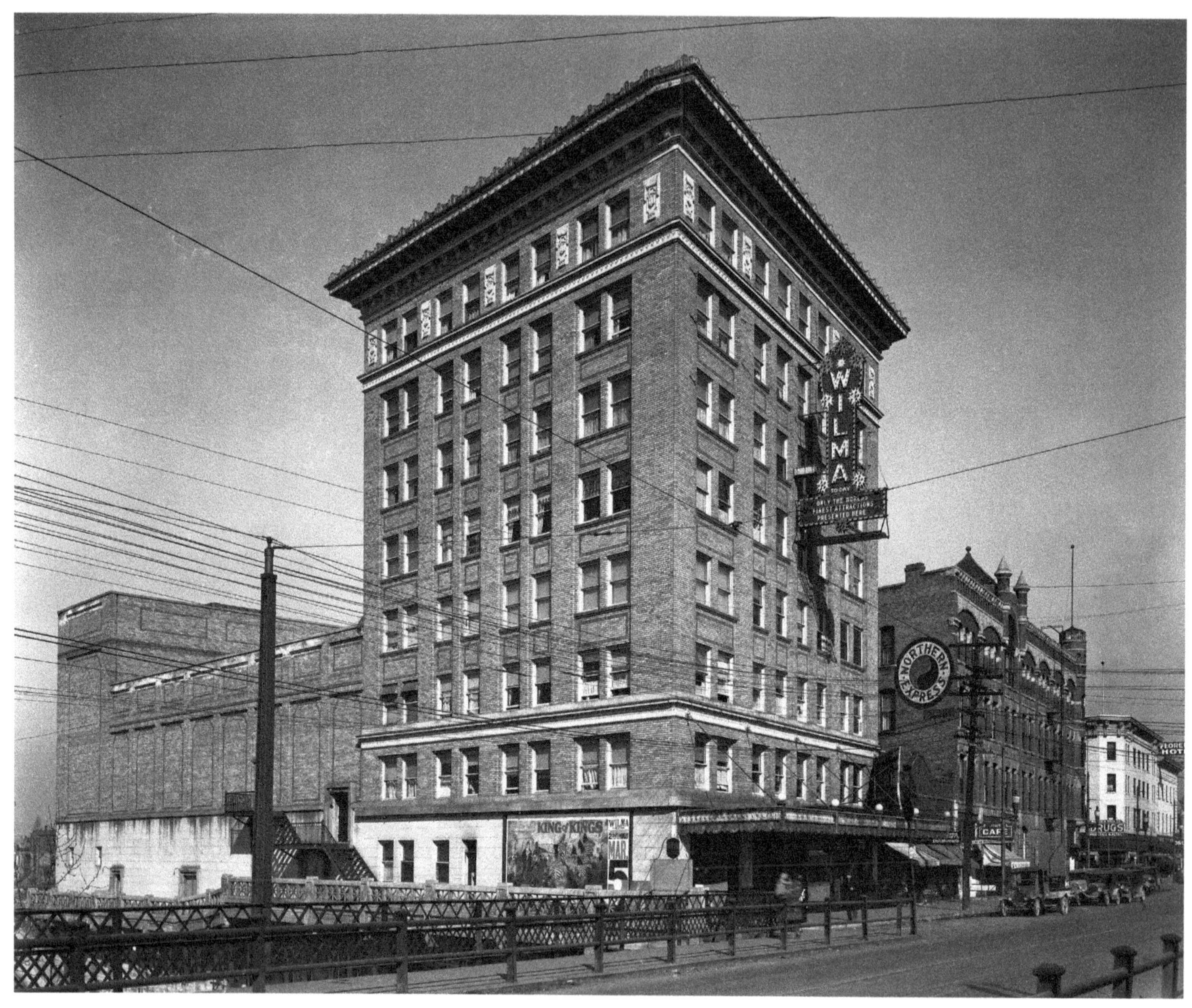

Missoula's Wilma Building is seen here from the Higgins Bridge. At eight stories, the Wilma was the tallest building in western Montana in the 1920s. Besides housing a theater, the building boasted an Olympic-size swimming pool, a restaurant, shops, a dozen apartments, and 50 offices.

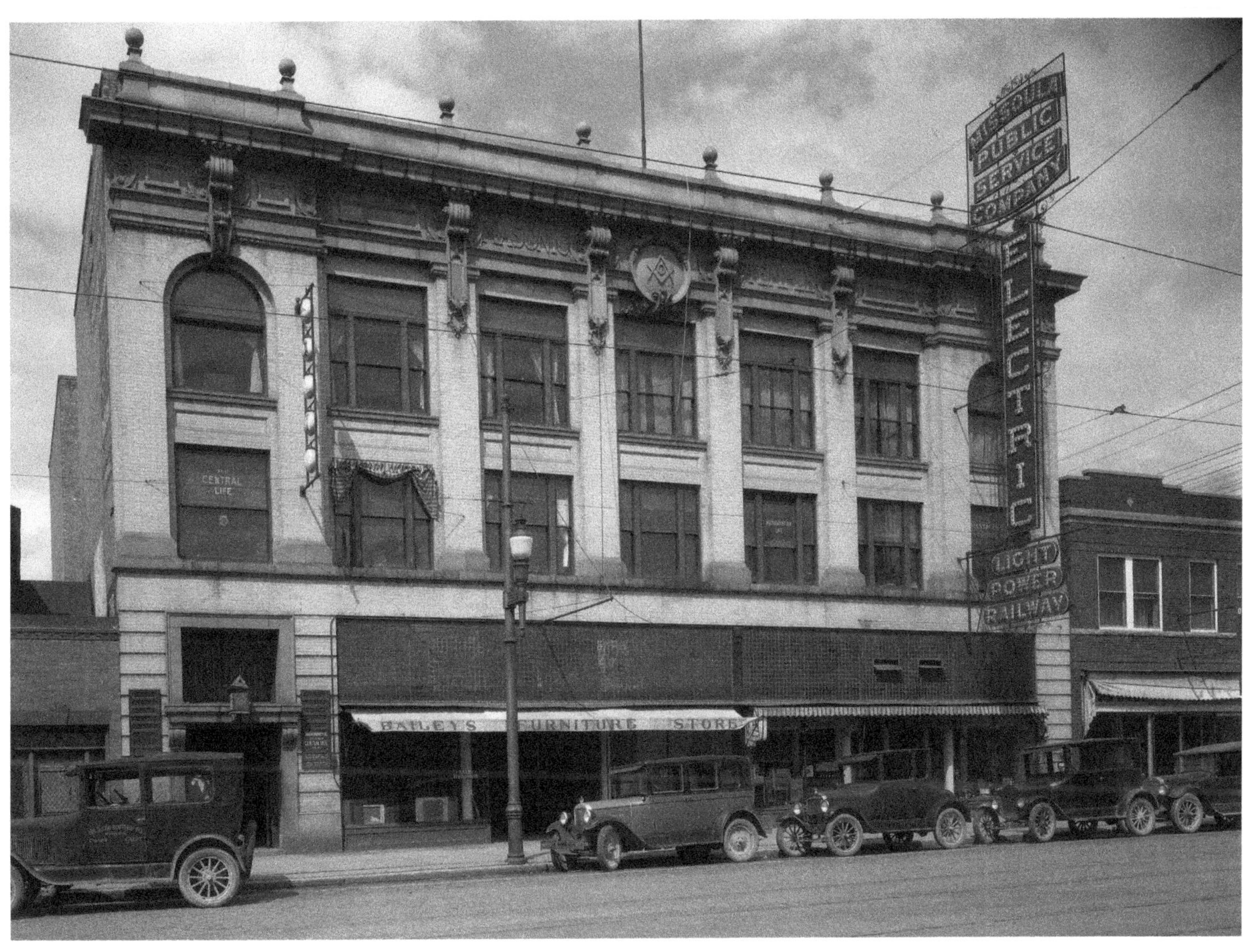

Missoula's ornate Masonic Temple on Broadway was built in 1909 and is seen here in 1928. Beginning in the 1860s, Masons worked to bring law and order and a sense of community to Montana's rough-and-tumble mining camps. The Missoula Public Service Electric Company was once housed in this building.

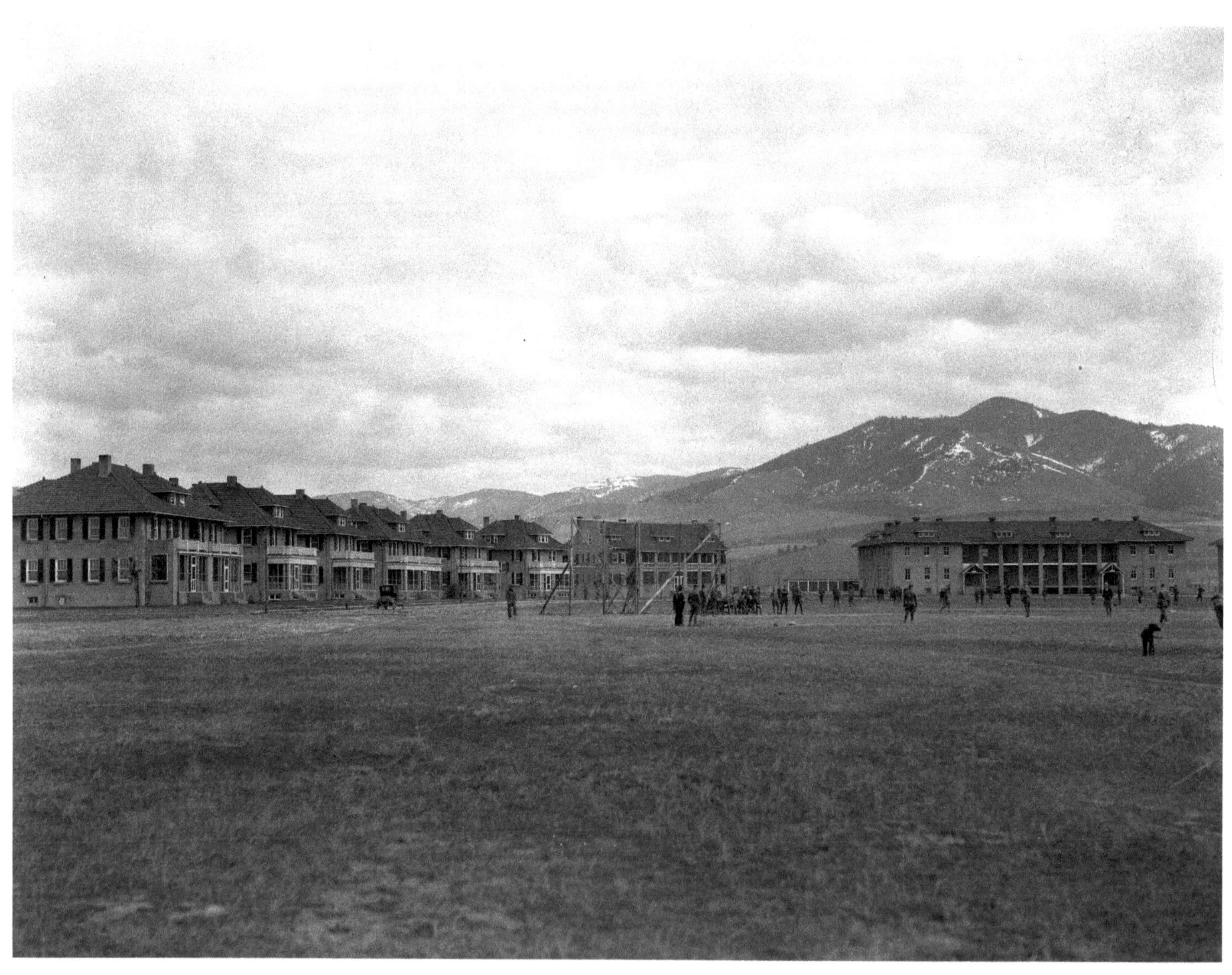

The parade grounds at Fort Missoula doubled as a baseball field in this October 1931 view. Officer's Row is at left, while one of the enlisted men's barracks buildings is at right. Mount Dean Stone rises in the background. Officer's Row is now home to various nonprofit groups.

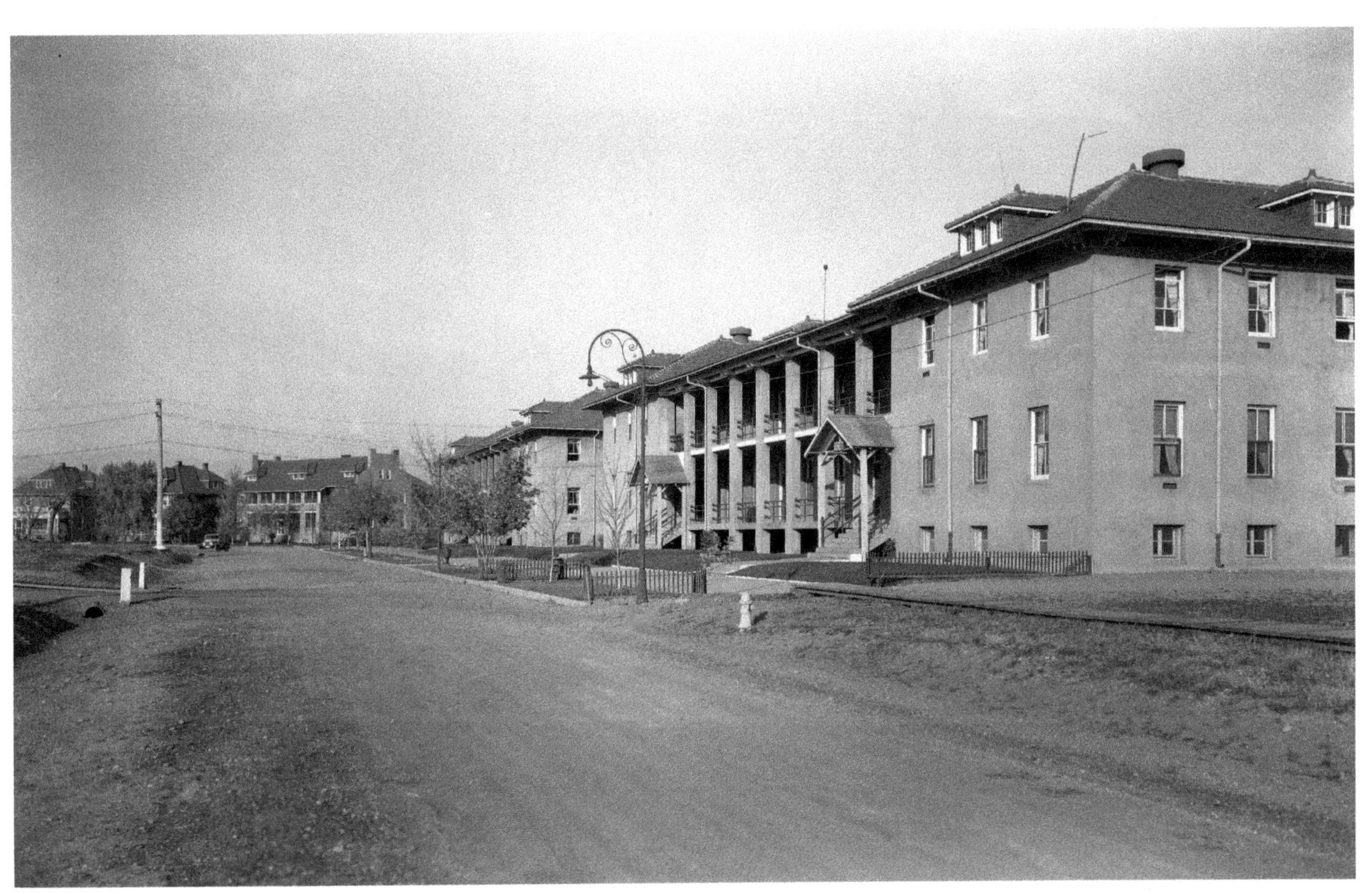

This 1931 view of the enlisted men's barracks at Fort Missoula looks north toward Officer's Row. During the 1930s the fort was home to a battalion of the 4th Infantry Regiment and also served as regional headquarters of the Civilian Conservation Corps.

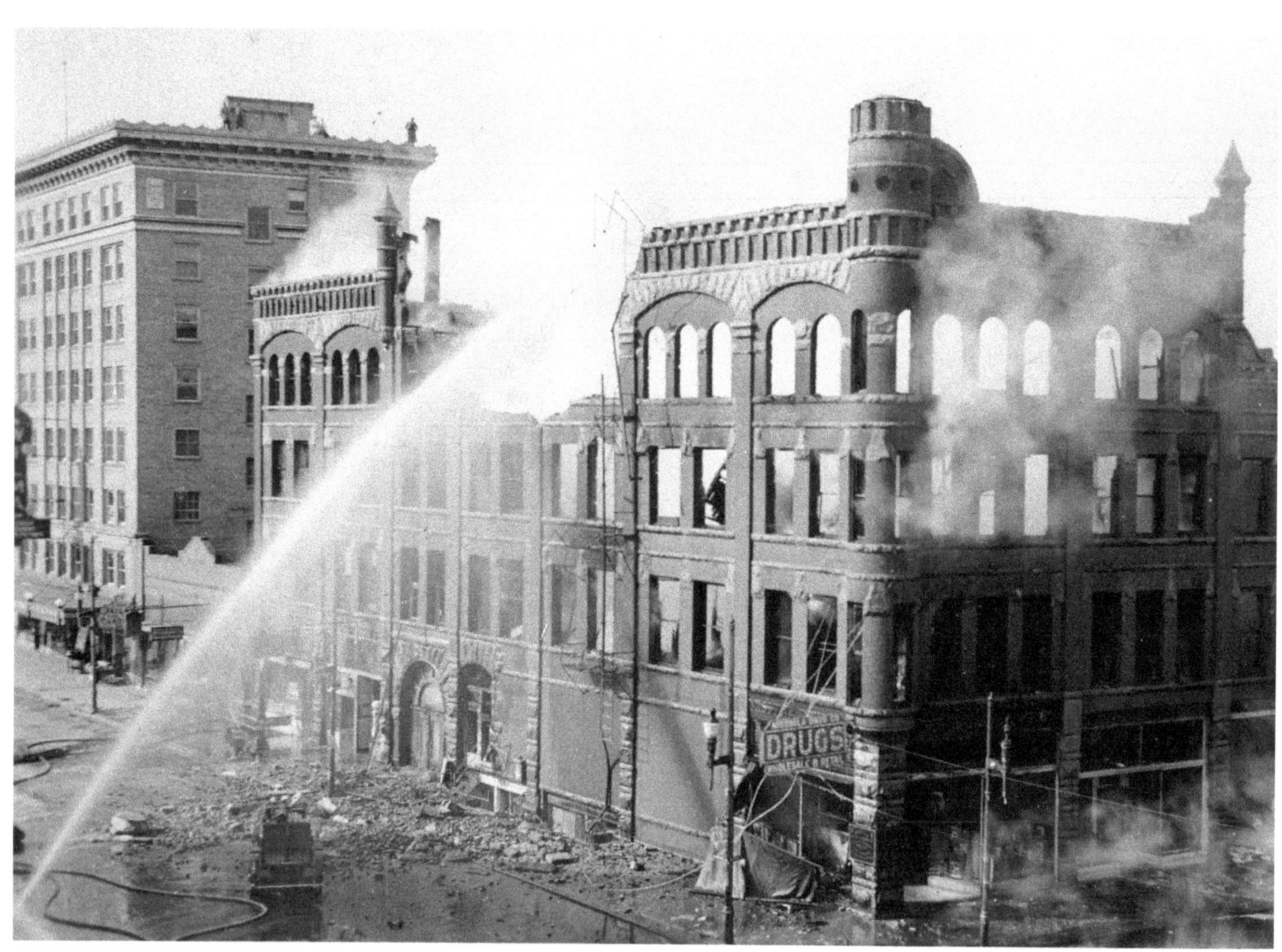

The castlelike Hammond Building in Missoula was destroyed by fire in 1932. The building served as headquarters for Andrew Hammond, a business rival of Marcus Daly and C. P. Higgins. Hammond built the nation's largest sawmill at Bonner and controlled the Missoula Mercantile, the Hotel Florence, and the First National Bank.

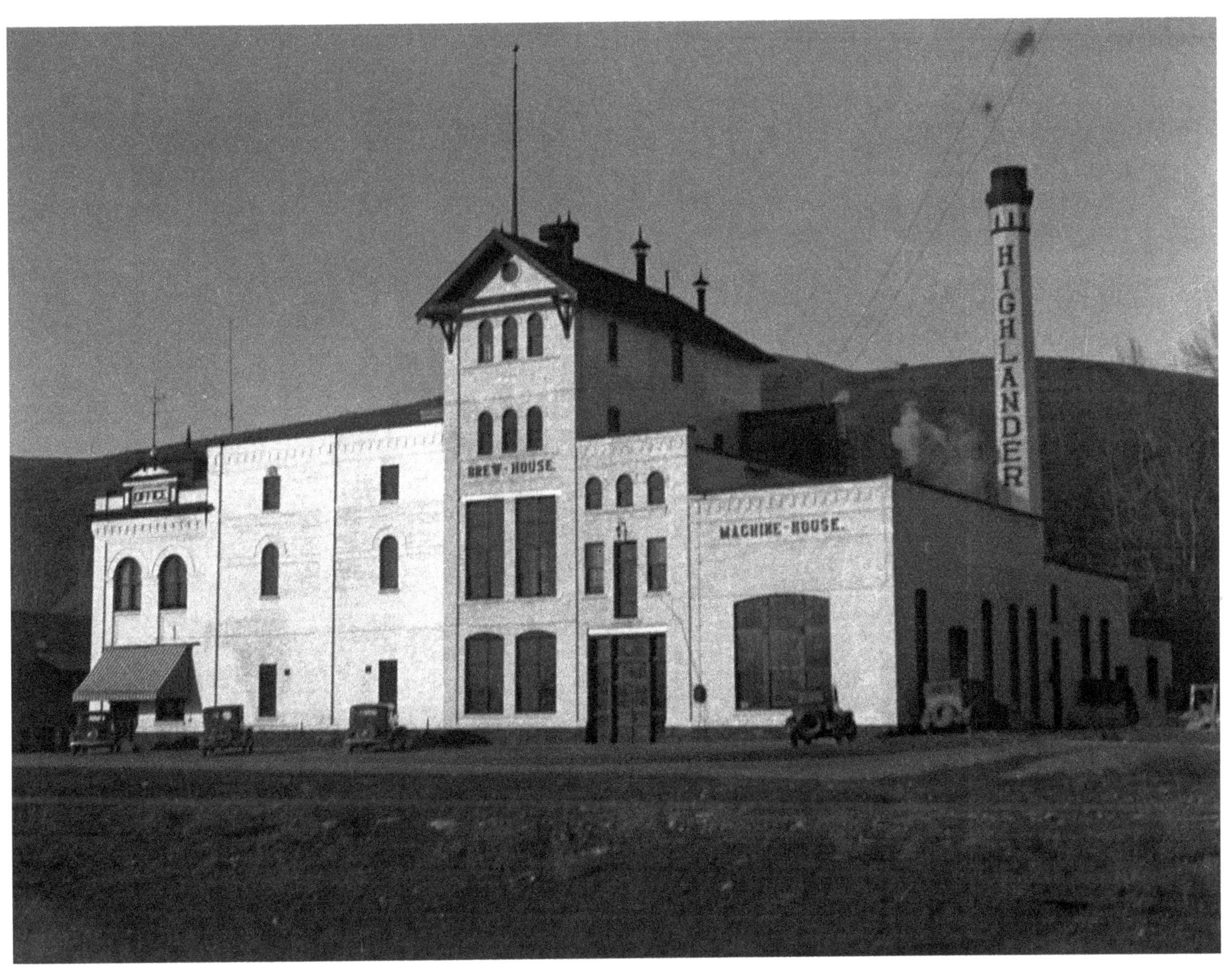

The Garden City Brewing Company was built in 1894 at the base of Waterworks Hill in Missoula. State Prohibition closed the brewery in 1918, but operations resumed in 1933 with the production of Highlander Beer. The brewery closed in 1964 to make room for the interstate highway.

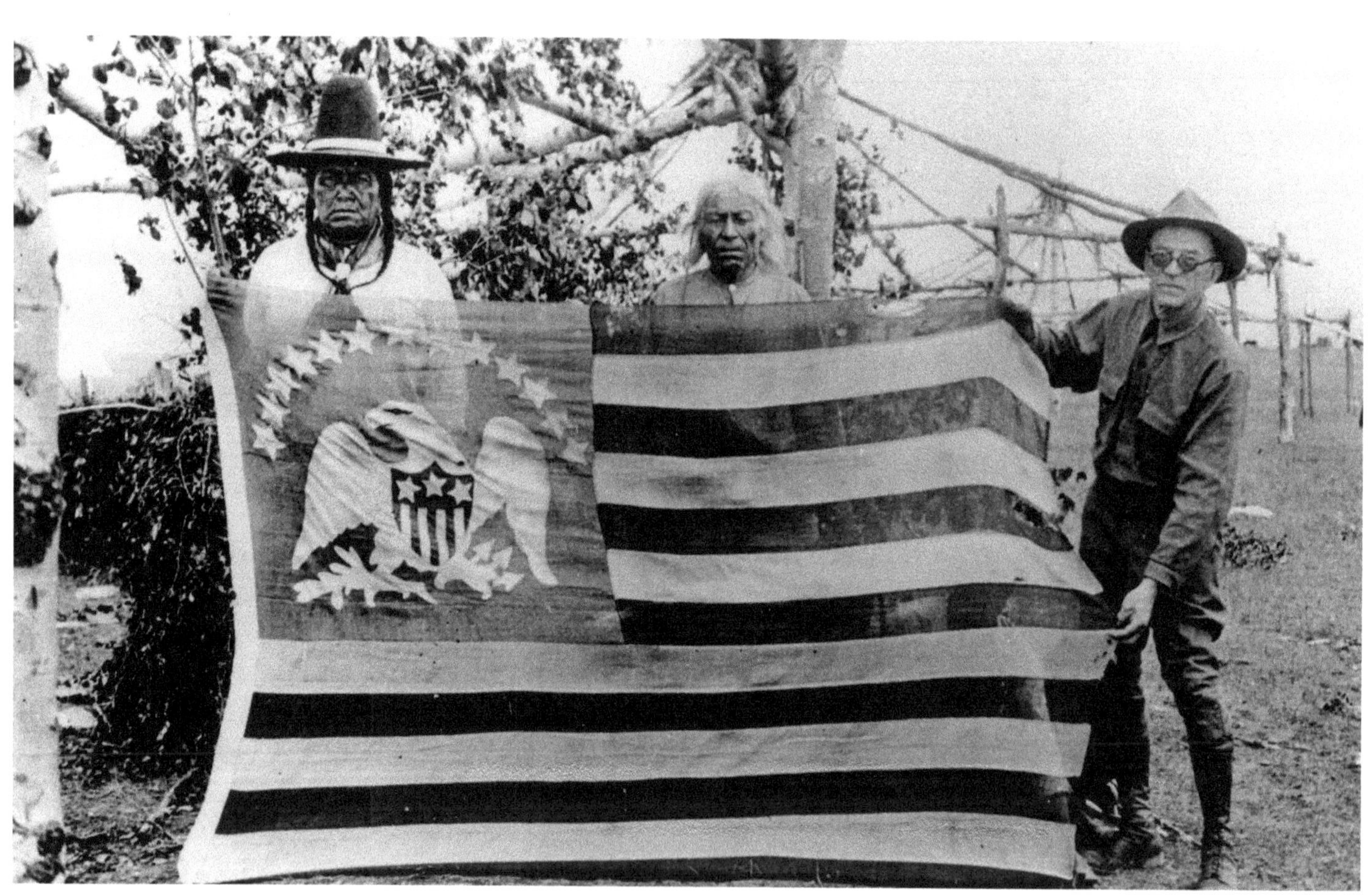

Loud Thunder (Jim Gopher), at center, displays the antique flag bearing the 13 stars of the original colonies that had been passed down through generations of his family. Frank B. Linderman, author of the book *Indian Why Stories,* stands at right in this 1933 photograph.

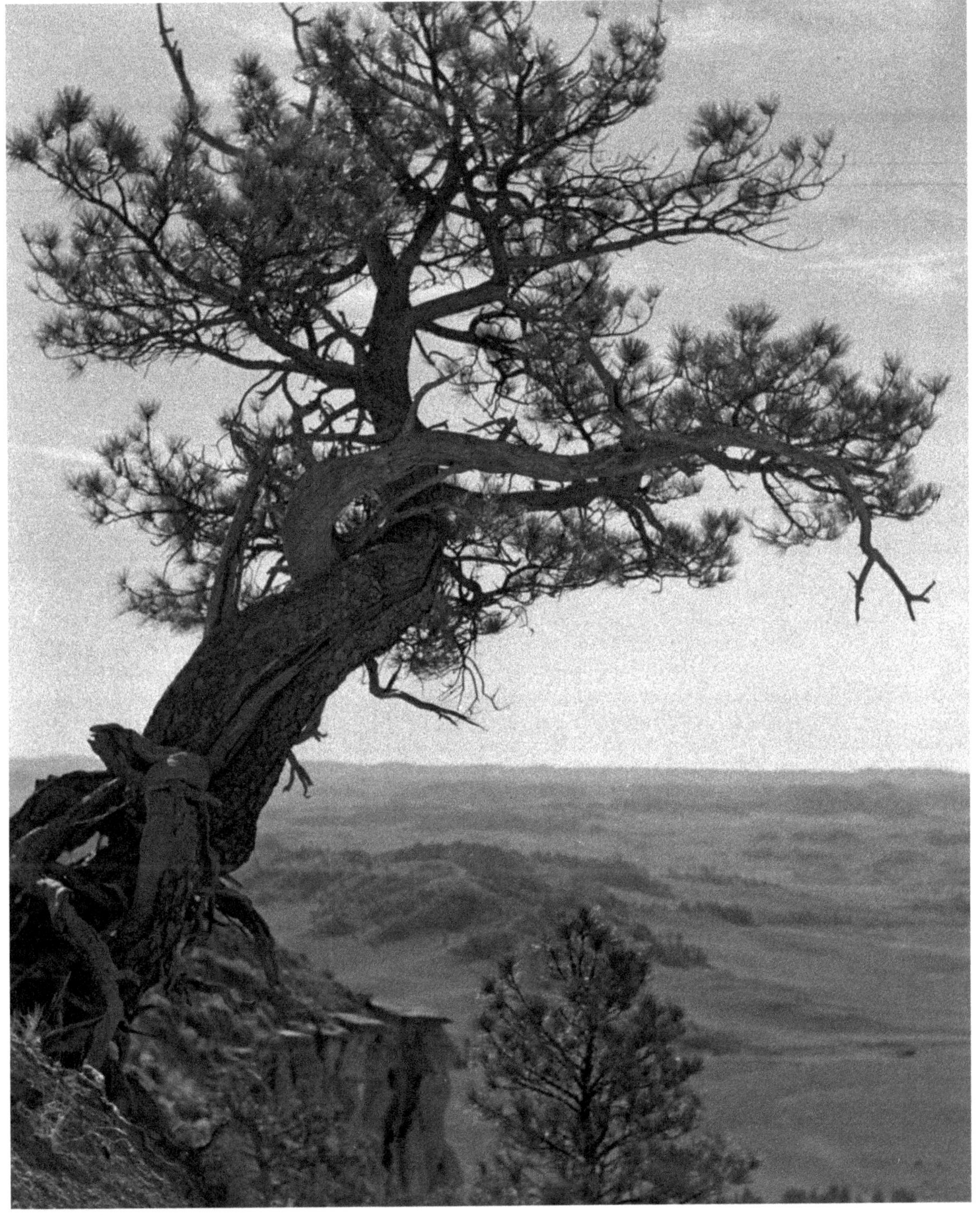

A twisted pine stands sentinel over the Beaver Creek area of the Custer National Forest in this 1934 image by the prolific photographer Kenneth D. Swan. Swan worked for the U.S. Forest Service and was instrumental in convincing the general public of the beauty and value of national forests.

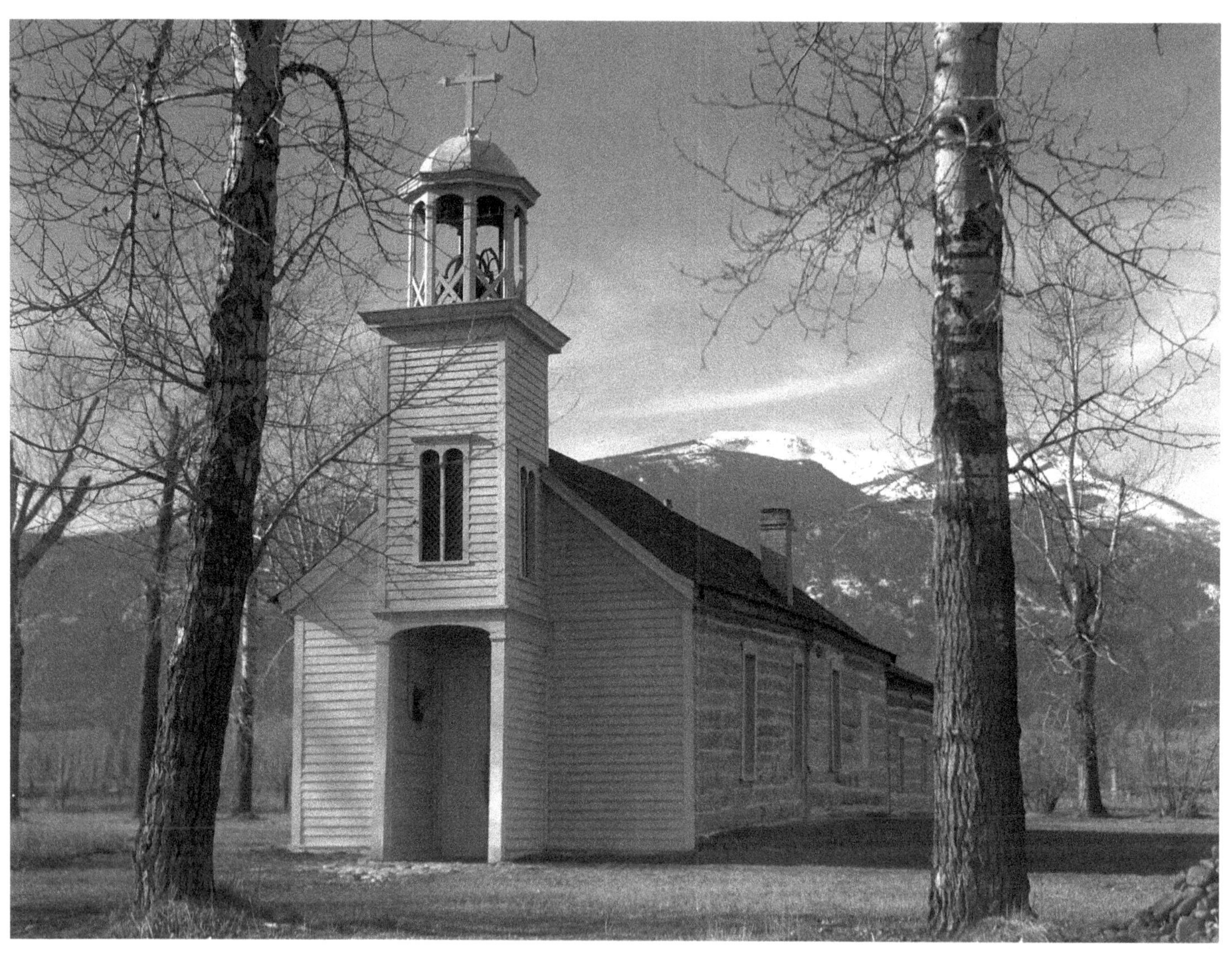

At the request of the Salish Indians, Father DeSmet and other Jesuits arrived in the Bitterroot Valley in 1841 and began construction on St. Mary's Mission. Stevensville, the state's first town, grew up around the mission. This view is from 1934.

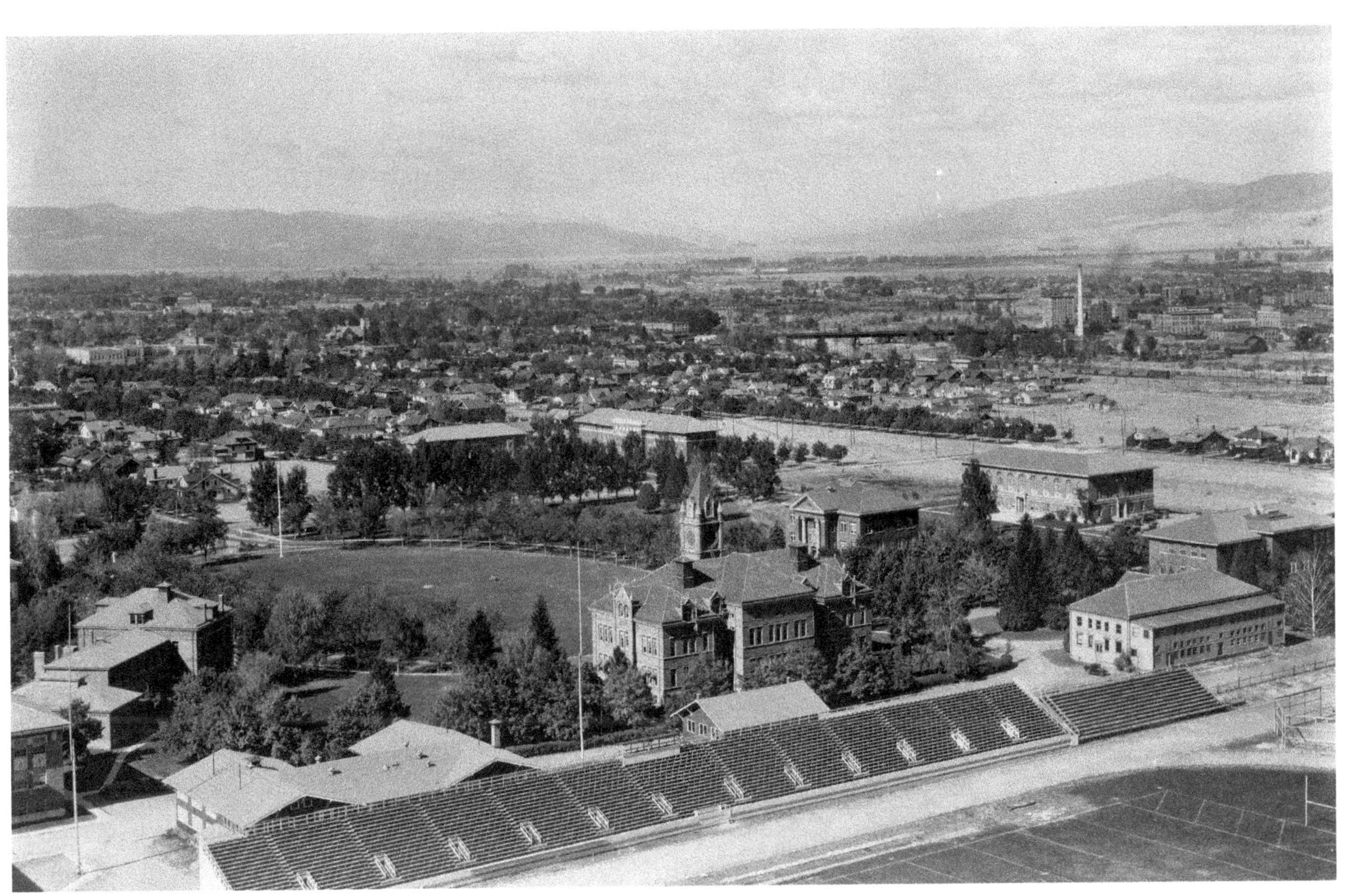

R. H. McKay snapped this photo of Missoula from Mount Sentinel in 1936. The University of Montana campus sits in the foreground. The Mansfield Library and University Center have since replaced the sports stadium seen here.

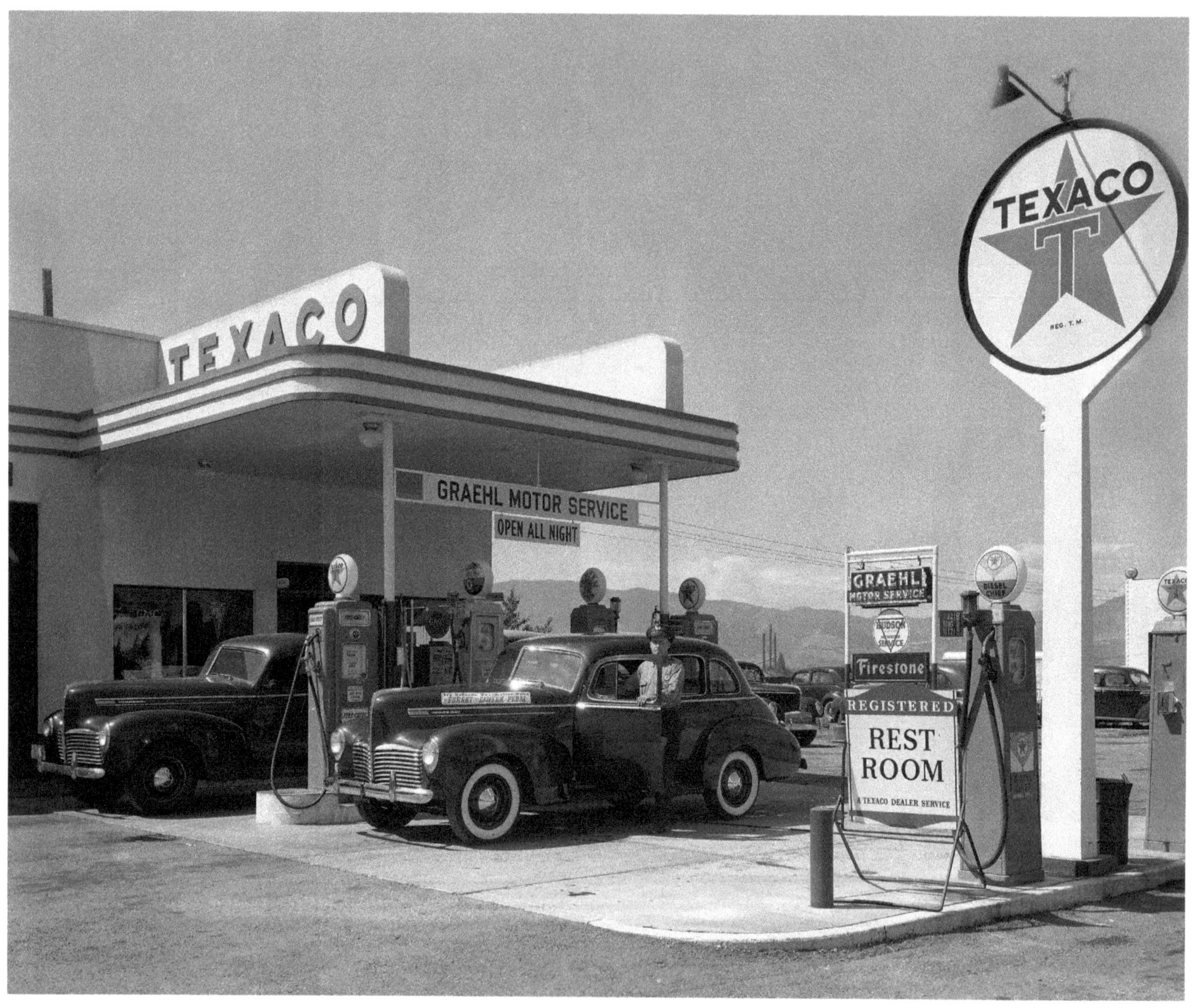

The Graehl Motor Service Texaco station in Missoula sold Hudson automobiles as well as gasoline. After the first Texaco station opened in 1911, the brand spread quickly across the country, with standardized signs, brochures, and advertisements.

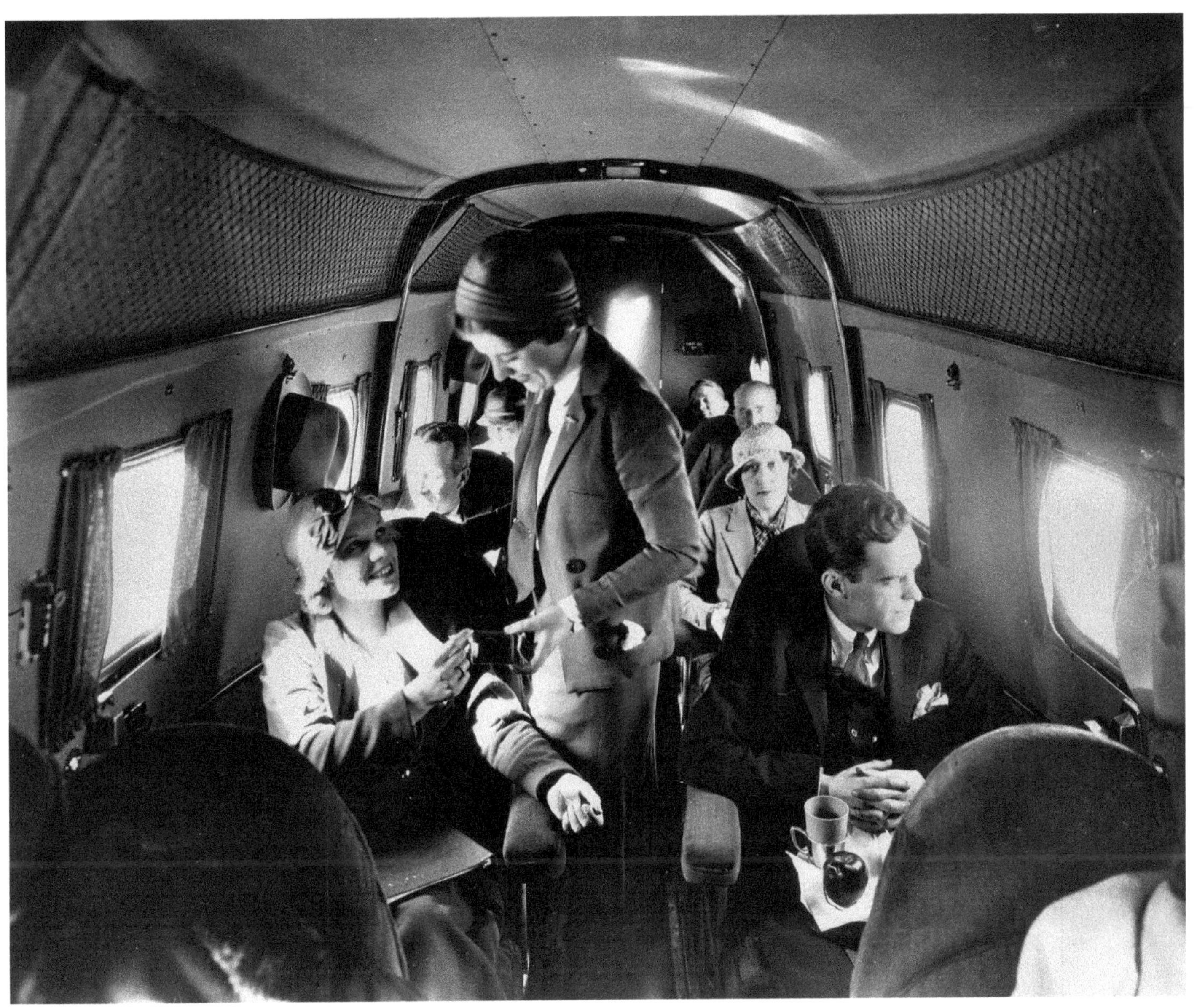

Northwest Airlines began regular service to Billings, Glendive, Miles City, Helena, Butte, and Missoula in 1933. This 1936 photo shows passengers aboard an early airliner at the Missoula airport.

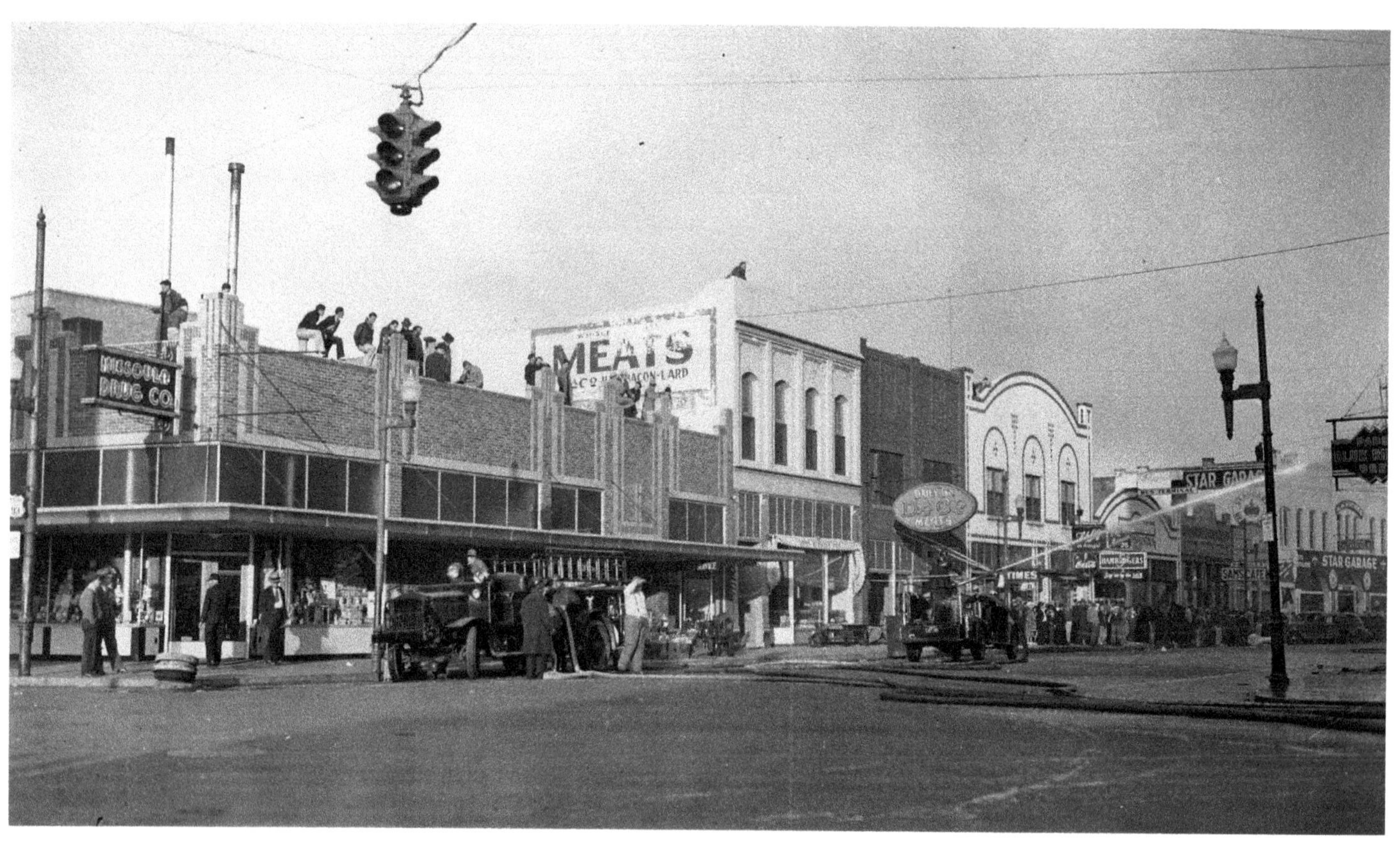

A Missoula crowd gathers at the corner of Higgins and Front streets to watch fire fighters attack the flames engulfing the Hotel Florence on September 26, 1936. The building was reduced to a hole filled with blackened rubble and remained so for a number of years. The Florence had burned once before, in 1912.

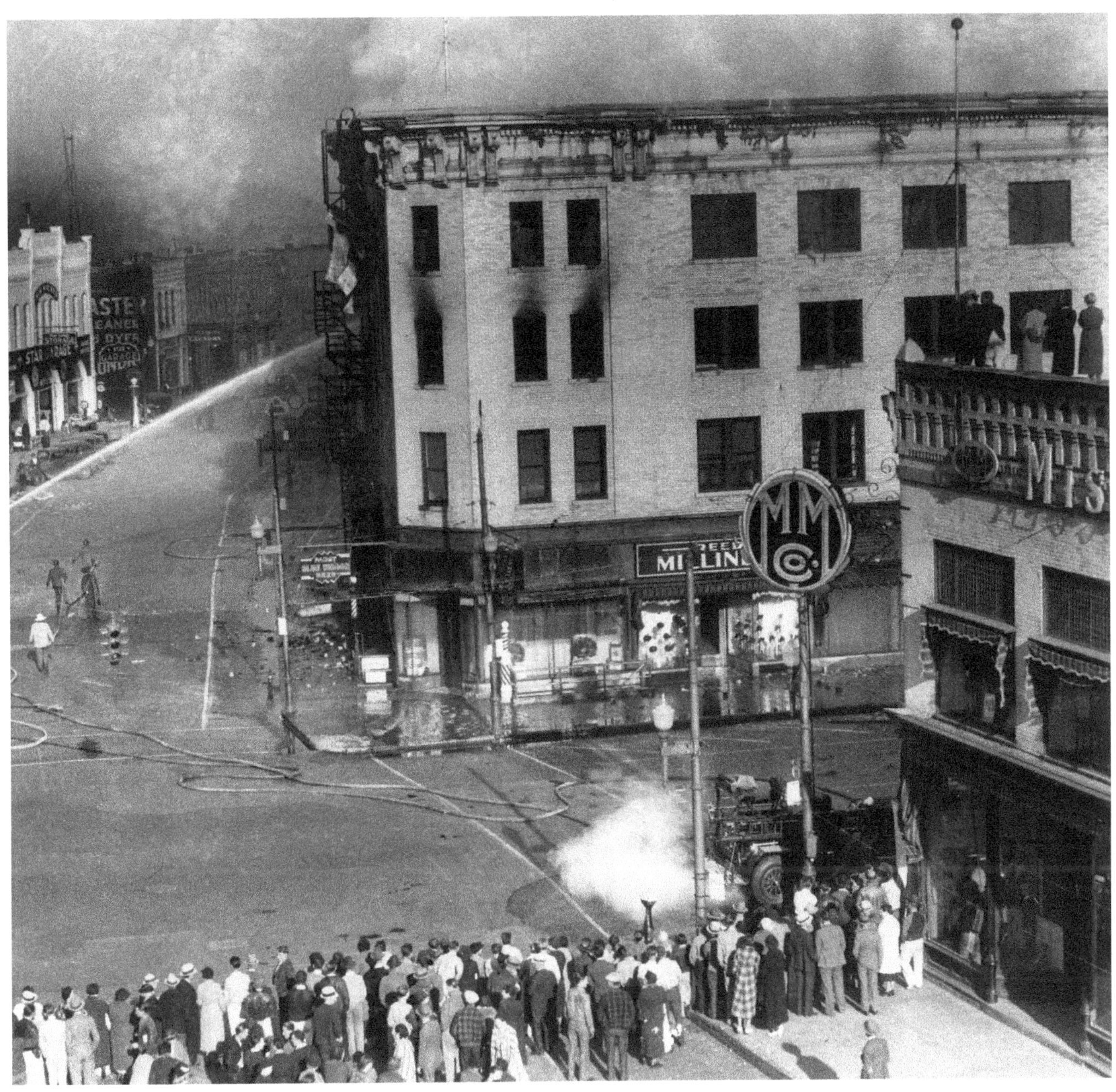

A crowd of onlookers gives the fire fighters room to work as they battle unsuccessfully to save the Hotel Florence. Five years after the 1936 fire, a new Hotel Florence was erected on the same site with financial backing from the owners of the Missoula Mercantile, located across the street.

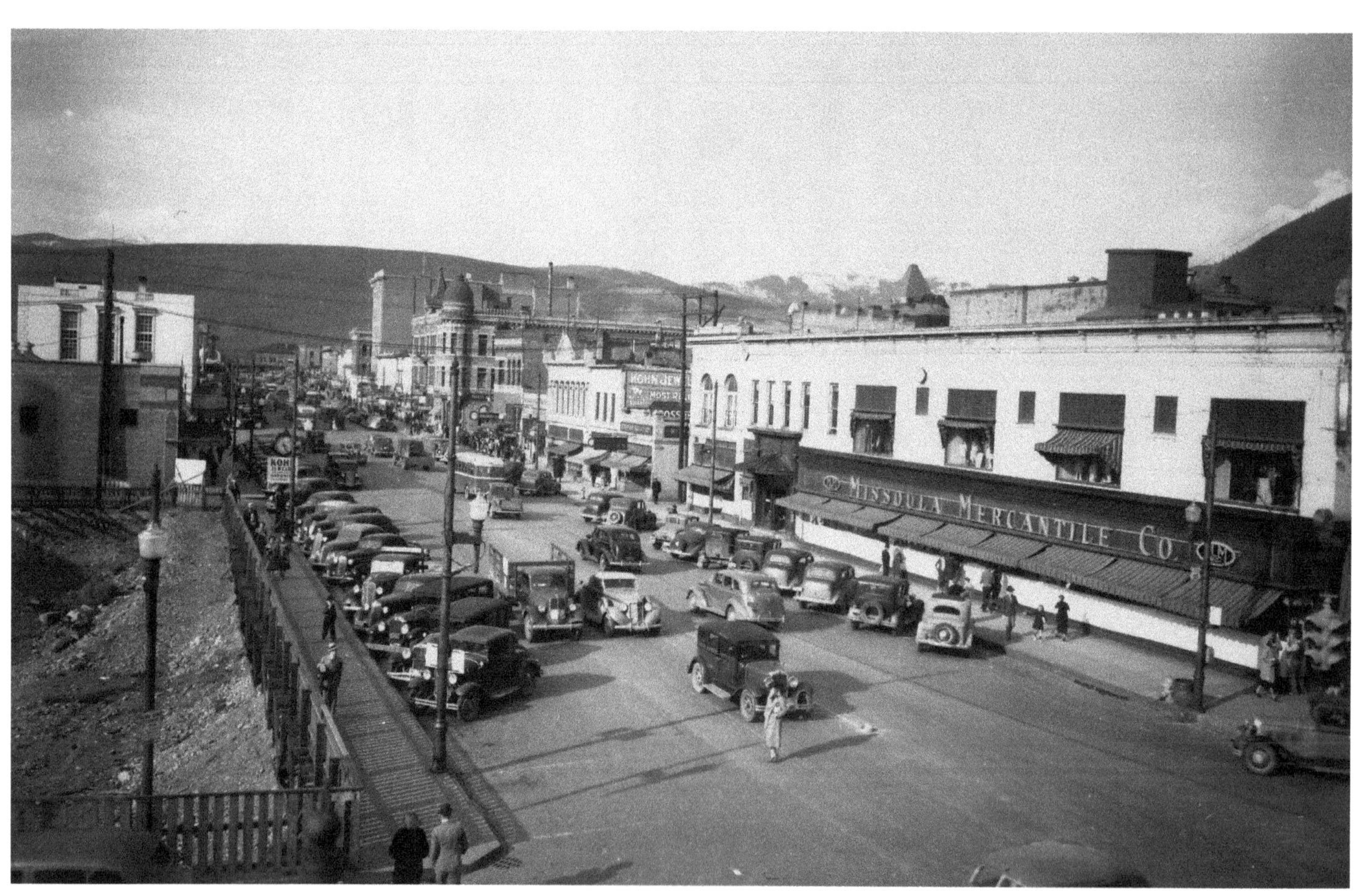

This view of the Missoula Mercantile and North Higgins Street was taken in the late 1930s. The remains of the burned-out Hotel Florence can be seen at left. W. H. McLeod of the Missoula Mercantile led a public fund-raising campaign to replace the Hotel Florence.

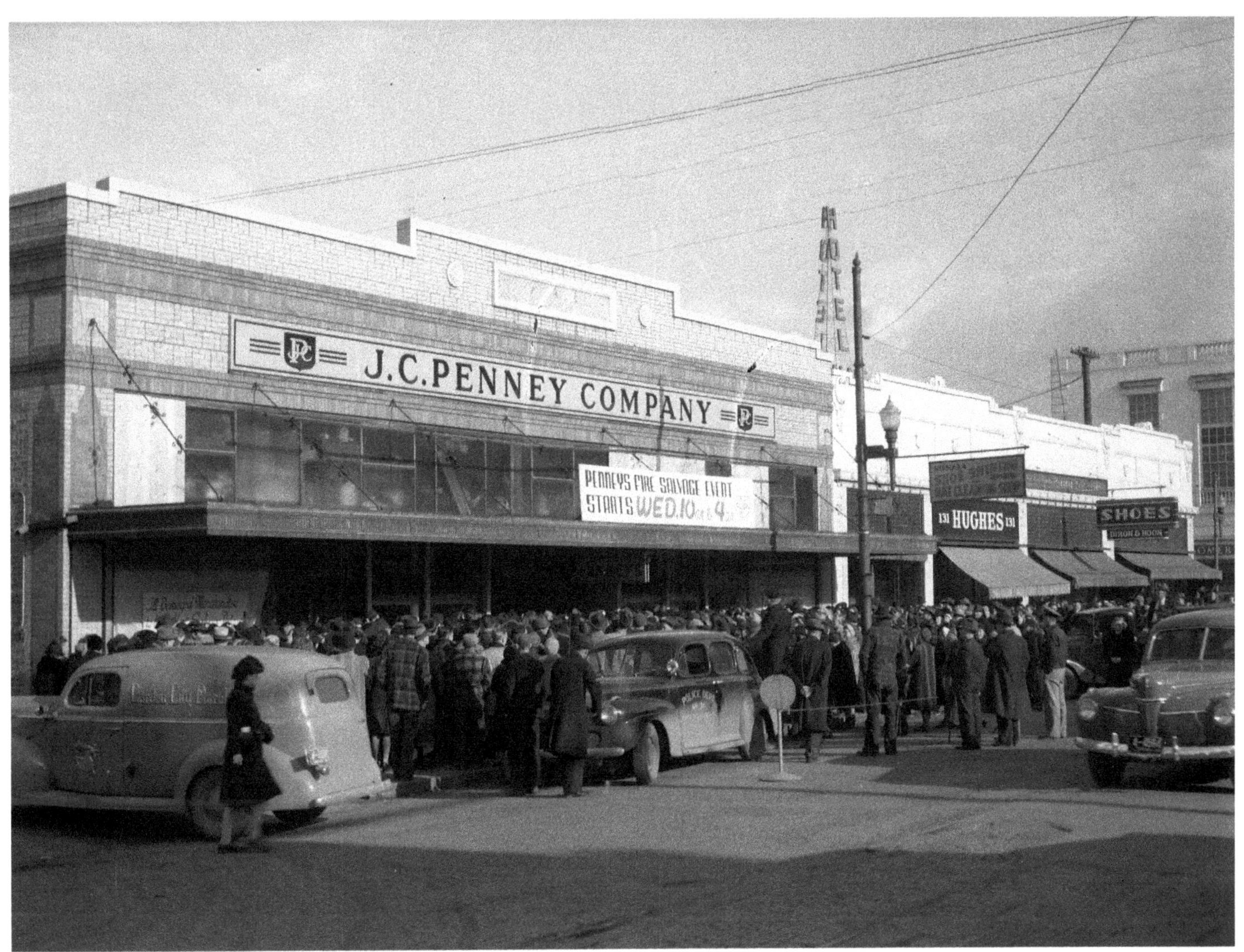

A crowd gathers outside the J. C. Penney Company store on North Higgins in Missoula. The company started in 1902 with a single store in Wyoming, called the Golden Rule, and quickly expanded to include hundreds more. A 1950 fire caused $100,000 in damage to this building.

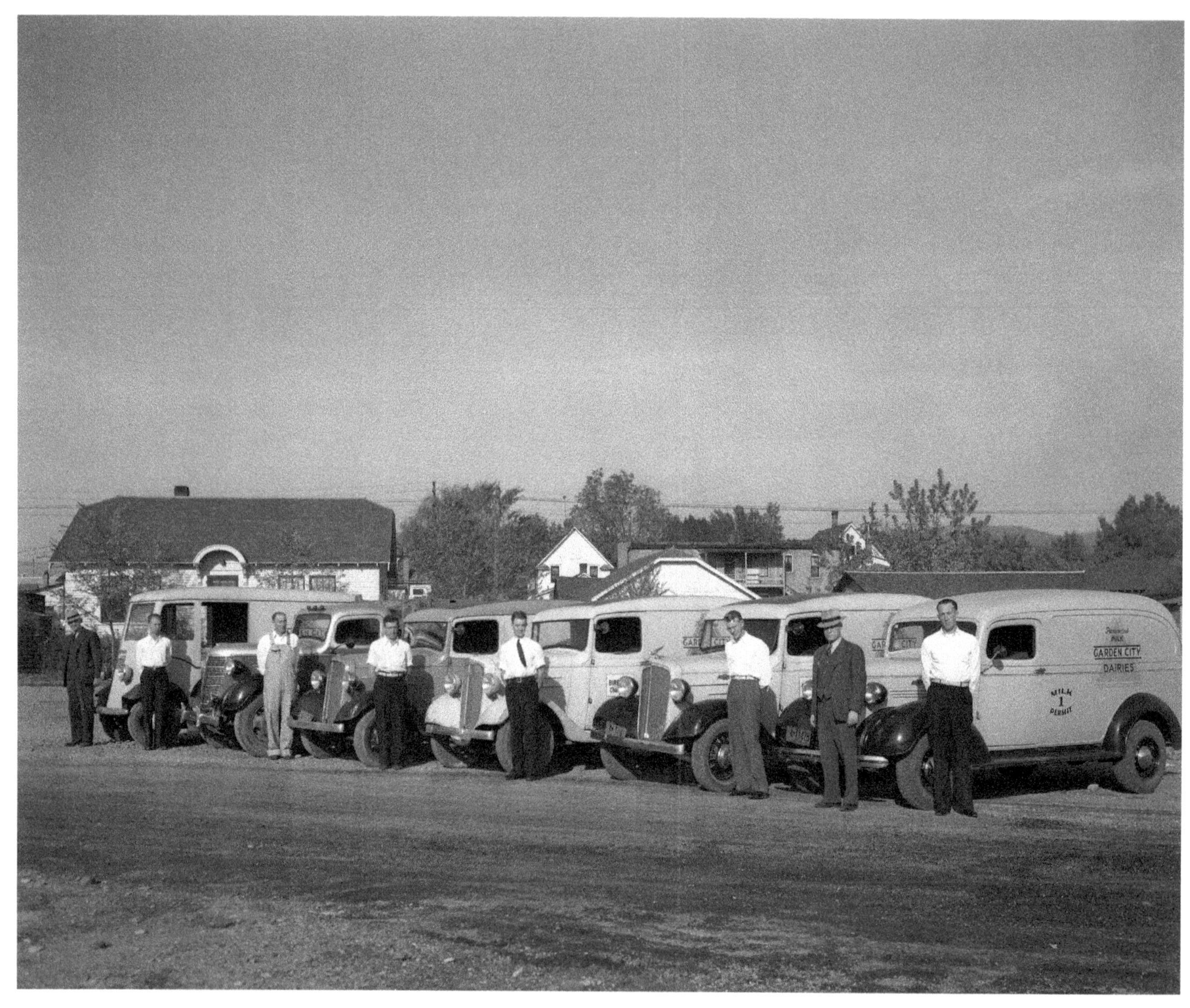

Delivery drivers for the Garden City Dairies pose before their fleet of milk trucks. These drivers were out before dawn each morning, delivering bottles of milk to nearly every household in Missoula.

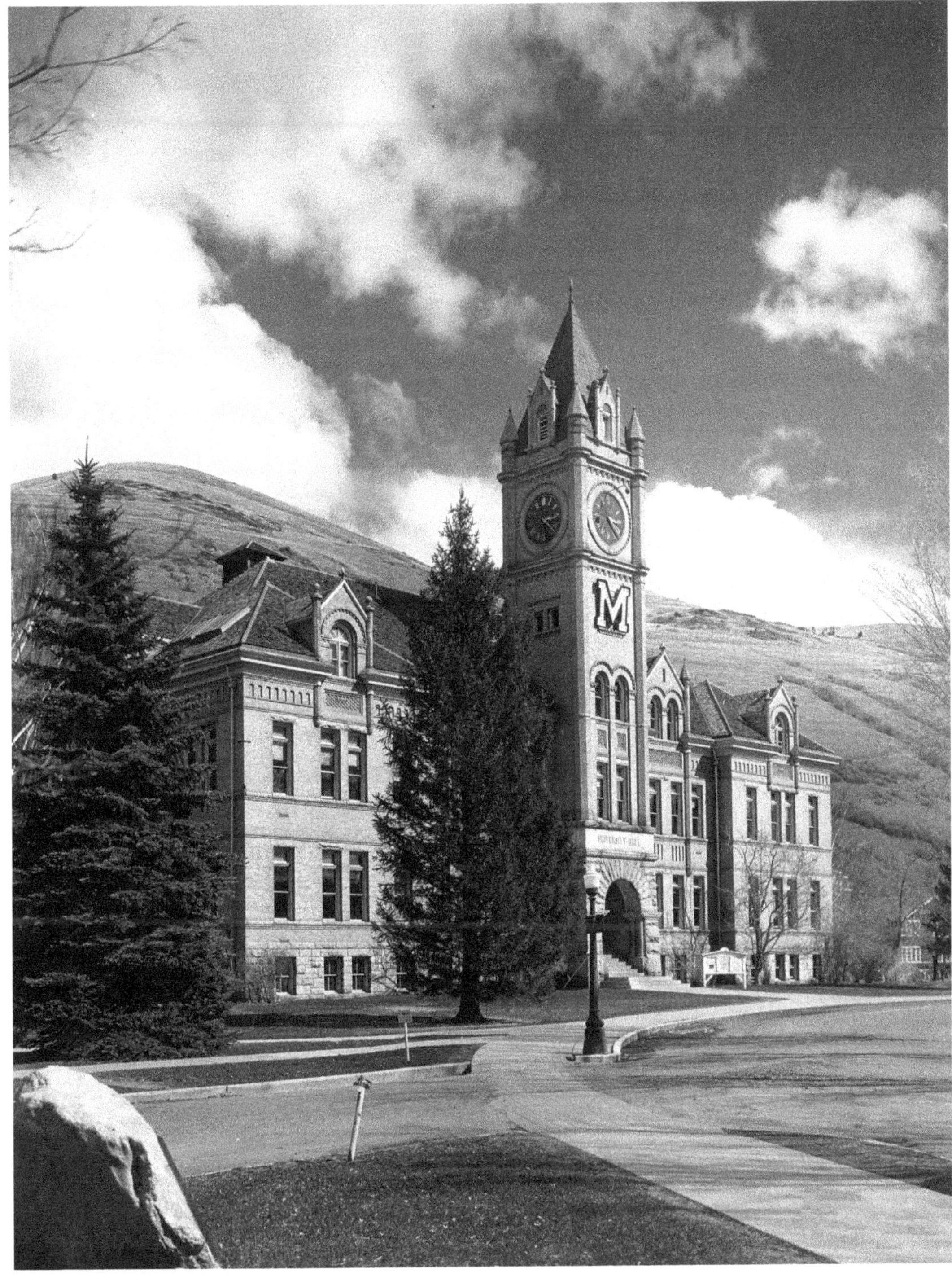

Noted architect A. J. Gibson designed the University of Montana's University Hall. Now known as Main Hall, it was the first building constructed on the Missoula campus. Taken 39 years after its construction in 1898, this photo shows the passage of time in the size of the trees.

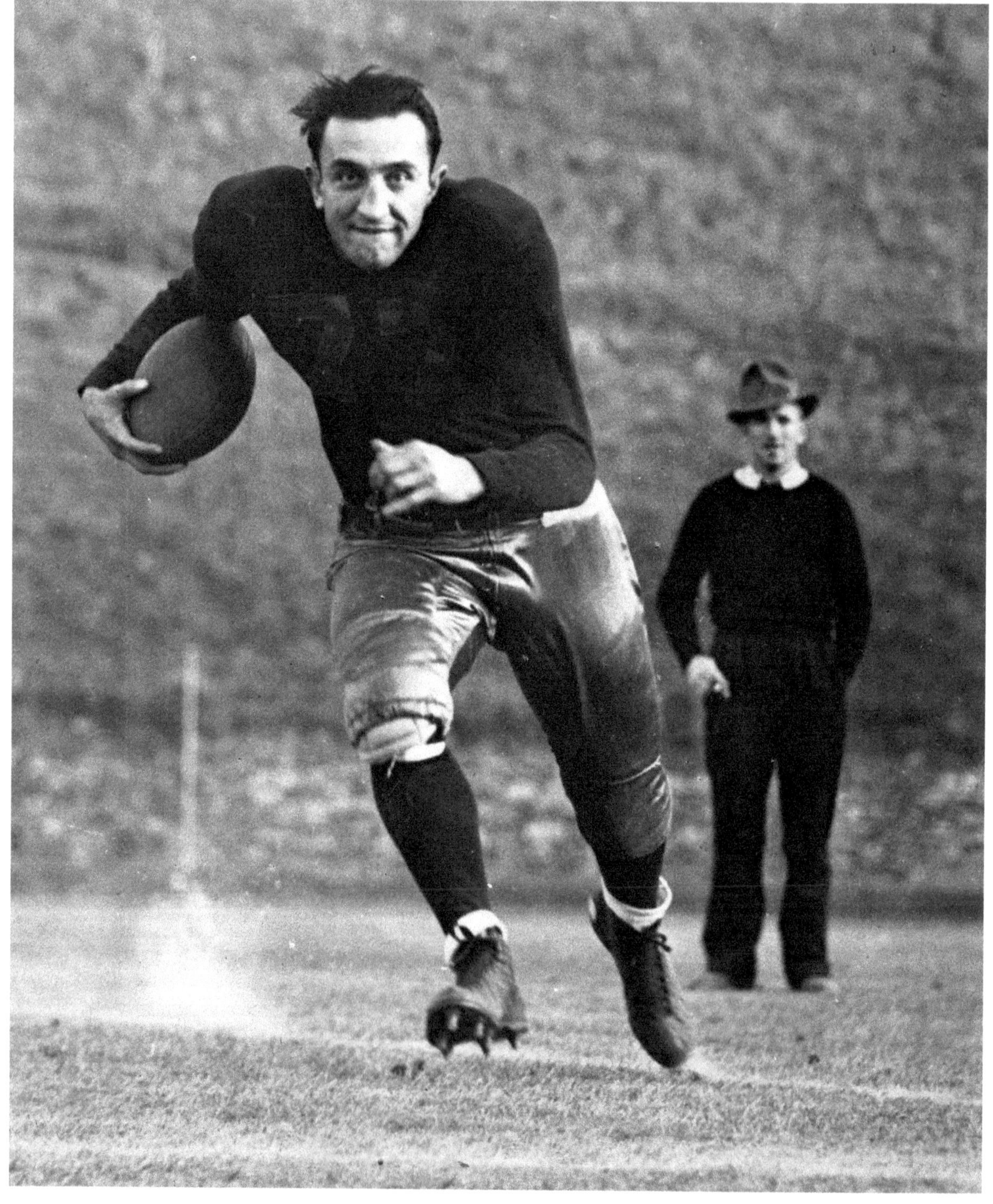

Butte, Montana, native and Montana Grizzly Milton Popovich scored two touchdowns in the 1936 "Cat-Griz" game against archrival Montana State. Popovich repeated that feat in 1937, a year in which he led the Pacific Coast Conference in scoring. After graduation he played for five years with the Chicago Cardinals of the National Football League.

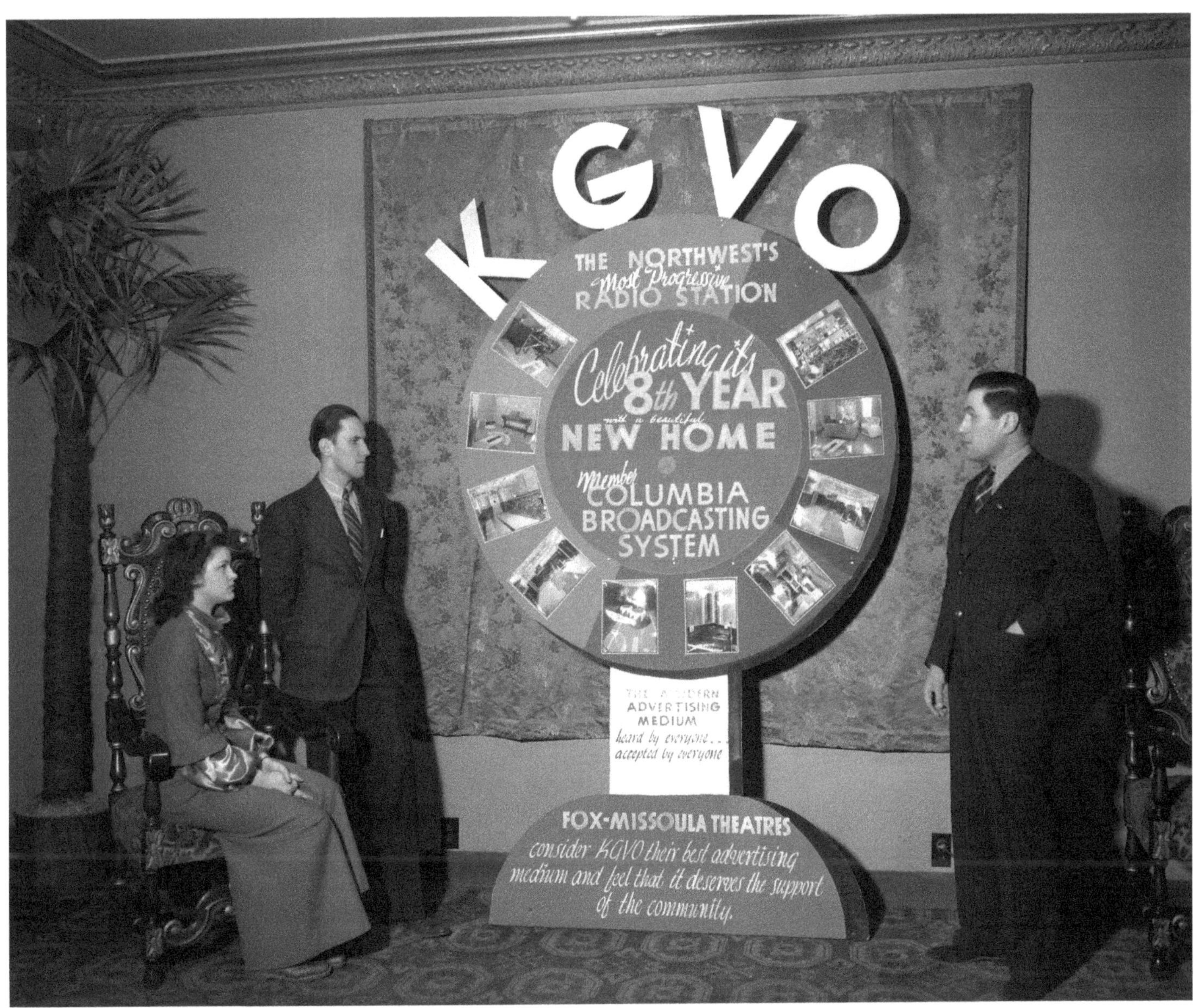

A display in the lobby of Missoula's Fox Theatre promotes KGVO, the "Northwest's Most Progressive Radio Station." The station was celebrating its eighth year as a member of the Columbia Broadcasting System, having started in 1931. KGVO radio is still on the air more than 75 years later.

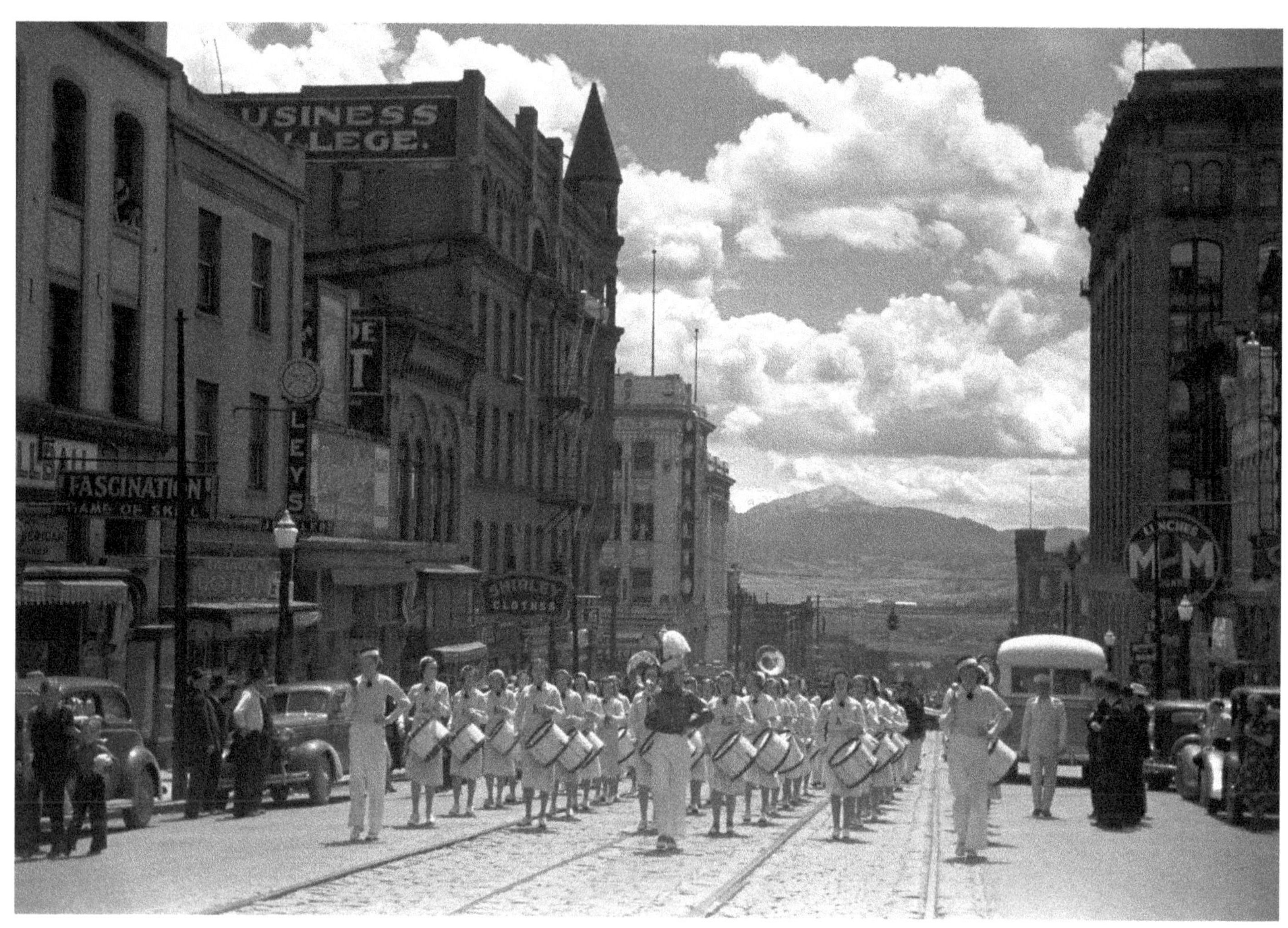

Using the trolley tracks for guidance, a high school band marches down Butte's Main Street in 1939. At right sits the famous M&M Cigar Store. After visiting it, the beat writer Jack Kerouac described the experience as "the end of my quest for an ideal bar."

PEARL HARBOR TO POSTWAR BOOM

(1940–1960)

Montana was recovering from years of depression and economic uncertainty when World War II broke out in Europe. During the spring of 1941, diplomatic relations between the United States and the Axis powers of Germany and Italy began to deteriorate. In May of 1941, the Immigration and Naturalization Service sent 1,200 detained Italian citizens to Fort Missoula. Most of these men were merchant seamen and workers from the 1939 World's Fair in New York who had overstayed their visas in hopes of staying out of the war in Europe.

Powerful Senator Burton K. Wheeler of Montana was a leading advocate for America's staying out of the war, a position supported by most of his constituents. That all changed with the Japanese attack on Pearl Harbor on December 7, 1941. Record numbers of outraged Montanans flooded recruiting offices across the state. At the same time, INS agents on the West Coast swiftly rounded up prominent Japanese American community and religious leaders and put them on a train for Fort Missoula. By the end of December there were 650 Japanese Americans interned under the big sky.

The 163rd Infantry Regiment, formerly the Montana National Guard, became one of the first units sent overseas. The Montanans spent the war trudging through the jungles of New Guinea and the Philippines, and later preparing for the invasion of Japan. The First Special Service Force, considered a forerunner to today's Green Berets, was formed and trained in Helena. The force invaded the Aleutian island of Kiska, then saw action at Anzio and elsewhere in Italy and France. A new air base near Great Falls was built to ferry thousands of warplanes and tons of supplies to our Soviet allies via Alaska.

The end of the war brought a housing boom, and the Montana economy improved markedly. There was a surge in industrial forestry with the construction of new lumber mills and increased clear-cut logging. Great Falls surpassed Butte as the largest city in the state but soon lost the title to Billings, which benefited from the oil boom of the 1950s.

Montana became a key player during the cold war of the late 1950s when hundreds of Minuteman intercontinental ballistic missiles were installed throughout north-central areas of the state. President John F. Kennedy once said that the missiles surrounding Malmstrom Air Force Base were the United States' "ace in the hole." President Kennedy visited Great Falls and Billings in 1963, just a few months before his assassination.

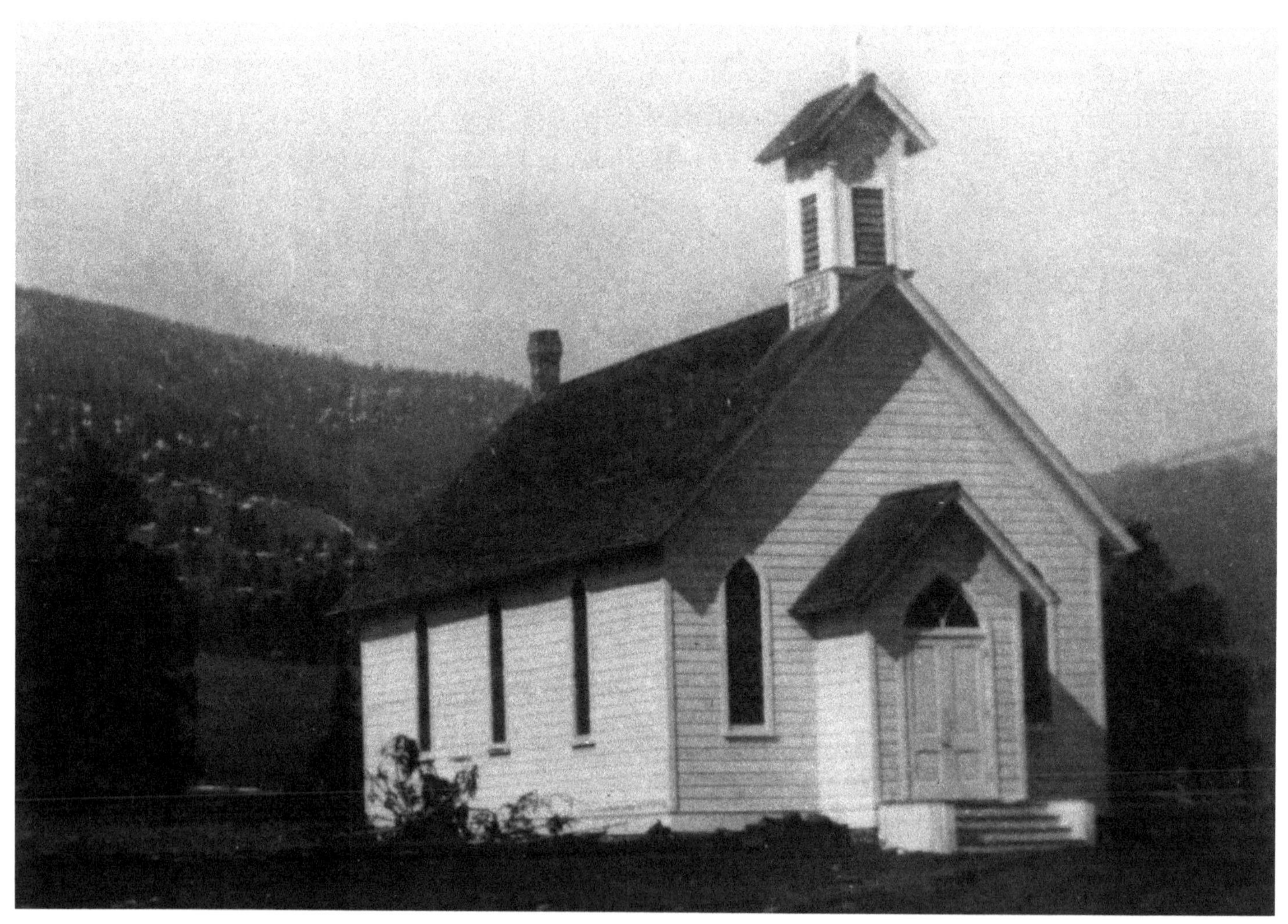

Robert Carlton, a resident of the northern Bitterroot Valley, deeded land for a community church north of Florence in 1883. The church was completed a year later and was actively used until 1924. After nearly 30 years of little use, a new congregation was formed in 1954, and in 1988 a modern church building was dedicated adjacent to the original church.

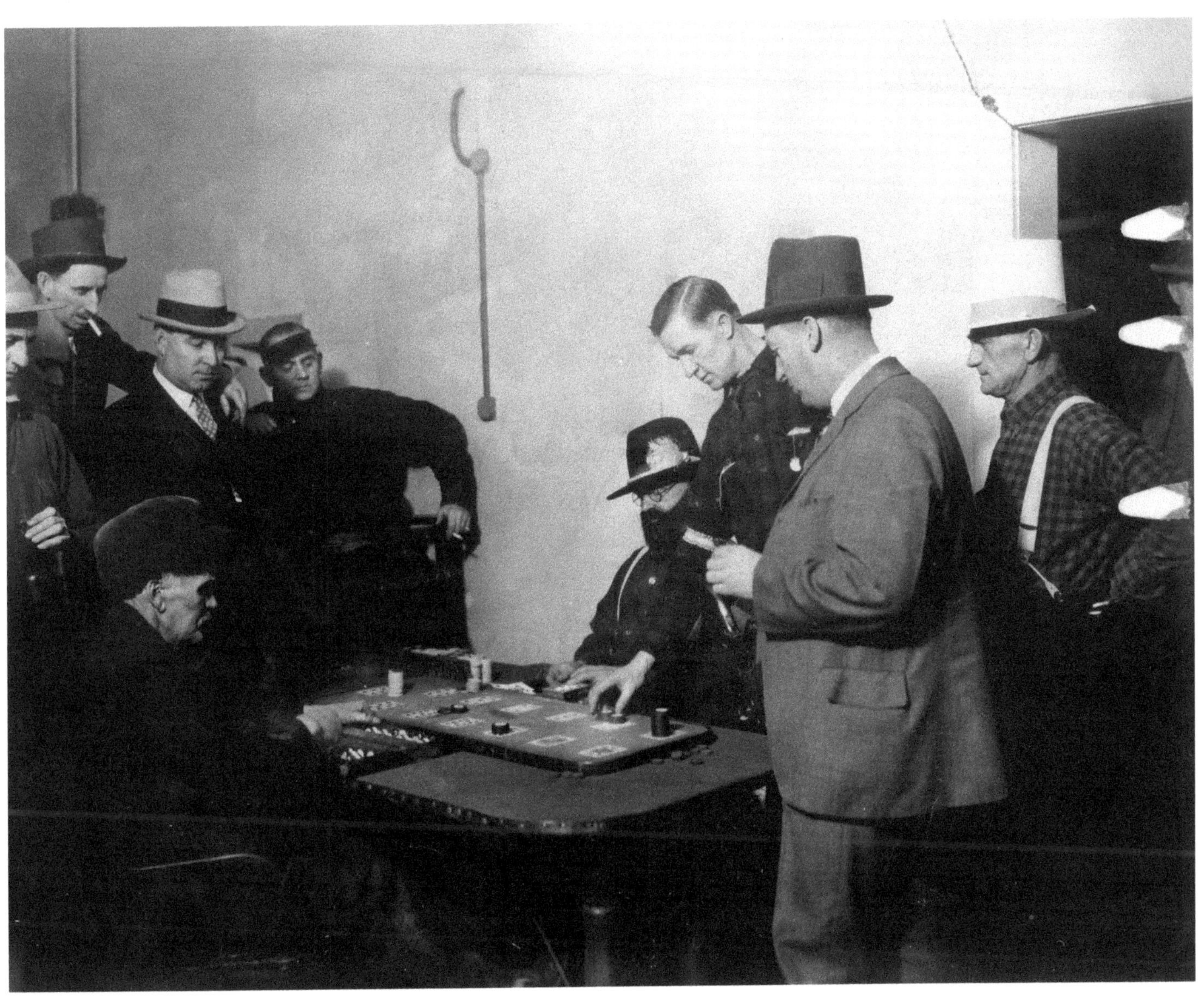

Gambling was declared illegal in Montana in 1889, but games of chance reappeared after the repeal of Prohibition in 1933. The state legislature legalized many table games in 1937 with passage of the Hickey Act. This photo was probably taken in Billings.

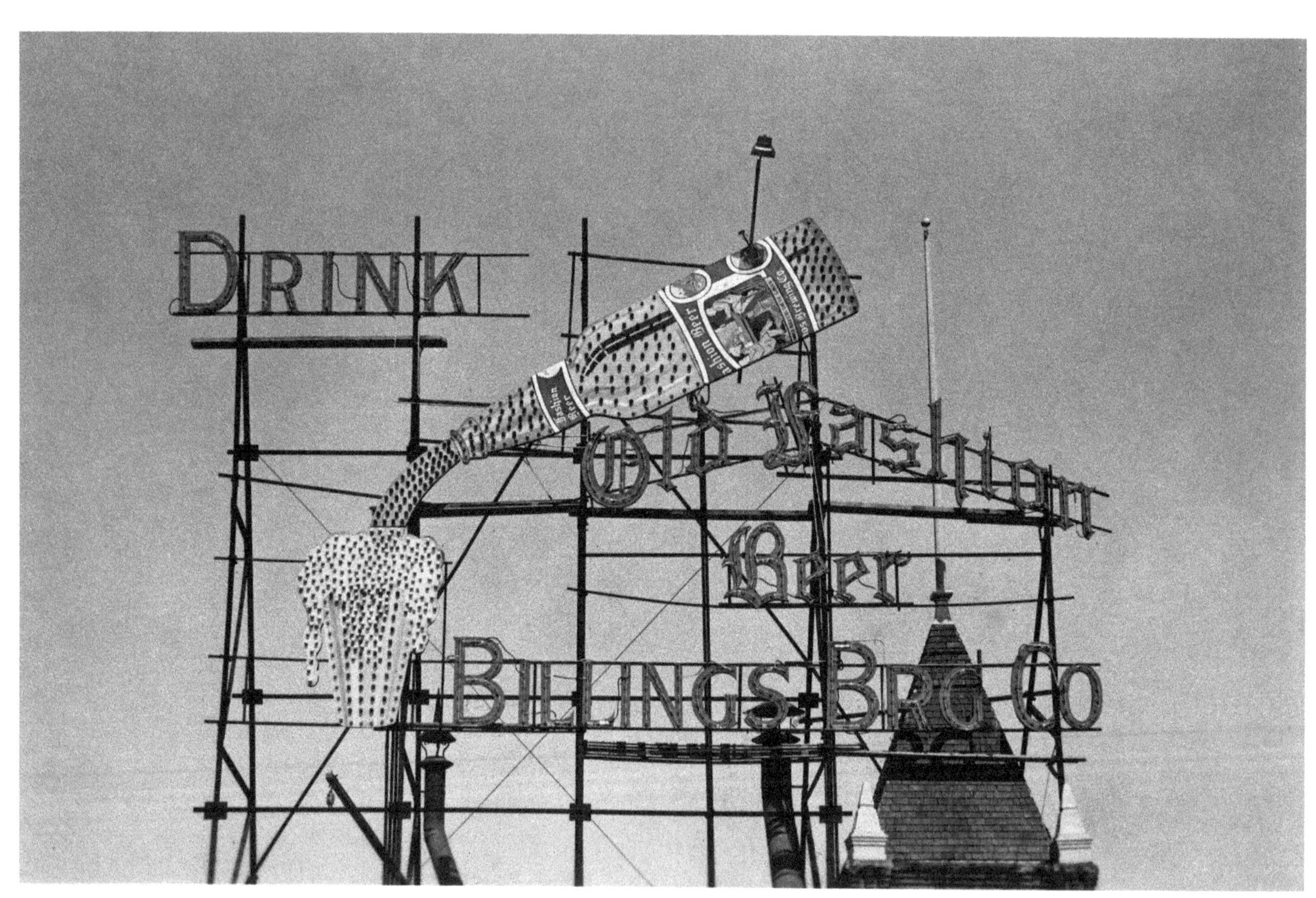

The Billings Brewing Company began producing Old Fashion Beer in the 1930s. This photo from around 1940 shows the company's roof-mounted electric sign. The brewery dropped the Old Fashion brand in the 1950s and replaced it with Tap Beer in cans. The brewery closed in 1952.

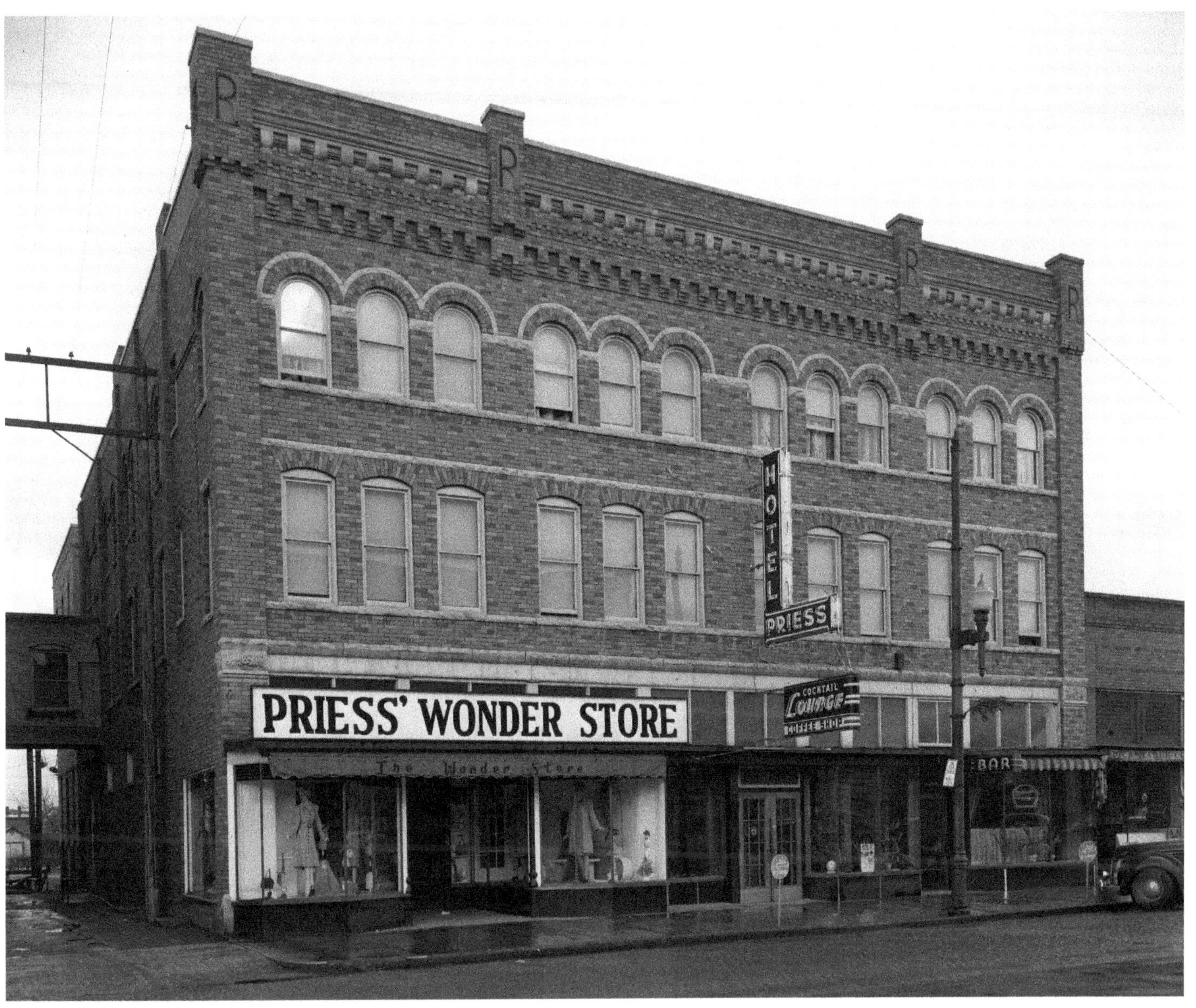

This exterior view of Missoula's Hotel Priess in 1940 shows the Wonder Store on the ground floor, along with the coffee shop and cocktail lounge. The hotel burned in 1972, killing a man named Robert Harvey Longabaugh who claimed to be the son of the Sundance Kid.

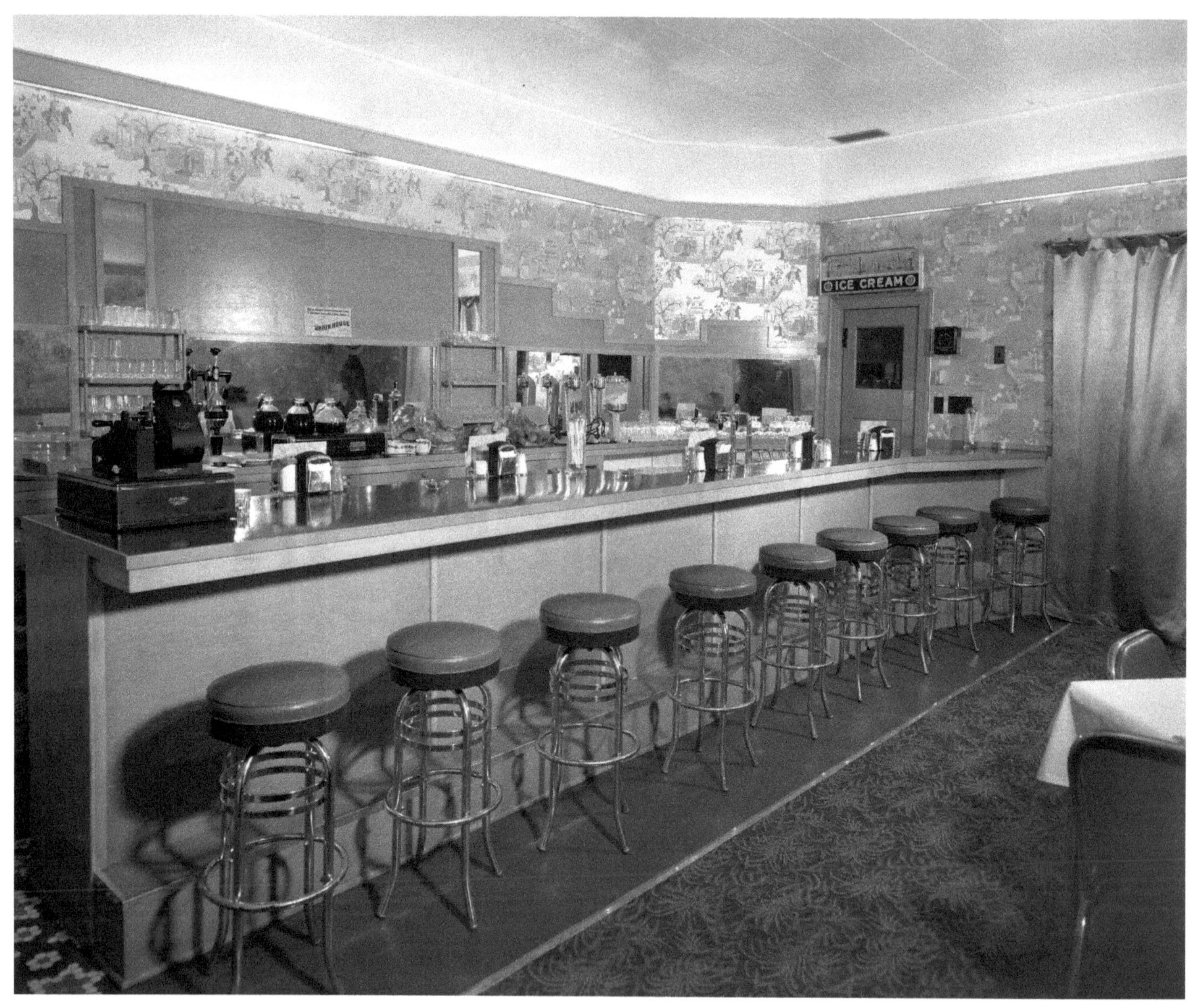

The coffee shop in the Hotel Priess featured modern decor and a typical lunch counter of the day.

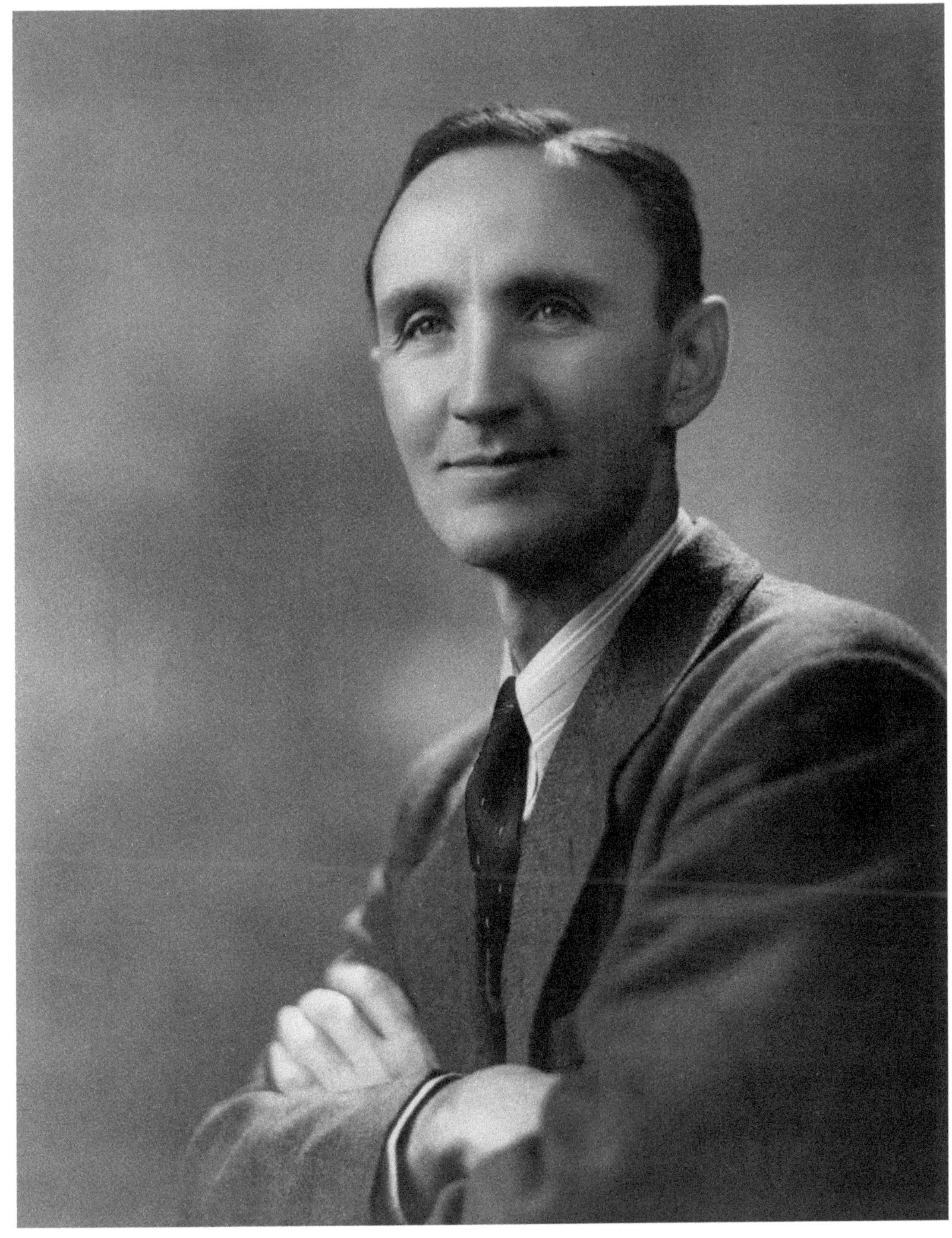

Mike Mansfield was a World War I veteran and a Butte miner turned university professor. Elected to the U.S. House of Representatives in 1942, the year of this photo, he served five terms and then was elected to the U.S. Senate in 1952. He spent 24 years in the Senate, 16 of them as majority leader. He was appointed ambassador to Japan in 1977.

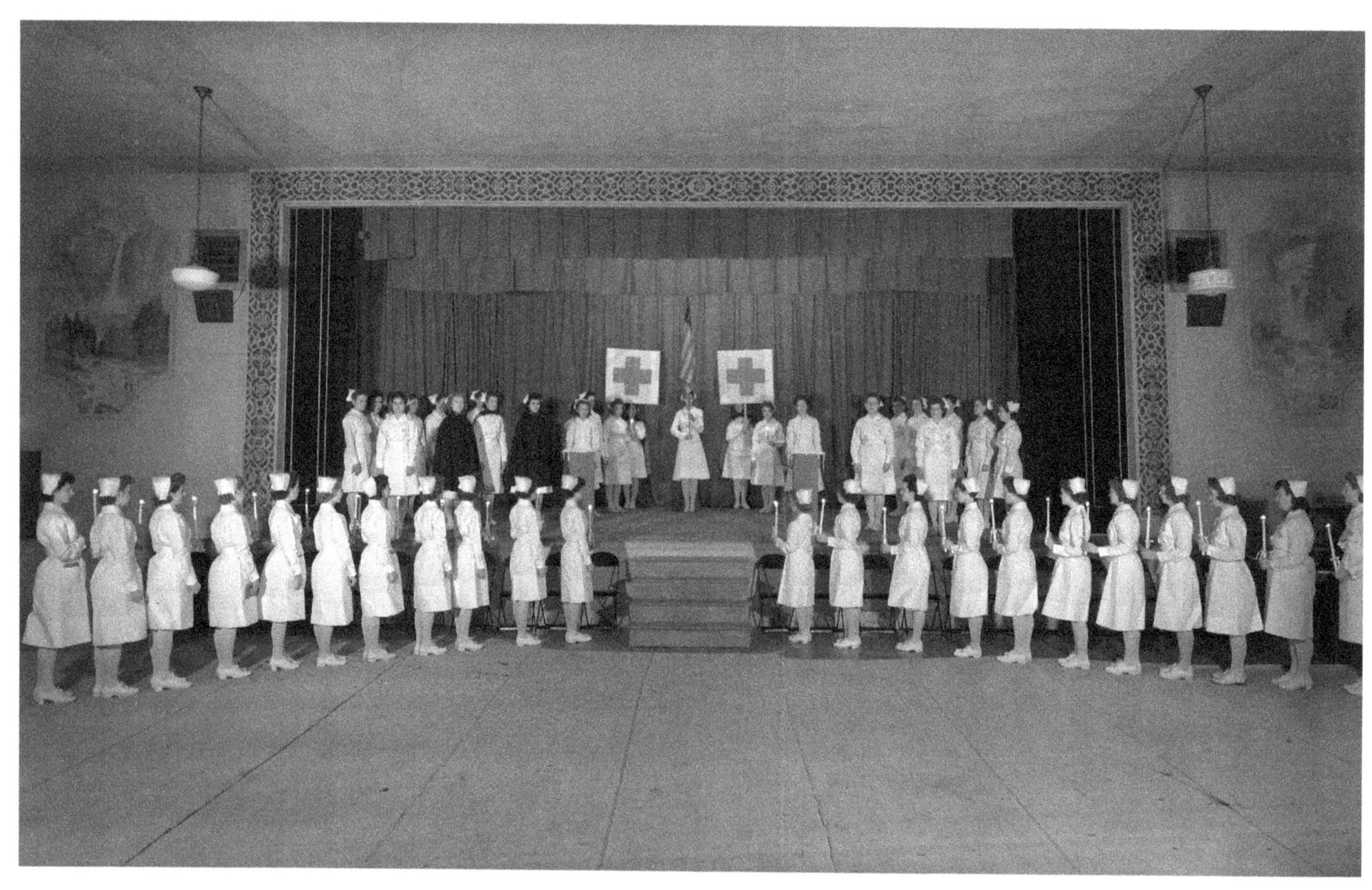

World War II had a profound effect on every aspect of life in Montana. In this 1942 photo by Missoula's R. H. McKay, uniformed nurses attend a Red Cross event in a ballroom. The American Red Cross enlisted more than 100,000 nurses for military service during World War II.

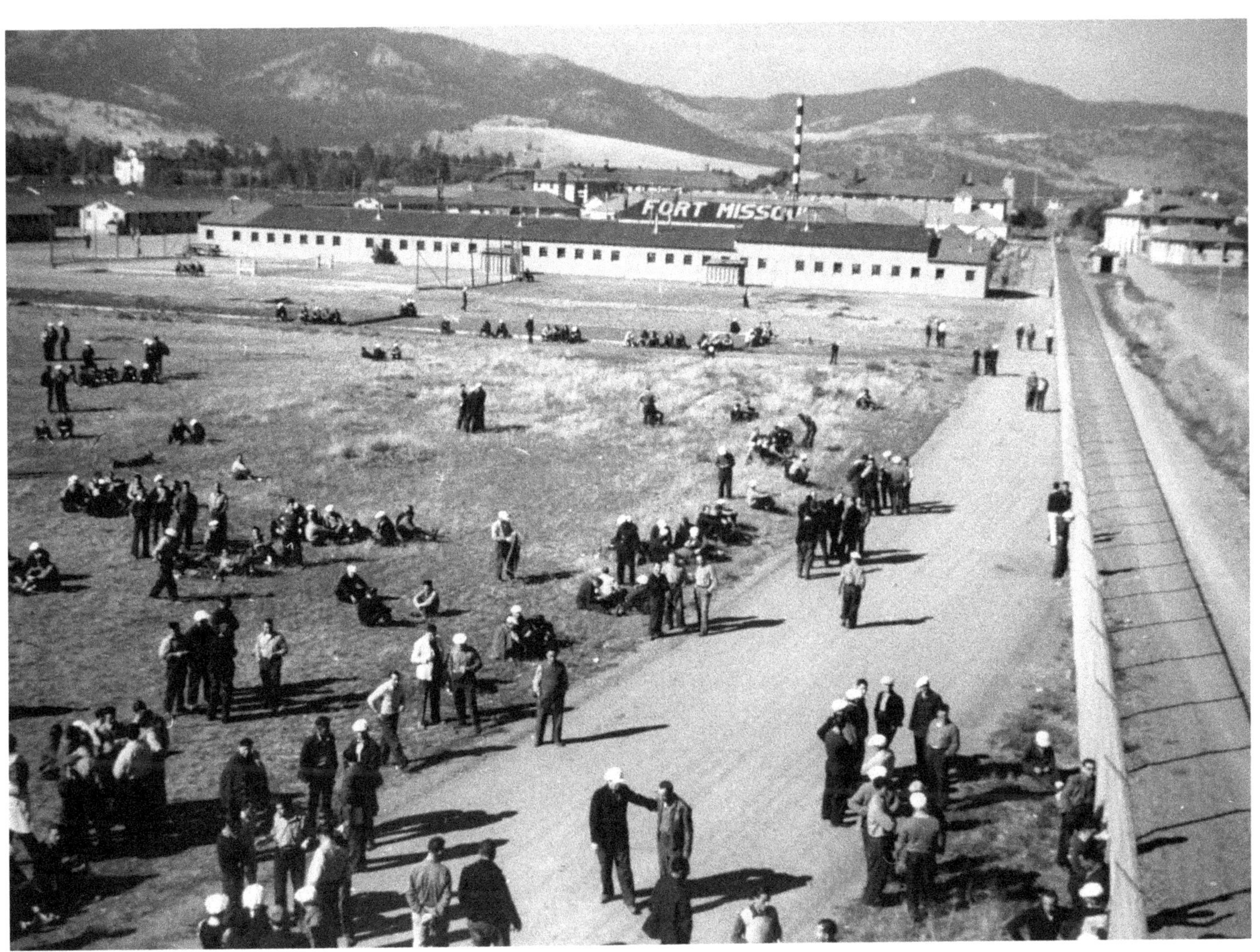

Fort Missoula was turned over to the Immigration and Naturalization Service in 1941. Six months before the United States' entry into World War II, the INS detained 1,200 Italian civilians on immigration charges and sent them to the fort. Hundreds of Japanese American men soon followed.

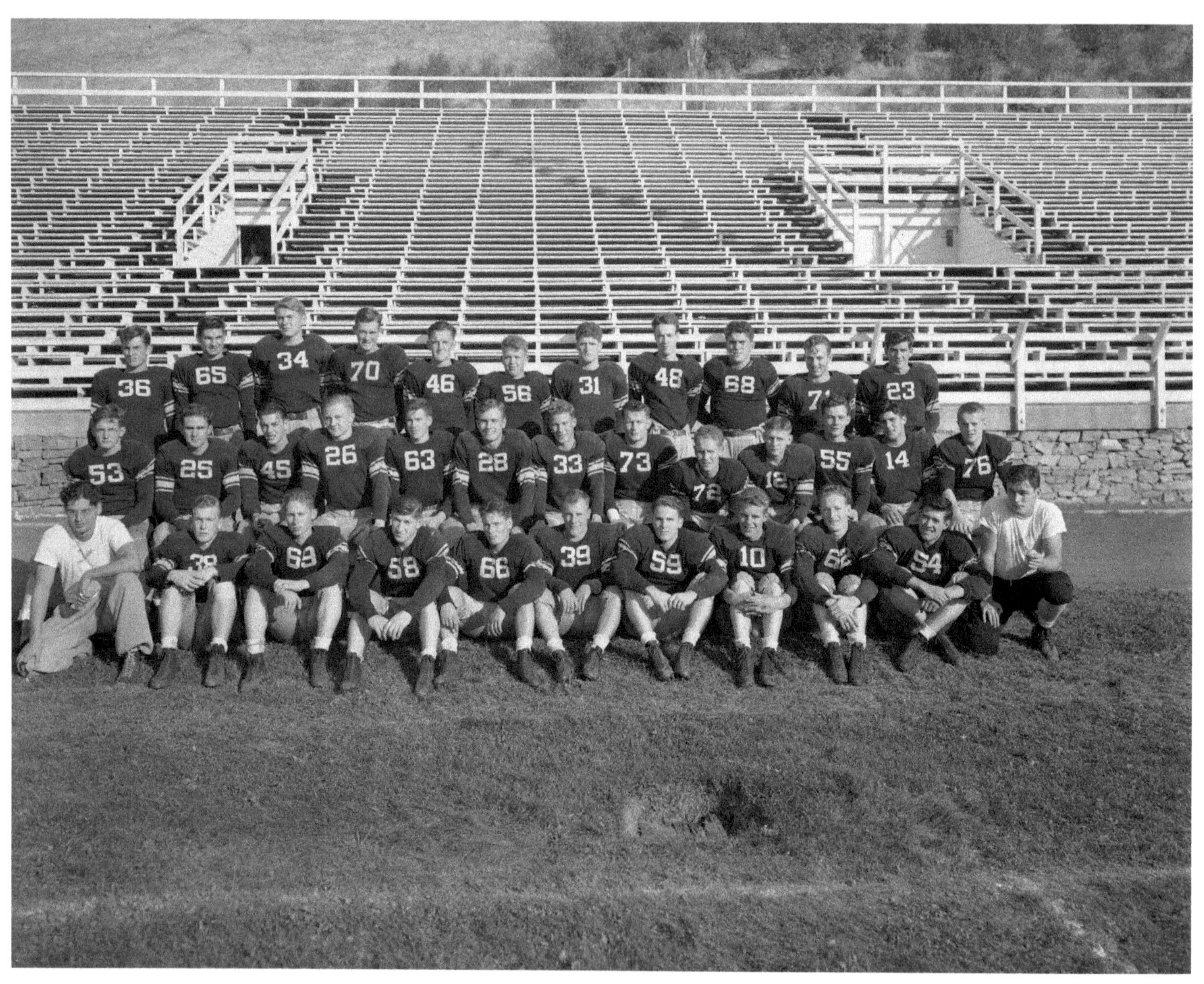

The University of Montana freshman football team poses for a photo in October 1942. The varsity team won zero games that season. The 1943 and 1944 football seasons were canceled due to the war.

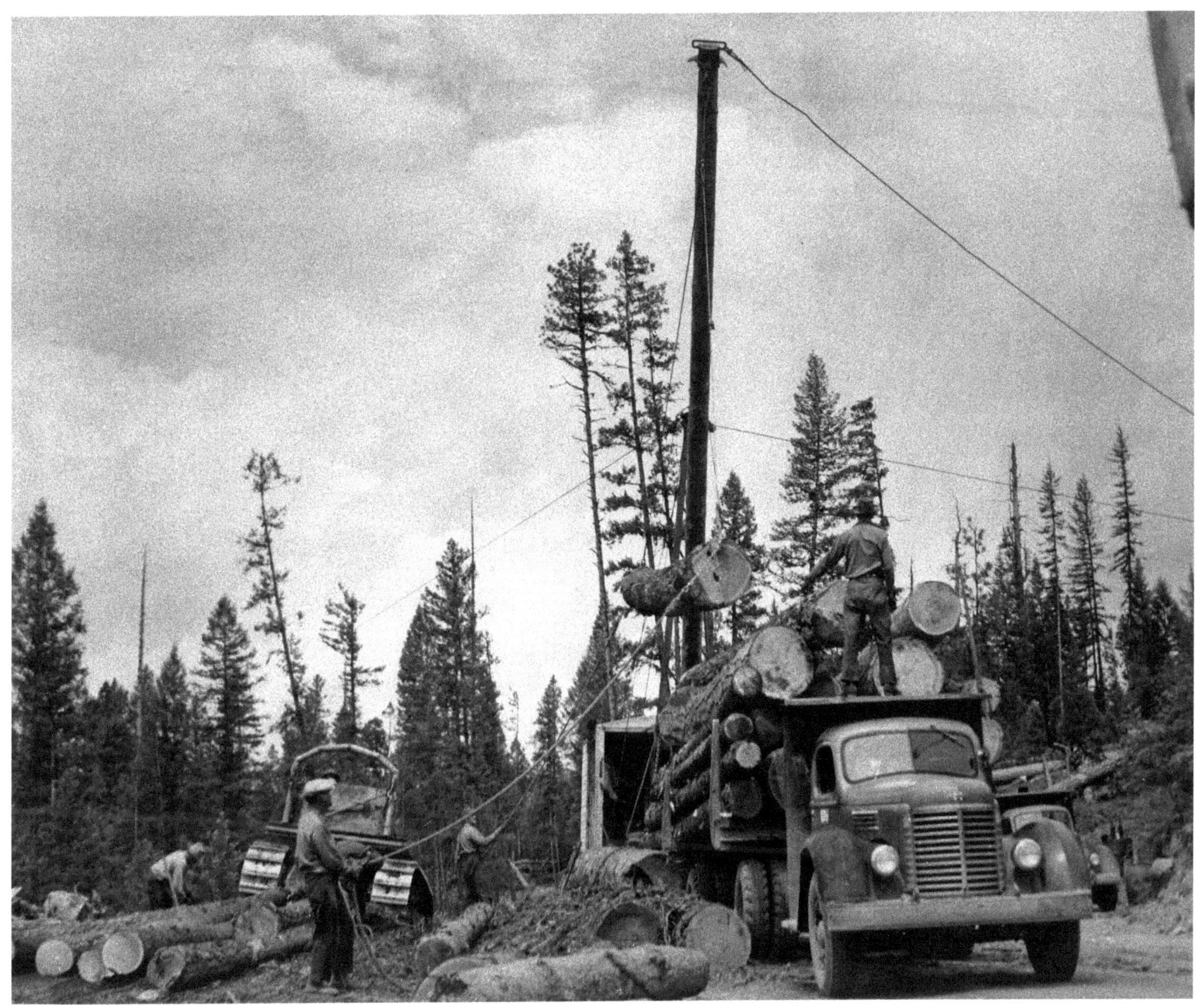

A crew working for the Anaconda Company loads logs near Woodworth, just east of Salmon Lake, in 1943. World War II brought a boom in demand for wood products, along with a serious labor shortage. Anaconda owned significant land in the Blackfoot and Clearwater drainages.

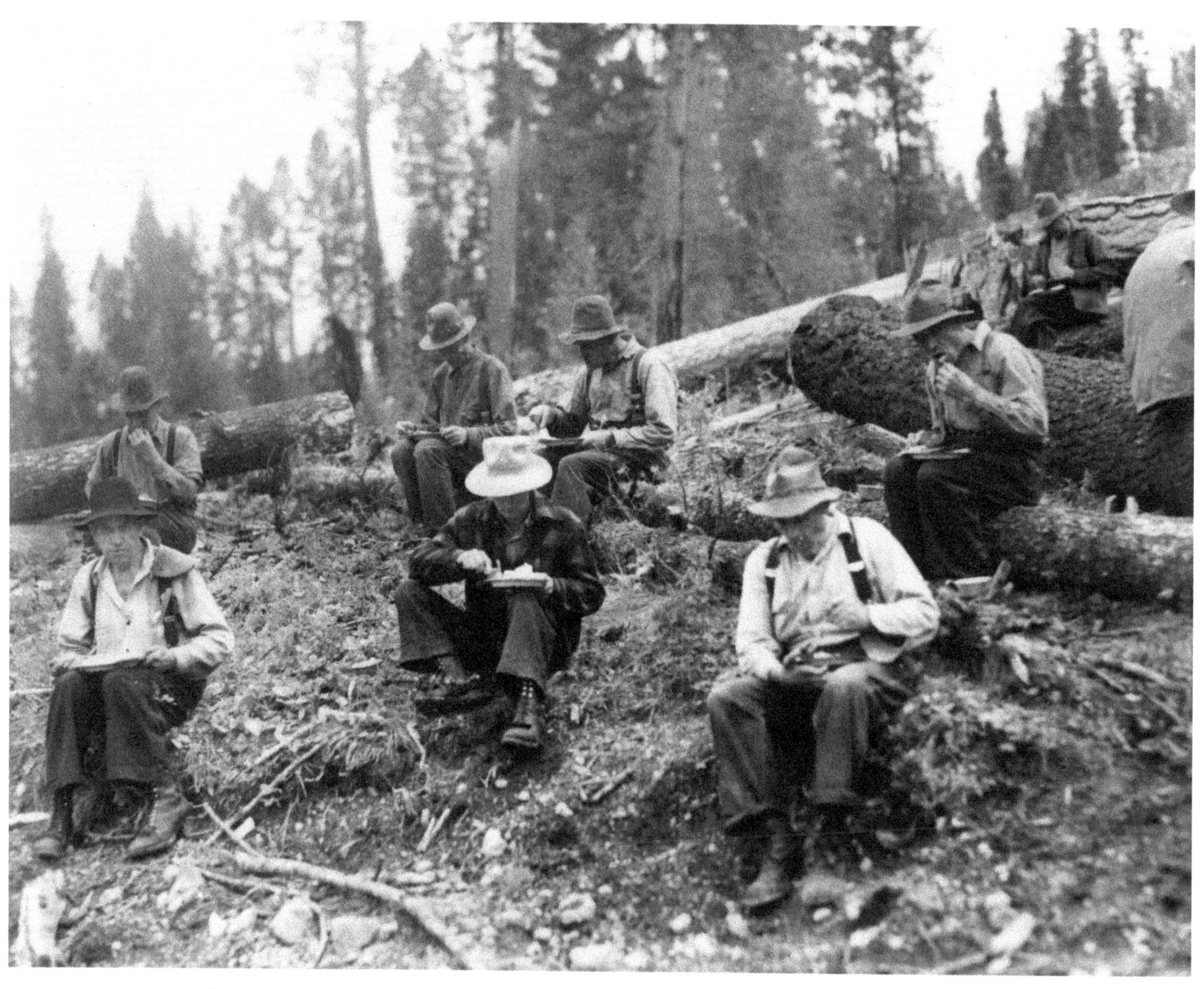

Loggers break for a hot lunch near Woodworth. Logs were loaded onto the Big Blackfoot Railroad and carried to the Anaconda Company sawmill in Bonner. Loggers had been working this same area for almost 50 years when this photo was taken in 1943.

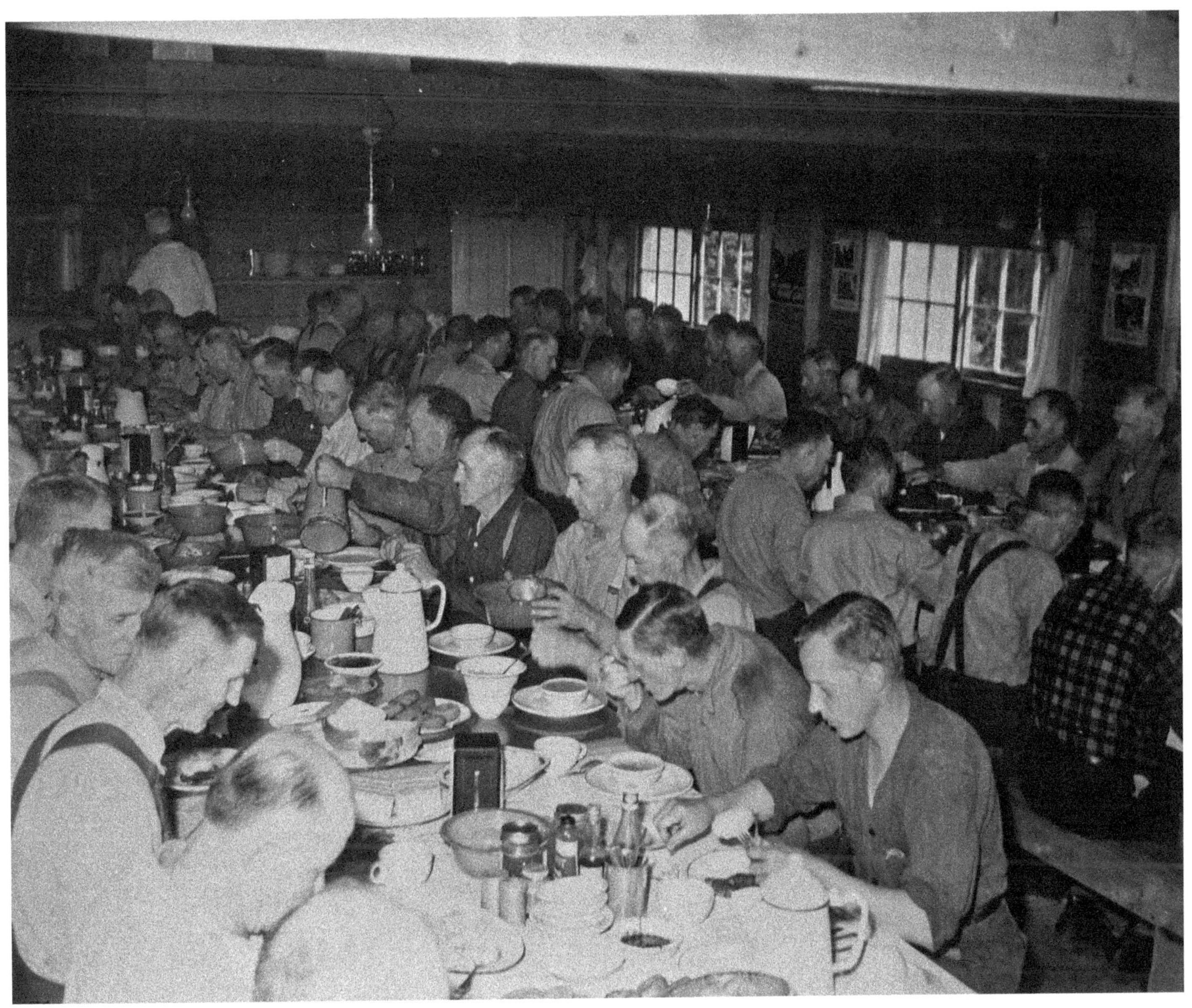

The small Powell County town of Woodworth was named for C. E. Woodworth, the first postmaster. Most of the residents were loggers, who often slept in railroad cars or camps built of portable buildings. This 1943 photo shows the loggers' cook shack at Woodworth.

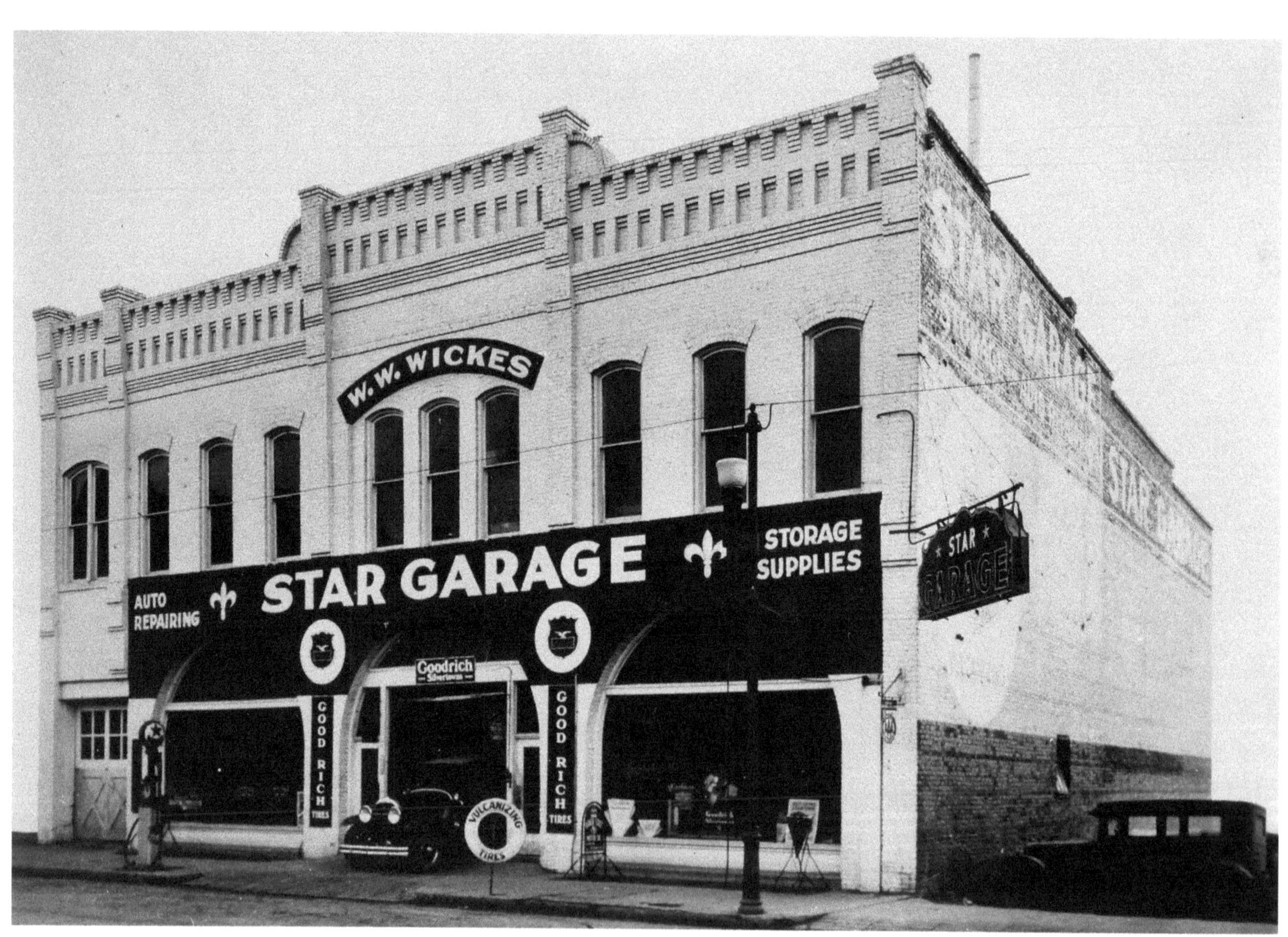

Conveniently located on West Front Street, the Star Garage was one of Missoula's larger service stations. When this photo was taken in 1944, rationing of gasoline and rubber tires was proving a hardship for citizens and businesses alike.

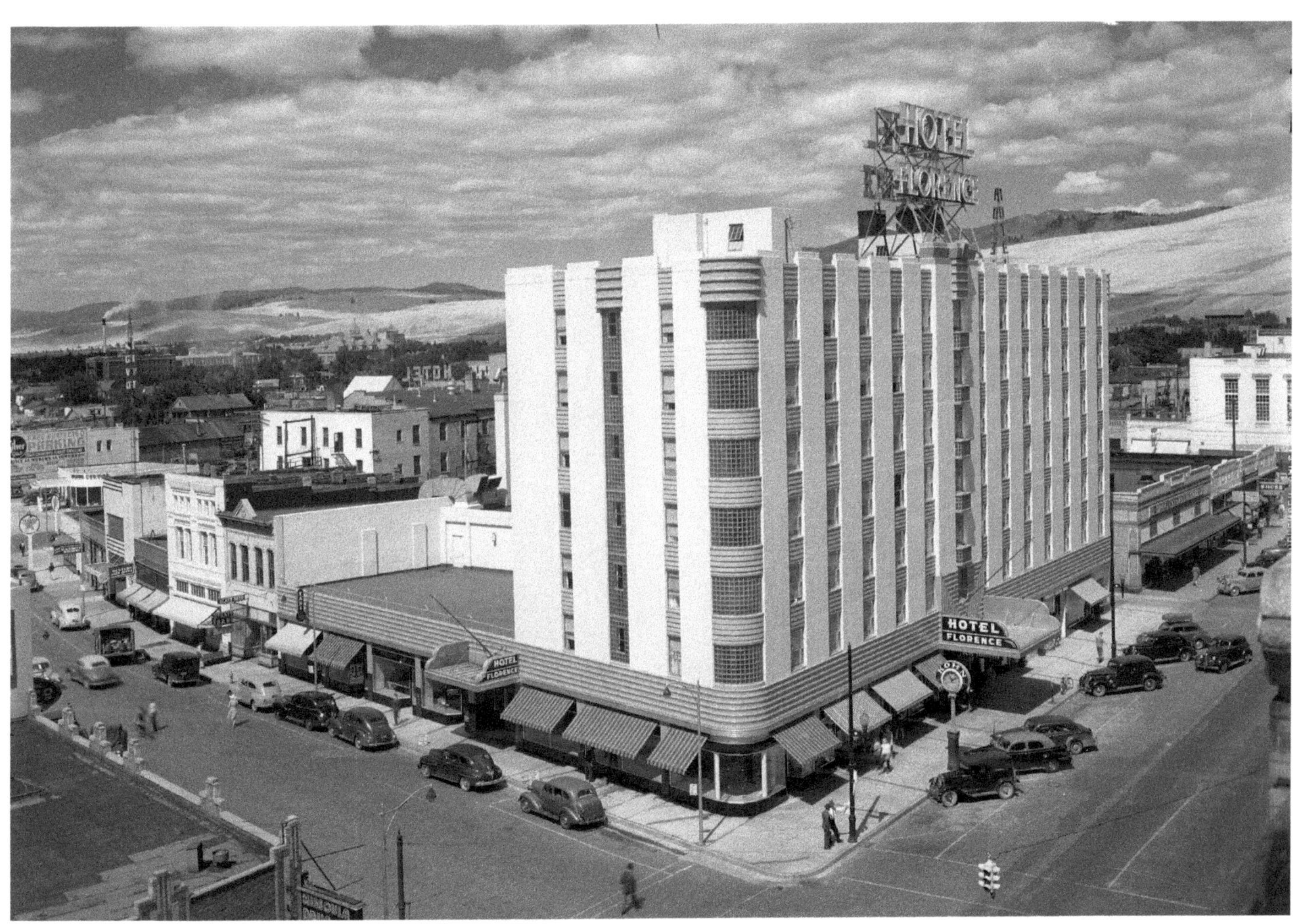

Burned to the ground in 1936, the Hotel Florence in Missoula was rebuilt in 1941 at a cost of $600,000. With a formal lobby, a spacious ballroom, and 75 rooms, the Florence billed itself as "America's Finest Small Hotel." The well-preserved building is on the National Register of Historic Places.

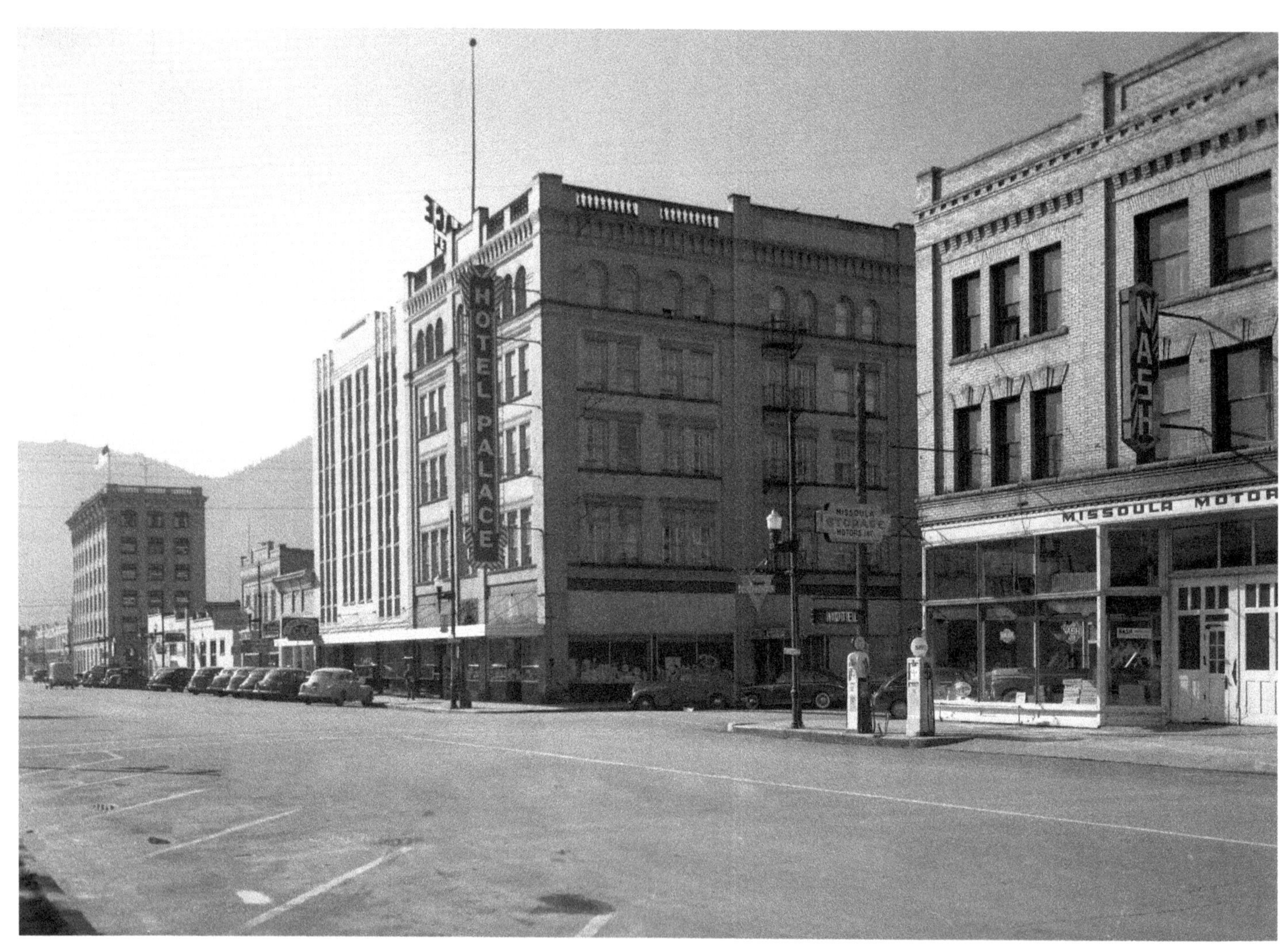

Built in 1909, the Hotel Palace in downtown Missoula was designed to cater to railroad passengers from the nearby Northern Pacific and Milwaukee depots. This 1947 view is to the east along Broadway Street. Missoula Motors, a Nash dealership, can be seen at right.

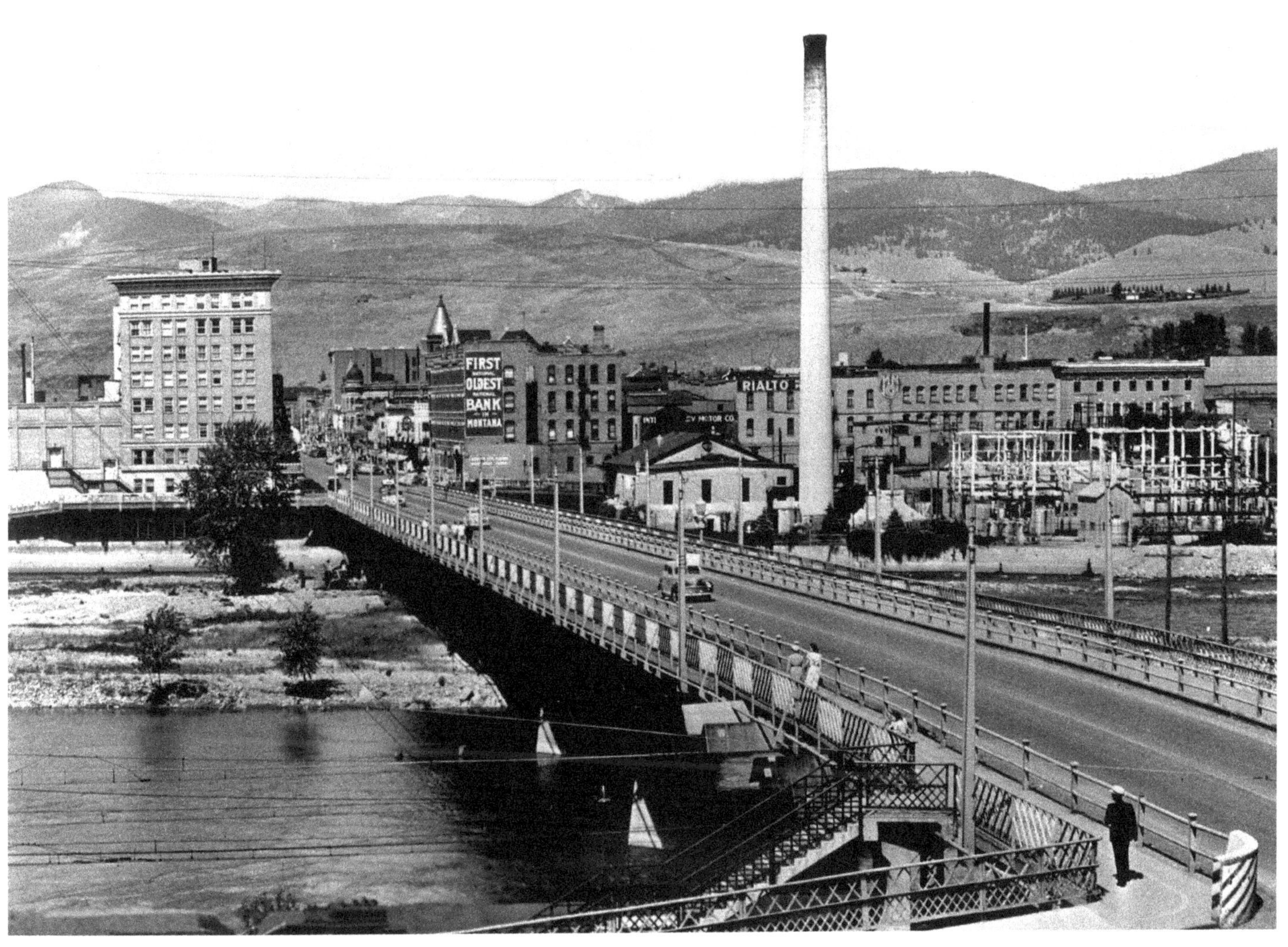

This photo of the Higgins Bridge and downtown Missoula around 1948 shows the smokestack of the steam plant that heated many of the downtown buildings. Numerous steam tunnels still remain under the streets and sidewalks. The imposing Wilma Building is at left.

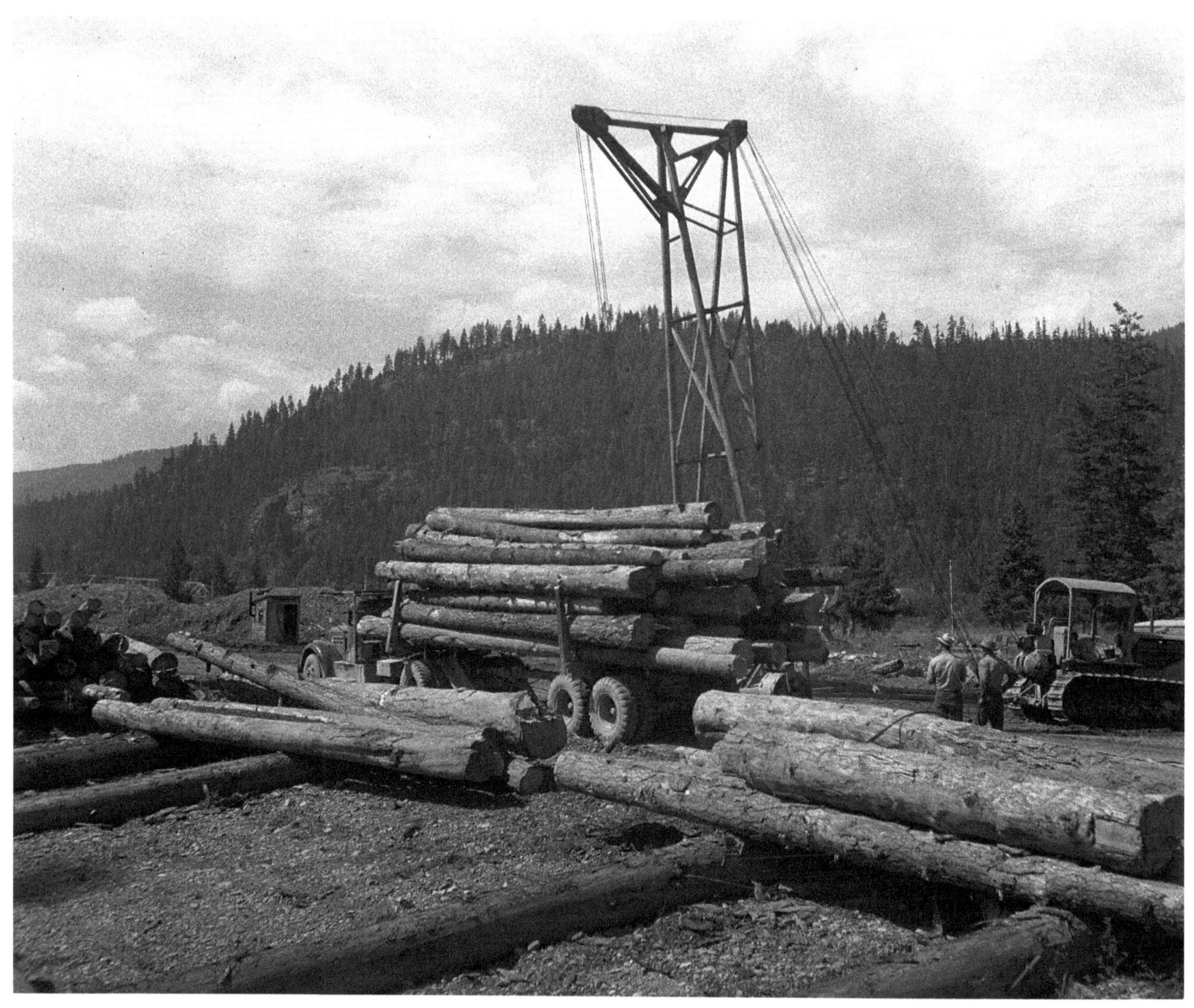

Workers with the J. Neils Lumber Company unload logs from a truck at a railroad landing in 1948. A major employer in the Libby area for more than 30 years, the J. Neils firm owned a sawmill, a plywood plant, and a railroad. The company merged with the St. Regis Paper Company in 1957.

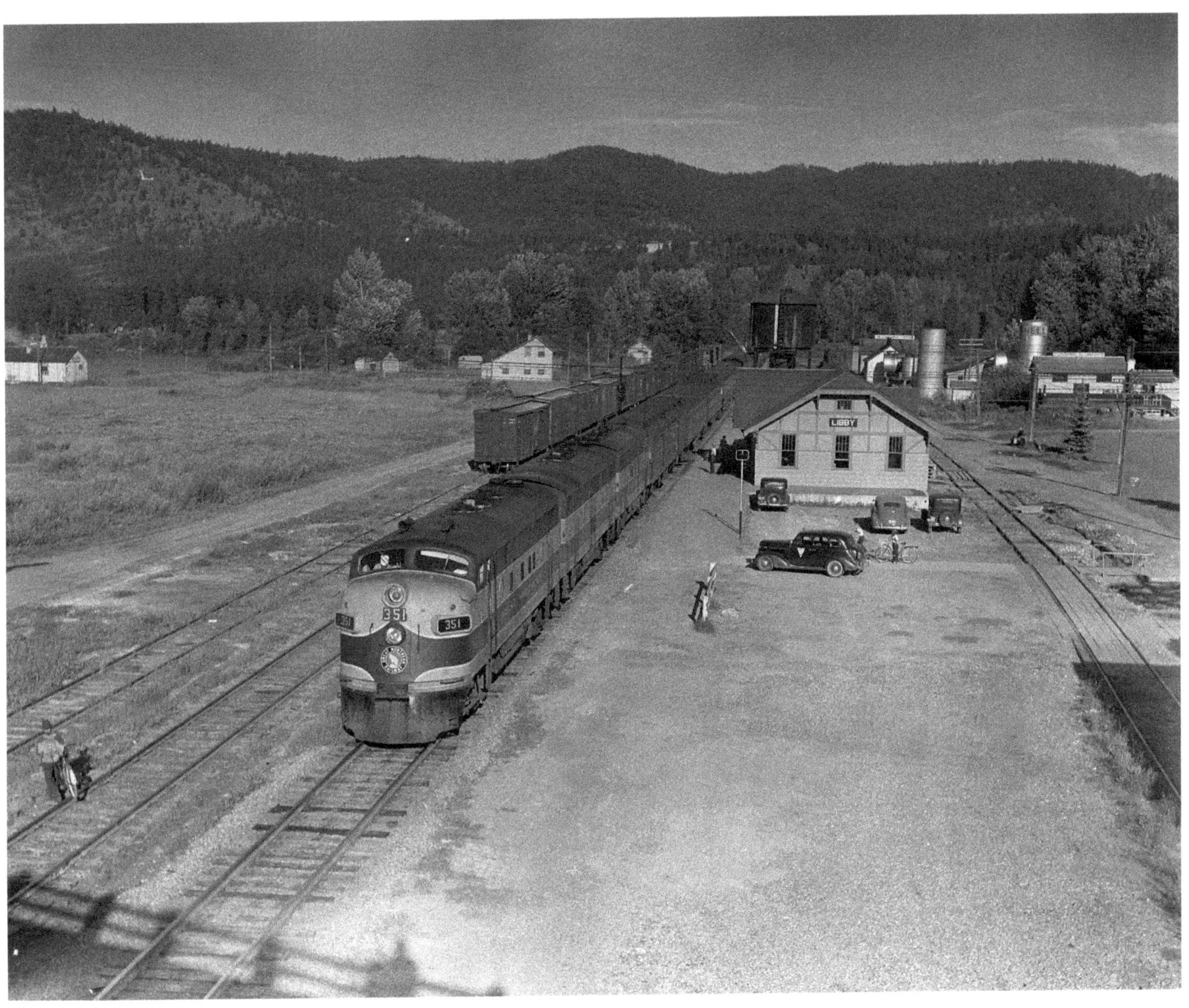

A diesel-electric locomotive pulls a Great Northern train into the Libby station in 1948. The Great Northern Railroad first reached the area in 1891, and the town of Libby was born. Major employers in the area included the Libby Lumber Company and the Zonolite asbestos mine.

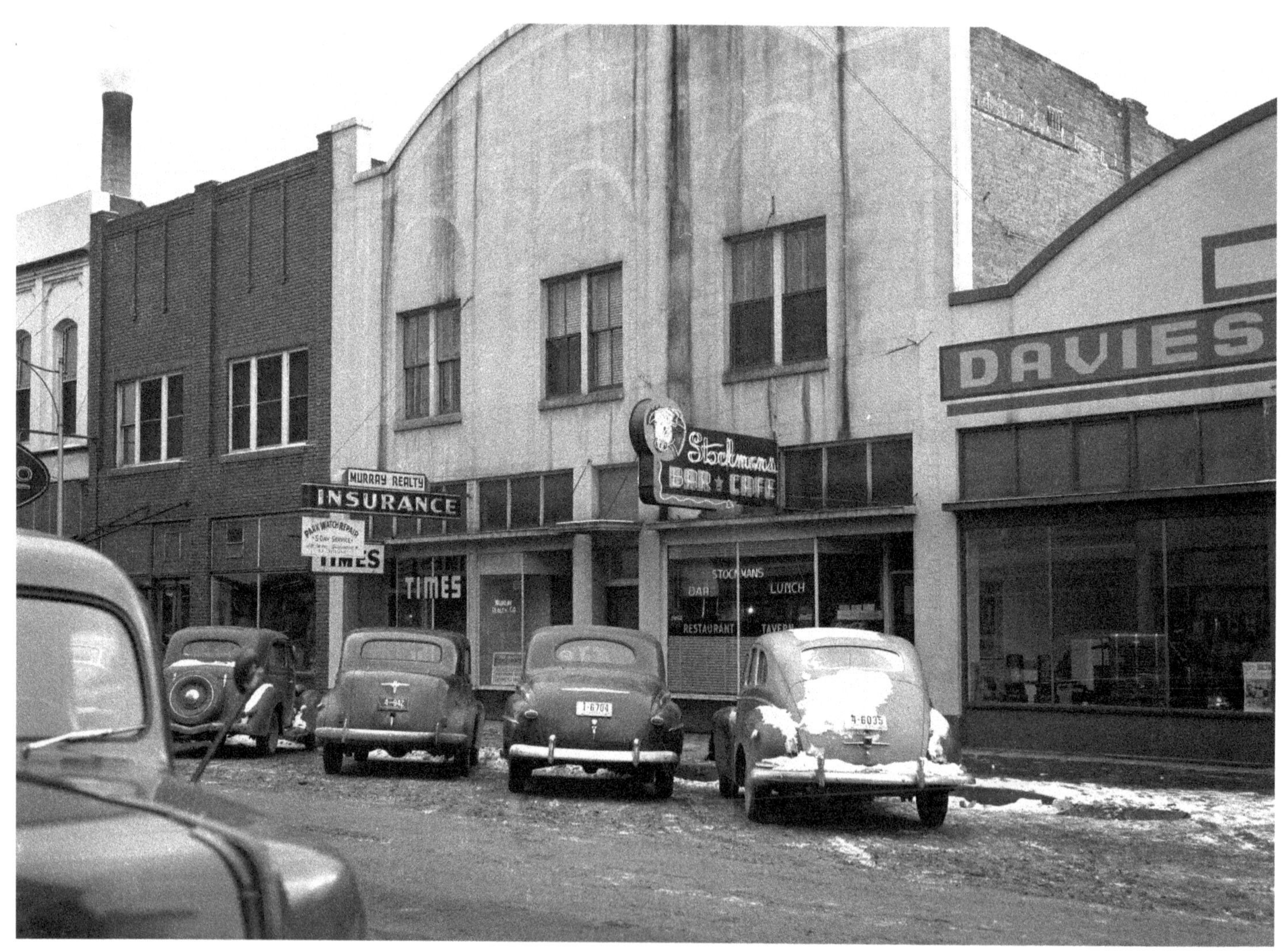

A downtown Missoula institution, Stockman's Bar has catered to a varied clientele of college students, businessmen, and sundry local characters for generations. Known locally as "Stocks," it includes a liquor store, card tables, and a classic wooden bar.

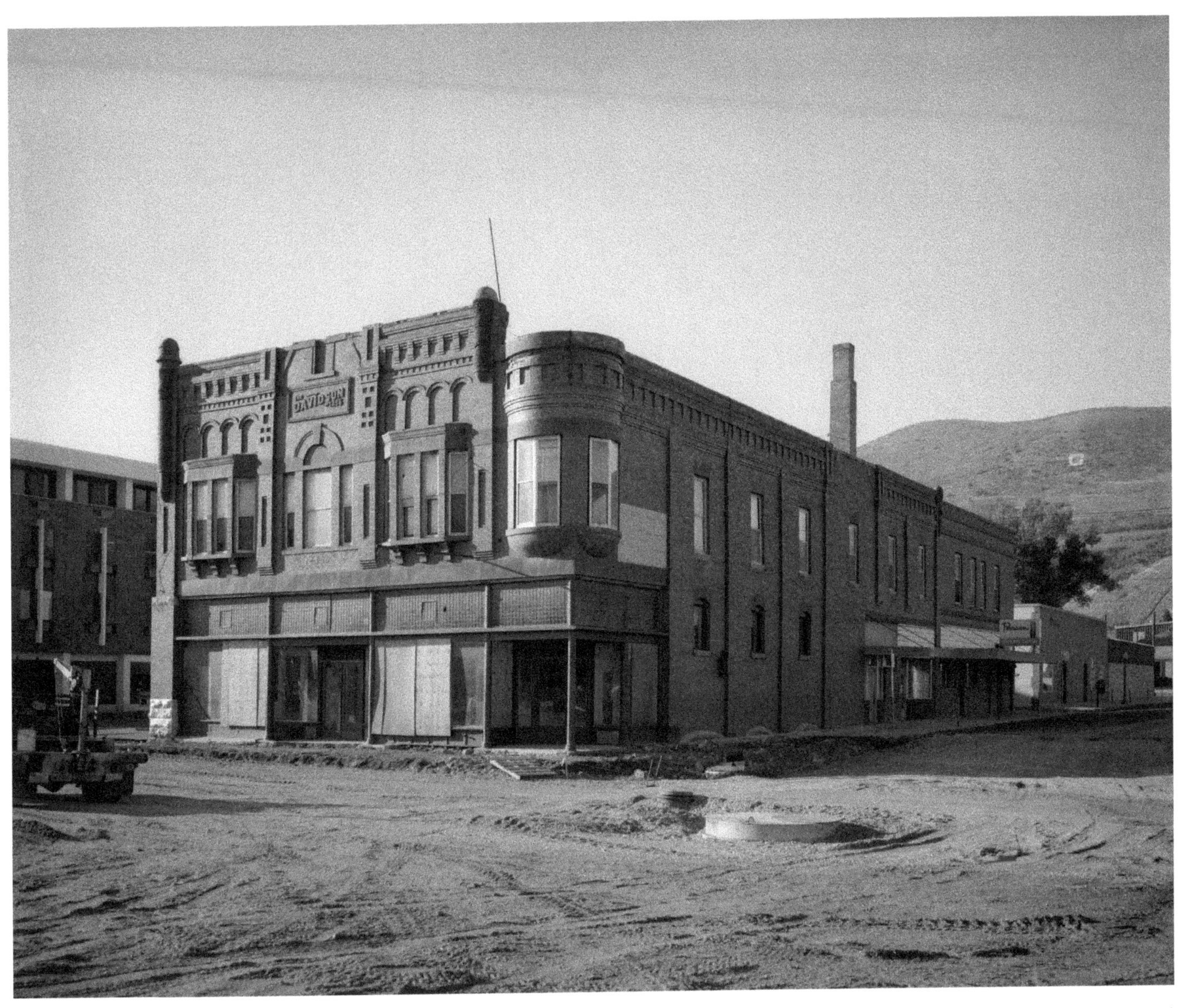

Anaconda's historic Davidson Building was erected in 1896 at a cost of $15,000. Seen here in 1950, the building was added to the National Register of Historic Places in 1983. The building houses two stores on the ground floor, with apartments above.

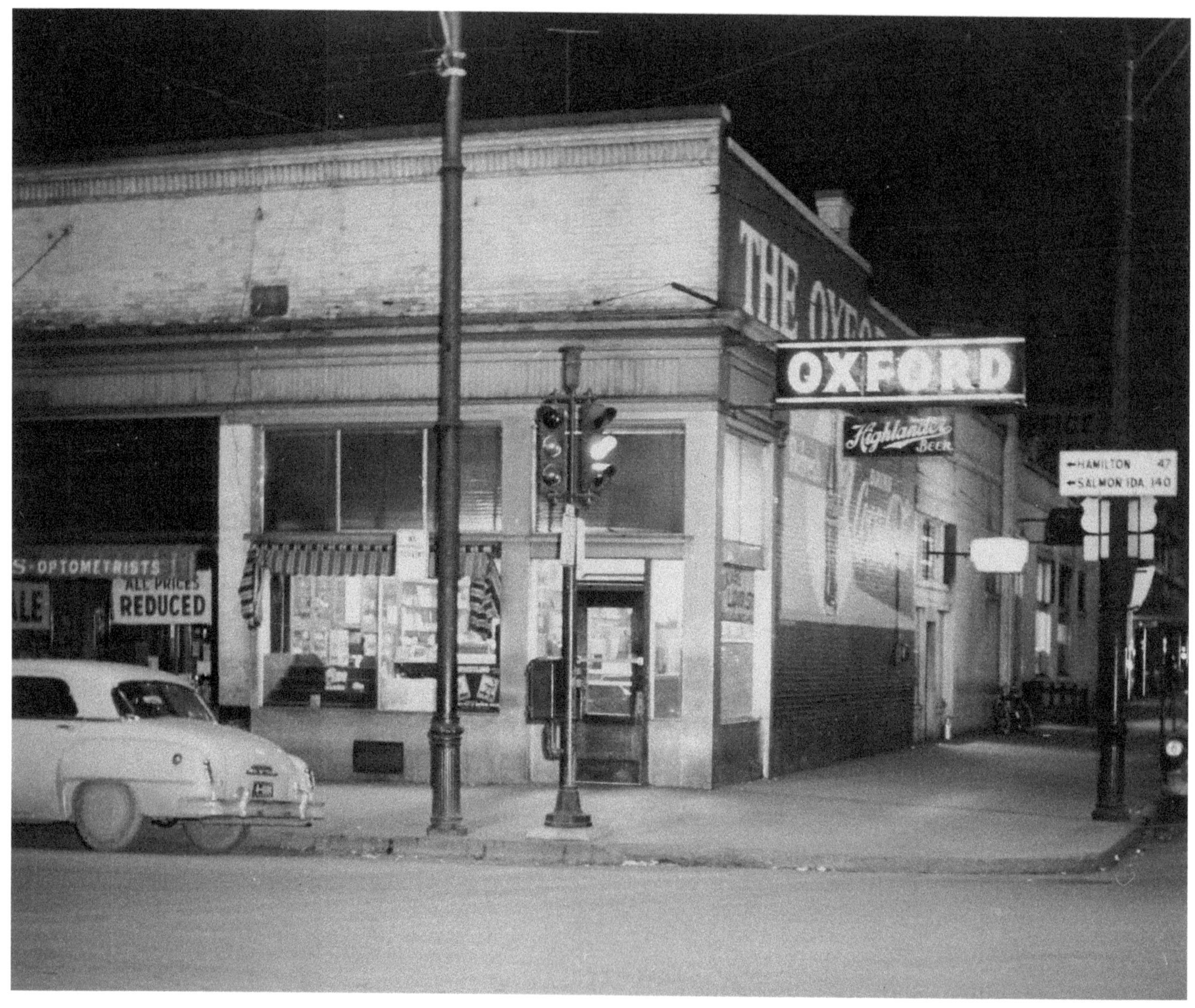

Missoula's famous Oxford Bar and Cafe, known locally as the "Ox," has been open 24 hours a day since the 1880s. Originally located at Higgins and Broadway, it moved a block north to this location in 1955. The Ox has been featured in both *Time* and *People* magazines.

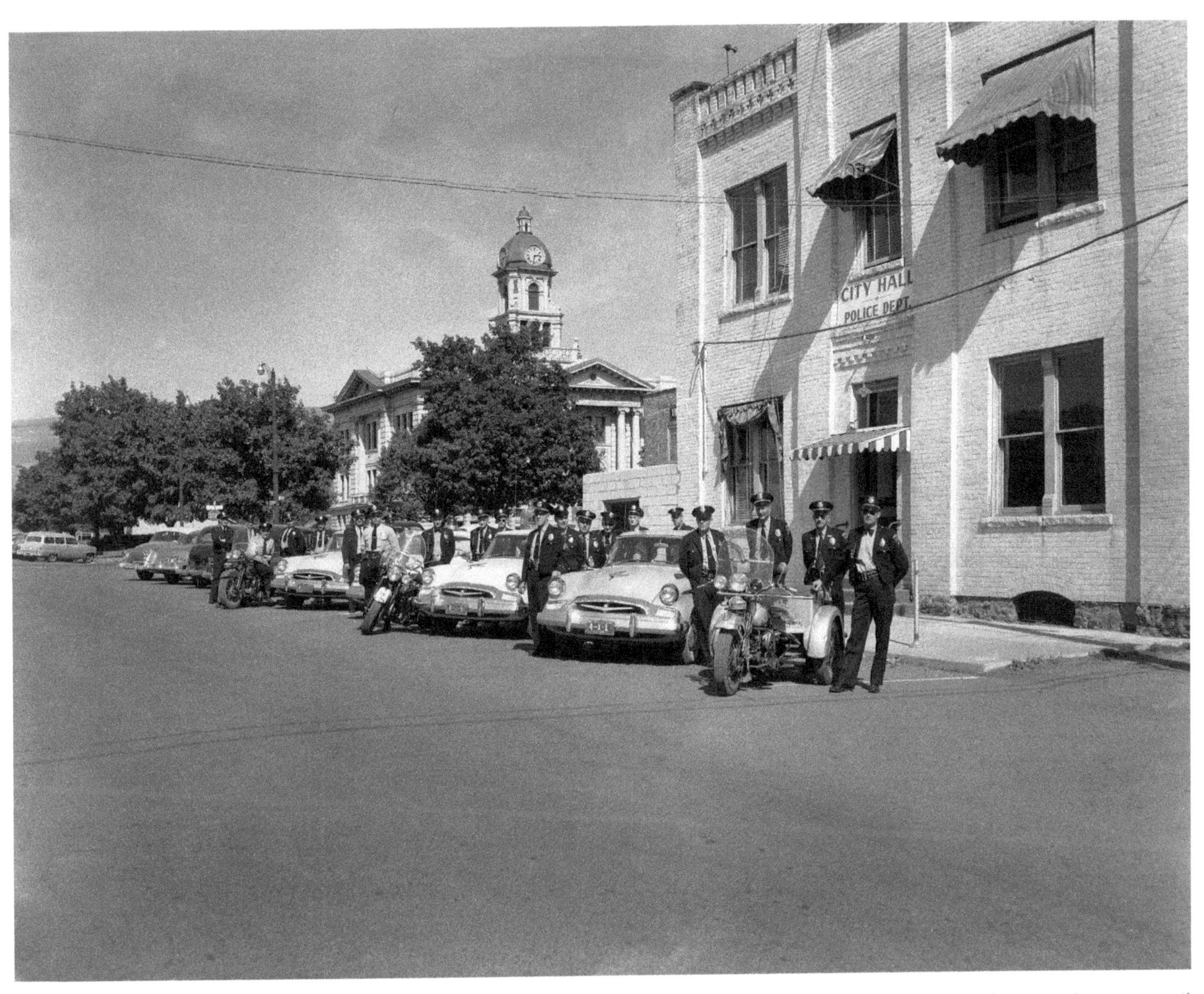

The Missoula City Council hired its first two police officers in 1883. The department had only one car and several foot-patrolmen up until the 1930s. This 1950s photo shows the expanded force posing with its three police cars and three motorcycles in front of City Hall.

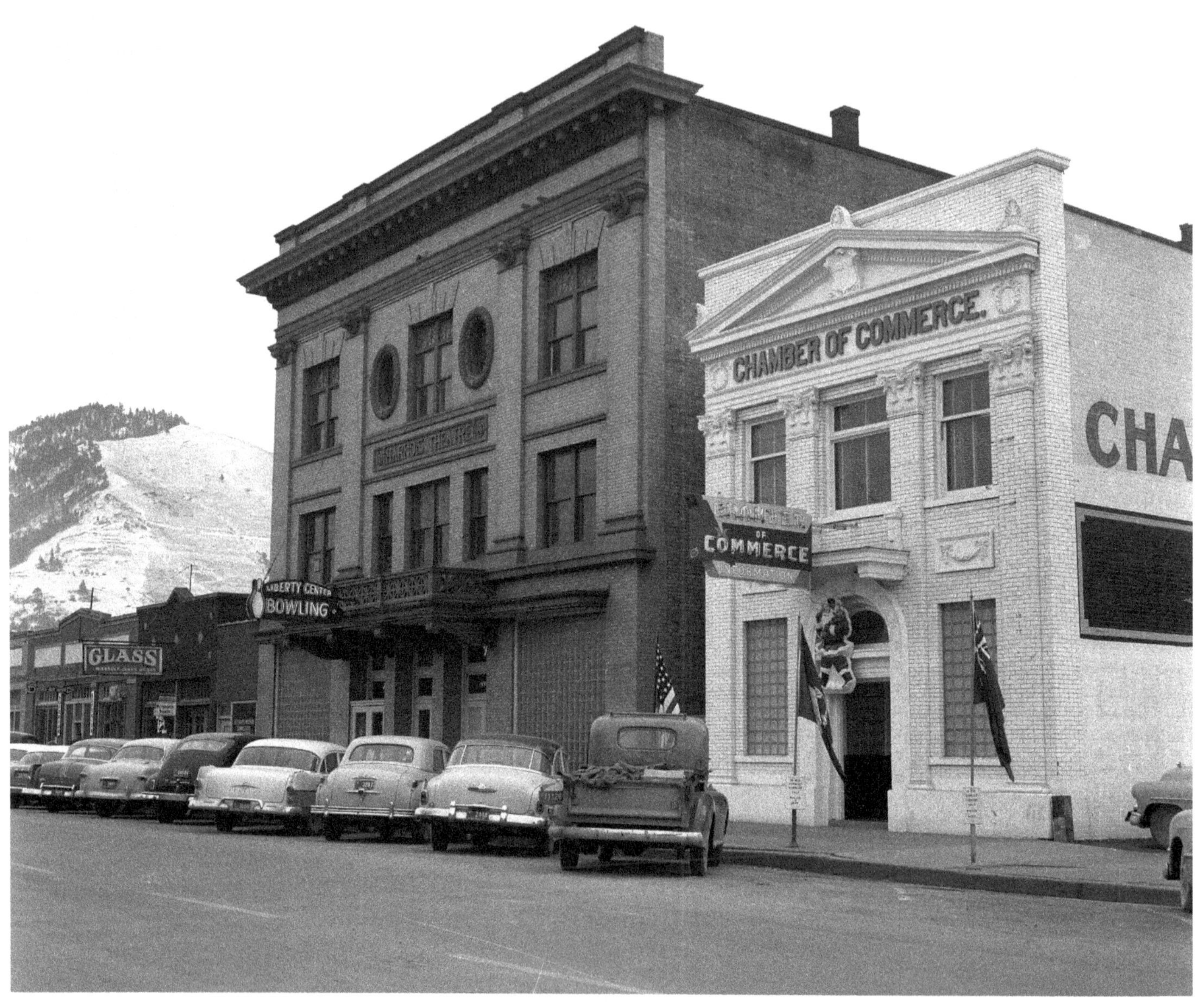

The Harnois Theatre, located next to the Chamber of Commerce on East Main in Missoula, was built in the 1890s, possibly by noted architect A. J. Gibson. The building went through several name changes and by the 1950s had been converted into the Liberty Lanes Bowling Alley. It was torn down for a parking lot in the 1960s.

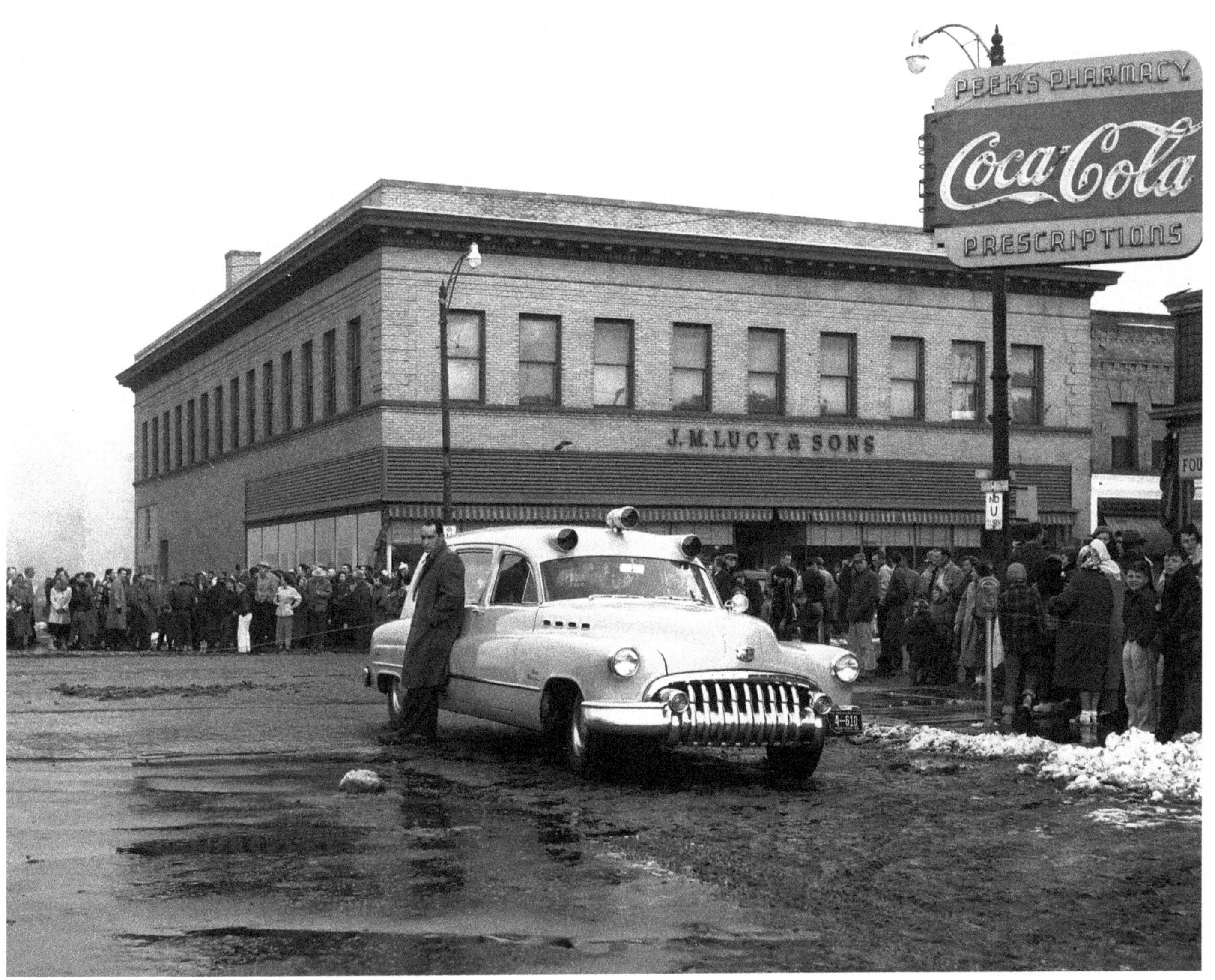

A crowd gathers in front of the J. M. Lucy & Sons furniture store to watch firemen battle a major fire that broke out in downtown Missoula on January 23, 1955. Stan Healy snapped this photo as flames raged (out of view) through the Gambles Store, Shapard Hotel, and Yandt's Men's Store.

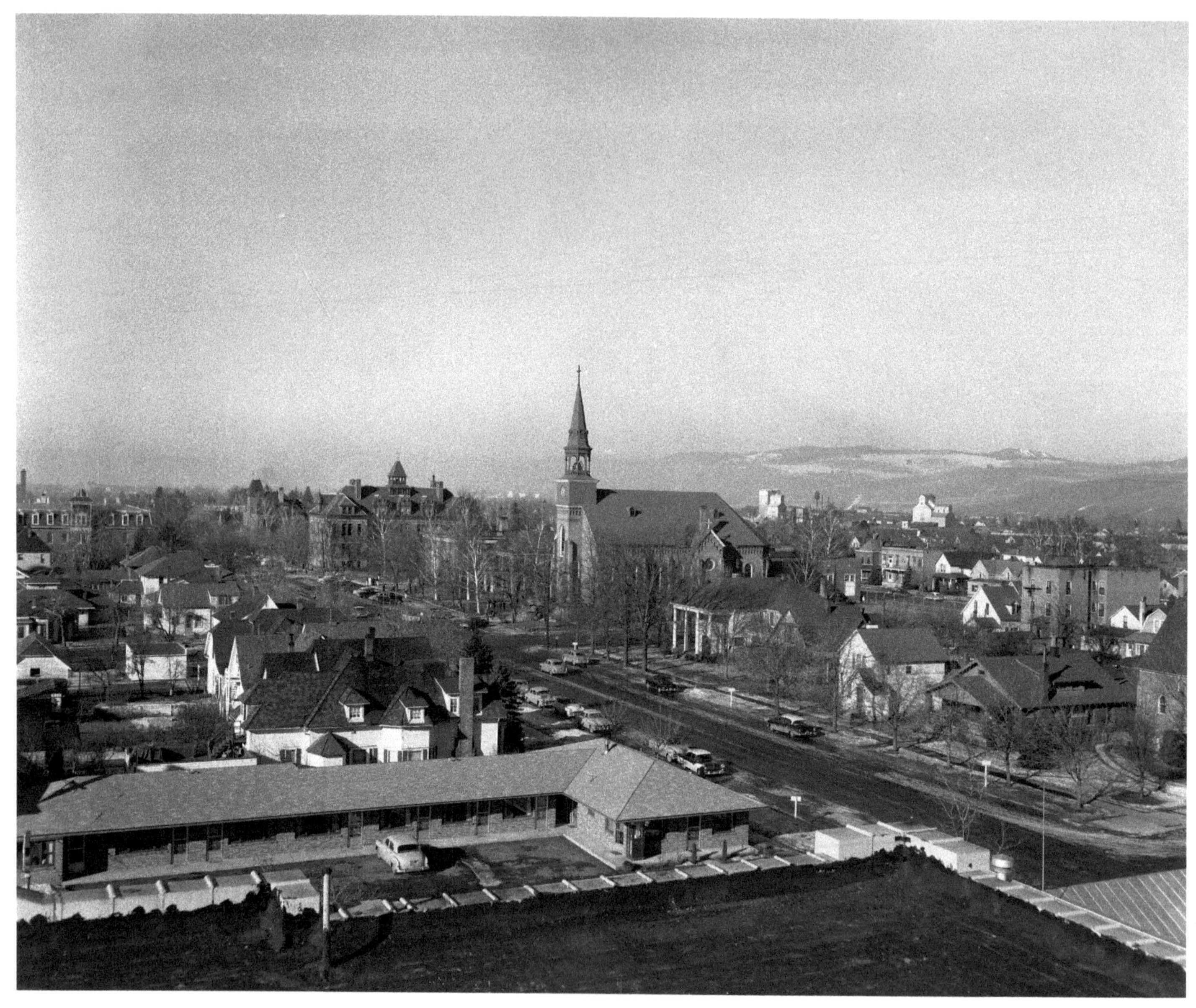

Stan Healy captured this panorama, facing west, from the dome of the Missoula County Courthouse on January 6, 1956. The spire of St. Francis Xavier Church on West Pine Street rises prominently at center.

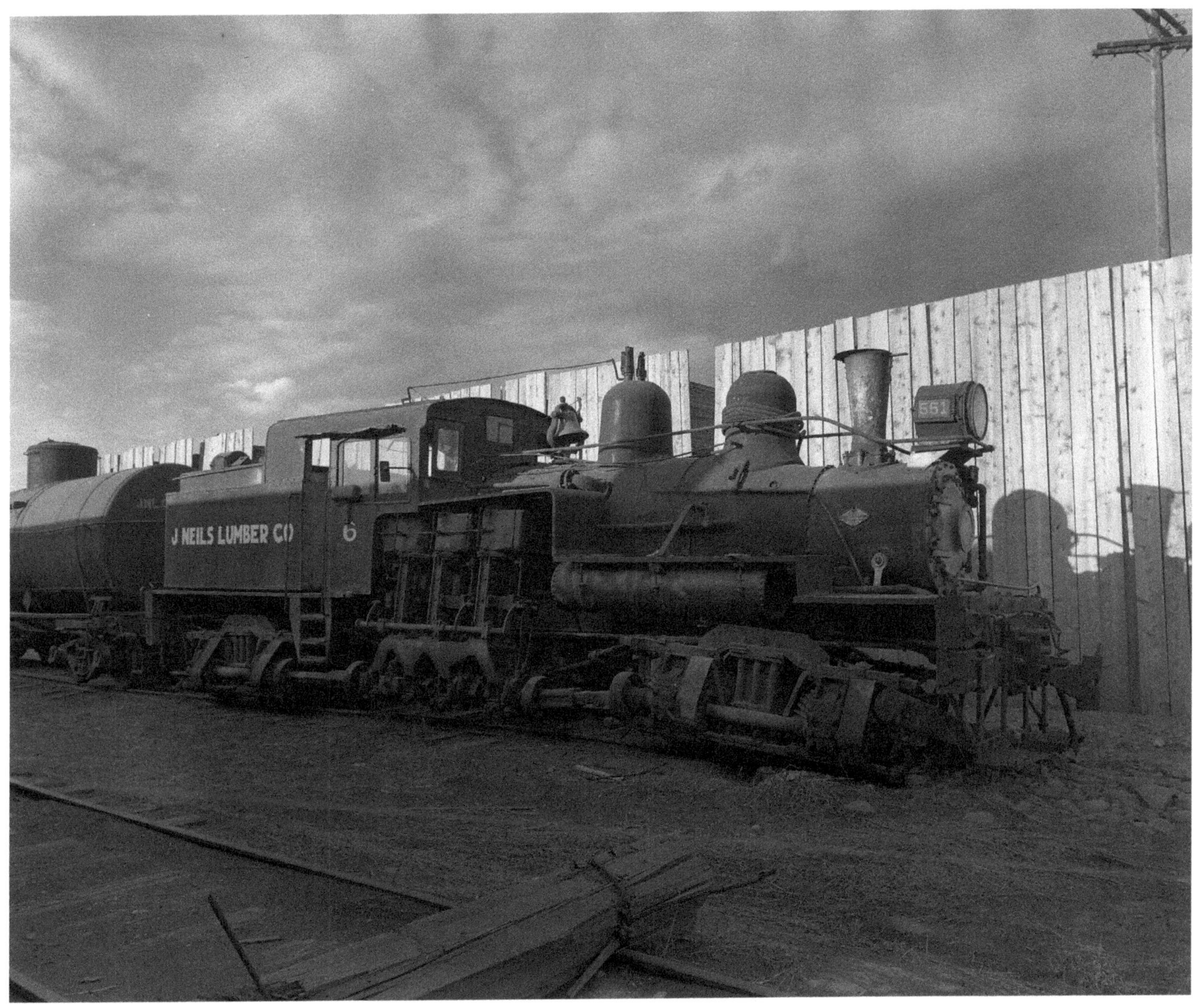

Shays were specialized locomotives designed to pull heavy logs up steep grades and around tight corners. Lima Shay No. 6 was one of several owned by the J. Neils Lumber Company in Libby, and probably operated in the woods from the early 1900s to the mid-1940s. It is seen here in 1960.

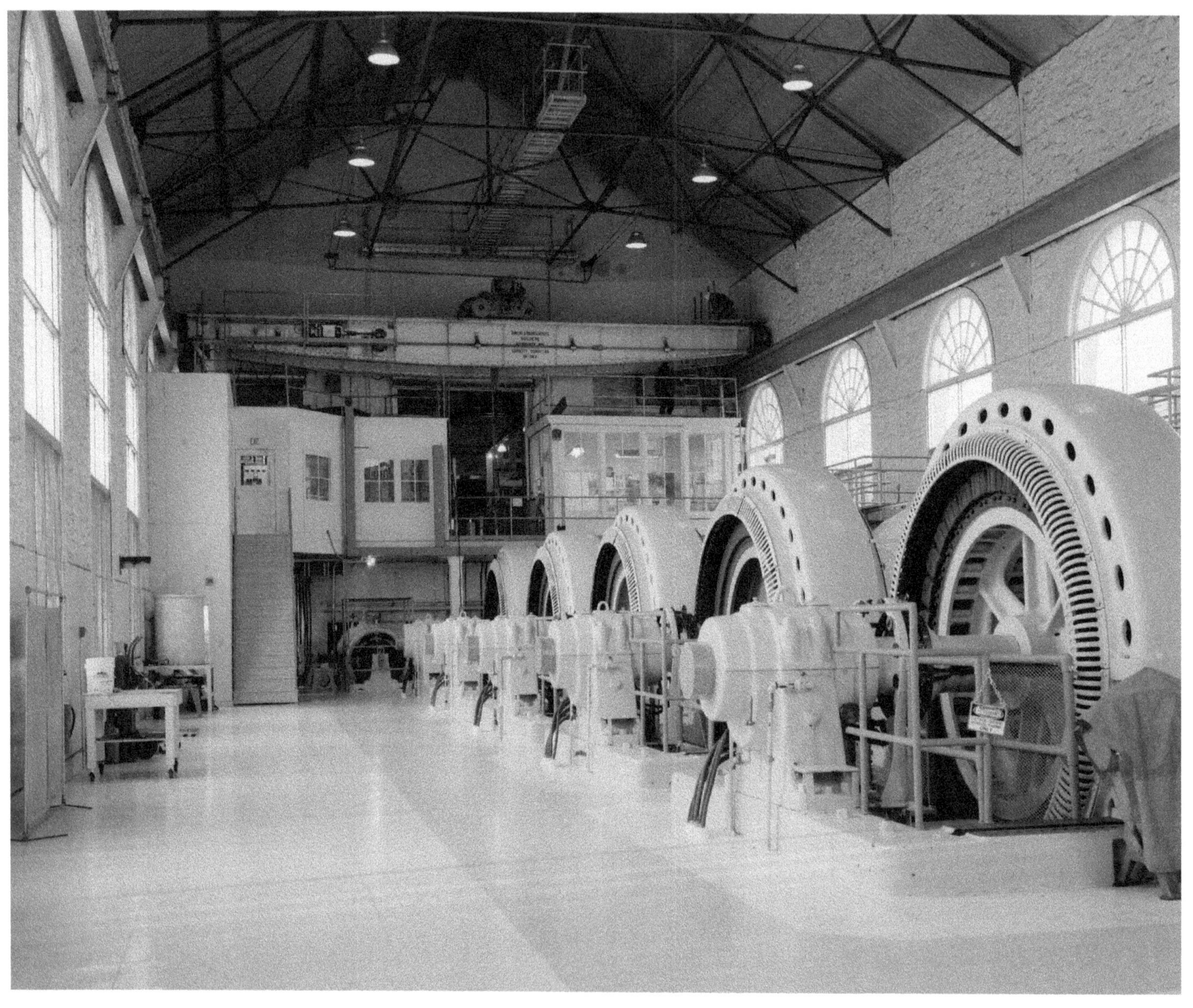

Located north of Helena, the six hydroelectric generators in the powerhouse of Hauser Dam have been generating electricity since 1911. Construction of the Missouri River dam began in 1905. It was named for Samuel Hauser, a Montana business pioneer.

NOTES ON THE PHOTOGRAPHS

These notes, listed by page number, attempt to include all aspects known of the photographs. Each of the photographs is identified by the page number, photograph's title or description, photographer and collection, archive, and call or box number when applicable. Although every attempt was made to collect all data, in some cases complete data was unavailable due to the age and condition of some of the photographs and records.

HISTORIC PHOTOS OF MONTANA

Montana is a land known for soaring vistas, towering peaks, and a rich heritage. The nearly 200 photographs in this collection celebrate the unique history of America's fourth-largest state. Ride along as photographers document life on the state's seven Indian reservations. Witness the birth, and sometimes death, of Montana's rough-and-tumble cities. Drawn from national and regional collections, *Historic Photos of Montana* offers a window into a vibrant past.

Whether taken atop a mountain in Glacier National Park, or on the banks of the Yellowstone River, these photos tell stories that celebrate the people of Big Sky Country. There are images of cowboys and loggers and miners, of course, but also of shopkeepers and schoolchildren, of politicians and housewives and other ordinary citizens who made their home in Montana. Sit back and enjoy the stories these photos tell, stories rich with the majesty, grandeur, and colorful history of the Treasure State.

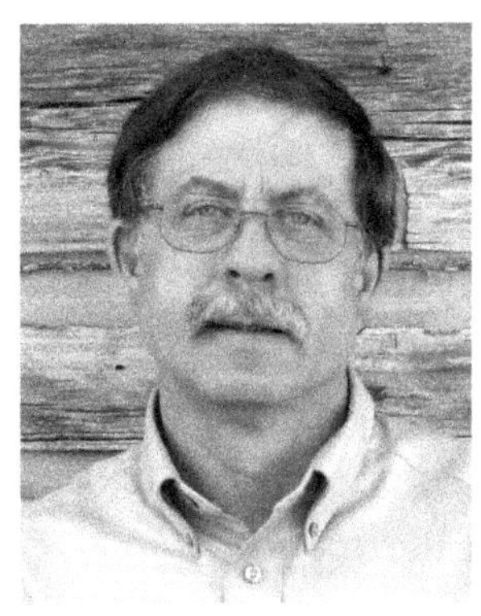

Gary Glynn has been writing about the Treasure State for more than 20 years. A fourth-generation Montanan, he grew up in Billings and received a degree in natural resource management from the University of Montana School of Forestry.

The author of *Montana's Home Front During World War II,* he has also written for a number of magazines and newspapers, including *American History, Montana Magazine, Aviation History, World War II,* and *Montana West.* He was a regular contributor to the *Missoulian* newspaper's award-winning coverage of the fiftieth anniversary of World War II, including the paper's six-part *Greatest Generation* project.

He currently serves on the board of his family's ranch, as well as on the Board of Trustees for the Historical Museum at Fort Missoula.